# VOEGELIN'S

# *ISRAEL*

# *AND*

# *REVELATION*

## An Interdisciplinary Debate and Anthology

EDITED BY

# William M. Thompson
and
# David L. Morse

## MARQUETTE
### UNIVERSITY

PRESS

MARQUETTE STUDIES IN THEOLOGY
No. 19

ANDREW TALLON, SERIES EDITOR

Library of Congress Cataloging-in-Publication Data

Voegelin's Israel and Revelation : an interdisciplinary debate and anthology
/ edited by William M. Thompson and David L. Morse.
   p. cm. — (Marquette studies in theology ; #19) Israel and Revelation is
vol. 1 of Voegelin's Order and history. Includes bibliographical references
and index.
ISBN 0-87462-643-9 (alk. paper : pbk.)
   1. Voegelin, Eric, 1901- Order and history. 1. Israel and revelation—
Congresses. 2. Judaism—History—To 70 A.D.—Congresses. 3. Judaism—
History—Philosophy—Congresses. 4. Bible. O.T.—Criticism, interpretation, etc.—Congresses. I. Thompson, William M., 1943- II. Morse, David
L. (David Lee), 1946- III. Voegelin, Eric, 1901- Order and history. 1. Israel
and revelation. Selections. IV. Series.
BM173 .V64 2000
296'.09'01—dc21
                                                    99-050791

Cover photo compliments of the Eric Voegelin Institute,
Louisiana State University

© 2000 Marquette University Press
Milwaukee Wisconsin 53201-1881

MARQUETTE UNIVERSITY PRESS
MILWAUKEE

The Association of Jesuit University Presses

# Contents

# PREFACE

We appreciatively acknowledge the cooperation and support of all those who helped bring this project to its completion. Along with the other contributors to this volume, we would list in first place the congenial and challenging company of the Eric Voegelin Society. Thanks are due in a special way to Dean Constance Ramirez and the McAnulty College and Graduate School of Liberal Arts of Duquesne University for a financial grant, to the always helpful and competent reference staff of the Gumberg Library of Duquesne University, and to the Department of Theology of Duquesne University. Joyce A. Bautch rendered extraordinary assistance to the project, assisted by Kathleen Contini Borres.

Chapter One was originally published in *Political Science Reviewer*, 1 (1971): 1-29, and in the revised and expanded form in this book in *Eric Voegelin's Search for Order in History*, Louisiana State University Press, 1978. Chapter Three has appeared in *Canadian Journal of Political Science/Revue canadienne de science politique*, 31 (1998): 61-90, © Canadian Political Science Association (l'Association canadienne de science politique) and/et la Société québécoise de science politique. Chapters Five and Six have appeared in *The Journal of Religion* © 1999 The University of Chicago Press. We gratefully acknowledge permission to publish these articles, all but the first originally written as a part of our interdisciplinary exchange for this volume. Each has been slightly edited. We acknowledge with most special thanks the permission to publish the selections from *Israel and Revelation*, reprinted by permission of Louisiana State University Press from *Order and History*, Volume 1, *Israel and Revelation*, by Eric Voegelin, copyright © 1956 by Louisiana State University Press.

We are all happily in the debt of Marquette University Press, and its Director, Professor Andrew Tallon, for taking on the publication of this project.

Most of all, we are in the debt of Eric Voegelin, to whom this book is dedicated.

"Tell us now, how did you write all these words?" (Jer 36:17 NRSV)

WMT

DLM

# CONTRIBUTORS

Bernhard W. Anderson is Professor Emeritus of Old Testament Theology at Princeton Theological Seminary. He is the author of numerous works on the Old Testament, including the standard textbook, *Understanding the Old Testament*.

Marie L. Baird is Assistant Professor of Theology at Duquesne University. Her areas of specialization and publication are Christian Spirituality, Holocaust Studies, and the thought of Emmanuel Levinas.

Aaron L. Mackler is Associate Professor of Theology at Duquesne University. His areas of teaching and publication are Health Care Ethics and Jewish theology and philosophy.

David L. Morse is the Senior Pastor of Monroeville United Methodist Church and Adjunct Professor of Theology at Duquesne University. He is a coeditor of volume 4 of Voegelin's *History of Political Ideas, Renaissance and Reformation*. His doctoral dissertation was on Voegelin's contribution to theological hermeneutics.

John J. Ranieri is Associate Professor of Philosophy at Seton Hill University, and the author of *Eric Voegelin and the Good Society*. Among his special interests are the works of both Eric Voegelin and Bernard Lonergan.

Ellis Sandoz is Hermann Moyse Jr. Distinguished Professor of Political Science at Louisiana State University and Director of its Eric Voegelin Institute. He has written numerous books and articles on Voegelin and political theory and a general editor of *The Collected Works of Eric Voegelin*.

William M. Thompson is Professor of Theology at Duquesne University. He is the author of numerous books and articles in the areas of Christology, theology, hermeneutics and philosophy of religion. He is a coeditor of Volume 4 of Voegelin's *History of Political Ideas, Renaissance and Reformation*. His most recent book is *The Struggle for Theology's Soul: Contesting Scripture in Christology*.

Glenn Tinder is Professor Emeritus of Political Science at the University of Massachusetts, Boston. He is the author of well known works, including *Political Thinking* and the highly acclaimed *The Political Meaning of Christianity*.

# Theme and Variations in Voegelin's *Israel and Revelation* and in His Interpreters[1]

# David L. Morse

The purpose of this introduction is to describe the history of this collection of texts and to alert the reader to the recurring theme and some variations that one can find throughout this book, both in the interpretive essays and the selections from *Israel and Revelation*. I will not attempt to summarize the essays in any detail. I assume that the reader can read them for himself or herself, allowing the texts to speak for themselves. Moreover, these texts reflect the interdisciplinary nature not only of Voegelin's work but of the interpreters and their respective disciplines. This diversity with respect both to style and content is one of the features of the text that reflects Voegelin's own interdisciplinary work as a philosopher, and it is an intentional effort to create a continuing conversation with Eric Voegelin, with readers and with continuing issues that arise out of *Israel and Revelation*.

This text is offered as a way of introducing the reader to the work of the political philosopher Eric Voegelin. The particular purpose is to introduce the reader to a specific Voegelin text, volume one of *Order and History*, published under the title *Israel and Revelation*. Voegelin is certainly one of the leading political philosophers of the twentieth century whose creative work was undertaken in the midst of and in response to the major political and social events of this century, especially the ideological mass movements that swept across Europe. Although Voegelin published many manuscripts on a wide range of subjects, his most famous text is the five volume work *Order and History*. Volume One presents Eric Voegelin's interpretation of the political experience of Israel summarized under the symbol "revelation."

The contents of this collection invite the reader to experience the work of Eric Voegelin in two ways. Through representative selections from *Israel and Revelation* the reader is invited to engage Voegelin's insightful penetration into the depths of the experience of Israel, an experience which can be summarized as the revelation of the transcendent God as the source of order represented in the formation of the people of Israel. We have tried to select portions of the text that reflect Voegelin's style both as a writer and interpreter of human culture, political experience and the particular experience of Israel. Through these selections we hope that the reader will not only be drawn into an engaging reading of the Hebrew scriptures but come to a new appreciation of Eric Voegelin's use of those texts as a political philosopher. The reader is also invited to continue his or her conversation with Voegelin through the various interpretations of *Israel and Revelation* that are represented in the essays that make up this volume.

Most of the essays were originally the basis of one of the panels at the twelfth annual meeting of The Eric Voegelin Society held in San Francisco, August 30-31, 1996. A roundtable discussion celebrating the fortieth anniversary of the publication of *Israel and Revelation* was proposed, organized, and subsequently chaired by Dr. William M. Thompson. Various persons, drawn from different academic disciplines and professions, were invited to read or re-read *Israel and Revelation* and then present a paper on some aspect of the work or a disciplined reflection on the text as a whole. The papers were circulated to each panel member prior to the meeting of the society. The essays then became the basis of the round table discussion. Due to the constraints of time, and the number of papers presented, the discussion was limited to a summary of each essay and a general conversation among the participants. Following the roundtable discussion there was a response by Paul Caringella, one of the general editors of *The Collected Works of Eric Voegelin.* His observations constitute an important part of the horizon of this book's essays for which the panelists are grateful. The editors thought that the complete essays, along with representative selections from *Israel and Revelation*, ought to be offered to a wider audience of interested readers in various fields, including biblical studies, history, political science, theology and philosophy. These are but a few of the areas in which this work, as well as all of Voegelin's labors, make a contribution to the understanding of human experience, in both its historical and transcendent dimensions.

In approaching these essays, as well as the selections offered from *Israel and Revelation,* I would like to suggest that the reader bear in mind the basic theme of Eric Voegelin's work along with variations of that theme that are sounded throughout these essays. The basic theme is the statement that opens the preface to *Israel and Revelation* and serves as the introduction to the entire five volume work: "The order of history emerges from the history of order." For Voegelin this is a guiding and presiding principle, however much or little his project changed over the years. The search for order, for Voegelin, is never an abstract search apart from the concrete realities of persons, societies and cultures. It is always a search that emerges out of the actions of human beings and their personal and corporate experience in history. The search for order is to be undertaken through the efforts of concrete persons and societies to discover that order in the midst of their experience, more often than not in response to the trauma of disorder that threatens to overtake and overcome the social order in which the searcher finds himself or herself. It emerges with particular clarity, often even leaps forward in being, when sensitive individuals, aware of the disorder that is taking place in their society, seek to correct that disorder through new insights and action flowing from the order of being. This is in fact how Eric Voegelin understood his own work. It was a type of intellectual therapy for the disordered existence that was thrust into the twentieth century by the massive ideological distortions that were present in the world.

Four variations on the theme of order and history emerge in these essays, which we can summarize under the headings of: (1) the universal and the particular, (2) the transcendent God and historical society, (3) ontology and ethics and (4) finally, Judaism and Christianity. I would argue that each of these themes is, as the different essays note, a variation on the basic theme of order and history. The essays in one form or another wrestle with Voegelin's thought on order and history and the balance between the poles of these various subthemes. Since balance as well as life in the metaxy, were important linguistic symbols for Voegelin, these essays honor his work by wrestling with these continuing issues, hoping to contribute to a further, constructive interpretation of them.[2]

## ORDER AND HISTORY

In one way or another all of the essays presented in this volume take up this basic theme. It is brought to special focus in the essay by political scientist Ellis Sandoz, which sketches major themes in Eric Voegelin and provides the context needed for an overall understanding of Voegelin's work and *Israel and Revelation's* place within that. As such this essay is especially helpful to the reader who may be coming to Voegelin's work for the first time. Sandoz treats the general range of Voegelin's thought, the major emphases, and something of the history of various Voegelin texts, so as to help the reader see not only the place and argument of *Israel and Revelation* but the entire purpose and scope of Voegelin's efforts. Although concentrating primarily on original works of Voegelin, Sandoz also places Voegelin in the context of contemporary scholarship, and through the notes provides the reader with further secondary literature.

Glenn Tinder's essay, also from the perspective of political science, falls into this same general category, but his focus is not so much on an exposition of Voegelin's thought as it is a careful reflection on continuing issues that emerge in Voegelin's work. Under the rubric of "impulses" he suggests directions in which Voegelin's thought may lead and certain issues that will have to be taken up as we move beyond the text of Voegelin's thought. As such, Tinder's essay is a good example of how a conversation with Voegelin's work can continue. He notes five areas in particular in which the issues raised in *Israel and Revelation* might well be fruitfully carried on in further discussion. These are eschatology, institutional pluralism, universalism, personalism and historicism. This essay invites the reader to carry on further reflection on some of the major issues in *IR* that continue to be an intellectual challenge. In so doing it fulfills one of Voegelin's own purposes, that is, to invite the sensitive soul to a continued reflection on the meaning of life in history and the continued search for order in one's own soul, in society and in history.

## UNIVERSAL AND PARTICULAR

This theme is treated in the essay by Aaron L. Mackler, an ethicist and theologian in the Jewish tradition. His essay examines, as its title indicates, *Israel and Revelation* from the perspective of Judaism. The essay is a review both of Voegelin's interpretation of particular texts in the Hebrew scriptures as well as an evaluation of Voegelin's hermeneutical method in approaching the experience of Israel. While finding much that is positive in this volume, Mackler raises throughout the essay the question of whether Voegelin has not gone too far in affirming the general at the expense of the particular, especially in his treatment of specific biblical passages as well as of the broader social, ethical and historical experience of Israel. Mackler acknowledges that Voegelin often brings out rich dimensions of the text, but in so doing tends to neglect others. This is, Mackler's essay argues, due to Voegelin's philosophical methodology, which tends to privilege the general over the particular. This, in turn, leads Voegelin to read specific texts as a confirmation of the general assumptions that he brings to them. To this extent, some of the things that Voegelin highlights in the texts of the Hebrew scriptures are not, according to Mackler, necessarily the central concerns of the biblical writers. Mackler also suggests that they may not be some of the most important points of significance for contemporary readers. Mackler clearly values Voegelin's voice in the conversation, but concludes that Voegelin's principal contribution should be appreciated as one more particular perspective that contributes to the discussion. That perspective is important, creative, and insightful, but not the only voice that speaks or the only interpretation that connects the text with our experience of order. Mackler expresses this theme very well in the closing sentence in his opening paragraph, where, alluding to a saying from Rabbinic lore, he then notes, "While some readings may be better than others, multiple readings may coexist and fruitfully complement one another, as different interpretations develop varying dimensions of significance for communities of readers." Voegelin would agree with this, but would probably do so only as long as the interpreter remains attuned to the universal as well. Mackler's essay, on the other hand, suggests that it may be important not to try to discern in each particular reading anything more than its own particular witness to the truth.

The essay by John Ranieri, a political philosopher, moves in a direction similar to that of Mackler's. Ranieri's essay proposes to show how the particular experience of Israel has been "tamed" by Voegelin, already beginning with *IR*, but increasingly as he continues to develop his political philosophy. Ranieri pays special attention to what he sees as a change in Voegelin's thought regarding the experience of Israel. He concludes that the very logic of Voegelin's thought leads to this gradual taming of Israel. This also is due to Voegelin's tendency to favor the universal over the particular. As such, the concrete experience of Israel becomes problematic. The experience of Israel, while an important example of a new differentiation in being, raises the key problem of the universal and the particular for Voegelin. Israel experiences the power of the transcendent God, the one who is Beyond. That experience occurs, as it always does, in the context of a specific history. This produces a tension for Israel. Voegelin characterizes Israel's response to this tension as not only inadequate but dangerous. Ranieri's essay argues that Voegelin comes to the conclusions he holds because he favors Plato over Isaiah, Hellenistic culture over Hebrew culture. The result, for Ranieri, is that in the end the experience of Israel and the scandal of particularity is lost from his work. This is a loss for political discourse. Ranieri closes his essay with the suggestion that this loss of the biblical voice in Voegelin through his favoring of the universal needs to be demythologized. The myth of being needs to be critiqued with the myth of justice, which may be another way of saying that the universal needs to be balanced by the particular.

## GOD AND SOCIETY

Another variation on the theme of order and history is the relationship of the transcendent God to the social order. The famous essay by Bernhard Anderson, premier Old Testament theologian, falls into this general category. The essay was first published in 1971, and was republished in a revised form in 1978. It is included in this collection in its revised form. Anderson has also included an additional essay prepared for the roundtable, which he characterizes as a "footnote" to his first essay. In both essays Anderson wrestles with several variations of Voegelin's theme. The relationship of the transcendent God, differentiated in Israel's experience, to the actual social order, is one of the themes of most interest to Anderson. In both essays he expresses positive comments about the contribution Voegelin makes not only to political philosophy but also to the interpretation of Israel's experience. In the relationship between the revelation of the transcendent God and concrete social organization, Anderson does raise the question, however, of whether or not Voegelin has done justice to the experience of Israel. In particular he finds Voegelin's concept of the "mortgage" of the world-immanent and concrete existence on transcendent truth to be problematic. Anderson wonders if this does justice to the dynamic character of the transcendent God in relation to the concrete human drama of Israel. He is less reserved than Voegelin about conceiving God's action in history and the change that this action can bring to bear on the particular order of any society in general and on Israel's mundane order in particular. He also discusses in his first essay the thorny problem of evil and how this is interpreted in the experience of Israel. Anderson, as other essayists, highlights the problematic character of a fundamental aspect of Voegelin's method, namely, his philosophy of being. He doubts that Voegelin's philosophy of being can do justice to the fullness of the biblical revelation, and in particular to this question of the relationship of God to society. While articulating Israel's experience of transcendence has been one of Voegelin's strengths, especially in contrast to other political philosophers, Voegelin nevertheless is said to fall short of appreciating the positive dimensions of Israel's concrete political organization.

My own essay on Voegelin's reading of Isaiah is a variation of the same theme of the relation of God to society. It is an effort to describe Voegelin's reading of Isaiah and his claim that Isaiah is a metastatic thinker, that is, according to Voegelin, someone who expects a change in the constitution of this world's being without its ceasing to be the world as we know it. For Voegelin, because Isaiah's solution to specific political problems is an example of metastasis, it is an inadequate solution. In fact, what Isaiah offers as political advice to the kings of Israel in their particular situations is not only inadequate, it is dangerous. The essay evaluates this reading of Isaiah by comparison with other readings. Since the issue for Voegelin is how the revelation of the transcendent God impacts concrete society, and the related question of whether or not it is possible to make any application of revelation to history that is not a deformation, the essay raises the question as to whether in Voegelin's writings there is some example held up where a vision of transcendence has been applied to the organization of a specific society. This leads to a comparison between Voegelin's reading of Isaiah and his reading of Plato's *Laws*. The latter is held up by Voegelin as an example of a successful, if modest, effort to move from a vision of the transcendent ground of being to a particular social organization.

## ONTOLOGY AND ETHICS

The essay by Marie Baird, a theologian whose work is focused on the area of spirituality, addresses the issue of ontology and ethics through a comparison of Voegelin with Emmanuel Levinas. Baird reviews Voegelin's work in the light of one of her own special concerns, the development of a post-holocaust spirituality. Given the great ideological movements of the twentieth century, and in particular the human destruction that these movements have wrought, Baird seeks to develop a form of spirituality that is rooted in the efforts to stay alive in conditions of extremity. This concern provides the basis of Baird's dialogue between Voegelin and Levinas. She begins by examining the movement toward personalism and ethical responsibility represented in Voegelin's analysis of Israel's experience, especially in the work of the prophets. She identifies an ethical dimension in Voegelin's account of the prophets. That dimension, she argues, is grounded in Voegelin's ontology. The movement toward ethical responsibility in the prophets, in Baird's presentation of *IR*, is based on an attunement

to and a participation in being, and in particular the tension toward
the divine being that has been revealed to Israel. There is, however, a
potential problem for any system of ethics based on ontology. Ethical
responsibility that is grounded in attunement to divine being can
become another totalizing system that ends up knowing, grasping and
even destroying "the other." This is the danger that Levinas saw in all
forms of ontology, and which he set forth in his work *Totality and
Infinity* (Levinas 1969). Ontological systems become tyrannical systems that destroy the other along with our obligations to the other.
Baird identifies this as a potential danger in Voegelin's own analysis
of ethics and being. She critiques, and endeavors to correct, this
tendency in Voegelin's analysis of Israel's prophets by inviting the
reader to consider Levinas and his affirmation of the ethical relationship to the other as prior to any ontological relationship. Her essay sets
forth what she considers to be the differences between Voegelin and
Levinas on the question of ontology and ethics. According to Baird,
what is most basic for Voegelin is the fundamental relationship to
being. What is most basic for Levinas is the relationship to the other
and the claim that the other makes on my existence prior to any
knowledge of being. These represent two distinctly different ways to
live and act in the world. Baird concludes with the observation that in
the kind of world in which we live, it becomes all the more important
to hear the voice of Levinas as a correction to all forms of ontology that
become totalizing systems that destroy our ethical responsibility for
the other. As such, the work of Levinas can become an important
corrective to the dangers of ontology, dangers that she sees in
Voegelin. This essay invites the reader to wrestle with whether, if
ontology is thought to be prior to ethics, that in the end destroys ethics
and one's responsibility for the other? Is this a danger in Voegelin, and
in all systems that begin with ontology?

## JUDAISM AND CHRISTIANITY

The final variation on the theme of order and history can be seen in
the question of the relationship between Judaism and Christianity in
*Israel and Revelation* and in Voegelin's other works. Not surprisingly,
several of the essays address this theme. It is a topic that is of
continuing significance in interfaith dialogue today. Mackler's essay
raises questions about Voegelin's treatment of Judaism, and in particular about the harsh language that Voegelin uses in reference to it
in various places. Mackler encourages the reader to note these flaws in
*Israel and Revelation* as well as how they have been developed, and

possibly corrected or not, both in later works and in other interpreters of Voegelin.

Anderson's essays, especially the most recent one, discuss this question directly and suggest an alternative way of viewing the relationship between Judaism and Christianity. He also notes again that part of Voegelin's difficulty involves his privileging of personal ontology over social being in community.

The most sustained discussion of this question is to be found in the essay by William M. Thompson, a Christian theologian, who examines the place of Christ and Christianity in *Israel and Revelation*. The essay opens with a summary of what is a close reading of the work yielding a detailed survey of the places where references to this theme appear. Following a very careful and thorough presentation of the actual references, Thompson then takes the reader through an extended dialectical conversation about Christ and Christianity in *Israel and Revelation*, with attention to the claims of both those who think that the work is too Christian and those who think that it is not Christian enough. This involves pushing the dialogue to the limits of what can be determined on this theme from this particular text. Thompson also imaginatively analyzes the concepts of figura and prefiguration as those bear on Voegelin's view of the relationship between Judaism and Christianity. The essay concludes with a discussion of some significant references to Christ and Christianity in later works, especially Voegelin's comments on the famous Colossians passage in "Gospel and Culture" and Voegelin's intriguing remarks about pre-Nicene Christianity. Thompson notes the extent to which Voegelin's work is compatible with orthodox Christianity and the role that doctrine, especially that of the trinity and incarnation, plays in Voegelin's thought.

## A Concluding Note

It is, in one sense, arbitrary to place these essays under the variations that I have identified. Each of the essays has it own particular style and its own individual theme. Moreover, many of the essays could have been placed under several of the categories that I have identified. This, of course, illustrates something of Voegelin's own extensive writings. There is an underlying unity in Voegelin's work and the issues it raises. Each of these themes is but one variation of that question that emerges out of the search for order and history.[3] Some thinkers display great depth, analytically surveying nearly all that can be mastered in a particular area of study. Other thinkers display great breadth, cover-

ing an unusually wide range of thought and putting together a
synthesis of insights from many different fields. Eric Voegelin is one
of those rare figures who has both breadth and depth. He has applied
that skill to his life's work, that of resisting disorder and in so doing
pushing the question of order to new levels of spiritual insight. His
work is a response to his world and to history. It contributes to, and
participates in, an ongoing conversation in many disciplines and has
a relevancy to all of life. Voegelin never claimed novelty. Indeed, for
him, the criterion of truth was not the production of something new,
but the rediscovery of something enduring. Truth was marked by its
very lack of originality (EESH, 122ff.). Truth is to be found in the
continued reflective, meditative participation in the process of history
that is itself "a mystery in the process of revelation" (*OH* IV, 6). These
essays are offered to the reader in the hope that they will keep the
question alive, nurture the conversation, and deepen the participation
of the reader in the search for order in history.

## NOTES

[1] This title is obviously a variation of the title of Gregor Sebba's essay, "Prelude and
Variations on the Theme of Eric Voegelin," in Sandoz 1982, 3ff.

[2] The term *metaxy* is a symbol for humanity's participation in existence, a participation that has the character of an "in-between." The term is a Greek word, taken
from Plato, which is used by Voegelin to characterize the tension that is
experienced in existence, a tension that can be expressed in a variety of ways. For
more detail on Voegelin's use of this important symbol, the reader may consult
the essay, "Eternal Being in Time," found in *AE*, 116-40, where the term first
appeared in Voegelin's work, and the succinct description of existence as having
the structure of the In-Between in EESH.

[3] With respect to the symbol of "the question," the reader might want to take note
of what Voegelin has written in *OH* IV, 316-35.

# POLITICS AND THE TRANSCENDENT:
## VOEGELIN'S PHILOSOPHICAL AND THEOLOGICAL EXPOSITION OF THE OLD TESTAMENT IN THE
### CONTEXT OF THE ANCIENT NEAR EAST

# Bernhard W. Anderson

The task of government is to actualize the order within which people may live together in peace and justice. In our revolutionary period, when conservatives to the right defend established political structures by appealing to law and order and idealists to the left advocate the overthrow of political forms which are seen to impede human fulfillment, this political task evokes with new urgency the question of the source and basis of world order. The question becomes insistent at a time when technological society has developed massive centers of power, which frighten the imagination with apocalyptic visions of cosmic catastrophe. Yet today, as we well know, the search for a meaningful interpretation of reality must be carried out in a post-Christian age, when the Christian symbols that once endowed Western civilization with eternal meaning have lost their power. Charles West describes the current "climate of opinion": "The structures of order, on which man has depended through the millennia to give his existence eternal meaning and direction, no longer control the reality in which we live. To put it in simple terms, God as the symbol of the unchanging transcendent being, the measure and the goal of all that happens in the transient realm, the ultimate reality in which all our partial realities participate, is no longer there ... His place is taken by man and man's activity" (West 1970, 277). Many social thinkers would swear that this is the truth—"honest to God!" If, however, it is difficult to believe in God in the modern world, it is equally difficult to believe in man—whether man the planner whose reason opens up new vistas of technological development, or man the revolutionary who shoulders the responsibility for his self-emancipation and the creation of the new order of the future. Indeed, "disenchanted intellectuals," for whom the spell of the Enlightenment has been broken, wonder whether man can create a social order without a recovery of transcendence, according to an illuminating essay (Havard 1962). Where does man encounter the "Reality" which from the outside, so to speak, lays claim upon his existence, providing a motive for political responsibility, a source of meaning in the midst of social change, and a ground of ultimate hope?

In his impressive study of the theme of "order and history," Eric Voegelin boldly undertakes a renewal of the perennial philosophical investigation into the metaphysical source of order. Philosophical inquiry, he says, is a way of diagnosing "modes of existence in untruth" and, as in the case of Plato, is "the means of establishing islands of order in the disorder of the age." He states at the outset that his work "should be read, not as an attempt to explore curiosities of a dead past, but as an inquiry into the structure of the order in which we live presently" (*OH* I, xiv). This structure is not something which man may create by taking charge of his historical destiny, through technological planning or social revolution; rather, it has its source in divine being. Accordingly, Voegelin's first volume, *Israel and Revelation*, sets forth a philosophy of history informed by a philosophical reflection upon the mystery of being and an analysis of the symbolization expressing man's participation in being. In its courageous synthesis of Old Testament revelation with classical philosophy, in its viewing of the whole human struggle for meaningful order *sub specie aeternitatis*, in its grappling with the problematic interrelation of the divine and the human order, this study displays a scope and penetration which have rarely been achieved since Augustine's monumental work, *The City of God*.

One of the great heresies of our time, if one may be permitted to speak in this manner, is the separation of theology and politics. "We fail to recognize the indivisibility of the world," wrote Thomas Mann in *Joseph the Provider*, "when we think of religion and politics as fundamentally separate fields, which neither have nor should have anything to do with each other; to the extent even that one would be devalued and exposed as false if any trace of the other were to be found in it. For the truth is that they change but the garment, as Ishtar and Tammuz wear the veil by turns, and it is the whole that speaks when one speaks the language of the other" (Mann 1963, 908ff. [I am grateful to my daughter, Carol Hanawalt, for directing my attention to this passage.]). The great merit of Voegelin's work is that he seeks to recover "the whole" by penetrating to the dynamic of human existence—existence which, as he says, is not a given, static fact, but "a disturbing movement in the In-Between of ignorance and knowledge, of hope and fulfillment, and ultimately of life and death." It is from the experience of "man's participation in a *move-*

*ment* with a direction to be found or missed" that the question of meaning arises; and this question which concerns "the humanity of man," Voegelin maintains, leads the inquiring mind to search for the divine ground of being (GC, 63).

It is surprising that Old Testament theologians, for the most part, have paid little attention to Voegelin's work, which will probably be read long after much of the current literature has been forgotten. Undoubtedly this neglect is the result of the parochialism that afflicts professional disciplines and also of the present disarray of biblical theology. In any event, it is refreshing to find that one of the greatest political philosophers, who is also acclaimed as one of the greatest philosophical minds in the United States, has taken it upon himself to interpret the scriptures of Israel, having studied carefully the original sources and the secondary literature up to the time of his writing. If the Old Testament for many people is a "valley of dry bones," to use Ezekiel's figure, then Voegelin has made these bones live! Indeed, this is one of the few books on the Old Testament that has so captured my interest that I have eagerly wondered what would be on the next page.

In reviewing a work of such compact richness, it is tempting for an Old Testament scholar to turn aside to some of Voegelin's specific contributions to a field which, as he observes, has too often been lacking in philosophical clarity. It would be profitable, for instance, to discuss his forceful challenge to literary critics who have inherited the presuppositions of Julius Wellhausen; it is equally tempting to explore the implication of Voegelin's philosophy of symbolization for current hermeneutical discussions of biblical language, or his always-provocative, if not always-convincing exegeses of particular passages. In this essay, however, I shall concentrate on the main outline and thrust of *Israel and Revelation* (1956), the first in the projected *Order and History* series. As the series progressed over the years Voegelin's plan was modified; indeed, the appearance of the fourth volume, *The Ecumenic Age* (1975), has occasioned discussions of a shift in thinking that Voegelin himself has confessed (Altizer 1975; RANH; Niemeyer 1976; McKnight 1975). Nevertheless, the first volume, despite subsequent refinements in thinking, remains foundational. In view of its rare and illuminating exposition of the Old Testament, it deserves to be considered in its own right as a classic of our period.

Since the volume appeared more than twenty years ago, it is appropriate, first, to recollect its central theme, giving some attention to relevant studies of the Old Testament and the Ancient Near East.

Then I shall examine from several angles the tension between the divine order (kingdom of God) and Israel's existence as a people in political history. And finally, I shall raise some questions as to whether Voegelin's ontology takes full account of Israel's experience of reality, especially the problem of evil. Since Voegelin limits himself in this volume to the scriptures of Israel, the "Old Testament" in Christian terms, and alludes only occasionally to the New, my observations will largely remain within the context of Old Testament theology and will not venture too far into the question of the relationship between the Testaments or, in Voegelin's terms, "the experience of an extraordinary divine irruption in the existence of Jesus" (GC, 80; Douglass 1976).

## I

The presuppositions of Voegelin's analysis are set forth in an introductory section entitled "The Symbolization of Order." This discussion, which merits careful pondering, provides the ontology or philosophy of being which informs Voegelin's treatment of Israel's reception of revelation in the context of the civilizations of the Ancient Near East. The history of mankind, Voegelin maintains, is to be understood as a drama of being in which man takes part as an actor— not a spectator. Man participates in being, for being is "consubstantial" with him. The meaning of the drama in which man is involved is veiled in mystery. The divine mystery, however, is partially illumined when the compact symbols of man's participation in being are differentiated—that is, when some aspect of the total experience of reality is, so to speak, lifted out or sharpened up in human consciousness. Voegelin emphasizes that the sharpened consciousness of one aspect of reality does not completely invalidate the other elements of the compact experience, but rather provides the vantage point for a clearer awareness of man's existential participation in the divine order of being. When this happened in Israel, there appeared "a new type of man on the world-political scene" (*OH* I, 222), a man who stood forth as an individual and who lived and acted politically *vis-à-vis* God, the transcendent author and source of the divine order in creation and history. The main outlines of the emergence of this new historical consciousness are as follows:

1. In the Ancient Near East man existed within a "cosmological civilization," that is, one whose symbolization expressed "the mythical participation of society in the divine being that orders the cosmos." In Mesopotamia the empire in its spatial organization was re-

garded as the archetype of the order of the cosmos, on the principle of the correspondence between macrocosm and microcosm. At the *omphalos* (navel) or sacral center, where heaven and earth meet and divine being flows into society, the social order was periodically re-generated. During the New Year celebration the king, as the ana-logue of the deity, took part in the annual victory over the powers of chaos. Egyptian culture, too, was grounded in the consubstantiality of the divine order with the pharaonic order, Pharaoh being the me-diator through whom the divine *Maat* (order, justice, truth) ema-nated into society. Pharaonic order was "a continuous renewal and reenactment of cosmic order from eternity." Through Pharaoh, in whom the presence of God was manifest, the humblest subject par-ticipated in the "timeless serenity" of cosmic order. The Egyptian style of attunement of society with divine being created a static and stable civilization that survived without essential change for more than two thousand years.

2. In these civilizations there were tendencies toward a breakthrough into "the radical transcendence of divine being" over against mun-dane society. This was especially the case in Egypt, as evidenced in the Memphite theology and the reform of Akhenaton. But these ten-dencies toward the differentiation of compact experience and sym-bolization never achieved the transcendence that could become the ordering force of a religious personality who, in turn, could become the center of a new kind of community. Rather, gods and men, heaven and earth, "nature" and "history," the rhythms of fertility and reali-ties of politics, were bound up in one compact whole; and the "pri-mary experience" of the oneness of being and order was expressed in a mythical pattern of symbolism, each element of which was an inte-gral part of the whole.

3. It was in Israel that "the search for the true order of being was carried one step forward." Under Dynasty XIX, which struggled in vain to break the limits of imperial symbolization, Moses led an "exodus from cosmological civilization" in the thirteenth century B.C. The Exodus, Voegelin rightly observes, was not a mere event of pragmatic history but was, according to the witness of the Old Testament, an event of divine liberation. This theophanic event Voegelin interprets as "an irruption of the spirit [which] transfigured the pragmatic event into a drama of the soul and the acts of the drama into symbols of divine liberation" (*OH* I, 113). Israel was liberated from the Sheol (realm of the dead) of Egypt for a new life in historical form. The "divine choice" of Israel resulted in a differentiation of the formerly compact experience through a heightened awareness of the

gulf between immanent existence, in which gods and men coexist in a "consubstantial community," and the transcendent deity who is beyond the order of society regarded as an integral part of the cosmic order. The "leap in being" toward more perfect attunement with transcendent reality, however, was primarily an event in the soul of Moses, though one that was anticipated in the case of Abraham. The "inrush of divine reality" created a new order of the soul and, through the agency of Moses, a new type of society living in immediacy under the kingdom of God. History was "the inner form" of Israel's existence under God, in contrast to other civilizations of the time that existed in the form of cosmological myth. Voegelin states that without Israel there would be no history—only the recurring rhythms of cosmological civilization.

4. From the very first, however, this life of the spirit was difficult to maintain, owing to "the pressures of mundane existence." Tradition portrays the history of Israel in the prestate period as an undulating movement of recessions from and returns to the covenantal order of existence given in the Mosaic revelation. The "greater derailment" came when, under the duress of political necessity, the people demanded a monarchy like the nations round about. This fateful development brought about a reversal of the Exodus and reentry into the Sheol of cosmological civilization—that is, a fall from true existence under God to the inauthentic existence of cosmological empire. From this point on the perpetual task of history was to regain the order of God which had been eroded or eclipsed by the influences of mundane existence.

5. Israel's history would have been an indefinite undulatory movement of defections from and returns to the order of the covenant had it not been for the Prophets. These "new carriers of meaning" rejected the institution of the monarchy and awakened the universalistic potentialities of Yahweh's revelation to Moses that lay dormant in the tradition. To them, the existence or non-existence of the kingdom was irrelevant to "life in righteousness before the Lord." Their mission was to recall Israel to the covenant mode of existence which was "transparent for the order of transcendent reality." The prophets were, as Voegelin puts it, spokesmen of "the new Israel in search of an effective organization" (*OH* I, 231)—the new order, or one might even say the "new creation."

6. Since, however, the prophetic call to return to the true order of being fell on deaf ears, the *omphalos* shifted from the Chosen People to the Prophet himself (e.g., Jeremiah) who, at odds with society, entered into the suffering of God and by faith participated in the

divine constitution of history. The climax of Old Testament prophecy was Second Isaiah's portrayal of the Suffering Servant, said to be the Prophet himself, and subsequent individuals of this type. The keynote of Second Isaiah's message, according to Voegelin, is "Israel's exodus from itself" in order to penetrate all mankind with God's revelation. Thus the Servant represents a new community, one which no longer has to reside in Canaan but, with a universal outreach, includes each individual whose personal soul is "the sensorium of transcendence" and becomes the center of an ecumenical mankind under God.[1]

7. The end result was a differentiation of *theologia supranaturalis* from *theologia civilis*, both of which were united compactly in primitive societies. The history of mankind, Voegelin says, was punctuated by "other irruptions of transcendent reality, such as the illumination of a Buddha or the opsis of Plato"; but the in-breaking of divine reality found its "optimum clarity" in the Bible where history is "structured" by crucial events such as the Exodus or the Incarnation.[2] From this standpoint of faith, the whole history of mankind is viewed as a drama in which every society, in its allotted time and space, struggles for attunement with divine being and, in some measure, approaches "the maximal clarity of divine revelation."

Before turning specifically to Voegelin's exposition of the Old Testament, it is worth noting that this philosophical approach throws new light on discussions about "historical revelation." Some scholars have challenged the view, regnant in the period of the so-called biblical theology movement, that Yahweh, the God of Israel, was known as the God of history and that history was the chief mode of divine revelation.[3] A Scandinavian scholar, Bertil Albrektson, has extended this criticism beyond the Old Testament. By means of quotations from Mesopotamian sources, he attempts to show that the testimonies to divine activity in history were not peculiar to the Old Testament. This, however, is a very deceptive argument, especially since Albrektson admits at the conclusion that "the idea of divine acts in history," in Israel on the one hand and in Mesopotamia on the other, "may well have occupied a rather different place in the different patterns of beliefs" (Albrektson 1967, esp. 115). The issue is not whether texts from both Babylonia and Israel witness to God's historical activity. That has really never been disputed. Rather the question is the semantic field, or as Voegelin puts it, the pattern of symbolization within which the respective statements are made. And this in turn raises the question of whether the gods—cosmic natural forces who were also coparticipants with men in society—were truly transcendent to "the consubstantial structure of the community of being" and therefore supracosmic, supernatural.[4]

Voegelin is right, I believe, in saying that Israel's knowledge of God brought about a sense of history which was a novelty in a cultural environment dominated by a mythical view of reality. History was, indeed, "the inner form" of Israel's existence before Yahweh. Unlike some modern theologians—Jewish, Catholic, and Protestant—Voegelin does not speak of *Heilsgeschichte*, or a history of salvation that is distinguished from profane history. Indeed, in his recent volume, *The Ecumenic Age*, he abandons the view that history as a linear course of events was a discovery of Israel, since historiogenesis had its inception, at least in a mythopoeic form, by the end of the third millennium B.C., as evidenced, for instance, by the Sumerian King List.[5] He is concerned to stress "the leap in being" which brought a new historical *consciousness*. It should be added, however, that Israel's experience of the Holy as redemptive concern and ethical demand was expressed in terms of a "story" or "history" (Exod 1-24) and in due course led to a historiography which had its counterpart not in ancient Mesopotamia or Egypt, but in Greece.

Israel's breakthrough into a new historical consciousness poses a problem to which we must give attention. The fundamental dilemma of Israel's existence, according to Voegelin's interpretation, is "the relationship between the life of the spirit and life in the world" (*OH* I, 183). The "spiritual meaning of the Exodus," he maintains, was never fully freed from the concrete Exodus, and the transcendent kingdom of God was never completely disengaged from "the sensuous, concrete symbols of Canaan." The Old Testament, to be sure, witnesses in various ways to the struggle of the spirit to escape confinement in a particular form of social organization and to separate the kingdom of God from the collective life and institutions of a people. But the attempt was never completely successful. Just as new wine could not be contained in old wineskins, so the leap in being for a life of the spirit in worldly existence could not be expressed adequately in Israel's historical symbols. Or, to use Voegelin's figure, the Old Testament carries a "mortgage" of the mundane upon the transcendent. The mortgage was reduced, especially by the Prophets; but it was not liquidated until the time when Christianity, announcing that the *Logos* had become flesh, united Israel's prophetic witness with the Greek philosophical "love of being through love of divine Being" which is the end of all existence.

## II

With this summary of Voegelin's volume in mind, our task is to consider what bearing "revelation" has upon man's historical existence, which is inescapably political. It is not accidental that Voegelin devotes the first volume of his projected *opus magnum* to ancient Israel. Theologians have often observed that if the Bible speaks anywhere to man's existence in the political forms of society, it does so primarily through that part of the biblical canon Christians term the Old Testament. The New Testament, heavily under the influence of apocalyptic ways of thinking, made a virtue of "patient endurance" until the end, which was believed to be imminent. Therefore, except for a few passages like Romans 13 and 1 Timothy 2, it does not address itself to the problems of ongoing political life. On the other hand, the Old Testament, in which apocalyptic expectations stand on the periphery (e.g., the book of Daniel), struggles with the question of what the revelation of God means for this world in which we live and move and have our being. We are reminded of the down-to-earth quality of the Old Testament by the fact that its two major motifs—the covenant (treaty) between two parties and the kingdom of God—are drawn from political experience. According to the Old Testament, God's revelation touches human existence in a society whose symbols provide the form of man's self-understanding and his knowledge of God. As Voegelin observes, even the course of pragmatic history can be transfigured, in the vision of faith, into "sacred history," whose "single events become paradigms of God's way with man in this world" (*OH* I, 121).

The Dutch theologian, Arnold van Ruler, has emphasized that Christianity would be impoverished, particularly in those areas having to do with political organization and social responsibility, if the Old Testament with its "overplus" were not part of the Christian canon (Ruler 1971). Voegelin would agree, I believe, that the New Testament presupposes this overplus; but he does not fall into van Ruler's error of supposing that the state is a theocratic order, a creation of God. On the contrary, Voegelin maintains that, because of the gulf between the transcendent and the mundane, the divine order can never be incarnate in a particular form of government or in any ethnic community. No "chosen people," he insists, can be "the *omphalos* of history."

This is a valid warning against the notion, which has proved to be pernicious in recent history, of a chosen race (e.g., the white) or a *Herrenvolk* that arrogates to itself a position of superiority. It is important to bear in mind, however, that "Israel" was constituted as a "people" (Hebrew: *'am*) long before the rise of the state under David. As the Jewish scholar, E. A. Speiser, has pointed out, Israelite tradition speaks of "the people of Yahweh" but not "the nation of Yahweh" (Speiser 1960). The sacral term, *Israel*, which once referred to a tribal confederacy loosely bound together in covenant relationship with God, has suffered the fate of corruption into the name of a state, as happened when Jeroboam I appropriated the term for the northern kingdom, or again in recent history when it was adopted to designate a secular state of the Middle East. The plain fact is that "state" or "nation" does not describe the unique calling and self-understanding of the "people of Yahweh" whose life-story is recorded in the Old Testament. The late Martin Noth began his *History of Israel* with the sober observation that Israel, despite its similarities with contemporary peoples, appeared on the historical scene as "a stranger in the world of its own time, a stranger wearing the garments and behaving in the manner of its age, yet separate from the world it lived in" (Noth 1960, 2; Anderson, 1971). Voegelin himself asserts that "there was apparently no factor in original Yahwism that would have imposed a particular political form on the faithful" (*OH* I, 219). One could agree to this statement readily if it were to mean that Israel's existence as a people was adaptable to various political forms. Voegelin, however, seems to press the point to the conclusion that Israel's attempt to adapt to any political organization was from the outset doomed to failure. The failure of the Israelite experiment was not just a failure in pragmatic history—the fate of a small nation overwhelmed by the imperial might of Assyria and Babylonia. Rather, owing to the transcendent character of the divine order, Israel's history in the world—that is, in the realm of political struggle and political organization—was intrinsically a history of failure.

This evaluation of Israel's existence as a people should not be confused with that of Rudolf Bultmann who, from existentialist premises, regards Israel's history as a *Geschichte des Scheiterns*—an abortive history. The miscarriage occurred, according to Bultmann, because the motifs of the covenant, the people of God, and the kingdom of God were deeply enmeshed in worldly existence; therefore, the sacred history, as Israel understood it, moved toward the innerworldly goal of the covenant people living in its God-given land under a Davidic messiah. The Old Testament, he says, is not a revelation for the Christian and its history is not "our history." Only from the standpoint of faith in Jesus Christ can this abortive history be understood, in a curiously negative sense, as "promise." For it demonstrates the impossibility of the realization of God's kingdom in worldly history and points beyond failure to God's gracious action in Jesus Christ, which transposes man into an eschatological existence and makes him a "new creature" (2 Cor 5:17). The meaning of history cannot be understood by surveying the whole course of human history; rather, its meaning is given in the present when man, critically reflecting upon the heritage of the past and with a view toward the open future, realizes his true historicity (*Geschichtlichkeit*) in decision and responsibility (Bultmann 1963, 1962). Voegelin has directed a penetrating criticism against this existentialist view which, in the manner of Gnosticism, "annihilates the world and history" by seizing a fragmentary truth out of the whole and eliminating or omitting other aspects of man's experience and symbolization of reality. The experience of "eschatological existence," he says, is not in itself wrong; for "we have indeed experiences of alienation; of being strangers in a world that is not ours; of a true measure of existence that is not taken from existence in this world; of a true reality, not of this world, whence this measure comes to us."[6] But the differentiation of one element of the whole truth, he insists, does not justify dismissing other aspects of the more compact experience. The leap in being was not "a leap out of existence into world-transcendent reality."

Nevertheless, Voegelin maintains that God's revelation to mankind did not reach its optimum clarity in the Old Testament because it was too closely bound up with Israel, the people who lived in a concrete society on the land of Canaan. The Mosaic leap in being had to be disengaged from the collective symbolism of Israel's self-understanding so that the individual personality might emerge as the locus of "the new order of the soul." For in the last analysis it is the psyche which is "the field of right order." The personal attunement with the order of divine being is said to have been realized in a measure by the Prophets, who struggled to emancipate the psyche from the collectivism of the Chosen People. Perhaps, Voegelin suggests, the Prophets were handicapped by the lack of a positive philosophical vocabulary such as was found in Greece. In any case, prophetic personalism was unable to break through to philosophy and to the idea of an immortal soul, perfected through grace beyond death (*OH* I, 232-42). Furthermore, "the prophets apparently were not only unable to see, but not even interested in finding, a way from the formation of the soul to institutions and customs they could consider compatible with the knowledge and fear of God" (446-47).

It is not my purpose to challenge the philosophical position from which this judgment is made. Here the question is whether Voegelin's analysis does justice to the materials of the Old Testament. Admittedly, the Old Testament as a whole does not break through into universalism, at least the kind of universalism that excludes the people whom Yahweh has called and formed for his special service in the world. There is one major exception to this, and Voegelin could have made much more of it. I refer to the wisdom literature, represented by such writings as Proverbs, Ecclesiastes, Job, or the Wisdom of Ben Sirach. It is well known that literature of this type, in contrast to the historical and prophetic literature of the Old Testament, makes little use of the historical experiences and symbols of Israel: promises to the patriarchs, Exodus, Sinai covenant, entrance into Canaan, Davidic covenant, and so on. Israel's sages turned their attention away from the unique events and the great historical sequences to what remains constant as a pledge of God's faithfulness. For them "the fear of Yahweh is the beginning of wisdom" in that it leads to a confidence in the ordering will of Yahweh manifest in creation, society, and individual life.[7] It is doubtful, however, whether tendencies toward "the idea of the psyche" can be traced in the parts of the Old Testament that come under Voegelin's scrutiny: the Pentateuch, the historiographical works, and the prophetic literature. From the very first the Mosaic "leap in being" demanded a *people* in historical form. Voegelin acknowledges this; but it should be emphasized that peoplehood was not accidental but essential to the revelation, as evident from the recurring covenant formula (e.g., Jer 31:33): "I will be their God and they shall be my people." To be sure, the relationship between God and people, according to the prophetic understanding, did not guarantee success in the world. Indeed, the Prophets perceived two Israels: the empirical Israel which stood under the severe judgment of God, and the new Israel that would arise out of the purging fires of suffering with whom Yahweh would continue his work in history. Voegelin fails to emphasize that Jeremiah's prophecy concerning "the new covenant" (Jer 31:31-33) portrays a covenant with "the whole house of Israel." Although the Prophet condemns externalization and speaks of the inwardness of the covenant, whose law is written on the heart, he does not propose a new individualism, nor does he suggest that the former collectivism was a deformation of the Mosaic covenant. Furthermore, Second Isaiah's prophecy (Isa 40-55), which Voegelin regards as the climax of the Old Testament, begins with Yahweh's message of consolation to "my people," although the Prophet understands the election of Israel in the spacious perspective of the divine purpose for creation and all mankind.

## III

Once we start from the premise that Yahweh constituted a people, a historical community within which the individual has his being, the question arises as to what bearing the knowledge of God has upon man's life in society where one must act politically and assume social responsibility. Yahweh's controversy with Israel, as found in Micah 6:1-8, indicates that the historical symbols of Israelite tradition (i.e., the "righteous acts" of Yahweh summarized in verses 4-5) provide the standard for action in society: "He has showed you, O man, what is good; and what does Yahweh require of you but to do justice, and to love kindness, and to walk humbly with your God?"

It is important to begin by recognizing that divine revelation induces a "tension," as Voegelin says, between the spiritual order and the temporal. This tension is inescapable if, as Micah's prophetic exhortation suggests, the standard by which human actions are judged is derived from the experience of the "transcendent," not from the realm of pragmatic politics. Voegelin deals effectively with the tension that existed in Israelite tradition between the kingdom of God and the kingdom of David. Old Testament traditions show that the rise of David as king brought innovations that evoked the sharp criticism of representatives of the old theocratic confederacy known as Israel. The controversy over kingship was precipitated in part by the pragmatic adoption of a centralized form of government capable of coping with the new realities of political power—initially the threat of the Philistines to establish an empire in Palestine. Samuel reminded the elders of Israel that if they were to have a king, "like the nations," the royal power would divest them of the liberties they had enjoyed during the days of the tribal confederacy (1 Sam 8:10-18). In a deeper sense, however, the struggle over kingship was a theological one which went to the very heart of Israel's faith. In the ancient world, as Voegelin observes, kingship was understood in the context of a mythical view of reality. The king was regarded as the mediator of the cosmic order evidenced in the rising and setting of the sun, the rhythmic regularity of the seasons, and the stability of heaven and earth. Historical changes, according to this view, occurred within a cosmic setting that gave ultimate meaning to man's historical existence and delivered him from the recurrent threat of chaos. Under David, Israel emerged from the restricted sphere of the tribal confederacy and "entered the cosmos," thereby gaining a broadened view of Yahweh's sovereignty over creation and history. No longer was Israel's self-understanding expressed primarily in the pastoral imagery of a seminomadic people; rather, the key image came to be the City (Zion), at the center of which was a complex of buildings (temple and palace) whose architecture, designed by Phoenician architects, reflected the mythical views of the environment: Canaan, Mesopotamia, and Egypt.[8] Under the assumption that a correspondence exists between the heavenly *tabnith* or model (cf. Exod 25:9) and the small-scale earthly replica, it was possible to maintain that Yahweh was present in the Jerusalem temple and at the same time enthroned in his heavenly palace (as in Isaiah's inaugural vision, Isa 6) (Clements 1965). This urban theology, reflected in a number of the psalms, provided the metaphor for Augustine's work, *The City of God* (Ps 87:3).

The adoption of the symbols of cosmological civilization, however, was qualified by a particular kind of covenant theology sponsored by the Jerusalem court. According to the royal covenant of Zion, which is associated with the court prophet Nathan (2 Sam 7), Yahweh made a *berîth 'olam*, or covenant in perpetuity, with David, promising to uphold his dynasty regardless of the strengths or weaknesses of particular kings. Unlike the Mosaic covenant, the "everlasting covenant" was fundamentally unconditional: Yahweh bound himself with promises of grace to David and, through David, to the people. This "theology of social stability," as it has been called, dealt effectively with the problem of the transfer of power to a new royal administration. By minimizing the risks of social disorder that attended the death of a king, it undoubtedly contributed to the unbroken duration of the Davidic dynasty for some four hundred years.

Moreover, the royal theologians, by drawing freely upon the cosmic symbolism of the Ancient Near East, brought the faith in Yahweh as creator—a faith which previously had been somewhat peripheral to Israel's traditions—into the very center of theological interest (Anderson 1967, 43–77). These theologians, who stressed the "everlasting covenant" with David, were vitally interested in the creation symbolism of ancient civilizations which also were concerned for social order and stability. In Jerusalem the everlasting throne of Yahweh, who is enthroned over the insurgent powers of chaos (Pss 29, 93), was regarded as the heavenly complement of the order and stability of the Davidic throne. The decrees by which Yahweh established cosmic order (Ps 93:5) were considered to be analogous to the mandate by which he installed his king on Zion (Ps 2:7).

Voegelin rightly emphasizes that Israel's covenant symbols did not require the rejection of everything else known as true in cosmological civilizations. Indeed, Israelite tradition was immeasurably enriched and deepened when mythical elements, liberated from their context of cosmological symbolization, were appropriated to express divine transcendence.[9] This point deserves emphasis, for man's existence is defined not only by his place in the continuum of history, but by his relation to the constancy of the cosmic order, as wisdom literature testifies. Yet, while the two kinds of symbolization were not mutually exclusive, it should also be said that the mythical language was transformed when brought into the Israelite context of interpretation.

A case in point is the divine kingship of the Ancient Near East. Although Israelite poets could adopt Egyptian court style in speaking of the Davidic king and could even address the king in one instance as "God" (Ps 45:6), this extravagant court language should not be pressed too far. Did the Davidic king, as Voegelin maintains, really become the mediator of the divine order in the sense of Pharaoh (*OH* I, 272)? Evidence for this is lacking, despite the contentions of some Scandinavian scholars. An interesting aspect of the problem is the *imago Dei* of Genesis 1:26 (cf. Ps 8:5). In both ancient Mesopotamia and Egypt the king, ex officio, was regarded as the "image" of the deity; indeed, in Akkadian texts the cognate of the biblical term *selem* (*salmu*) is used (Schmidt 1964, 127-48; Wildberger 1965).[10] Whether the king was divinely commissioned (Mesopotamia) or divine (Egypt), the intention was to say that he was a mediator, through whom the deity was present in society, preeminently at the temple, the cosmic *omphalos*. In Israel the king was regarded as the *elected son* of God, but the expression "image of God" was never applied to him. Rather, this Near Eastern motif was "democratized" and applied to man. Man is the image of God, the one in whom God manifests his presence on earth and through whom God's rule is to be manifest. As God's vicegerent, man is to rule benevolently over his environment and other forms of life, and thus is to bring the natural would into the drama of God's history with his people (Anderson 1976c). If Psalm 8 comes from the period of the monarchy, as is probable, the democratization of kingship theology took place early in the history of the Jerusalem cult. In any event, this reinterpretation of royal theology is a significant illustration of Voegelin's thesis concerning "the shift from the cosmic *omphalos* to the soul of man."

It must not be supposed that the covenant was a homogenous form in the Old Testament. As a matter of fact, there are several covenant theologies. Standing in rivalry with the Davidic covenant discussed above was the Mosaic covenant, which formally was similar to the suzerainty covenants or treaties made by Hittite kings with vassal states.[11] The Hittite covenant form includes the self-identification of the covenant maker, a recitation of his benevolent deeds on behalf of the vassal, a stipulation of laws binding on the vassal in gratitude for benefits received, and an appeal for obedience under the sanction of blessings and curses. The pattern of the Mosaic covenant is so similar to this that many scholars believe Israel understood its relationship to Yahweh in terms of this political form, perhaps from the time of the tribal confederacy which presumably was instituted at Shechem under Joshua (Josh 24). If this is true, Sinai (i.e., covenant and law) was not "a rival center of meaning" alongside the Exodus, as Voegelin asserts (*OH* I, 137f.). Rather, Exodus and Sinai belonged inseparably together. In the Torah story, as Emil Fackenheim points out (1972, 8-16), God's presence in history is manifest through two interrelated "epoch-making events" or, as he prefers to say, "root experiences"— namely, "the saving experience" and "the commanding experience." One of the tasks of Old Testament theology, in my judgment, is to understand how the Israelite experience of divine Reality, or in Voegelin's terms the Israelite "leap in being," was expressed in two major forms of symbolization: one based on an international treaty form (suzerainty treaty) and the other profoundly influenced by the cosmological symbolism of king and temple; both were alien to Israel's earliest traditions. The important thing to observe in this connection is that the Mosaic covenant, in contrast to the Davidic, was essentially conditional in character: "*If* you will hear my voice and keep my covenant, you shall be my own possession among all the peoples" (Exod 19:5). While the Davidic covenant sought to insure social stability in the midst of historical change and the constant threat of chaos, the Mosaic covenant called man to decision, placed an awesome responsibility upon him, and set before him a future that, under the judgment of God, was contingent upon his behavior. There is good reason to believe that after the revolt of the northern tribes from the Davidic empire, this type of covenant theology was revived in the circles of North Israel, as represented by Hosea and Deuteronomy. Unlike the South (Judah), the North did not develop a theology of social stability. No dynasty—not even that of the great king Omri—was able to maintain itself, and the kingdom finally came to an end in a wretched state of social disorder (Hos 7:1ff.).

Prophets who stood in the northern Mosaic covenant tradition held out the prospect of the dissolution of the covenant and the end of the people, because of Israel's betrayal of the covenant obligations. In the face of the persistent disloyalty, manifest in Israel's history and in contemporary social life, the covenant formula, "my people," would be inverted to "not my people," for as Hosea announced, Yahweh's verdict was "you are not my people and I am not your God" (Hos

1:8). On the other hand, Isaiah of Jerusalem, a southerner who was profoundly indebted to royal theology, declared that the impending historical judgment of Yahweh would bring about a purification of Zion, but the City would stand and a descendant of David would rise to govern a remnant of the people. These two major covenant theologies existed in tension with one another, as Voegelin observes. They converged, however, in the prophecy of Second Isaiah, in which the Prophet drew deeply upon the symbolism of the Exodus tradition (though ignoring the Sinai covenant) and announced that Yahweh had transferred the promises of the Davidic covenant to the *people* (Isa 55:3) (Anderson 1976b). In the message of this prophet, the "everlasting covenant," based unconditionally upon divine grace and forgiveness and not upon the contingencies of human history, opened a new future for Israel and, through the Suffering Servant, for all mankind.

## IV

We come, now, to the heart of the problem—namely, the "mortgage" that characterized Israel's existence in the Metaxy, or "In-Between." Israel's covenant symbolization, Voegelin says, was "a perpetual mortgage of the world-immanent, concrete event on the transcendent truth that on its occasion was revealed" (*OH* I, 164). Moses experienced a breakthrough into transcendence that went beyond the dim apprehensions of divine reality in Egypt or Mesopotamia, but the transcendent reality was couched in the sensuous, collective symbols of the Exodus and the conquest of Canaan. The question was whether, in the course of Israelite tradition, "the mortgage of the historical circumstances of revelation" could be gradually reduced so that the universalistic and transcendental implications of divine revelation could be acknowledged by people in the present (369).

Voegelin maintains that the mortgage was made permanent by the book of Deuteronomy, which codified the Torah, thereby mummifying the historical revelation and bequeathing to the future the legalism based on a "canonical" book. The great Prophets, however, sought to liquidate the mortgage. The prophetic struggle, he says, went through three stages. First, Amos and Hosea expected the political restoration of Israel under the conditions of pragmatic history. Second, Isaiah's awareness of the gulf between present society and the divine order prompted a metastatic faith in the rule of a future king under completely changed mundane conditions. And finally, Jeremiah turned the futuristic faith back to the present, and the Prophet *himself*, as one who enacted the fate of his people, became the *omphalos* of God's order in history. Thus the messianic hope moved toward separating the eternal from the temporal, the spiritual from the political, the universal from Israelite collectivism. The end of the mortgage, which occurred with Christianity, was anticipated by Second Isaiah's message of Israel's exodus from itself to communicate God's revelation to all mankind.

In Voegelin's ontological perspective, the Israelite decision to establish a kingdom "like the nations" was the great aberration from the Mosaic revelation or, in his terms, "fall from being." The witness of the Old Testament on this political development, however, is ambivalent. This is particularly clear in the historical traditions, some of which approve the kingdom as a providential development, though others frown upon it as Yahweh's grudging concession to Israel's improper demand. The Prophets, too, are not unanimous on the subject. Hosea, to be sure, has a predominantly negative attitude, for he traces the corruption of Israel's society to Gibea, presumably a reference to the home city of Saul, the first king of Israel (Hos 9:9); and he states flatly that Yahweh gave Israel kings in his anger (Hos 13:11). But this antimonarchic stand did not prevent the prophecy from being received in the south (after the fall of Samaria, 721 B.C.), where it was understood to anticipate a return to "Yahweh their God and David their king" after a period of corrective punishment (Hos 3:5). Of course, southern Prophets were bitter in their attacks upon the reigning kings, but, in varying degrees, their faith in "the messianic royal ideal" prompted them to believe that the Davidic dynasty would not be broken (Engnell 1969, 160-62).[12]

The fact is that the Prophets do not always say the same thing in regard to the shifting scene of politics. Nathan, as we have seen, provided an oracle concerning Yahweh's covenant with David and his dynasty. Elijah returned from the traditional mount of the Mosaic covenant to sponsor political revolutions in Syria and North Israel (1 Kgs 19:15-18). Isaiah of Jerusalem spoke of the inviolability of Zion, while his contemporary, Micah, insisted that the Assyrian dictator was the rod of Yahweh's judgment against Israel (Isa 10:5-19), and Second Isaiah, who stood in the same Isaianic circle of tradition, announced that Cyrus of Persia was Yahweh's instrument (literally, "messiah") for liberating Israel from political bondage in Babylonia (Isa 44:24-45:13). In short, "nothing is taken for granted," as Kornelis Miskotte remarks, and thus there is ample room in Israelite tradition for what we would call "experimental thinking" in the realm of politics (Miskotte 1967, 274, 278).

At one point Voegelin's discussion prompts the question of whether the word of Yahweh, spoken by the Prophet, may exert a power for social reform. In the context of a comparison of Isaiah and Jeremiah, he remarks: "The order of society in history is reconstituted in fact through the men who challenge the disorder of the surrounding society with the order they experience as living in themselves. The word of the prophet is not spoken to the wind, it is not futile or impotent, if it does not reform the society which he loves because it has given him birth" (*OH* I, 483). There was a profound difference, he maintains, between Isaiah and Jeremiah. Isaiah envisioned reform through *metastasis*—a term that refers to a "change in the constitution of being." In doing so, he "tried the impossible: to make the leap in being a leap out of existence into a divinely transfigured world beyond the laws of mundane existence" (452). Later, in a virtual *tour de force*, Jeremiah returned the prophetic word to "the untransfigured present," the world in which we live. This achievement, however, made an impact not in the reform of society, but in the formation of a new community: the "remnant" of Israel which is a "continuation of order in history, when its realization in the pragmatic order of a people is in crisis." "In Jeremiah," writes Voegelin, "the human personality had broken the compactness of collective existence and recognized itself as the authoritative source of order in society" (485). Despite metastatic visions of Prophets like Isaiah, the Israel that was organized as a kingdom "went the way of all organization, their government, and kings in history." What is left, however, is a residue of individuals, like Jeremiah, who attune their existence in the present to "the order of being."

In his understanding of the Prophets, Voegelin thus seeks to correct the delusion that man can achieve the promised land or the perfect social order in history through evolution or revolution. "The will to transform reality into something which by essence it is not," he states, "is the rebellion against *the nature of things as ordained by God*" (*OH* I, 453, emphasis added). His deep concern about this matter is voiced in the preface to this volume, where he says that "the prophetic conception of a change in the constitution of being lies at the root of our contemporary beliefs in the perfection of society, either through progress or through a communist revolution." He goes on to say: "Metastatic faith is one of the great sources of disorder, if not the principal one, in the contemporary world; and it is a matter of life and death for all of us to understand the phenomenon and to find remedies against it before it destroys us" (xiii). Time and again he reminds us that the problem of history cannot be solved by "Canaans or Utopias."

There is a ring of biblical truth in this, though Voegelin's warning against "metastatic visions" applies more to modern use of the Prophets than to the prophetic message itself. Will Herberg, a convert to biblical faith form Marxism, has shown persuasively that modern perfectionist views, such as that of communism, are secularized versions of the prophetic understanding of history (Herberg 1976a, 180-89; 1976b). I cannot agree, however, that the prophetic view itself is the root of our contemporary troubles. To be sure, Isaiah contrasted his corrupt society, which was completely lacking in health (Isa 1:5-6), to the new society in which an idealized Davidic king would inaugurate a region of unprecedented peace and justice (Isa 9:1-7); but the portrayal concludes with the emphatic statement that this would be accomplished through "the zeal of Yahweh of hosts," that is, through wonderful divine intervention. Moreover, the vision of the ecumenical age, when nations will stream to the *omphalos* of Zion and learn of war no more (Isa 2:1-4), is placed in the immediate context of vivid portrayals of the Day of Yahweh—the Day which will be against every symbol of civilizational achievement and human presumption, when men will flee into caves of the cliffs before the terrible manifestation of the divine majesty (Isa 2:6-22). Clearly there is no basis anywhere in prophecy for the modern illusion that man can build the kingdom of God on earth, either through technological planning or revolutionary zeal. This notion is completely alien to the prophetic understanding of history.

Having said this, however, we come back to the fundamental problem of human existence in society, and specifically to the "gulf" that separates God and man. Voegelin suggests that the impulse for social reform is located in the soul of the persons, or the remnant community, who experience the order of being in themselves. But the Prophets have a much more dynamic view of God's activity in the political arena. They insist that Yahweh himself has chosen to implicate himself in human affairs and that his presence, rather than upholding "things as they are," provides the dynamic for social change. Difficulties inevitably arise, of course, when the poetic and concrete idiom of the Old Testament is translated into philosophical categories such as transcendence and immanence. It is appropriate to use the word *transcendence* to express the truth of the second commandment of the Mosaic decalogue: the God whom Israel worships cannot be domesticated within man's world. He is not the captive of man's theology or philosophy, the prisoner of man's political schemes, or the guarantor of man's values and priorities. When men build a "golden calf," attempting thereby to bring the divine into cultural or historical visibility, this "god" must die.

Yet there is another side of the matter, which is just as important in the Israelite tradition—namely, the announcement that God has "condescended" to take part in the human story, speaking his Word in human words and making his presence known redemptively. This theology of "divine condescension" is found in paradigmatic form in the Exodus story. The story goes that he "knew their sufferings," and that he had "come down" to rescue them from bondage to the mightiest political power of the day and to bring them into a new land where they could find their freedom in his service (Exod 3:7-8). The narrator goes on to say that, even though the slaves preferred the fleshpots of Egypt to the possibility of freedom, Yahweh refused to leave them in a no-exit situation where the future was closed but led them "out of the old" and "into the new." It is not surprising that recent "theologies of hope," especially those produced by the black community, have made much of this story.

The Prophets spoke of Yahweh's "transcendence" in such a way as to portray his awesome presence in history. For Hosea, Yahweh was "the Holy One in your midst" (Hos 11:9); and even Amos could subscribe to the belief in Immanuel ("God with us"), with the proper reservations (Am 5:14-15). Jeremiah, it is true, countered the message of the false prophets by saying that Yahweh is the God who is "afar off," not a subjective phenomenon of the dream world; but his purpose was to stress that God is the inescapable One, from whom there is no hiding place (Jer 21:23-32). The social arena, according to the Prophets, is the sphere where Israel must prepare to meet her God (Am 4:12), who is actively involved in history. Hence, they spoke to those who have power—political, economic, or social—and were in a position to act. The justice they demanded was not an abstract moral standard, but the exercise of power in setting things right, in restoring oppressed individuals or groups to their proper place, in giving persons the freedom to be human in God's covenant society. Since justice is a requirement that must be faced from case to case, they offered no overall plan for social reform. Rather, they attacked the abuses of privilege or power, such as the land-grabbing from the poor by those who have economic power, the callous indifference of rulers to the welfare of the people, the capitulation of religious leaders to national interests, or the failure of the law courts to administer justice impartially. Neither pragmatists nor idealists, they proclaimed

the actuality of God in the world—the God who was actively engaged in the human struggle to create the peace (*shalom*) which is a
wholeness and healthiness manifest in the midst of time as a pledge
and foretaste of his ultimate intention for mankind.

For me it is a serious question whether Voegelin's theme of the
"mortgage" does justice to the dynamic character of human existence
and the participation of God in the human drama. There is much in
the Old Testament which indicates that God, in his own way, acts to
change the world as it is. A philosophy of being is inadequate for
dealing fully with this literature, if it emphasizes the attunement of
the individual soul to the transcendent order of being. According to
Israel's witnesses, there is no true being unless it is a being-in-relation-
ship, and there can be no attunement with God unless it is manifest
in the social sphere of man's life. This is the reason, I believe, that the
Old Testament never approaches anything like the Greek doctrine of
the immortality of the soul and why at its frontier, where it begins to
touch the New Testament style of expression, it adopts the apocalyptic view of the resurrection of the body (self) at the consummation of
the whole historical and cosmic drama (Dan 12:2-3). In contrast to
other cultures, Israel did not develop a mortuary cult and displayed
surprisingly little interest in a transcendent solution to the problems
of human existence beyond the grave. In the Old Testament, life and
death are understood dynamically. Death is regarded as a power that
extends its empire into the land of the living, manifesting its aggres-
sion in any limitation, bodily or social, which reduces man's historical being in relationship with God and his fellow men. And life, on
the other hand is measured by the wholeness and fullness of man's
being in the context of historical relationships, within which one can
join the worshipping community in praising God for his goodness
and faithfulness. The laments of the Book of Psalms, which sound
the depths of our experience of alienation in society today, are cries
of distress to God for deliverance here and now from faceless "enemies" (often described in mythical imagery) that reduce "the vitality
of the individual" to the verge of the non-being of death. And the
thanksgivings of the Psalms are praises to the God who, as the vindi-
cator of justice, manifests his righteousness by restoring the suppli-
ant to some measure of the fullness of human life.[13]

Voegelin touches on this dynamic aspect of God's revelation when,
in an illuminating discussion of the Tetragrammaton (YHWH =
Yahweh), he speaks of the name of God as the "frontier" of God's
presence with man (*OH* I, 411, 413). The context of the disclosure
of God's name (Exod 3:13-15) indicates that this frontier is the fu-

ture which lies under the sign to Moses, "I will be with you." God's being, as it is turned toward man, is manifest as a being-with, a going-with. The God who goes with his people into the future, however, cannot be reduced to human size or visibility, but remains free to have mercy on whom he will have mercy (Exod 33:18-20; cf. Rom 9:15). He is free to act as he will and to manifest himself in any way he chooses. He retains the initiative and, consistent with his character and faithful to his purpose, alters his course of action from time to time in view of the changing responses of man in history. The name of God, by which the people call upon him in worship and by whose authority Prophets speak, is indeed the frontier of God's presence in the world. Those who face this frontier are called to act in the world: to assume responsibility for changing the relations of power so that justice may prevail, and to rule over their God-given natural environment in a way that will sanctify human life and glorify the Creator. Life in the spirit versus life in the world is not an alternative for Prophets, narrators, and psalmists who stand before the mystery and majesty of the God who has chosen to become involved in human history.

## V

Finally, any philosophy that deals with order and disorder in history has to cope with the problem of evil. The problem is peculiarly inescapable if one attempts to understand the tragic dimension of Israel's history. The Jewish philosopher, Emil Fackenheim, points out that when Israel's "root-experience" of God's presence in an epoch-making historical event (the victory over Pharaoh's hosts at the sea) is subjected to philosophical reflection, the theophanic event is "shot through" with three "dialectical contradictions," namely, transcendence and immanence, unlimited divine power and human freedom, and universality and historical particularity. In regard to the latter he observes: "If the God present in one moment of history is the God of all history, He is in conflict with the evil which is within it" (Fackenheim 1972, 16-19).

The problem of the evil that mars God's creation is portrayed in dramatic form in the biblical narratives of the primeval history (Gen 1-11). The Flood story, for instance, is introduced by the announcement of God's decision to destroy the earth owing to the *hamas* (violence, lawlessness) that had corrupted it (Gen 6:11-13). In the present form of the story, the divine judgment takes the form of a cosmic catastrophe in which the earth almost returned to precreation chaos, the watery abyss of Genesis 1:2. This story is "prehistorical" in the sense that it preserves the elemental experience, common to all peoples at all times, of the threat to human existence—existence that is suspended, so to speak, over the abyss of chaos. It portrays an *Urgeschehen*,[14] in which case *Ur-* refers to a primal or primary occurrence in mythical consciousness.

Voegelin effectively demonstrates that this "primary experience" survives even when the transition is made from mythical consciousness to historical consciousness. The "spiritual irruption" that occurred in Israel did not cancel out the experience but raised it to articulation, with the result that there is a polarity of creation versus chaos, order versus disorder, existence versus nonexistence (McKnight 1975, 5-6; Anderson 1967). A similar "leap in being," discussed by Niemeyer (1976, 32-33), occurred in ancient Greece, where philosophers, like Plato, were influenced by the insight of Anaximander, expressed in his fragments: "The origin (*arche*) of things is the Apeiron ["Boundless"] . . . It is necessary for things to perish into that from which they were born; for they pay one another penalty for their injustice (*adikia*) according to the ordinance of Time."

Here, however, I am especially concerned to see how the ancient myth is reinterpreted in biblical tradition. It is noteworthy that in the story of the Flood the "violence" that corrupts the earth is traced to the human "heart" (mind, will): for "Yahweh saw . . . that every imagination of the thoughts of [man's] heart was only evil continually" (Gen 6:5; cf. Gen 8:21). We are told, furthermore, that this flaw evoked the *sorrow* of Yahweh, who perceived that only an almost complete erasure of the slate could provide the possibility of a new beginning. It may be that the *Urgeschichte* expresses in its own way the theme of *hybris* and *nemesis*, though I think that commentators have exaggerated this.[15] In any case, here we are given a view of reason that is different from the mainstream of the philosophical tradition stemming from Plato and Aristotle. The "heart" is the organ of "historical reason"; the mind and the will are inseparably one. Hence evil is traceable to the human heart which is capable of deceit, blindness, and perversity. The mystery of human freedom, according to the biblical narrator, was a puzzle to God himself and called forth his "sorrow!" Voegelin, too is troubled by this mystery, which poses difficulties for his philosophical view. Why is it that rational people everywhere do not share the noetic vision of reality? Why is it that only certain people at certain times are given the insight? And why is it that, once the vision is gained by Prophets, philosophers, and saints, it is rejected, deformed, or eclipsed and must be rediscovered anew?[16]

Israel's Prophets were troubled by this question too. For them, the gulf between man and God was measured by a lack of "knowledge of God," that is, the willful refusal to recognize the God of the covenant. In their view, the fault lay in man's will, in his misplaced devotion. They rebuked the people for their "hardness of heart," for "turning away" (apostasy) from Yahweh and "forgetting" him, for their rejection of "knowledge of God"; and they called for repentance, that is, a redirection of the will and a consequent change of lifestyle. They spoke to a people who refused to hear, with the result that they had to retreat into their own prophetic circle (Isa 8:16-17) or, as in the case of Jeremiah, were driven into personal suffering and near despair. In a key text in Jeremiah 17:9 we read: "The heart [mind] is deceitful above all things, and desperately corrupt; who can understand it?" The popular Prophets only aggravated the problem by pandering to the people's desire for security. They lacked the vision of Yahweh's transcendence for, as Jeremiah said in pictorial language, "who among them has stood in the [heavenly] council of Yahweh, to perceive and to hear his word, or who has given heed to his word and listened?" (Jer 23:18). On the other hand, the faithful Prophet, to continue the figure, is one who received his commission in the heavenly council and whose task it was to translate the heavenly vision into the mundane realm of political and social reality. If in the face of the repeated appeals of Yahweh's messengers and the impact of political crisis, the people refused to respond and to return, disaster was inevitable, and they had no one to blame but themselves. "Your ways and your doings have brought this upon you," Jeremiah announced; "this is your doom and it is bitter; it has reached your very heart" (Jer 4:18).

The Prophets, though speaking with different theological accents, display an amazing consensus in their interpretation of the disorder and suffering of their time. They do not portray human beings as the victims of fate or demonic powers of chaos; rather, the problem, in their view, was the human mind and will ("heart"), and the people were fully responsible and culpable. Hence, they did not hesitate to draw the conclusion: the sufferings experienced in the political arena at the hand of the world empires (Assyria and Babylonia) were *deserved punishment* for "sin." Yahweh was performing his *opus alienum* (Isa 28:21), using a foreign power as "the rod of his anger." The coming of the foe from the North, which threatened to return the earth to chaos, was actually the expression of Yahweh's judgment upon the sin of the people (Jer 4:23-28). The purpose of the seismic shaking of the foundations was to bring the people to their senses (to reason) and to effect a purification and renewal through catastrophe.

This prophetic view of evil, however, was too simplistic to do justice to the brutal realities of history.[17] When the Babylonian army was rolling over the world, careless of all moral distinctions and with military power as its "god," Habakkuk's prayer poignantly raised the question about the "violence" that seemed to eclipse the presence of God and the justice of his ways (Hab 1:2-3). He was given the answer that the righteous should live by faithfulness, trusting in Yahweh's promise and waiting for the time when the historical enigma would be clarified (Hab 2:1-4). But this answer was not existentially or theologically satisfactory, especially to apocalyptists whose writings began to appear on the margins of prophecy (Isa 24-27; Isa 55-66; Zech 9-14). These writers perceived that the evil in history, with which God enters into conflict, is more sinister than anything conceivable in terms of covenant theology, with its call to repentance and responsibility. Therefore, they revived the mythical imagery of the powers of chaos represented by the sea, the floods, many waters, Rahab, Leviathan. Thus in an apocalyptic passage, which has striking affinities with the Canaanite (Ugaritic) myth of Baal's conquest of *Yamm* (Sea), it is said: "In that day Yahweh with his hard and great and strong sword will punish Leviathan, the fleeing serpent, Leviathan, the twisting serpent, and he will slay the dragon that is in the sea" (Isa 27:1). Similarly in Daniel 7, the beastly empires, each one more terrible than the preceding, arise from the depths of the sea. No longer is the issue "sin" and its deserved punishment, as in prophecy, but the "divine warrior's" victory over radical evil that infects human history itself in the period between *Urzeit* and *Endzeit*.

In my judgment, it is too extreme to say that apocalyptic was an escape from historical reality in the manner of Gnosticism; for apocalyptic shares with prophecy the vision of God's transcendence and the coming of the kingdom on earth as it is in heaven. The major roots of apocalyptic are found, not in Zoroastrianism or in proto-Gnostic wisdom, but in prophecy. Apocalyptic is prophecy in a new idiom. The difference between the two is evident in their respective views of God's relation to human history and of the evil at work within it. While the Prophets understood their task to be translation of the vision of the heavenly council into the realities of political history, the apocalyptists believed that the vision was untranslatable and could be given only in a symbolic code, intelligible to the esoteric group of the faithful. "Prophecy was transformed into apocalyptic," Paul Hanson observes, "at the point where the task of translating the cosmic vision into the categories of mundane reality was abdicated" (Hanson 1971, 469; 1975). This literature was the idiom of a minority group that found itself victimized by the evil manifest in empires and political institutions. But at least in the case of the book of Daniel, which was a tract for a political revolution (the Maccabean), apocalyptic was not an otherworldly retreat from the political sphere. Faith in the transcendent sovereignty of God, whose victory over the evil powers within history was imminent and inevitable, provided a motive for action regardless of how great the odds against the relatively powerless minority. "The people who know their God," we read in a key apocalyptic text (Dan 11:32), "shall stand firm and take action."

Voegelin's philosophical interpretation of the Bible challenges us to rethink the relation between prophecy and apocalyptic, and in particular, to reconsider how these biblical perspectives converge in the New Testament. It is indisputable that apocalyptic eschatology has profoundly influenced the writings found in the New Testament. The last book of the New Testament, the Apocalypse of John, has striking affinities with the book of Daniel. The apocalyptic perspective, however, is not on the margin of the New Testament. The earliest Gospel, Mark, contains a "little apocalypse" (Mk 13) and the Gospel as a whole portrays the victory of the Messiah (*Christos*) over Satan and his hosts and the inception of the kingdom of God on earth. Furthermore, Paul, the great theological interpreter of the Christian story, is indebted to the apocalyptic perspective as evidenced not only by his Thessalonian correspondence but by magnificent chapters like Romans 8 and 1 Corinthians 15 where he draws a distinction between the present age, which is under the dominion of the "principalities and powers," and the age to come which is under the dominion of God's triumphant love.

Christian interpreters, however, have profoundly modified the apocalyptic perspective with the announcement that already the power of the age to come has broken into the present evil age in Jesus of Nazareth: His words and deeds, His crucifixion and resurrection. Early Christians found themselves living in the Metaxy; but this was understood, especially by Paul, as the interim between the Already and the Not-Yet, between the first resurrection that had already occurred and the final, general resurrection at the end when God, through Jesus Christ, will have overcome every enemy hostile to his purpose, including "the last enemy," death (1 Cor 15:24-28). Voegelin softens Paul's language by speaking of "a vision of the Resurrected," presumably a vision of the final reality when the paradoxes of history are overcome in the new creation intended by God's creative activity from the beginning. But this interpretation does not do full justice to the actuality and factuality of God's saving activity manifest in history through the historical person, Jesus of Nazareth.[18] Paul affirms that God's decisive victory over the powers of evil, chaos, and darkness has already occurred through Jesus Christ. Jesus' resurrection, in Paul's language, is the "first fruits" (*aparche*) of the final consummation (1 Cor 15:20), and the Spirit is the "guarantee" (*arrabon*) of the inheritance that awaits (2 Cor 1:22 and 5:5; cf. Eph 1:13). In the Metaxy—between the first resurrection and the final resurrection—God is involved in the human drama, overcoming the powers that are hostile to his purpose and establishing "islands of order" (to use one of Voegelin's expressions) in which the new creation is proleptically evident.

It is no devaluation of Voegelin's work to say that his philosophy of being cannot encompass fully the meaning of the biblical revelation. It is difficult, indeed impossible, to fit the biblical story into any philosophy without remainder. As a biblical theologian, I am profoundly impressed with the depth and breadth of Voegelin's exposition. Above all, he has enabled us to plumb, in some degree, the mystery of existence: nascent in mythical consciousness and brought to articulate consciousness through the "leap in being" in ancient Israel and in Christianity. The dogmas of the church are only surface manifestations of the fundamental experience of divine reality, to which the Bible bears witness in many and various ways. Hence, I share Voegelin's appreciation of Paul's theology of history expressed in his epistle to the church at Rome, chapters 9-11 (HG, 75-77, 85). In this great passage Paul is overwhelmed by the "mystery" (Rom 11:25) of history whose meaning, partially revealed, is finally lost to human comprehension. What awes him, however, is not a vision of the "structure of history" but the wonderful constancy of God's faithfulness to his promises to Israel and the amazing freedom of his grace. At the end of his anguished struggle with the problem of the church existing *vis-à-vis* the community of Israel, both sharing the same scriptural heritage and both belonging to God's elect people, he finally breaks out into doxology to the God whose judgments are unsearchable and whose ways are past finding out (Rom 11:33-36). There is, to use Paul's expression, an "Israel of God," composed of those upon whom God shows his mercy, and which bears witness to the faithfulness of God which underlies the whole creation and the whole human drama. Those who are drawn into this community of strangers and pilgrims are called to actualize in the present the peace and justice which, in some measure and in some sectors of society, signify the purpose of God which he intended in the beginning and which he will fulfill in the end. Such people who respond with such active faith to God's involvement in mundane existence represent, in the words of Voegelin, "the new type of man on the world-political scene."

## NOTES

[1]Voegelin highlights Second Isaiah's vision of the universality of the "spiritual exodus" and its relation to the imperial conquest of Cyrus, whom the prophet hailed as Yahweh's "Anointed" (Isa 45:1) in *OH* IV. See Altizer 1975.

[2]Voegelin's view of the encounter with the Incarnation as a "structuring event" in human history is presented succinctly in his GC, esp. 82ff.

[3]On the American scene this view was forcefully presented by Wright in his influential (1952) monograph. The view was sharply criticized, without the offer of a positive alternative, by Barr (1966). The first and third chapters of Barr's book elaborate his inaugural address at Princeton Theological Seminary (1963). Barr now maintains, however, that the dominant form of Israelite traditions is "story" which is "history-like" (1976).

[4]As observed by McKnight 1975, 358, who also remarks that ranking scholars, like Mircea Eliade, fall into the error of speaking of the intracosmic gods as transcendent.

[5]See Altizer 1975, 758, who wonders whether Voegelin has surrendered "a unilinear conception of history even while conceiving the process of history as an eschatological movement in time" (763).

[6]See GC, 83 and passim, wherein Voegelin responds to Bultmann's essay "The Significance of the Old Testament for Christian Faith" and other writings.

[7]See Rad 1970, esp. 364-405, where the peculiar Israelite character of wisdom is discussed, and 1973.

[8]Poulssen's (1967) traditio-historical study demonstrates that the building plans of David and the building activity of Solomon are to be understood against the cultural background of the Ancient Near East, where king and temple were intimately associated in mythical symbolizations.

[9]The appropriation of mythical elements began even before the time of the Davidic monarchy, according to Cross 1966. "Even in the cult of the [tribal] league," he writes, "themes of mythological origin can be detected, standing in tension with themes of historical memory or enhancing redemptive events by assimilating them to cosmic events" (18). See further Anderson 1975.

[10]The view that "man" of Gen 1:26 and Ps 8:5 is *Urmensch* and *Urkönig* (Bentzen 1948, 6, 12) has not been demonstrated exegetically.

[11]See the basic work by Mendenhall (1954), now available as a monograph; also Baltzar 1960. A clear discussion of the major covenant theologies is found in Hillers 1969.

[12]Engnell goes so far as to say that the prophets "ultimately reflect a positive understanding of the king" (62).

[13]On the dynamic conception of life and death, see Johnson 1949; on the psalms of lament and thanksgiving, see Barth 1947.

[14]This view of the *Urgeschichte* is advocated by Westermann 1975, a commentary illuminated by the phenomenological study of religion. See Anderson 1972 and my review of the completed volume in a forthcoming issue of that journal.

[15]See Gowan 1975, who shows that the best examples of this theme are found elsewhere in the Old Testament in regard to *political* powers, e.g., Assyria (Isa 14:4-21) or Tyre (Ezek 28), who arrogate to themselves the sovereignty that belongs only to God.

[16]See Niemeyer 1976, 36f., for a summary of Voegelin's wrestling with this question.

[17]For elaboration of the above discussion of prophecy and ensuing paragraphs on apocalyptic, see Anderson 1976a, 5-11.

[18]See the perceptive comments in Newmeyer 1976, 34-35.

# Revisiting Voegelin's *Israel and Revelation* after Twenty-Five Years
## Bernhard W. Anderson

### Introduction

The monumental character of Eric Voegelin's work, *Order and History*, is evident in the fact that some forty years after its inception, with the publication of the foundational volume *Israel and Revelation* (1956), it was the subject of two major symposia, one held in San Francisco in connection with the annual meeting of the American Political Science Association (Aug. 1996) and another at the University of Manchester, England (July 1997). The explanation for this extraordinary persistence of interest must lie, at least in part, in the philosophical boldness of the project and the creative imagination of a mentor who unleashed an "impulse"[1] that urges disciples to appreciate, reevaluate, and go beyond. Revisiting Voegelin's *Israel and Revelation* after a quarter of a century is intellectually exhilarating.

Normally we think that political science deals with, and is restricted to, pragmatic history; but here is a work, in the philosophical tradition of Plato, Aristotle, and Augustine, that lures us into political philosophy. In a time when metaphysics has been put on the shelf in many citadels of learning, it is refreshing to be invited to think philosophically about "the metaphysical source of order in history." This kind of philosophical interest is rare in my field—so rare that when I, a modest biblical theologian, come into this professional company which speaks with philosophical charisma, the ancient proverb is relevant: "Is Saul also among the prophets?" (1 Sam 10:12)

I am neither a political scientist nor a philosopher. My task is to respond to Voegelin's work as a biblical scholar, particularly as an Old Testament Theologian, as I did years ago in my essay "Politics and the Transcendent" [republished here as chapter one]. In fact, the present essay is an extended footnote on that earlier essay. Essentially I stand by what I wrote then, although the discussion has to be qualified and updated in view of the vast changes that have taken place in the field of biblical studies in the past generation.

It is important for this symposium to take account of biblical scholarship for Voegelin himself wanted to avoid reading extraneous mean-

ings, derived from Christianity or philosophy, into the biblical historiographical work; therefore, he said, "the interpretation must be kept
as close as possible to the Biblical text" (*IR*, 163). Accordingly, he
became a serious biblical student himself (many of his biblical excurses
are quite illuminating) and even engaged in an extended "note on
the state of Old Testament science" since Julius Wellhausen, the
founder of modern biblical criticism (147-62).

## Beyond History

When Voegelin immersed himself in biblical studies in the
mid-twentieth century, Old Testament research had already moved
beyond the historicism of Wellhausen, with its focus upon historical
methodology and putatave "sources" (the documentary hypothesis ),
into a form-critical study of the preliterary and literary "forms"
(*Gattungen*) in which Israel's faith found expression and the history
of traditions that led from early combinations and compositions of
discrete literary units to the final canonical conclusion of the process
(redaction criticism).

The dominant figure in the field at that time was the eminent Old
Testament theologian Gerhard von Rad, to whom Voegelin was profoundly indebted. Von Rad maintained that the subject of Old Testament theology is not pragmatic history but the "history of traditions," that is, a study of how the Israelite story, found in core confessions of faith (e.g. Deut 26: 5-9), was appropriated and "made
present" (the German verb, *vergegenwärtigen*) in the changing circumstances of Israel's historical journey.

On the American scene the school of W.F. Albright, the distinguished archaeologist, maintained that the biblical record is more
closely tied to the pragmatic history that is open to historical inquiry
and archaeological corroboration. The Albrightian view was given
forceful theological expression in *God Who Acts* (1952), an influential monograph by George Ernest Wright, one of Albright's illustri-
ous students. Israel's faith, he said, is not based upon creedal formulations but upon the recital of the "mighty acts of God"—crucial
events including guidance of the ancestors, exodus from Egypt, taking of the land. The *magnalia Dei*, however, were not just a "story"
(*Geschichte*) but belong to "history" (*Historie*), to invoke the distinction drawn in those days. Therefore, it is possible to speak of "the
revelation of God in history," a theme of the Biblical Theology movement that flourished in the United States in the period immediately
following World War II.

Voegelin's work relies on the approach of the German school. Indeed, von Rad's emphasis on form criticism and tradition-history enabled Voegelin to interpret the history of Israel's traditions as a "history of symbolization" from Moses through the Israelite experiment with monarchy and on to the emergence of Christianity out of Judaism. With his own philosophical accent, he drew a distinction between the transcendent order of the Kingdom of God and the mundane affairs with which the historian or political scientist deals.

For various reasons the view of God's revelation in history whether understood as ordinary history or a history of traditions, was tried in the balance and found wanting. For one thing, scholars demonstrated that portrayals of God acting in history were not particularly unique with Israel; similar claims were made on behalf of other deities of the Ancient Near East. Also, the emphasis upon meaning in history or history moving toward a goal was difficult, if not impossible, to maintain in the face of the colossal violence of the twentieth century, including the holocausts of Auschwitz and Hiroshima and the apocalyptic threat of atomic disaster during the Cold War. Furthermore, there was a rising skepticism about the validity or viability of probing behind biblical documents, composed primarily to confess faith in God, in search of historical referents. Archaeology, which is as close to historical science as one can get, complicated the picture, as in the case of the fall of Jericho or the "conquest" of Canaan as a whole.

In that situation, theologians like Paul Tillich insisted that faith cannot rest upon historical possibility, or at best, probability, which is all the historian can give us (cf. Ernst Troeltsch). So, for various reasons, many biblical interpreters have revolted against the dominance of history and historical method and have adopted methodologies that deal with the biblical text, rather than a "history behind the text." Indeed, so-called historical criticism, it is said repeatedly these days, is based on the rationalism of the Enlightenment and is unsuitable for the "post modern" period that is dawning. The changed situation in the biblical field is well described in a recent book by Leo Perdue, *The Collapse of History* (1994).

The latest theological venture in the Old Testament field, Walter Brueggemann's *Theology of the Old Testament* (1977 [remarks based on the unpublished manuscript available at the time of writing]) is very critical of the whole historical-critical enterprise, regarding it as a legacy of the Enlightenment and its Cartesian epistemology. He maintains that Old Testament theology deals with Old Testament *texts* in their "multiplicity and density" (this sounds like a legacy from

historical criticism!), not with some reality behind the text such as
"history" or "being." Under the influence of linguistic hermeneutics
(cf. Paul Ricoeur) he insists that God is, so to speak, in the world of
the text, not behind or beneath the text in some other dimension.
According to his scheme, 1) Israel makes its core testimony to God,
2) then Israel (and the nations) makes a counter-testimony; 3) this
linguistic dialectic leads to new advocacy of Yahweh's reality and sovereignty. Brueggemann finds a model for this theological presentation in the genre of the court trial before the nations, as in the poetry
of Second Isaiah.

In my judgment Voegelin's work is not fundamentally invalidated
by the fate of historical criticism. He is not really interested in revelation *in history*, that is, a process of events, or even in a sacred history
(*Heilsgeschichte*), a sequence of crucial historical events charged with
revelatory meaning. Rather, he is concerned with revelation in historical consciousness, or better, in the psyche of sensitive ("inspired")
persons (Moses, Jeremiah, the "genius" of the Suffering Servant, and
above all Jesus) - persons so attuned to the order of being that their
souls are "a sensorium of the transcendent." In a Voegelinian perspective, the hermeneutical disarray arising from "the collapse of history" and the failure of the hermeneutic of the Enlightenment only
go to show that revelation does not occur in pragmatic history, or in
any special sacred history. In this time of hermeneutical confusion,
Voegelin would probably advise the theologian to turn from the
dead-end road of "history" and concentrate on those persons, presented in the Bible though found outside too, in whom the order of
being, in which all human beings participate, became a powerful
force to reshape society according to the transcendent will of God.

This is a powerful challenge. I am deeply impressed with Voegelin's
emphasis upon symbolization, a breath of fresh air after the literalism of conservatives (often "fundamentalists") and the "historicism"
of liberal followers of Wellhausen. In the future, Old Testament theology, I believe, must take seriously the symbolic dimensions of scripture (Miller 1977; Anderson 1999). Also Voegelin witnesses effectively to the holy, transcendent God who cannot be imprisoned in
creedal statements or—we should perhaps add—in human language,
even the most poetic. Whether or not one follows Voegelin philosophically, the pressing issue is still whether the struggle for order in
history has a transcendent dimension that is given expression in the
language of religious imagination. In his view, when one looks back
over the biblical tradition, it is possible to trace "the trail of sym-

bols," as he nicely puts it, that show defection from and return to the transcendent ground of human history.

## THEOLOGY AND IDEOLOGY

Since the 1970's, with the rise of a sociological approach to biblical studies, the question of transcendence has been raised in a new way. Sociology attempts to reconstruct the history and religion of Israel by studying the changing forms of social organization. Biblical traditions, it is maintained, were produced by social groups and therefore reflect their needs and aspirations and how they perceive the world or "construct" reality. Therefore a primary concern is the sociology of knowledge, an approach advocated, for instance, by the sociologist Peter Berger, in works such as *Invitation to Sociology, The Social Construction of Reality*, and *The Sacred Canopy.*

Some sociologists, especially those under the influence of Karl Marx, go further. Not only do the traditions of the Bible reflect the interests of social groups, but they disclose the interests of those *in power*, the so-called "establishment." In other words, theology may be an ideology, the attempt of the established powers to legitimate their authority and hold others in subjection.

On the American scene, Norman Gottwald has been the primary protagonist for a liberation theology based on this view (Perdue 1994, chap. 4). He has been followed, though with some reservations, by Walter Brueggemann in his *Old Testament Theology* mentioned above. In sociological perspective, the history of biblical traditions is the history of a struggle for power, with this special twist, that Yahweh, the God known and worshiped in Israel, is the God who takes the side of the powerless and creates out of Egyptian slaves an egalitarian society. In his view, the Mosaic ''revelation'' was an Exodus (a real event in pragmatic history) from an imperial structure of power into a new form of social life in history, namely, a people's confederacy (*qahal*, assembly) based on a covenant (*berith*). The Israelite decision, under the pressure of pragmatic history, to have a king "like the nations," was a fall from grace, a return to the alien ways of nation and empire. Prophets arose to appeal to the people to cast off the extraneous imperial symbolization and return to the covenantal way of life.

Voegelin, it will be recalled, says something similar as he reflects on the problem of living the life of the spirit within the confines of mundane society. He is very critical of the Israelite experiment with monarchy, and the adoption of royal cosmological symbolism under

David. This fateful development was tantamount to "a reentry into the Sheol of cosmological civilization" and hence a "fall from being." Furthermore, Voegelin maintains that the Kingdom of God enters the mundane sphere at a terrible cost: a "mortgage" of pragmatic history upon the transcendent truth of being. This seems to be a philosophical way of speaking about theology becoming ideology: the attempt to legitimate the established power structure and its social or national interests.

Voegelin, however, is so concerned with the universal order of being that he is unable to deal constructively with the struggle for justice in the mundane sphere. The prophets, he maintains, emphasized "the right order of the soul" (*IR*, 440). But a close reading of the biblical text shows that they called for social order based on a right relation with God manifest in caring for the orphan, widow, and resident alien. Aaron Mackler called attention to the deficiency in an excellent paper in this book. By way of contrast, he effectively quotes the Jewish philosopher, Abraham Joshua Heschel's classic study, *The Prophets*:

> A student of philosophy who turns from the discourses of the great metaphysicians to the oration of the prophets may feel as if he were going from the realm of the sublime to an area of trivialities. Instead of dealing with the timeless issues of being and becoming, of matter and form, of definitions and demonstrations, he is thrown into orations about widows and orphans, about the corruptions of judges and affairs of the market place. Instead of showing us through the elegant mansions of the mind, the prophets take us to the slums (Heschel 1962, 1:3).

Voegelin, however, is concerned with "revelation"—the irruption of the order of divine being into history, manifest in the souls of persons like Moses. It is this irruption, as I understand it, that may lead to social change, in so far as sensitive individuals (poets, prophets) are prompted to speak a critical word against social abuses and power-holders and to fire the imagination with the "ideal" of the Kingdom of God. To speak of "revelation" is to reach beyond the competence of sociological method and, I may add, is to go beyond most current discussions of biblical theology. A leading sociologist, Peter Berger, has written an interesting little monograph, *A Rumor of Angels*, in which, addressing himself to theologians, he wonders whether there is any way out of the limitations of sociological method into the realm of "transcendence." In our mundane experience he finds a few *intimations* of transcendence, one of which is the human longing for order, in which connection he refers to Voegelin's *Order and History*. In every age, he writes, human beings have believed "that the created order of society, in one way or another, corresponds to an underlying order of the universe." "The human propensity to find order," he declares, is a "signal of transcendence" (Berger 1969, 60-61; Anderson 1985). That little book does not give much comfort to the theologian, though it may relax somewhat the tension between science and faith. These intimations of transcendence are a far cry from Voegelin's discussion of "revelation," or as he puts it, the irruptions of transcendence into the souls of persons living in mundane society. Indeed, it is significant that the foundational work in Voegelin's massive study of history starts with Israel as the bearer of *revelation*, irruptions that find expression in revelatory symbolism.

In this whole discussion, the fundamental issue is the relation between order and freedom. I began my essay on Voegelin long ago with the remark: "The task of government is to actualize the order within which people may live together in peace and justice." Liberation theologians will find difficulty with Voegelin because he gives a divine warrant for order, and is fearful of revolutionary expressions of human freedom which are aimed at taking power from the rich and established and distributing some of it to the poor and marginal. According to Brueggemann, Israel's "core testimony" is a revolutionary emancipation from the power structure of Egypt, showing that Yahweh is the God who demands and brings justice. In his discussion of theodicy, he goes so far as to say that "in its deepest vexation, Israel is able to make a distinction between Yahweh and the reality of justice . . . Justice is held up as ultimate, and Yahweh as an agent of justice is critiqued for failure about justice" (Brueggemann 1977, 721-22). This is surely a one-sided reading of the Old Testament. For there are many texts (or "countertestimonies") in which Yahweh upholds and maintains order. There is a danger in placing too much emphasis on the revolutionary event of the Exodus and ignoring or discounting the corresponding account of the revelation of Sinai, where Yahweh gives the "teaching" (*torah*) that provides order for the covenant community, an order which gives the *shalom* (peace) that means well-being, wholesome relations, and righteousness.[2]

## JEWISH-CHRISTIAN RELATIONSHIP

One of the major developments in the twentieth century has been that, despite the terrible tragedies brought about by anti-Semitism, supremely the Holocaust, relations between Jews and Christians have improved. Without surrendering their identities, Jews and Christians have worked together on biblical interpretation (as in the Society of Biblical Literature) and have engaged in constructive dialogue from their respective positions (Rothschild 1990[3]). As is evident from the title of Voegelin's foundational work (*IR*), the phenomenon of Israel, especially in the biblical phase of its existence, is crucially important in his thinking. He maintains that in Israel the revelation of the order of being found expression, preparing for the supreme revelation in Jesus Christ.

How, then, does Voegelin understand the relationship between Judaism and Christianity, or—stated another way—the relationship between the Old and the New Testaments? At first Jews and Christians shared the same body of scripture (*TaNaK*); indeed, whenever the word scripture(s) (*graphe, graphai*) appears in the New Testament it refers, probably without exception, to the Jewish scripture which in the Christian community was read in Greek translation (Septuagint). These two communities of faith, having the same Bible, somehow belong inseparably together in the mystery of God's purpose, as Paul argued in his agonized discussion in Romans 9-11.

In *Israel and Revelation* the relationship between Israel and Christianity proves to be a thorny problem, as William Thompson has observed in his perceptive study in chapter nine of this book. Thompson draws attention to "the contentious page 144" where Voegelin attributes to Talmudic Judaism a failure to be the carrier of the truth of being for all humankind owing to an inability to get rid of the cultural mortgage, that is, the territorial claim on the land of Canaan and ethnic ("communal") exclusivism that separates the Jewish community from humanity. Hence the promise to Abraham, originally intended to include all humankind, was forfeited to Christianity which was able to free the truth of being from land and *Volk*.

It is ironic that Voegelin, for whom revelation to Israel is the foundation and starting-point, winds up with a negative assessment of the future of Israel in God's purpose. As a Christian, he finds much that is true and good, but those benefits are under the shadow of the "mortgage" to the concrete realities of this world: social relations, ethical action, life on the land (earth). Hence just as Israel made an exodus from cosmological civilization under Moses, it must—owing to the particularity of its existence in the mundane sphere—engage in an "exodus from itself." More than that, having accomplished its temporary purpose in the creation of living symbols, it is the destiny of Israel to die, and to be superseded by the universal revelation of God in Christ (*IR*, 315, 506).[4]

As I see it, the relation between the Old and the New Testaments, and in a larger sense between biblical Judaism and New Testament Christianity, is a dialectical movement of continuity and discontinuity. The dialectic is clearly stated in Matthew, a Jewish Gospel, in the Sermon on the Mount (the new Sinai!), where Jesus announces, "I have not come to destroy but to fulfill the Torah and the Prophets"; yet almost in the same breath he says in radical reinterpretation of the Law, "It was said to you of old, but I say unto you . . ." The dialectic of continuity/discontinuity is also expressed profoundly by Paul in his Epistle to the Romans. Converts to the Christian faith are children of Abraham in so far as they share Abraham's faith, yet the promises to Abraham are not limited by ethnicity. Moreover, God's promise to Abraham that he would inherit a land is endorsed by God's revelation in Christ, yet *'eretz* is taken in its larger meaning of "earth, world" to bring out the universal scope of the promise (Rom 4:13 ).[5] The irruption of the Kingdom of God in Jesus Christ has brought about a new mission for the New Israel: to proclaim the gospel to the world and to invite all into a community of faith where there are no boundaries: neither male nor female, Jew or Gentile, slave or free (Gal 3:28).

The universal outreach and inclusivity of the Christian community, however, need not conflict with the special calling of Israel to be the people of the Torah. The two vocations could be complementary in the economy of God's purpose, as Franz Rosenzweig argued in his classic, *The Star of Redemption.*

On the controversial page 144 and perhaps elsewhere Voegelin seems to get into trouble because he consistently stands by an ontology that is primarily personal (being of the soul) and only secondarily social (being in community). That personalism accounts for his dismissal of royal covenant theology, with its symbolization of king and temple, as a "derailment" on to a false social track; and it stands behind his indictment of the prophet Isaiah for a "metastatic faith" that envisions a transformation of society (see my remarks in chapter one of this book). In the background of this discussion lurks the threat of supersessionism; for if the truth of being received its maximum clarity in Jesus, divested of mundane attachment to promised land and ethnicity, why should we turn to earlier stages in the history of symbolization found in the Old Testament?

I find two main difficulties with a hermeneutic based on this ontology. First, it is arbitrary to single out individuals, like Moses, and say that in them a "leap of being" occurred. We know Moses only through the traditions in which he is portrayed and in these portrayals Moses cannot be separated from the community of Israel and its aspirations for a promised land. Almost the moment Moses appears on the historical scene, the issue is God's promise to set Hebrew slaves free and lead them into a promised land, at the cost of the dispossession of the native populations (see Exod 3:7-8). God's revelation to Moses instilled in him a new consciousness of personal identity and vocation but it did not free him from the territorial needs of pragmatic history and from ethical responsibility to his people. In sociological terms, theology was contaminated by ideology from the very first; in theological terms, the Word of God was given within the limitations of human words. Further, Israel, as the carrier of revelation, has boldly accommodated to the pragmatic history of nations, as we well know; even the church, represented by the Vatican, preserves some trappings of empire.

Secondly, repeating what I said in chapter one, I am not satisfied with Voegelin's dismissal of the royal covenant theology as a derailment (wasn't the association of Mosaic revelation with Canaan also a derailment?). The adoption of cosmological symbolization was indeed a new step, which called for a new understanding of Israel's traditions and its covenant relation with God. This symbolization, however, did not replace the Mosaic symbolization but ran parallel to it, or interacted with it, thereby enriching Israel's understanding of God's relation to the people, human society, and the whole creation.

In the illuminating Introduction to *IR*, "The Symbolization of Order," where Voegelin discusses human participation in the order of being, he speaks about "pluralistic symbolization." "Every concrete symbol," he writes, "is true in so far as it envisages the truth, but none is completely true in so far as the truth about being is essentially beyond human reach" (*IR*, 7). Here Voegelin is speaking about symbolization of the order of being found in Israel and elsewhere in the Ancient Near East. But symbolic pluralism itself is something that needs to be taken more seriously. In the Old Testament there are three major patterns of symbolization: 1) the priestly symbolization of the "tabernacling presence" of God in the midst of the people that dominates the Pentateuch in its final priestly version; 2) the Mosaic symbolism of the Mountain of God and the covenant formulary (comparable to ancient suzerainty treaties) that governs Deuteronomy and the Deuteronomistic History (Joshua through 2 Kings); and 3) the David symbolization of monarch and temple that is dominant in the book of Psalms and the Chronicler's History. When one stands at the canonical conclusion of the history of traditions, looking back over "the trail of symbols," to use Voegelin's nice expression, one sees a plurality of symbolic formulations. Each expresses distinctively the presence of the holy God in the people's midst, and all are necessary to express in human speech the revelation of the holy God whose being is beyond the reach of human conceptuality but who is nevertheless "God with us."

## THE ROLE OF THE MESSIAH

Judaism and Christianity share the mystery of the presence of the holy God "in our midst" (cf. Hos 11:9b). They differ over the christological confession that Jesus is the Christ. The question is whether the christological difference is reduced or sharpened by a Voegelinian ontology which posits the "consubstantiality" of human being and primordial being, or of the human and the divine. Commenting on the trajectory of the title Son of God, which moves from the Egyptian Pharaoh to Israel (Hos 11:1), from the people to the Davidic king (Ps 2), and from the king to the prophet (cf. Jer 1:5), he says that finally in the Christian revelation it becomes clear that "only God can be the son of God" (*IR*, 467).[6]

Some years ago J.C. Rylaarsdam, a scholar at the university of Chicago, wrote an illuminating essay, "Jewish-Christian Relationships: The Two Covenants and the Dilemmas of Christology" (1972). He provided an excellent discussion of two symbolic trajectories, one associated with Moses and the other with David.[7] The Mosaic pattern of symbolization moves in the horizontal dimension of history, from promise to fulfillment; the Davidic symbolization, on the other hand, moves in the vertical dimension of the primordial and the cosmic. His thesis was that the Jewish community flourishes in the Mosaic symbolic world, whereas Christianity is at home in the Davidic world. In the Davidic covenant theology, the key symbols are God as cosmic King (Isa 6:1-5) and the City of God which signifies God's rule on earth through the Davidic king, called "the Son of God" (2 Sam 7:14; Ps 89:26-27).

This essay does not solve the problem of the relation between the Jewish and Christian communities. The two patterns of symbolization are present, and interact, in both the Old Testament and the New. It is not a matter of either-or. However this essay does lead to the christological question, specifically the question of whether God's revelation in Jesus Christ is to be understood in terms of Old Testament messianism or in the primordial perspective of creation. What is the meaning of Peter's confession at Caesarea Philippi: "You are the messiah, the Son of the Living God" (Mt 16:16)?. Does this refer to agency or being, to historical function or ontological relationship?

It is well known that the Hebrew word *mashiach*, translated as Messiah or Christ, refers to function or role. The one who bears the title, whether the earthly Davidic king or the ideal king who is to come, is the Anointed One (the meaning of Hebrew *mashiach*), one who is anointed for a task. In this functional sense Cyrus of Persia could be called Yahweh's "messiah" (Isa 45:1); for the foreign king was chosen to be instrumental in God's saving purpose. In the New Testament, when people asked whether Jesus was the messiah, they wanted to know, at least initially, whether he was God's chosen agent through whom a new age ("the kingdom of God" or in apocalyptic terms the "new creation") would be introduced.

In the Matthean version of Peter's confession, the title "Son of God" may seem, at first glance, to go beyond historical function to ontological status. The language echoes exalted language used in ancient Israel of the king. In royal psalms the Anointed One is declared to be God's Son *this day*, originally the day of coronation (Ps 2); he is portrayed as seated at the right hand of God sharing the divine rule (Ps 110); and in one instance, if we follow "the difficult reading" of the received text rather than sidestepping it (as in some modern translations), the king is addressed as divine: "Your throne, O God, endures forever" (Ps 45:6). Most scholars understand this language to be the hyperbole of oriental "court style." The king was extolled in extravagant terms, especially on festival occasions (enthronement, royal wedding). In the Old Testament there was no serious departure from the view that the king was God's agent, anointed for a task. This is undoubtedly true in the well-known messianic passage in Isaiah 9 ("Unto us a child is born, a son is given") where the coming king is given the most glorious throne-titles: "Wonderful Counsellor, Mighty God, Everlasting Father, Prince of Peace" (Isa 9:6). The king, even the One who was to come, was not regarded as consubstantial with deity. The theologian Elizabeth Johnson rightly says that "Jewish scriptural symbols," such as Messiah and Son of God, do not "connote divinity." A significant step, she adds, was made when interpreters used Wisdom categories (e.g. Prov 8:22-31) to explore the messiah's "ontological relationship with God" and the cosmic status of the messiah who is active with God in the creation (Johnson 1994, 98).

The motif of the *imago Dei* is no exception (Gen 1:26-28; cf. Ps 8:5-8). In Genesis the view is that human being, mortal humanity (*'adam*), is commissioned to be God's representative. Humans, constituted as "male and female," are crowned as viceroys who take part in God's administration of earthly affairs so that peace and righteousness may prevail (chap. 1, sec. III, of this book), which I have discussed at length (Anderson 1994, chap. 7).

It was not in the Old Testament but in the New that a momentous shift took place: from a functional christology inherent in the word "Messiah" or "Christ" to an ontological christology concerned with the being of Christ in relation to God. This is evident when one moves from the symbolic world of the Synoptic Gospels to the quite different symbolic world of the Fourth Gospel, which is introduced by identifying Christ with the Logos that in the beginning was "with God" and "was God." This shift to ontology is also evident in Deutero-Pauline writings such as the Epistle to the Colossians which declares that God created the world in Christ (Col 1:15-17) and that in him "all the fullness of deity" dwelt (1:19; 2:9). Statements like these have no real parallels in the Old Testament.[8]

Revisiting *Israel and Revelation* after all these years has helped me to see more clearly that there are two different ways of thinking christologically. One is to say with St. Paul (as in 1 Cor 15) that in Christ the *New Age* has begun, his resurrection being a foretaste or "the first fruits" of that final historical consummation. The other is to say that the *New Being* has appeared, representing a personal life in which all are invited to participate by faith.[9] Perhaps these two christologlcal affirmations—one historical and the other ontological—belong together, as in the New Testament. That is a matter for theological reflection and debate. In any case, as others have observed, Voegelin's interpretation clearly moves in the direction of the trinitarian discussion of the early Christian church.

## Notes

[1] See Glenn Tinder, "The Voegelinian Impulse," chap. 4 of this book.

[2] See Jon Levenson's (1993, chap. 6) forceful criticism of a one-sided emphasis on the Exodus.

[3] The outlooks of five Jewish thinkers are presented (Leo Baeck, Martin Buber, Franz Rosenzweig, Will Herberg, Abraham J. Heschel) with responses by Christian theologians.

[4] The relevant pages are cited and discussed by Mackler in this book in the section, "Ethical Action and the Kingdom of God."

[5] The divine promise of land/world is discussed further in Anderson 1995, 145-154.

[6] Discussed in chap. 9 of this book.

[7] Discussions of Old Testament theology have largely ignored the priestly pattern of symbolization which focuses on "the tabernacling presence." See my discussion of "the priestly point of view," Anderson 1997, 406-416.

[8]Voegelin strains exegesis when he argues (*IR*, 399) on the basis of the spokesperson simile used in the Exodus story (Exod 4:16-18; 7:1) that although Moses is "not God" he is "something more than man."

[9]This is written in the light of a stimulating paper by Victor Nuovo, professor of Philosophy at Middlebury College, "Resurrection, Realism, and Truth: Reflections on Paul Tillich" (June 1996).

# Voegelin's Philosophy of History and Human Affairs:
## With Particular Attention to *Israel and Revelation* and Its Systematic Importance

# Ellis Sandoz

Eric Voegelin's masterwork is *Order and History*. It appeared over a period of three decades with the fifth and final volume being published posthumously in 1987. While the focus of attention here is on the first of these volumes, *Israel and Revelation*, that book is only a part of the larger enterprise. Thus, a few words reflecting on the range of Voegelin's thought may be helpful in order to suggest something of the context of discussion.[1]

By the time Voegelin came to the book before us, he had researched and written a sprawling study of "The History of Political Ideas" running well over 4,000 pages in typescript (*HPI*), published five books in German and dozens of articles in German and English, and he had achieved a degree of celebrity in America through publication of *The New Science of Politics* (*NSP*) whose thesis that Gnosticism is the essence of modernity evoked *Time* magazine's editors' feature story, "Journalism and Joachim's Children," for their thirtieth anniversary issue (*Time* 1953). The two succeeding volumes of *Order and History*, entitled *The World of the Polis* and *Plato and Aristotle,* actually already had been written, apart from prefatory and introductory materials, so that *Israel and Revelation* can properly be read as their intellectual sequel.[2] At age fifty-five and the height of his powers, Voegelin by this time had at his disposition a remarkable range of philological and scholarly capacities and a distinctive philosophical perspective on major theoretical and historical issues. But he had practical purposes in mind, too, in writing *Israel and Revelation*, as he explained in 1954 to an editor at Macmillan, which had first intended to publish Voegelin's studies. The work on Israel and especially on Moses, Voegelin enthusiastically wrote, "will make [the book] a 'must' in theological seminaries and for reverends, because (though that may sound almost unbelievable) no book on the political ideas of Israel has ever been written at all. Besides the part on Israel is particularly well written and should, therefore, appeal to a general public that is interested in Jewish history" (*HPI* I, 10).

## SCOPE OF THE PHILOSOPHY OF HUMAN AFFAIRS

In his mature work, Voegelin constantly invokes the participation of man in all the spheres of reality identified from Aristotle onward as participation in the hierarchy of being and, most especially, in transcendent divine Being whose consideration is ineluctable and central to philosophy as engendered by the ancient Greeks, and now energetically resumed by Voegelin. The restoration of wholeness in human affairs—in *personal, social* and *historical* dimensions—is radically dependent upon the scholarly recovery of the facts of human experience as they register through time the participatory dimension that defines the human condition. The inquiry in its several (over-lapping) stages is conducted in terms of a philosophical anthropology which gives way, in turn, to a theory of politics, a philosophy of history, a philosophy of experience-symbolism (or of symbolic forms) and a theory of consciousness that is fundamental to the entire enterprise. Voegelin's method is the critical method, by which is meant that he writes on the basis of a mastery of all of the chief philosophical and meditative writers from the pre-Socratics to Anselm to Husserl, Bergson and Whitehead—and of the principal secondary literature—, critically adapting and modifying the analyses in the light of their cogency as accounts of *reality experienced* and of his own command of the sources of knowledge. Thus there is the constant silent asking of the Socratic question: Look and see, is this not the case? The form of the inquiry is primarily a search of the historiographic record as the available evidentiary material of human experience over the 5,000 years of civilized existence. As explained in the preface to *OH* III:

> *Order and History* is a philosophical inquiry concerning the principal types of order of human existence in society and history as well as the corresponding symbolic forms. The oldest civilizational societies were the empires of the ancient Near East in the form of the cosmological myth. And from this oldest stratum of order emerged, through the Mosaic and Sinaitic revelations, the Chosen People with its historical form in the present under God . . . In the Aegean area emerged, from the stratum of order in cosmological form, the Hellenic polis with the symbolic form of philosophy (iv).

As will have become clear, the *empiricism* of Voegelin's philosophy and philosophical (noetic-pneumatic) science of politics (or human affairs) insists on an accounting of the entire range of human experience-symbolization, with the accent falling on the highest reaches of reality as formative of the distinctively human reality. The problem of transcendent Being, of the divine Ground of being, is the central problem of all philosophy from the time of the pre-Socratics into the present, in his view. *Philosophy* itself is defined as "the love of being through the love of divine Being as the source of its order" (*OH* I, xiv). The love of Being and resistance to untruth take shape as a struggle against pervasive "climates of opinion" that tend to form a veritable iron curtain of the soul in the modern world, enforcing spiritual blindness through massive control of communication and action (*OH* III, 79). The *truth* to be recovered in openness to reality, then, embraces personal, social, historical and ontological dimensions as disclosed through the most differentiating experiences-symbolisms left as the trail of the human pilgrimage through time with God. This is the record of participatory reality in the In-Between of divine-human encounter (Plato's *metaxy*) given in events and artifacts from the Neolithic Age onward. The search requires great respect for all relevant testimony. It also requires a redefinition of *empiricism*—and of *science* itself—so as to include cardinal modes of non-sensory experience fundamental to moral, religious, aesthetic, mystical and noetic life and representation. In result, it can be said that comprehensive reality becomes intelligible in terms of *apperceptive* experiences central to a philosophical science that seeks adequately to account for the heights and depths of human existence. Polarities traditionally identified as religion-science and faith-reason tend to blur and almost to disappear as they find redefinition as noetic-pneumatic experiences-symbolizations in the course of meditative analysis, especially in such capital late essays as "Reason: The Classic Experience" (RCE) and "The Beginning and the Beyond: A Meditation on Truth" (BB) and the final volume of *Order and History (OH* V).

## RESISTANCE AND BALANCE

The vast effort whose monument is *OH* I-V is an act of resistance aimed especially against the contemporary ideological enterprise first identified in antiquity in the prophets' excess as "metastatic faith" (*OH* I, 452-58), that is, the attempt magically to transform reality through divine intervention—and in its modern forms the transformation of the world through human volition and coercion by this or that gnostic revolutionary movement. Such attempts involve the ideologues' mutilation of philosophy, which merely seeks to interpret the world in various ways: first by undertaking to change the world, thus perverting philosophy into comprehensive knowledge through various systems; then by proclaiming autonomous Man (meaning this or that libidinous elite) master of reality—often with lethal consequences for millions of human beings. Voegelin's resistance and therapeutic purpose is the recovery of truth and reality as far as philosophy (ever the *love* of wisdom, not its definitive possession) permits (*AR*, 93-107). Further, he urges it as a *duty* that the massive social means deployed in deformation and corruption of our common human reality be *resisted by everyman* to the limits of each person's capacities: "No one is obliged to take part in the spiritual crisis of a society; on the contrary, everyone is obliged to avoid this folly and live his life in order" (*SPG*, 15; *WPG*, 33).

Thus the center of resistance arises in the evocation of the inviolable integrity of the individual human person, *qua* participant in the ever-mysterious transcendent divine Ground, whose reflective mind and conscience lie tensionally at the core of society and history—and of reality experienced, in its ontic and knowable dimensions. The social "Amnesia" (or forgetfulness of what ought to be remembered) (*OH* I, ix) that obscures the recollection and understanding of reality historically attained over centuries, and woven into representations of true order reflective of the struggle of existence, is dispersed in the act of recovering differentiated truth from the historical record. This work of resistance to socially enforced forgetfulness and the reconstitution of philosophy as the noetic-pneumatic means of critically ascertaining the truth of being yield consequences for political and social order.

Certain of these consequences can be stated as *Postulates of Balance*, as follows (*OH* IV, 11-30, 227-38):

1. The unspeakable depth of the Mystery of being must not be allowed to overwhelm the truth of being critically ascertained through the philosophers' noetic-pneumatic inquiry: that is, *we know only what we know*! That vision and knowledge (modest as it sometimes seems to be) is to be prized, nurtured and refined against all opining, scepticism, fanciful imagining and (today) nihilistic disdain of deconstructionists and other power-intoxicated predators (Sandoz 1996).

2. Human reality is persuasively represented as the stratified participatory reality of the In-Between (Plato's *metaxy*), each level of

which, from material to divine reality, possesses its dignity, worth and rightful claim. Thus, man is neither God nor brute; and human reality is both hierarchically structured (from *apeiron* to divine Nous, founded from the "bottom" up, formed from the "top" down through the individual man's participation in transcendence), as well as directionally oriented toward eschatological fulfillment, a suspense of time-space in the mysterious eternity called God (RCE, 287-91; Sandoz 1981, 214-17). *Reality*—comprised experientially of *Thing-reality* and the comprehensive divine *It-reality* in later work (*OH* V, chap. 1)—thus, manifests itself as "a recognizably structured process that is recognizably moving beyond its structure" (*OH* IV, 227).

3. The philosophical or noetic science of human affairs rests upon a triadic structure historically evinced as: [a] *spiritual outbursts*, the leaps in being or flashes of eternity into time, whereby universal divine transcendent Being is apperceived in a variety of modalities, especially pneumatically in Israel and Christianity and noetically in Hellenic philosophy (although that distinction sharply narrows in Voegelin's late work); [b] *historiography*, whereby the before-and-after of the divine irruption is articulated as a recognizable epoch under the particularities of culture and ethnicity in time, space and place, thus creating history; and [c] *power constellations*, such as the ecumenic empires, recognizable as social and political entities organized for action in history and expressive of the concupiscential or passionate dimension of existence, including especially man's *libido dominandi*. These aspects ramify variously through the reality spheres termed *Person*, *Society* and *History*—with the strict understanding that the individual person constitutes core human reality.

4. Human reality with horizontal (time-space) and vertical (ontological) dimensions is always recognizably human as in tension toward the Ground and thereby so structured as incipiently *to constitute history and historical existence itself.*

In compact form, human reality arises in an indeterminate distant past (20-50,000 years ago) and moves directionally toward an indefinite and uncertain future open to its horizon. The structure-process of reality ranges from compact to differentiated through stages identifiable as cosmological, anthropological and soteriological (*NSP*, 76-77). These stages (if they may be so termed, in light of post-1974 work when unilinear development is sharply qualified or rejected) in the movement from compactness to differentiation present complicated problems. They are understood to be cumulative rather than discrete, so that earlier insights retain their truth. But they are subject to reversal and deformation, and they do not necessarily lie along any time line at all. Rather, they open into a complex pluralistic field of historical development, one concretely characterized by reversal, rebellion, loss of clarity, and decline as much as by advance and greater luminosity (*OH* IV, 1-11). Finally, the noetic-pneumatic dimension always appears concretely in the context of material reality, that is, in the life experiences of a human person in bodily existence, in the form of specific historical configurations and in tension with concupiscential demands as well as in attraction to the Good. The steely cords of passion are no less real than the golden cord of *Nous*. All are pulled by the divine Puppet master, to remember Plato (*Laws* 644d-645b, 903d; *OH* III, 231-36).

## Consequences of the Leap in Being

The convictions regarding the process and structure of history and the nature of man that emerge in *Israel and Revelation* are permanent gains to Voegelin's understanding of these vast issues, as reflected in the foregoing comments. He took stock of matters in the introduction to *The World of the Polis,* entitled "Mankind and History":

> The leap in being, the epochal event that breaks the compactness of the early cosmological myth and establishes the order of man in his immediacy under God—it must be recognized—occurs twice in the history of mankind, at roughly the same time, . . . and the two experiences differ so profoundly in content that they become articulate in the two different symbolisms of Revelation and Philosophy . . .
>
> The primary field of order is the single society of human beings, organized for action to maintain itself in existence. If, however, the human species were nothing but a manifold of such agglomerations, all of them displaying the same type of order under the compulsion of instinct as do insect societies, there would be no history. Human existence in society has history because it has a dimension of spirit and freedom beyond mere animal existence, because social order is an attunement of man with the order of being, and because this order can be understood by man and realized in society with increasing approximations to its truth. Every society is organized for survival in the world and, at the same time, for partnership in the order of being that has its origin in world-transcendent divine Being; it has to cope with the problems of its pragmatic existence and, at the same time, it is concerned with the truth of its order. This struggle for the truth of order is the very substance of history; and in so far as advances toward the truth are

achieved by the societies indeed as they succeed one another in time, the single society transcends itself and becomes a partner in the common endeavor of mankind. Beyond the primary field of order there extends a secondary field, open toward the future, in which mankind is constituted as the subject of order in history (*OH* II, 1-2).

The emergence of the truth of order in the present under God as experienced in revelation and symbolized in the paradigmatic history of the Old Testament is the primary concern of *Israel and Revelation*. The strength of the study is the power and care with which Voegelin delineates the meaning of the familiar account in terms of spiritual experiences. Herein lies the vital thread of revelation through the response of Israel by its representative personalities and by Israel as the chosen representative of mankind in the passage of history from Abram and Moses to the Suffering Servant of Deutero-Isaiah. Accordingly, it will be useful to organize the further presentation by attempting to clarify briefly with respect to Israel the experiences symbolized, the truth of order, the meaning of history, the problem of universality and the enduring significance of Exodus as emblematic of the human quest.

## EXPERIENCES SYMBOLIZED

The core of the experience is a break with the truth of the myth of the divine cosmos as deficient truth or outright untruth through discovery of the truth of divine Being beyond all cosmic representation by the leap in being. This concretely occurs especially in the drama of Exodus as symbolized in the *berith* or Covenant between God (Yahweh) and His Chosen People of Israel as this unfolds at the Burning Bush through Moses and on Sinai with the People and their acceptance of the Decalogue. The reality of experience-symbol thereby is differentiated by the polarities of immanent and transcendent divine being. The experiences are presented as a passion of being chosen and of responding to the commands of the divine partner in reality as the means of securing more perfect attunement through existence in truth.

> They entered into a covenant with [God], and thereby became his people. As a new type of people, formed by God, Israel conquered the promised land. The memory of Israel preserved the otherwise unimportant story, because the irruption of the spirit transfigured the pragmatic event into a drama of the soul and acts of the drama into symbols of divine liberation.

The events of the Exodus, the sojourn at Kadesh, and the conquest of Canaan became symbols because they were animated by a new spirit. Through the illumination of the spirit the house of institutional bondage became a house of spiritual death. Egypt was the realm of the dead, the Sheol, in more than one respect . . . When the spirit bloweth, society in cosmological form becomes Sheol, the realm of death; but when we undertake the Exodus and wander into the world, in order to found a new society elsewhere, we discover the world as the Desert . . . When the world has become Desert, man is at last in the solitude in which he can hear thunderingly the voice of the spirit that with its urgent whispering has already driven and rescued him from Sheol. In the Desert God spoke to the leader and his tribes; in the Desert, by listening to the voice, by accepting its offer, and by submitting to its command, they at last reached life and became the people chosen by God (*OH* I, 112-13).

Voegelin explores the texture of the experiences with care. To begin with, the condition of revelation is the human response, and if there is no response there is no revelation (*OH* I, 417). But, as with Moses, to hear the voice means to have become a servant of Yahweh, for the command could be rejected only by one who could not hear it: "the man who can hear cannot reject, because he has ontologically entered the will of God, just as the will of God has entered him. When the consciousness of the divine will has reached the clarity of revelation, the historical action has begun" (407). The symbolism continues through various permutations throughout subsequent time. The call of the past and call of the present blend in prophetic consciousness as parts of a continuum of revelation, "which creates historical form when it meets with the continuum of the people's response" (429). The attunement to the timeless revelation of the eternal God must be preserved as a constant tension of existence in the concrete community of the people to prevent a fall from historical form under God into the Sheol of civilizations from which they had been delivered. This dynamic is expressed in the prophetic effort as the people are exhorted to do justice and seek truth, and as "listen!" becomes a fundamental command in Jeremiah (434). The inability of the people to maintain this tension moves the symbolism of chosen people toward the symbol of the chosen man in Jeremiah and the Suffering Servant, a mark of increasing spiritualization and a breaking of the collective experience by differentiation of the individual human personality in the present under God. Spiritual autobiography emerges as a new symbolism, and prophetic existence is experienced as "participation in the suffering of God" (485-88).

## TRUTH OF ORDER

Differentiation of the truth of order in Israel through the leap in being achieving existence in the present under God in historical form places the divine Ground in a beyond of the cosmos. Yahweh is experienced-symbolized as Creator and sustainer of the world and its order. The order of Israel becomes therewith historical, and its exodus from Egypt marks a liberation from the death of existence in the compact cosmological order. Israel experiences itself as living in an emphatic partnership with Yahweh as a peculiar people, the carrier of a new truth in history through attunement with transcendent Being. The record of this relationship is the content of the Old Testament understood as paradigmatic history. "Israel alone constituted itself by recording its own genesis as a people as an event with a special meaning in history" (*OH* I, 124). The content of the truth of order is given especially in the Decalogue and other aspects of the Sinaitic Covenant. And the truth experienced and symbolically elaborated is sensed as not only parochial truth for Israel alone but as truth for a mankind that Israel has been divinely chosen to represent, even if the universalist components are long in differentiating fully.

But the problem Voegelin first emphasizes in the introduction to his study has its place in this aspect of our discussion, namely that the leap in being is not a leap out of existence (*OH* I, 11, 452). Thus, the differentiation of the truth of being that marks the emergence of existence in historical form leaves untouched the large range of reality not directly related to divine truth. This raises the question of the relationship between pragmatic and paradigmatic history—or profane and sacred history—in a consideration of the historical form. In terms of the truth of existence it is observed that the order of Israel as a practical matter denotes the history of a society with a core of ethnic identity that is formed through living memory of the Sinai Covenant. The shortcomings as an order fit for action in the world came to a crisis with the desire to have a king like the other nations and the Davidic Covenant. For the Berith "provided for the right relation between God and man, as well as for the relations between the members of the Chosen People, but made no provision whatsoever for a governmental organization that would secure the existence of the people in the power field of pragmatic history. This gap was now filled by the organization of David's conquest in the wake of the Philistine wars" (300). This brings to attention the fact that the vacuum is filled at the time of David with the cosmological symbolisms that attend to the basic problems of existence in the world quite satisfactorily, and remain of permanent validity even after the differentiation of transcendent Being.

The interaction with the historical form, however, also effects a differentiation of the old cosmological symbols themselves. And in this connection two developments are noted. One is the immanentization of the transcendent symbols of Israel in certain respects, as reflected in what Voegelin terms "the imperial symbolism." For example, the opening of Psalm 93 (*Yahweh malak*), "The Lord reigneth!" in the King James Version of 1611, has the original meaning of "Yahweh has become King!"—"right here and now in the cult of Yahweh's enthronement which the faithful in the time of the monarch attended . . . And . . . nobody can say with certainty at which point in the history of Israel the *Yahweh malak* in the sense of a present rule of the God over his Chosen People has begun to taste bitter on the tongue of the singer who suffered the misfortunes of Judaite history, and out of despair arose the hope that someday Yahweh would be really the king of his people in a perfect realm of peace. That would be the point at which the ritual renewal of Yahweh's rule in the cosmological sense began to shift into the eschatological hope of a restoration of order, never in need of renewal, at the end of time." "When the revelation of the transcendent God has become the experiential center of order and symbolization," Voegelin concludes, "the transcendental implications of the compact symbols are set free; and correspondingly the volume of meaning in the symbols shrinks until the ritual renewal of order in time becomes a prefiguration of its ultimate restoration in eternity" (*OH* I, 302-303).

The other, related development is the prophets' attempt to distend the terms of the Covenant to cover pragmatic exigencies that eventually derails the revelatory experience into the excesses Voegelin calls *metastasis* and *metastatic faith*, as previously mentioned. At that juncture, Voegelin the spiritual realist steps forth to write two of the most arresting pages in a great book and, in so doing, touches on "the fundamentals of a philosophy of history."

> "The prophets had no doubts about the ontological presuppositions of their problem of order: Without the God who 'knows' his people and the prophet who 'knows' God, there would be no Chosen People, no defection from the commandments, no breaking of the Covenant, no crisis of Israel, no prophetic call to return, and no suspense between destruction and salvation. Existence in historical form presupposes the existence of the world-transcendent God, as well as the historical fact of his revelation . . . For the

prophets lived concretely as members of a people called Israel, which experienced its order, in historical continuity, as constituted by the Sinaitic revelation. While they anticipated disasters for the empirical humanity surrounding them, they never doubted for a moment that the dispensation of history created by the Message would continue, whatever 'remnant' of Israel or 'offshoot' from the House of Jesse would be its empirical carrier in the future. History, once it has become ontologically real through revelation, carries with it the irreversible direction from compact existence in cosmological form toward the Kingdom of God. 'Israel' is not the empirical human beings who may or may not keep the Covenant, but the expansion of divine creation into the order of man and society. No amount of empirical defections can touch the constitution of being as it unfolds in the light of revelation. Man can close the eye of his soul to its light; and he can engage in the futility of rebellion; but he cannot abolish the order by which his conduct will be judged . . . In the surrounding darkness of Israel's defection and impending political destruction—darker perhaps than the contemporary earthwide revolt against God—the prophets were burdened with the mystery of how the promises of the Message could prevail in the turmoil. They were burdened with this mystery by their faith; and history continued indeed by the word of God spoken through the prophets. There are times when the divinely willed order is humanly realized nowhere but in the faith of solitary sufferers" (*OH* I, 464-65).

In this blazing affirmation of the truth of being inspired by his meditation on the plight of the prophets, even as they are driven to the excess of trusting in divine intervention to salvage the physical well-being of Israel, Voegelin's own faith shines through as a matter of more than mere reflection.

The primordial quaternarian structure of being—experienced-symbolized as God, Man, World, and Society (*OH* I, 1)—differentiates historically through revelation and philosophy. The differentiation yields the truth of reality in human consciousness. Noetic-pneumatic consciousness of the participatory tension toward the ground is the constitutive presence that cognitively defines the *specific nature of man* as Reason *(Nous),* in the philosophical language of Plato and Aristotle. It is cherished as the prize of personal existence in prophetic and in Christian experiences, to the limits of divine disclosure variously symbolized as *Ruach, Logos* or *Nous*:

The Deutero-Isaianic drama moves from the compact revelation from Sinai toward the Logos of God. From Aeschylus the movement goes toward the Platonic Vision of the Agathon; from Deutero-Isaiah it goes toward the Incarnation of the Logos. When man is in search of God, as in Hellas, the wisdom gained remains generically human; when God is in search of man, as in Israel, the responsive recipient of revelation becomes historically unique (496).

Thus, "the substance of the creative action is the 'word.'"

> From the Beginning, reality is the divine word speaking in succession the evolution of being from matter through plant to animal life, until it speaks man who, in the persons of patriarchs and prophets, responds by his word to the word spoken by god in history . . . In the Hellenic context, the sense of close relationship between reality and the word that renders it truly engenders the meaning of *aletheia* as both reality and truth; in the Israelite context, the relationship is traced back to its source in the divinely creative word-reality. The word of man when he articulates his consciousness of reality emerges from the reality that is the word of god (*OH* IV, 13; cf. *OH* I, 222; *OH* V, 18).

With respect to the core meaning of *reason*, then, Voegelin summarizes matters from the philosophers' perspective in the following remarkable language:

> Reason did not exist in language in the history of mankind until it was formulated in the Greek fifth century [BC] as a word denoting the tension between man as a human being and the Divine ground of his existence of which he is in search. The consciousness of being caused by the Divine ground and being in search of the Divine ground—that is reason. Period. That is the meaning of the word *reason.* That is why I always insist on speaking of "noetic" and use the term *nous:* in order not to get into the problems of the ideological concept of reason of the eighteenth century. The word *nous* is applied by Plato and Aristotle to the consciousness of being in search of the ground of one's existence, of the meaning of one's existence—the search, the *zetesis.* One is in the state of ignorance, of *agnoia;* one asks questions, the *aporein;* and the answer is that the Divine *Nous* is the cause that moves me into the search . . . It is a divine pull that pulls you. It is not a [merely] natural movement (*CEV,* 138).

This is a substantive and extended meaning of reason (Sandoz 1971, 301-302; Germino 1995), summarizing a more detailed analysis by Voegelin (RCE), including a comparative analysis of key philosophical and New Testament texts (GC; QDD). Voegelin has argued that the distinctions traditionally separating faith and reason are empirically insupportable: "We can no longer ignore that the symbols of Faith express the responsive quest of man just as much as the revelatory appeal, and that the symbols of Philosophy express the revelatory appeal just as much as the responsive quest. We must further acknowledge that the medieval tension between Faith and Reason derives from the origins of these symbols in the two different ethnic cultures of Israel and Hellas, that in the consciousness of Israelite prophets and Hellenic philosophers the differentiating experience of the divine Beyond was respectively focused on the revelatory appeal and the human quest . . ." (BB, 211; Caringella 1991). Voegelin's exchange with Thomas Altizer is particularly relevant here (Sandoz 1982, 179-98; RANH).

## MEANING OF HISTORY AND UNIVERSALITY

While history as a whole has no identifiable essence and no knowable meaning as extending into an indefinite future and being thereby inexperientiable as a noetic matter (*NSP*, 120), the philosophical impediment does not wholly hinder the prophets' pneumatic experience of history as the movement through time in partnership with God toward an eschatological fulfillment in Canaan, the Kingdom of God (*OH* I, 345n). The limitations of philosophy give rise to paradox in Voegelin's work. "The fact of revelation is its content" (*NSP*, 78). "Philosophy can touch no more than the being of the substance whose order flows through the world" (*OH* I, 411). And the paradox is expressed in the late work where Voegelin, in reflecting again on the tetragrammatic God of Thomas Aquinas, writes: "The God who is experienced as concretely present remains the God beyond his presence. The language of the gods, thus, is fraught with the problem of symbolizing the experience of a not-experientiable divine reality . . . Not the Beyond but its Parousia in the bodily located consciousness of questioning man, the experience of the not-experientiable divine reality has history: the history of truth emerging from the quest for truth" (*OH* V, 68; cf. 103). While Voegelin freely acknowledges the importance of pragmatic history, it is history as the "inner form" of Israel's existence that is his concern, as it is the concern of the prophets who struggle to maintain attunement to the intended order of the people under God against the inroads of actual disorder (*OH* I, 355, 409). The work of the prophets is most especially "to clarify the meaning of existence in historical form." The universalist implications emerged in the reliving of the Berith drama by "solitary spiritualists tortured by the destiny of the Chosen People" (430). One urgent question was whether the Kingdom of God had to take the form of a political Israel, or a political society at all, where constitutionalism, legalism and dogmatism transform the living faith into spiritually deadening ritual conformity of action, both political and religious. Moses therewith becomes no longer the author of his people but merely the author of a book. The conflict between the mundane and divine orders as exemplified in the drama of Jeremiah and his trial are seen in parallel to the conflict in Athens two centuries later with the trial and condemnation of Socrates that also yields mutual death sentences to the man and to the corrupt society (436). "From the middle of the eighth century BC to the fall of Jerusalem, the histori-cal order under a universal God is the constant concern of the proph-ets . . . The order of society and history participates in the order of God only in as much as the universal, transcendent God is experi-enced as such in the faith of men who order their existence in the light of their faith . . ." (471-72).

The prize of existence and the pulse of historical form is the living faith of individual persons under God, and this experience is at the heart of prophetic existence and their call to the community to re-turn to the life of salvation. Anything less is defection from truth. Thus Voegelin interprets the prophetic effort as "a struggle against the Law" as a deadening of the spirit of Yahweh (*OH* I, 447n.). Ad-mittedly, their attitude seemed to contradict common sense and the pragmatic need for effective community action based on political and religious cohesion. The prophets' point in their exhortations, rejections and demands is to overcome externalization and the su-perficial in life by disengaging the existential from the theopolitical merging of divine and human, and by rejecting the mundane order. Even absent philosophy and its symbolization of the order of the immortal *psyche* developed in Hellas, the prophets nonetheless "rec-ognized the formation of the soul through knowledge (Hosea) and fear (Isaiah)." They were not only unable to see, but "not even inter-ested in finding, a way from the formation of the soul to institutions and customs they could consider compatible with the knowledge and fear of God" (446-47). This rejection of institutional order on prin-ciple, that marks the prophetic attitude and defies common sense, "adds up to an ontological denial of the conditions of existence in the world" (455). At the heart of the attitude is the metastatic yearn-ing of the prophets for a new world so that "the constitution of being is transfigured into a state of perfection" to be achieved through "a divine act of grace that will bestow ultimate order on the world." The real issue is to reorder existence through knowledge (*da'ath*) of God, and at least in Hosea, this is not a disturbing factor but an effort to "bring the Kingdom of God in the souls of men forth from its theopolitical matrix" (456). The prophetic effort's insistent spiritualization leads toward the insight in Jeremiah "that the order from eternity is not incarnate in a people and its rulers in pragmatic history." It also leads to the contraction of the Chosen People into the existence of the chosen man who has to act out the fate of Israel in his own life.

The prophet had become the City of God, the sole representative of divine order (*OH* I, 466-67, 490). The authority in existence has shifted from the king to prophet. The stages of prophetism pass through the institutional (Amos and Hosea), the metastatic (Isaiah) and existential (Jeremiah). Behind the problem of metastasis lie the problems of balance and faith. To repeat: "the order of society and history participates in the order of God only in as much as the universal, transcendent God is experienced as such in the faith of men who order their existence in the light of their faith and thereby become the representative center of society and history (472, 474). Metastasis is explored to its end in Isaiah, who envisions the spirit of God filling a glorified world so that "the wolf shall dwell with the lamb, and the leopard shall lie down with the kid" (Isa 11:3-5). The vision of transfigured Israel grows into a vision of world peace with God the judge of nations: "'they will beat their swords into plowshares' and learn no more the art of war (Isa 2:4). Governmental institutions and their human incumbents are no longer mentioned" (480). Metastatic faith, thus, precludes any sort of fulfillment through pragmatic action, and one could only wait for the miracle to happen (481). The balance can be recovered only when divine presence is rescued from futurism and recognized as the tension of existence at once ontologically present and eschatologically directed.

## Exodus as Enduring Symbol

The Exodus of Israel from itself forms the final act of the drama as it is resolved in the eschatological hope of the Suffering Servant of Deutero-Isaiah. There is a "terrible truth" to be glimpsed from the prophets' suffering participation in the divine suffering. This is that no concrete society of any sort whatever can resolve the problem of order in history or serve as the chosen vessel or People and center of the true order of mankind.

When Abram emigrated from Ur of the Chaldeans, the Exodus
from imperial civilization had begun. When Israel was brought
forth from Egypt, by Yahweh and Moses his servant, and constituted as the people under God, the Exodus had reached the form
of a people's theopolitical existence in rivalry with the cosmological
form. With Isaiah's and Jeremiah's movement away from the
concrete Israel begins the anguish of the third procreative act of
divine order in history: The Exodus of Israel from itself (*OH* I,
491).

The present as lived in the experience of the Servant as a participation in divine suffering becomes the experience of redemption in the
here and now, thereby completing the last act in the drama of Exodus in the movement "from the order of a concrete society toward
the order of redemption (501). But the meaning of *completion* must
be clarified. "It means that the order of being has revealed its mystery
of redemption as the flower of suffering. It does not mean, however,
that the vision of the mystery is the reality of redemption in history:
The participation of man in divine suffering has yet to encounter the
participation of God in human suffering" (501). The Exodus from
the cosmological order of empires is completed in the Servant, and
the history of Israel as "the people under God consummated in the
vision of the unknown genius, for as the representative sufferer Israel
has gone beyond itself and become the light of salvation to mankind" (515). The revelation is not a transfiguration of the order of
the world but "a revelation of God as Redeemer" (499).

Lastly, the force of the Exodus motif in Voegelin's philosophy of
man and history is an enduring symbolism of the mystery of history
with its open horizon, and of the quest of man as ever unfulfilled. It
is this aspect of his work that I would particularly stress for its pivotal
significance and wonderful nobility. It is a motif, sounded in the
opening pages of *Israel and Revelation,* that recurs in many passages
as abiding insight, one indicative of the man and his work, but also
emblematic of the human condition itself and of the quest of faith in
search of understanding that binds together prophets, philosophers,
saints and sages from Abraham onward. From the philosopher's perspective: "It means that the quest for truth is ultimately penultimate.
In the quest, reality is experienced as the mysterious movement of an
It-reality through thing-reality toward a Beyond of things . . . For the
questioner has to tell the story of his struggle for the unflawed order
from his position in the flawed order of thingly existence; and he can
tell it, therefore, only in the flawed language that speaks of non-things
in the mode of things . . . When the paradoxic experience of

not-experientiable reality becomes conscious in reflective distance, the questioner's language reveals itself as the paradoxic event of the ineffable becoming effable. This tension of effable-ineffable is the paradox in the structure in meditative language . . ." (*OHV*, 102-103).

The sense of quest and penultimacy in tension toward the Ground and its transformative pull is reflected in Voegelin's fondness for a passage in *Enarrationes in Psalmos* 64.2. It illustrates the understanding that the tension of faith is not a Christian monopoly but a trait of human nature, and that the structure-process of history is the same as that of personal existence. As exemplified in the cited passage, Augustine "lets the historical symbols of exodus and of Babylon express the movement of the soul when it is drawn by the love of God:

> Incipit exire qui incipit amare.
> Exeunt enim multi latenter,
> et exeuntium pedes sunt cordis affectus:
> exeunt autem de Babylonia.
>
> He begins to leave who begins to love.
> Many the leaving who know it not,
> for the feet of those leaving are affections of the heart:
> and yet, they are leaving Babylon.

His conception of history as a tale of two cities, intermingling from the beginning of mankind to its end, conceives it as a tale of man's personal exodus written large . . . History is Christ written large. This last formulation is not in conflict with the Platonic 'man written large'" (IES, 78).

With these reflections, we touch the meaning of Voegelin's steadfast insistence that the soul is the sensorium of transcendence and that the experience of transcendence is inseparable from the understanding of man as human—whether in his individual and personal or social and historical existence—, fundamentals of the philosophy of history and human affairs.

## Conclusion

In terms of genre, *Israel and Revelation* must be seen in the context of Voegelin's study of order in history and as a part of his philosophy of history. The concern with the Biblical sources is primarily directed toward discerning and analyzing the revelatory experiences symbolized therein. The thrust of the study, therefore, is to clarify the order of being beyond the primordial experience of cosmic divinity as this is articulated in Israel's leap in being. The ethical order as it finds primary expression in the response of Moses and of Israel for mankind in the Sinaitic Covenant and the Ten Commandments clearly is derivative *from* the revelation of Yahweh and grounded in the attunement to the truth of Being glimpsed in these indelible experiences and constantly recurred to in subsequent generations, centuries and millennia into the present as the heart of the living faith. An ungrounded ethical order is a dogmatic derailment and a deformative externalization of faith akin to legalism, by Voegelin's analysis. The same principle applies in philosophy in the Hellenic horizon where he is equally insistent that the formation of character through the experience of transcendence lies at the core of elaborations of order as consequences in the ethical and political spheres. An ungrounded ethics or politics constitutes a derailment of both Yahwism and philosophy.

The cardinal ethical principle that emerges, then, is the obligation of each person *to resist corruption and disorder* so as, thereby, to live in accord with the truth of the divine Ground. In the horizon of revelatory experience this requires the nurture of living faith of the kind Voegelin discerns in the tenacious prophetic effort to "listen" to the Word of God and bring with them the community of Israel they represent. This would seem to be a position wholly consistent with the resolute proclamation of the *Shema* and with its reiteration as the Great Commandment by Jesus (Deut 6:4-5;Mt 22:37;Mk 12:29-30;Lk 10:27). The basis for this stress in Voegelin is the emphasis in the sources themselves and in the perceived tendency of those who defect from truth to assert various false grounds to justify their deformation and disorder. Occlusion against the Ground is the abiding fallacy and mutilation of reality against which Voegelin contends as the root of evil, to the extent that it implies the sufficiency of man to himself as autonomous.

While there is an affirmation of the constancy and resiliency of being and its order as coming from the hand of God, there is also a sense of direction and pilgrimage in the process of history and the Whole in Voegelin's attention to the experiences-symbolizations of order. We have touched on this aspect of his account in terms of the experience of permanent exodus in recalling the passage from Augustine. The structure of reality is not a rigidly inflexible fixity but a structure in process of moving beyond itself. This is to say that history has ontological dimensions and eschatological process (Sandoz 1981, 243-51). These attributes also register in Voegelin's philosophy as he constantly revises and finds now one, now another figure or symbol to express in meditative discourse the experiences he tries to illuminate. The point is captured in many places but perhaps nowhere better than in the closing paragraph of *The Ecumenic Age*:

> Once the fallacies are removed, the hierarchy of being comes into view, not as a number of strata one piled on top of the other, but as [the] movement of reality from the apeirontic depth up to man, through as many levels of the hierarchy as can be discerned empirically, and as the countermovement of creative organization from the divine height down, with the *Metaxy* of man's consciousness as the site where the movement of the Whole becomes luminous for its eschatological direction. When the historical dimension of humanity has differentiated, the Question thus turns back to the process of the Whole as it becomes luminous for its directional movement in the process of history. The Mystery of the historical process is inseparable from the Mystery of a reality which brings forth the universe and the earth, plant and animal life on earth, and ultimately man and his consciousness. Such reflections are definitely not new, but they express, in differentiated form . . . the mode of questioning engendered in the contemporary situation by a philosopher's resistance to the distortion and destruction of humanity committed by the "stop-history" Systems. They are an act of open participation in the process of both history and the Whole (*OH* IV, 335).

## EPILOGUE

A few additional words may be of value for locating Voegelin's thought in the horizon of contemporary scholarship as it bears on some of the questions he himself addressed. Nothing but the barest hints can be given, and the rather paradoxical reasons for this need to be made clear at the outset. To begin with, and on several counts, Voegelin was something of a one-man band. William C. Havard (quoting Gregor Sebba) explains matters this way:

> Two things have prevented the appropriate recognition of the emergence of a new theory of politics . . . the first is that the advancement of that theory "is largely the work of one independent thinker, Eric Voegelin, who published his first book four decades ago . . . and is still forging ahead at a pace which leaves his best readers behind." The second is the "enormous demand" which the Voegelinian achievement makes on the "newcomer to such studies." Not only must the reader be able to follow abstract reasoning at its highest level; he must also know the history of ideas,

philosophy (in all its dimensions), theology, the full sweep of history from prehistory to modernity, and the present development of scholarship in fields as widely separated as anthropology, biblical criticism, comparative literature, and psychology . . . all of this is very far from the concerns of the practicing political scientist today" (Havard 1984, 97; Sebba 1968).

Sebba, who was a friend and colleague of Voegelin's in Vienna, from the 1930s prior to the Nazi *Anschluss* until the end of his life, engagingly writes elsewhere:

The philosopher Eric Voegelin has the distinction of being kept unread in [the philosophers'] storage basement, presumably as a contemporary fossil. Or perhaps they mistake him for a political scientist, as the political scientists do.

Voegelin has always defied departmentalization . . . One could almost speak of three Voegelins, in reverse chronological order. First comes the author of *Order and History* (1956-1987). Then there is the Voegelin of *The New Science of Politics* (1952), still a focus of fruitless controversy among political scientists. (Is he a kind of Saint Francis preaching to the birds in a positivistic aviary? A dangerous but happily unreadable reactionary? An irrelevant unscientific dilettante?) Finally, there is the virtually unknown Voegelin of the period from 1922 to 1938, the author of five books and nearly forty papers on topics from the Federal Reserve System to the Sun Hymn of Akhenaton. I took him at that time for a young sociologist of the Max Weber, Georg Simmel, and Max Scheler type, a born theoretician with an insatiable intellectual appetite, whose work was very hard to understand (Sebba 1991, 198).

Preaching to the birds in a positivistic aviary is both useful and colorful as a metaphor to describe Voegelin's relationship to so-called "mainstream" political science. This does not alter the fact, however, of Voegelin's life-long self-identification as a political scientist, nor of his ambition from the beginning of his academic career to develop a viable science of politics that might more adequately reflect human reality and permit its more precise scientific investigation. From the standpoint of the discipline and profession it is not too much to say that this is, indeed, the core of Voegelin's work as a revolutionary thinker. It would seem that not even Sebba understands this fully. What is entailed by the achievement passes over the heads of most other readers as well; so it is worth emphasizing that there is, indeed, a new philosophical science of politics awaiting more general discovery in Voegelin's work.[3]

Voegelin's singularity is further suggested by his employment of the previously mentioned technique of analysis variously called the "critical method" or "Aristotelian procedure" or "unoriginal thinking."[4] This has two aspects. The first is the spirit of comparative analysis that he admired in Max Weber and that involves the pursuit of questions on the basis of a mastery of the pertinent literature in all relevant languages to the point that the state of scholarly understanding can be assayed and, where possible, the issues then analytically penetrated a step or two farther. This method is well displayed in *Israel and Revelation*. The fact was noticed by Bernhard Anderson, the distinguished Old Testament scholar and theologian, who commented: "It is refreshing to read the work of a philosophical 'layman' in the field who has taken it upon himself to master the original sources and the secondary literature up to the time of his writing . . . This is one of the few books on the Old Testament which has so engrossed my interest that I have eagerly wondered what would be on the next page." In 1997 Anderson commented: "Revisiting Voegelin's *Israel and Revelation* after a quarter of a century is intellectually exhilarating . . . Essentially I stand by what I wrote then . . . " (chaps. one and two of this book).[5] Fittingly, Voegelin's appointment at the University of Munich in 1958 was to the chair of political science conveniently left vacant for the momentous three decades after the death of its previous incumbent, Max Weber.[6]

The other aspect of Voegelin's critical method is the leveling of much conventional thought because of its ideological, deformed or dogmatic character. Such doctrinaire thinking falls before the Weberian principle of intellectual honesty ("*intellectuelle Rechtschaffenheit*") (*AR*, 44) and it is enduringly symbolized on the model of the relationship between Socrates-Plato and Athens. It is biographically rooted in Voegelin's long effort to extricate himself from the methodological horizon of neo-Kantian positivism as a young academic, and in his personal and professional face-to-face confrontation with ideologues of left and right in the intellectual and political brawl that first climaxed in Nazi hegemony in Central Europe and persisted in various forms thereafter (Levy 1993, chap. 2; 1981; 1987). But it amounts to more than this, for a principle is involved: the philosopher *qua* philosopher, if true to the calling, inevitably stands in tension with— in some degree of critical opposition to—*all* received and conventional truth of what kind so ever, a message of the Allegory of the Cave. This is Voegelin's stance as a scholar who refuses to be bound by anybody's orthodoxies, friend or foe—not as a fetish, pose or ec-centricity but as the indispensable condition of what he takes to be requisite for the true servant of science, philosophy, and truth. He pulls no punches. This is not the Dale Carnegie School prescription for how to win friends and influence people, of course, and the truth-sayers of history typically have been notorious outcasts.

The attitude appears often enough in Voegelin's writings to be taken as paradigmatic. A good example that hits close to home and is, there-fore, of particular interest, is "The Oxford Political Philosophers." This essay consists of a critique of Liberal theory (specifically as found in writings by A.D. Lindsay, R.G. Collingwood, J.D. Mabbott, E.F. Carritt, G.R.G. Mure, C.H. Wilson, R.B. McCallum, J.W. Gough, Max Beloff, W. Harrison, and A.P. d'Entrèves), and after praising only Mure's "brilliant lecture" on *The Organic State*, ends with the following paragraph:

> I shall conclude on an Aristotelian point . . . The polis offers the opportunity for full actualization of human nature. The fully actualized man is the *spoudaios*, the mature man, who has devel-oped his dianoetic excellences and whose life is orientated by his noetic self. This is the decisive issue in a philosophy of politics, the issue which the distinguished authors whose work we have dis-cussed studiously avoid. Under pretext of respect for the freedom of conscience they ignore the fact that conscience, however "good" it may be putatively, can only be as good as the man who has it. A theory of conscience that shies away from ontology, and in particu-lar from a theory of the nature of man, is empty; it is a parlor game in which one can indulge as long as the surrounding society contains enough Christian substance to make at least the worst sort of good consciences socially ineffective; but even under such favorable conditions (as they still exist in England) this nihilistic theory of conscience contributes to the intellectual and moral confusion which paves the way for the best of all consciences, *viz.*, that of the totalitarian killers. All men are equal, to be sure, or they would not be individuals of one species; but sometimes it is forgotten that the point in which they most certainly are equal is their capacity for evil. Enough of that evil is rampant; and this is no time to pat the viciously ignorant on the back for being "sincere," or abiding by their "conscience." This is a time for the philosopher to be aware of his authority, and to assert it, even if that brings him into conflict with an environment infested by dubious ideologies and political theologies—so that the word of Marcus Aurelius will apply to him: "The philosopher—the priest and servant of the Gods" (OPP, 114, 100).

Thus the "paradox" of a thinker (seen as something of a loner) who took his vocation with utmost seriousness and expected colleagues to do the same; ransacked the sources in every field his inquiry led him into; conducted an enormous correspondence with scholars throughout the world on a vast array of subjects; constantly rejoiced in the collaborative achievements of the historical and theoretical sciences in the twentieth century, even while condemning radical modernity's Gnosticism; roundly rejected the characterization of himself as a solitary thinker, embracing in its place the image of a cosmopolitan scholar in touch with experts in every field; eagerly insisted that his own work be as completely informed as possible with all the latest scientific results. Voegelin's is not so much the loneliness of a Saint Francis preaching to the birds (even though his "ism"-ridden aviary is a hostile environment, to be sure), but that of the personality for whom Diogenes long before lighted a candle at mid-day.

If one considers the range of topics—dimensions of reality—Voegelin addresses and looks for connecting links and organizing centers among them in his writing and thought, the very top of the list belongs to his steadfast devotion to the integrity of the individual human being as *imago Dei*[7] and as the justification for the entire constellation of historical, social and intellectual activities and arrangements associated with civilization per se. The theory of human nature is central to that of community, political and social order and to the philosophy of history or historicity, symbolization and consciousness.[8] In a great variety of ways this emphasis and direction of inquiry is present from early writings onward. In the abandoned *Herrschaftslehre* "the person . . . is the intersection of divine eternity and human temporality . . ."[9] Man is more than merely biological or social and shares in the entire hierarchy of being from material reality to the spiritual and divine, Voegelin vociferously and repeatedly argues against the Nazi race "theorists" in his two 1933 books, *Race and State* and *The History of the Race Idea*.[10] He looks for a place to stand in addressing the crisis of modernity and that place is the development of a differentiated understanding of what it is to be a human being—this he calls a theory of human nature, a philosophical and political anthropology as part of a general ontology, to use the language of the *New Science of Politics* and of the initial volumes of *Order and History*. But what is the *differentia specifica* of man in his humanity but his soul or consciousness?—to maintain the continuity with classical and Christian philosophy, while at the same time basing himself indubitably in empirical or experiential, self-evident fact.

The theory of consciousness, noticed earlier, dominates the work of the final years and is seen to underlie all of the work from the 1940s onward, as the correspondence with Alfred Schütz about Edmund Husserl and phenomenology indicates (Opitz and Sebba 1981, 74-90, 431-65). The introduction to the American edition of *Anamnesis*, "A Remembrance of Things Past" (1978), is the key document, and what is perhaps the key sentence there reads: "What I had discovered was consciousness in the concrete, in personal, social, and historical existence of man, as the specifically human mode of participation in reality" (*AE*, 30). The anamnetic exploration of consciousness as the center of a critical philosophy of human affairs in palpable continuity with that of Plato and Aristotle animated all of the remaining work.

There are important qualifications, however. The unfolding of the potential of human nature is not given in full actualization immediately, either in individuals or in mankind as a whole, but develops (or atrophies) biographically in each person's lifetime and in exuberant diversity historically in multiple civilizational, religious and other communities of the one mankind down to the present (*OH* IV, introduction). This pivotal point is stated—with a warning against obsessive "intellectualism"—in the early *History of Political Ideas* in the chapter on Dante, as follows: "Our modern [philosophical] anthropology is enriched by insight into the historical structure of the human mind. It is no longer possible to identify the essence of man with ahistoric intellect . . . The unity of mankind is not intellectually static; it is an open field in which the possibilities of the human mind unfold historically and manifest themselves in the sequence of civilizations and of nations. To stop history at any point of time, and to elevate a civilizational crosscut, or more frequently a fragment of the crosscut, to the rank of an absolute and to call it the nature of man has become impossible. With this insight into the historicity of the mind, the idea falls that [any] static 'organization' can be the political answer to the idea of man. The drama of human history can not be caught in a governmental power organization, imperial or otherwise . . . " (*CW* 21, chap. 16, 6, b).[11] Voegelin adds later on, apropos Nicholas of Cusa: "The reception of the Aristotelian ranks [of human types] of the free *sapientes* and the slavish *insipientes* created a formidable problem, for the Hellenic idea of a natural slave is incompatible with the Christian idea of the spiritually free man . . . The principal obstacle to an integration of Hellenic political theory into the Christian is formed by the Hellenic idea of nature: *Hellenic nature is nature without grace*. The differentiation of types [of man] is a brute fact . . . In a Christian system, nature itself has to be penetrated spiritually in order to make natural differences psychologically bearable and systematically compatible with the fundamental idea of spiritual freedom" (*CW* 21, chap. 22, 23).[12]

When we concluded the body of the present essay with a suggestion of the open horizon of human and historical endeavor by remembering Augustine's experience of the translation of time into eternity and subtly striking an eschatological note, we found a fitting symbol for Voegelin's own open quest and search for order in exodus. Complementing it are such further clues and insights as the Question that is more important than the answers found; the knowing questions and the questioning knowledge that structure inquiry; the Socratic and Anselmian awareness of their ultimate ignorance before the abysmal mystery of being as faith seeks understanding; and recognition that the "temptation to fall from uncertain truth into certain untruth is stronger in the clarity of Christian faith than in other spiritual structures" (*SPG*, 75). These are some of the hallmarks of Voegelin's meditative science and theoretical achievement.[13]

## Notes

[1]So as to stay within space limits, the present essay—apart from the Epilogue— concentrates on Voegelin's writings themselves with little direct reference to the burgeoning secondary literature or to comparisons with the work of other writers addressing related issues. The primary intent is to get clear on Voegelin's presentation in an extensive body of work still surprisingly unfamiliar to many political theorists almost a half-century after *The New Science of Politics* first saw the light. There exists, indeed, a substantial secondary literature, and those interested in it can consult for guidance the excellent compilation of Price 1994. This extensive bibliography is periodically updated electronically in the *Voegelin— Research News*, archive address: vax2.concordia.ca/#vorenews. Another help for readers new to Voegelin's writings is the glossary appended to Webb 1981, 277-89. Since 1986, the Eric Voegelin Society has conducted programs of up to nine panels in conjunction with the American Political Science Association's annual meetings; see Eric Voegelin Institute website at http://www2.artsci.lsu.edu/ voegelin/voegelin.html for program, conference and bibliographic information.

[2]For a detailed account of these matters *see* Hollweck and Sandoz 1997, 1-48.

[3]See Sandoz 1981, chap. 7. Good presentations of Voegelin's political science are given in Cooper 1986, 1989, 1999; Germino 1967; Ranieri 1995. Voegelin's work considered as a new science under the aspects of epistemology and ontology has been studied in Baek 1989; Burchfield 1994; Myers 1997. Background in terms of the German context of *Geisteswissenschaft* and *Staatslehre* is concisely given in *CW* 1, ix-xxxv, where Jürgen Gebhardt outlines some of the key connections of Voegelin's work to Edmund Husserl, Max Scheler, Karl Jaspers and discusses his exodus from the neo-Kantianism of his mentor, Hans Kelsen,

and the pure theory of law (*Reine Rechtslehre*). Voegelin's intentions are directly suggested by his early article ZLS and more fully in the unpublished manuscript fragment entitled *Herrschaftslehre und Rechtslehre*, which dates from *ca.* 1931, and runs some 125 pages in typescript (Hoover Institution, Voegelin Archives, box 53, file 5). The developments of the early period in Voegelin's thought have been carefully studied by Chignola 1993.

[4]Cf. *NSP*, 31, 52, 117, 133. Unoriginal thinking is formulated as follows: "The validating question will have to be: Do we have to ignore and eclipse a major part of the historical field in order to maintain the truth of the propositions, as the fundamentalist adherents of this or that ideological doctrine must do; or are the propositions recognizably *equivalent* with the symbols created by our predecessors in the search of truth about human existence? The test of truth, to put it pointedly, will be the *lack of originality in the propositions*" (EESH, 122).

[5]For detailed analysis of Voegelin's writings from the perspective of theology and religion see Morrissey 1994, esp. the comparison with Bernard Lonergan, 171-226; Kirby and Thompson 1983; Thompson 1991, esp. chap. 2; Hughes 1993. Of particular interest for this dimension of Voegelin's work is *CW19*, esp. 30-47, 149-224.

[6]The Weberian aspect of Voegelin's political science is discussed in *AR,* 11-14, 16, 33, 45-46 and throughout. It is the subject of a lively debate between Jürgen Gebhardt and Frederick G. Lawrence, who favors Voegelin the mystic-philosopher, in McKnight and Price 1997, 10-58. This volume also includes a valuable classified bibliography by Price. That the imagined two Voegelins—scientist and mystic—are not mutually exclusive but complementary also can be seen from Voegelin's lecture, "On the Greatness of Max Weber" (*OBG*, 78-98), which concludes by suggesting that Weber considered himself to be a mystic.

[7]Levy 1993, 1981, 1987 explores this subject. The starting point for Voegelin, that is, in his work of the 1930s, was the Platonic-Aristotelian and Christian anthropology of Max Scheler and of one of his mentors at Vienna, Othmar Spann. See Scheler, 1913-1916, 1915, 1921, 1923; Spann 1923. For discussion and analysis see Petropoulos 1993, 36, who concludes that meditation as the basic form of philosophizing, and the person as imago Dei, remain of fundamental importance throughout Voegelin's philosophical career. See also Kessler 1995; Henriques 1992.

[8]Much of the secondary literature is taken up with these aspects of Voegelin's writings. To be mentioned here are only a few select items: Webb 1981, 1988; Aaron 1961; McKnight 1978. The issues of modernity and Gnosticism within Voegelin's theories of politics and history are addressed in Sandoz 1971a; Schall 1987; Opitz 1993; McAllister 1996; Langan 1996; McKnight 1991; 1992, which examines the Hans Blumenberg, Karl Löwith, Voegelin debate over modernity; Germino 1982; Cohn 1957; Vondung 1988; Walsh 1983; Zanetti 1989; Franz 1992; Keulman 1990. On various aspects of Liberalism: Forster 1960; Walsh 1990, 1997; Sandoz 1990, 1996; Syse 1996.

[9]"Die Person, sagten wir, sei der Schnittpunkt von göttlicher Ewigkeit und menschlicher Zeitlichkeit; in ihr offenbart sich die Endlichkeit also das Wesen der Welt. Person ist die Erfahrung der Grenze, an der ein Diesseitig-Endliches sich gegen ein Jenseitig-Unendliches absetzt" (*Herrschaftslehre*, MS, 7).

[10]See *RS*, 8-16, 19-36, 128-53, and passim, where the author begins with a condemnation of the race theorists: "A system of dogmas . . . that, in short, I will

call the system of scientific superstition" (9). Voegelin's two race books are analyzed in Heilke 1990; Winkler 1997.

[11]This line of analysis is palpably continued and elaborated, with attention to what is here termed the intellectualist fallacy as a major defect, in the philosophies of history of Hegel and Jaspers, in Voegelin's late work; see, esp. *OH* IV, chap. 7, 300-35.

[12]Italics added. The critical updating of Aristotle's philosophical anthropology is a prominent subject of "What Is Political Reality?" (*AE*, 143-214; see the summary at 172-74).

[13]Other contemporary authors whose work in some significant way is comparable to Voegelin's and/or influential upon it, and who are not otherwise cited or mentioned herein, include: Michael Oakeshott, Martin Heidegger, Alfred North Whitehead, Emmanuel Levinas, Talcott Parsons, Harry A. Wolfson, Martin Buber, Leszek Kolakowski, Albert Camus, Friedrich A. von Hayek, Carl Schmitt, Petrim Sorokin, Wolfhart Pannenberg, Etienne Gilson, Hans Jonas, John Hallowell, Jacob Taubes, Gottfried von Haberler, Gerhart Niemeyer, Jacob L. Talmon, Hermann Broch, Thomas Mann, Robert Musil, Heimito von Doderer, Mircea Eliade, Karl Kraus, Albert Paris Gütersloh, Flannery O'Connor, Hans Urs von Balthasar, Geoffrey Barraclough, Maurice Natanson, Paul G. Kuntz— among many others, but the list already is too long. It can be filled out and supplemented from *AR*. See also Voegelin's two *Festschriften*: Dempf, Arendt, and Engel-Janosi 1962; Opitz and Sebba 1981.

# THE VOEGELINIAN IMPULSE
## Glenn Tinder

Followers of almost any thinker, such as Aristotle or Hobbes, may use their studies of that thinker to engage in processes of reflection that bring out their own ideas. There are a few thinkers, however, that render such processes of reflection mandatory. They require a personal response. Plato is an obvious example of such a thinker; Nietzsche is another. This essay has been premised on the hypothesis that Voegelin is a thinker of this sort. He rules out any but a dialogical relationship with his readers. Plato did this, of course, by writing dialogues; Nietzsche did so by confining himself largely to somewhat cryptic aphorisms. Voegelin's dialogical posture derives from what one might call the unfinished character of his thought. Voegelin calls on his followers not simply to follow but to ponder issues and possibilities of development which his work presents. Mere assent is precluded; one has to go further. The present essay is an effort to define what going further might mean.

The "Voegelinian impulse," then, is in directions indicated but not explicitly followed. The phrase has a double reference. It refers first of all to possible lines of development leading into Voegelin's later work, particularly to the later volumes of *Order and History*. The later work is of course largely beyond the bounds of this paper. But assuming that some of the issues opened up by *Israel and Revelation* are not wholly settled later on and thus remain open at the end of Voegelin's life, it can be said that "the Voegelinian impulse" carries beyond the whole body of Voegelin's work. I am particularly interested in issues of this sort. This is partly because of my sense that they are numerous and important, and partly because of my belief that Voegelin's worth as a thinker lies not only in the questions he answered but in those he asked and invited his readers to answer. He asked not merely for agreement but for creative thinking.

My concern will be—in line with Voegelin's own major concern— with the principles of order. These, needless to say, are not the characteristics of an ideal society, since we cannot conceive of such a society, given the conflict between the demands of transcendence and the demands of pragmatic existence in history. Rather, the principles of order are permanently valid axioms bearing on the organization of society under a world-transcendent God; an example of such principles would be the very impossibility of an ideal society within history. A crucial feature of the principles I have chosen for discussion, however, is that they invite development—the articulation of presuppositions, for example, or the specification of institutional implications. In short, they are principles in which there is an impulse. An equally crucial feature of these principles is that the impulse they provide is one to which, so far as we can tell, Voegelin would be open. My discussion is intended to suggest ways in which Voegelin's thought might be filled out but not, properly speaking, contradicted or set aside.

I propose to discuss five principles of order that are either set forth or clearly implied in *Israel and Revelation*. These are: (1) Eschatology, that is, the idea that history has an end, with the end coming not only as a fulfillment of history but also as a break with, and a judgment upon, history. From beginning to end, eschatology implies, history comprises both progress and failure. (2) Institutional pluralism. The inconclusiveness of history mandates institutional polarities and tensions of some kind. For all the earth, and all realms of life, to be under one all-encompassing authority would invite an idolatrous neglect of the imperfections of collective life in history. (3) Universalism. The exodus from cosmological civilization is a universal event, bearing on the destiny of all humankind. In that sense, it relativizes every particular historical society and requires every individual to sustain, in some manner, a relationship not only with "the unseen measure," and with surrounding institutions, but also with the entire human race. (4) Personalism. This of course is Voegelin's term for the idea that the orientation toward transcendence is reflected primarily in personal, and only secondarily in societal, order; in other words, society after the Exodus is macroanthropic rather than microcosmic. And finally, (5) Historicism. An unsatisfactory term, owing to its diverse definitions, "historicism" is seemingly the only available term for designating the idea that history has meaning. In Voegelin's words, history is "the inner form of a people's present existence before God." Let us consider these five principles in order.

## I

(1) Eschatology. Voegelin's eschatological orientation is implicit in a theme running throughout his work: the insolubility within history of the requirements placed on society by a world-transcendent God. It is clearly indicated in such a statement as the following: "The

promised land can be reached only by moving through history, but it cannot be conquered within history. The Kingdom of God lives in men who live in the world, but it is not of this world" (*IR*, 114). The impulse arising from eschatology is to discover ways of safeguarding the very idea of an event bringing history to an end and thus being something other than an historical event in the usual sense of the term. Also needing to be safeguarded is the idea of a state of life that is brought nearer in the course of history but is incompatible with the fundamental conditions of history, such as alienation and temporality. The eschaton, symbolizing both the event and the state of life realized through the event, not only has never been seen; it never can be seen in the same way a material object is seen. Hence it is unimaginable and inconceivable. It follows that as soon as we begin to imagine the eschaton, which we are apt to do in the very act of thinking of it, we have lost the concept itself. In short, eschatology is unthinkable. How, then, can we even entertain the concept?

As every reader of Voegelin knows, he was acutely conscious of this problem. His tireless attacks on Gnosticism and metastasis were, in effect, efforts to defend the bulwarks of his eschatological faith. And I believe it is fair to say that his whole interpretation of the prophetic movement in Israel turns on the notion that the principles of order are falsified by claims to historical fulfillment. Thus he speaks of "the terrible truth" that "no Chosen People in any form will be the omphalos of the true order of mankind" (*IR*, 491). Beyond establishing these positions, which Voegelin did through careful and sustained argumentation, what more might be done? What further impulse is there in Voegelin's eschatology?

One possible answer to these questions lies in a further question: Is an eschatological attitude altogether secure if it is not grounded in a quite explicit concept of sin? A reader of Voegelin can gain the impression that he often regarded Gnosticism and metastasis as expressive of sin, but that he did not do so invariably; sometimes he seems to envision them as intellectual, or spiritual, errors. This is the case, for example, when he characterizes the prophetic experience as "essentially metastatic" (*IR*, 484). Does the possible innocence of metastatic distortions of history—distortions tending to undermine eschatology—reduce their gravity and leave them insufficiently defined? To put the question even more sharply, would Voegelin's eschatology be situated more soundly if it rested on a concept of original sin—of sin as characteristic not just of individual acts but, so to speak, of the human posture in the universe? It is regrettable that Voegelin did not comment on Reinhold Niebuhr's *The Nature and*

*Destiny of Man*, which appeared well over a decade before *Israel and Revelation* and which exhibited dramatically the role which the concept of original sin can play in an eschatological view of history.

In sum, it is arguable that a clearly articulated concept of sin would tend to protect eschatology against Gnostic and metastatic exaggerations of historical possibilities. Still, one might object, it would not render the eschaton any more imaginable or eschatology any more thinkable. But probably nothing would. Eschatology is a boundary concept in that it confronts us immediately with the mystery of human existence as it impinges on history. All we can do to safeguard eschatology is to conceive of history in a way which clearly demarcates everything within it from the kingdom of God, thus barring us from denying the final mystery of life by trying to cast it in historical terms. The value of the concept of original sin lies partly in the fact that it does this. Could that concept, then, be used to strengthen Voegelin's position without betraying in any way the spirit of his thought?

(2) lnsitional pluralism. The need for institutional diversities and balances arises from a condition which Voegelin seems to have held at the center of his mind throughout his intellectual career: that a society is a spiritual order which must maintain its existence amid material circumstances. Voegelin's poignant account of Saul's spiritual confusion as he approached his own death in battle dramatically evokes the tragedy which is invited when the supreme secular ruler is also the supreme spiritual ruler. How keenly attuned Voegelin was to the issue is evident when he notes, in concluding his discussion of Saul's plight, that Israel's historical situation did not permit an institutional solution to the problem of theopolitical order "comparable to the Christian development of the spiritual and temporal orders" (*IR*, 247).

The Voegelinian impulse in this area arises from the unfinished character of his ecclesiology, if indeed one may attribute to him an ecclesiology. I take it for granted that Voegelin was in some sense a Christian. Although not an orthodox or practicing Christian, he seemingly viewed Christ as the culmination of Israelite and Hellenic spiritual history. It is obviously not mere happenstance that the last word in *Israel and Revelation* is "Jesus." Yet the Christian tradition and the major Christian institution for fifteen centuries, the Catholic Church, apparently had relatively little spiritual significance for Voegelin. There is of course a good deal of evidence of this in the body of Voegelin's work. In *Israel and Revelation* the clearest sign of Voegelin's guarded attitude toward the Christian tradition and Church appears in a rather startling footnote. "The meaning of history under the Christian dispensation," he writes, "is as far from satisfactory positive expression today as it was at the time of Jesus and his generation" (*IR*, 345). Unless "the meaning of history" is understood far more narrowly than Voegelin probably understood it, Voegelin seems here to express a consciousness of profound failure on the part of Christian doctrinal development, and by implication on the part of the Christian Church, up to the present time. That attitude is in line with Voegelin's reservations (reminiscent of the early Barth) concerning religion broadly. In *Israel and Revelation*, these reservations are expressed in the observation that reliance on "the symbols of a creed," if it becomes "socially predominant," is apt to "kill the order [of the spirit] it is supposed to preserve" (377). Voegelin's views in this matter may be well-grounded. What is noteworthy in the present context, however, is that they give rise to serious questions concerning the political order. To use established terminology, these questions concern the duality of church and state. How is the separation of spiritual and temporal authorities, so vital to a proper earthly order, to be realized?

There is perhaps no sharper illustration of the unfinished character of Voegelin's thought, and of the possibilities of development which it puts before the reader, than this question. The question can be translated into various subordinate questions. Does Voegelin's philosophy, and in particular his epistemology, with its emphasis on experience over doctrine, offer a basis for reconceiving the Church? Is there any way of institutionalizing the role of prophets and philosophers in spite of what one might deem to be the essentially random and unorganizable nature of prophetic and philosophic genius, in order to realize the duality of the spiritual and temporal spheres apart from the Church? Or does Voegelinian thought preclude any spiritual-temporal duality of the traditional sort and thus urgently call for a theory of secular dualities and pluralities such as those embodied in American society and politics? To recall the revolutionary impact which the rise of the Church had on Western political theory and practice is to sense the importance of the Voegelinian impulse in this matter.

(3) Universalism. The issue of universalism can be discussed more briefly; this is mainly because it is deeply implicated in the issue of institutional plurality. The latter issue presents one central question, that is, how insitutionally to represent and symbolize the spiritual order. But the spiritual order is universal. The rise of the Christian Church not only established a sphere of life and thought marked off from, and superior in dignity to, the political sphere which in ancient thought and practice had been all-inclusive. It also gave institutional

embodiment to the idea of the human race as a single, unified entity. Although the Roman Empire did the same thing, yet if viewed from the perspective of a world-transcendent God it could not place that entity on the ultimate foundations that were accessible to the Church. Nor could any secular empire or political order. So here again we confront the questions Voegelin compelled us to ask in relation to the issue of institutional plurality. Does the Church, in view of its doctrinal failures, rest on foundations any deeper than those of the Roman Empire or of any secular empire? If not, how can the idea of human unity under a world-transcendent God be made vitally present in history?

It is a commonplace of late twentieth-century thought and discussion that the human race has been technologically unified while remaining politically diverse and scattered. Thus the question which Voegelin leaves open—that of finding institutional embodiment for the concept of human unity—the modern world finds pressing. But it also finds the question largely unanswerable; societies in a state of spiritual decay, as evident in phenomena such as crime and family disintegration, to say nothing of religious doubt and despair, are scarcely in a position even to think about the question. It must be asked, however, whether Voegelin offers a new and more promising point of entry into this discouraging situation. Voegelin worked out an original and profound conception of the relations of the human mind to ultimate being. He may in that way have provided new ways of conceiving of the unity of the human race. The question of whether indeed he did is surely one of the most significant manifestations of the Voegelinian impulse. Did he point toward a way of working on the problems of international relations and order that is more philosophically and spiritually profound than our chaotic century has so far been able to carry on?

(4) Personalism. Voegelin's "personalism," that is, his grounding of social order in the order of personal being, is undoubtedly one of the richest resources in his writings. *Israel and Revelation* contains numerous eloquent statements of the personalist concept. Voegelin writes, for example, that "the order of Israel has its origin in Moses; and the order in the soul of Moses has its origin in the leap in being" (*IR*, 402). And of Jeremiah he writes that "the prophet had to act out the fate of Israel in his own life, because the holy omphalos of history had contracted from the Chosen People into his personal existence" (466). And, in a fascinating formulation that immediately follows the preceding sentence he says of Jeremiah that "he had become the City of God above the doomed cities of the land" (466-67). Augustine may

have implied as much; but he did not embody the personalist principle in so explicit and challenging a formula.

The personalist idea seems particularly pertinent in an age of disorder and decay, such as the age of the prophets in Israel, or the era of the Peloponnesian War and its aftermath in Athens, or, of course, the twentieth century. In such times, individuals in danger of being swept away by the violence and disorder in worldly polities can, at least in some instances, inhabit their own inner polities. When outer citizenship reflective of the order of the universe becomes impossible, inner citizenship remains for those prepared to avail themselves of the possibility. And this means the redemption not only of individuals but also, in some sense, of societies in history. People who dwell in their own inner cities, even though living apart from the world or even in rebellion against the world, keep alive within the world the principles of a valid politics. In this way they have a role of some significance in human affairs. They become, so to speak, fortresses of authentic order. To take just one example from our own times, a figure like Alexander Solzhenitsyn, for most of his life isolated or exiled, might be held to have played as important a part in Russian history as did Lenin. The latter may have had a greater demonstrable impact on national circumstances; but Solzhenitsyn performed the indispensable function of preserving a sphere of true order, in his inward being, at a time when the principles of true order were being monstrously falsified by his own nation.

I suggest that exploring the politics of inward order is one of the most important tasks that Voegelin bequeathed to his followers. This might mean studying certain periods of history with particular attention to the interplay between crises of social order and the achievement and defense of true order within the souls of particular individuals. Or it might mean an effort to understand philosophically or theologically the conditions underlying such interplay. The Christian concept of Christ as the crucified Word, or Logos, is a particularly concentrated expression of the personalist idea.

Personalism offers other avenues of development, avenues not followed by Voegelin, but very much in the spirit of his thought. For example, personalism brings to our attention the indispensability of solitude, not only for individuals, who need solitude for working out their own personal destinies, but also for societies and polities. Without the solitude in which an individual's attitude toward social conditions and political problems can be decided, responsible citizenship is impossible. Yet today solitude is virtually forgotten. The fact that personal lives depend on a social context and that personal destinies can be realized only through narratives describing common destinies, has come to be so emphasized that the subject of solitude has largely disappeared from social theory. This can be seen in the prevalent condemnation of individualism, as though all real life is collective. Lost from sight is the truth that collective life is necessarily degraded unless it incorporates a sphere of individual life apart from the collectivity. Voegelin obviously cannot be charged with individualism of the kind social theorists justifiably criticize. He knew as well as anyone ever has that the history of the human race is a story of societies and civilizations. Nonetheless, his philosophy provides strong grounds for understanding that the story of societies and civilizations is enacted in some measure within the lives of individuals who, even if inspired by them, stand apart from and resist them. (D. H. Lawrence remarks somewhere that he is English "in the teeth" of England itself.)

Personalism is a sufficiently clear and important truth to deserve institutional recognition. For example, it implies the standard of privacy and points toward the necessity of private property, without which privacy can hardly be secure. At the same time, it implies the necessity of constitutional—that is, institutionally limited—government. Finally, it probably implies governmental policies of whatever kind are needed to protect personal liberties against social and economic conditions which tend to undermine them. These were relatively marginal concerns for Voegelin, but all are deeply congruent with his major insights.

Finally, it must be noted that personalism has egalitarian and democratic reverberations. I deliberately use the vague and metaphorical term "reverberations" rather than the more precise term "implications," for the latter term is too strong. It indicates that personalism is necessarily egalitarian and democratic. In truth all we can say is that by invoking the mysterious dignity of a few individuals who manifestly transcend historical chaos it impels us to ask whether there are seeds of such dignity in all individuals. It seems fair to say that Voegelin's attitudes were somewhat aristocratic. The achievements he studied were those of rare individuals. In that sense, his personalism was aristocratic rather than democratic. But there is nothing fundamental in his philosophy to bar a measure of social and political equality, and it could be argued, I believe, that some of his sympathies ran in this direction. There is one great political thinker who viewed equality and democracy with an ambivalence that is perhaps similar to Voegelin's. This is Alexis de Tocqueville. I suggest that a Tocquevillean reading of Voegelin, taking into account both the democratic and aristocratic reverberations of his personalism, would bring into view possibilities of rounding out Voegelin's thought in ways that Voegelin himself would be very likely to approve of.

## II

(5) Historicism. Voegelin's idea of the meaning of history is particularly rich with possibilities of development. An obvious set of such possibilities has to do with the differentiation of historical periods and eras. One of our major debts to Voegelin lies in his establishment of historical continuities that had heretofore been unrecognized or neglected. The best-known of these continuities is represented by his concept of Gnosticism. To seize on the flight from reality that was involved in ancient Gnosticism and to see that such a flight is inherent in modern revolutionary ideologies and was prepared for in the Middle Ages by Joachim of Flora's departure from orthodox Christian eschatology, was an insight of prime importance. In *Israel and Revelation* we see this insight expressed mainly in the discussion of the metastatic tendencies of the prophets. Another example of the constructive uses to which Voegelin was able to put his sense of continuity is seen in the way he placed writers of ancient Greece firmly within sacred history, along with the spiritual leaders of ancient Israel. With such continuities in mind, however, might it not be illuminating to look again at the discontinuities which remain even where there are strong continuities—for example, to distinguish more sharply than Voegelin did between ancient and modern Gnosticism? Or to elaborate more fully than Voegelin did on the difference between the "pull" manifested in the history of Israel and the "push" behind Greek philosophy? In other words, one of the impulses inherent in Voegelin's continuities is perhaps toward a more fruitful discussion of historical discontinuities than has hitherto been possible.

Probably the major discontinuity in Western philosophies of history is between the period before, and the period after, Christ. Some such discontinuity, it would seem, must characterize Voegelin's interpretation of history. But how is that discontinuity to be defined? Not, presumably, quite in the traditional Christian manner in view of Voegelin's dissatisfaction with standard Christian views of history. And if (as apparently is the case) Voegelin rejects such christological formulae as that which holds Christ to have been "begotten, not made," being thus different in nature from all other human beings, what are the implications for the structure of history? Is Christ still to be seen as the axis of history? If not, then how are we to envision the fundamental order of historical events? One of the most useful studies of Voegelin might be one comparing Voegelin with Augustine. Such a study would presumably center on christology and the meaning of history and might do much to clarify the basic thrust of Voegelin's thought.

Less obvious, although not less important, are the openings for development provided in Voegelin's views of historical action. There is, for example, Voegelin's emphasis on the need for realism in appraising the demands for action inherent in any particular historical situation. Voegelin detects a lack of adequate realism in Isaiah's assurance to the Israelites that their strength would be found in "quietness and trust" (*IR*, 451). It is noteworthy, however, that Isaiah's advice reflected, not only the political leanings of one prophet, but a spiritual ideal expressed at various places in the Old Testament: that of a general human posture before God, a posture of "waiting for the Lord." It may be, then, that the prophet had more in mind than Israel's proper response to a particular external threat. He may have been calling for a general attitude of trust in God—an attitude that would be highly relevant in any political situation. Hence, even though the prophet seemingly allowed his immediate political advice to fall into metastatic distortions, he may have provided a basis for developing a balanced concept of political responsibility, one taking into account the need both for waiting, in order to discern God's demands in a particular situation, and for acting accordingly. This interpretation of Isaiah's intentions is confirmed by the sequel to the passage which particularly concerned Voegelin; this passage contains the prophet's assurance that those who wait for God will in time be shown what to do (see Isa 30:21). In other words, "quietness and trust" might in some circumstances, instead of replacing action— which would exemplify the metastatic error—prepare for action.

The Voegelinian impulse is clearly toward a concept of action which takes into account the demands both of the spirit and of material circumstances. That Isaiah's call for "quietness and trust" might provide the key to such a concept did not escape Voegelin's notice, even though it was the danger of a metastatic misunderstanding of historical action that concerned him mainly. Thus in a footnote to his criticism of Isaiah he remarks that "the same passages, which reflect a dubious civic virtue, will appear in quite a different light when they are considered with regard to their spiritual implications" (*IR*, 211). And he adds that "the crude faith" in Yahweh as a military ally will then become "a compact expression of the insight that faith has its origin not in human initiative but in a divine *gratia praeveniens.*"

Granted, Voegelin is speaking of faith rather than action. Still, his words strongly suggest that Isaiah's overall attitude might be embodied in a more balanced formula governing historical action than his words explicitly offer. Voegelin himself seems to open the door for those who might work out such a formula.

Perhaps the most intriguing aspect of historical action which Voegelin brings to our attention concerns the place of suffering in action. In *Murder in the Cathedral*, T. S. Eliot says that suffering is action (and action suffering). What he may have had in mind is the principle, going back to Greek tragedy, that suffering can bring purification. In doing this, of course, it may (depending on the number and identity of those undergoing purification) bring historical change—which we usually think of as the province of action. As for Voegelin's views in *Israel and Revelation*, some of his climactic passages comprise eloquent statements concerning suffering. He writes, for example, that "prophetic existence is participation in the suffering of God" (*IR*, 488). A few pages further on he states that "the order of being has revealed its mystery of redemption as the flower of suffering" (501). And then, in one of the places where he suggests that Christ is in some sense the culmination of ancient spiritual history, he remarks that "the participation of man in divine suffering has yet to encounter the participation of God in human suffering" (501). My point is that such suffering, through its purifying powers, has historical consequences and is in that way in conformity with Eliot's dictum, a form of action. And not only that. It is an irreplaceable form of action, for action in the usual sense cannot destroy the underlying perversity of personal being which Christians call "sin." Not only does action issue from finite minds that are incapable of comprehending sin, and hence are incapable of acting effectively on it; it is itself infected with sin.

In our time there have been daring efforts to wipe out sin through action. These invariably have eventuated in the very opposite of the goal being sought: sin has assumed monstrous proportions. Voegelin's comments on suffering open up one of the most important avenues of reflection to be found in *Israel and Revelation*.

Finally, the most fascinating question which *Israel and Revelation* leaves in the mind of readers may be that of how to conceive of the meaning of history. At the outset, Voegelin assumes that the meaning of history becomes manifest primarily in a sequence of events and developments that, at least in principle, can be made the subject of a narrative account. This assumption is implicit in the famous dictum that "the order of history emerges from the history of order" (*IR*, ix).

This dictum is elucidated in the statement that "the great societies . . . have created a sequence of orders, intelligibly connected with one another as advances toward, or recessions from, an adequate symbolization of truth concerning the order of being of which the order of society is a part" (ix). This, it may be said, is one of the major premises adopted by Voegelin in setting out on his study of spiritual history. It conforms with what is obviously one of the major premises underlying Augustine's *City of God*. And it also conforms with what, by now, is common sense; if an event has any meaning, you can presumably tell a story about it. One of the most disquieting feelings arising from the chaos of the twentieth century is the suspicion that history does not make up a story but rather is merely "a tale full of sound and fury, signifying nothing."

But is the possibility of embodiment in a single narrative the sole test of whether history has meaning? Many twentieth-century novels have deliberately departed from narrative order. Are such novels merely exhibitions of disorder, or do they manifest a sense that there are other, perhaps more fundamental, kinds of order—or even kinds of meaning—than can be exhibited in narrative order? It might be arbitrary to raise such questions about *Israel and Revelation* had not Voegelin himself raised them later on in revising his original plans for *Order and History*. Although we are concerned here mainly with the first volume of this work, it would be a piece of needless artifice to speak as though none of us is aware that in the fourth volume Voegelin told of his discovery that his original plans were untenable because they "had not taken proper account of the important lines of meaning in history that did not run along lines of time" (*OH* IV, 2). Such statements as these contain a powerful impulse toward a new philosophy of history, or rather toward a fuller elaboration of the philosophy of history sketched out in the later volumes of *Order and History*.

It is worth noting that the relationship between narrative order and historical meaning can be of utmost interest to orthodox Christians, who are perhaps not quite as firmly wedded as one might assume to the principle that historical order is narrative order. Even for Augustine, after all, God—in contrast with human beings—did not understand history in the form of a narrative; this is clearly implied in the doctrine that God knows all of history at once, and that past and future both make up a single eternal present in the mind of God. Given these tenets of faith, Christians can hardly help asking whether even here on earth and in time the equation of historical meaning and narrative order is quite as inevitable as we often assume that it is.

Beyond the five questions we have been considering, there is a question which subsumes these questions and perhaps most of the others one might ask after reading *Israel and Revelation*. This question concerns Christ.

## III

We have already noted many intimations that only in Christ is the meaning of Israel's history and of the prophetic experience fully unfolded. As soon as this is noted, however, we become aware that it is not Christ as a solitary figure toward which Voegelin points. If God's word does not return unto him void, but accomplishes that which he pleases (Isa 55:11), then we are concerned not just with Christ, in Voegelin's thought, but with the consequences of Christ's appearance—with Christianity. Indeed, Christ is known to us only as interpreted by Christianity, rather than through any direct experience or merely factual account. Yet Voegelin's interpretation of Christ was not that of orthodox Christianity. This is clearly implied in the footnote I have already cited. That Voegelin's divergence from the orthodox tradition has profound repercussions is suggested in our earlier discussion of how the shape of history, determined traditionally by the before-and-after of Christ's appearance, is bound to be affected by any substantial revision in the traditional understanding of Christ. I suggest, accordingly, that the major thrust of the Voegelinian impulse is toward understanding these repercussions and rendering them explicit. This impulse might have been fulfilled by Voegelin himself in the final volumes of his great work as originally projected— *Empire and Christianity* and *The Protestant Centuries*. That he did not, however, strikes me as the most challenging opportunity he sets before his followers.

It would be difficult to indicate adequately where those responding to this opportunity might be led. Various possible directions come to mind. One of these, for example, might be to seek a fuller articulation of the priority of divine grace over human initiative. Voegelin clearly assumed that priority, yet his frequent characterization of grace as "pull" and human initiative as "push" sometimes left in the background the primal fact of God's historical sovereignty. Bringing it into the foreground could have important political implications—implications that Voegelin presumably would acknowledge and even may have been fully conscious of. Thus, in line with an earlier discussion in this paper, focusing clearly on the sovereignty of grace would lend plausibility to the notion of vicarious suffering as a form of political action. Human weakness could be seen as a medium of divine strength. In this way, the theme of the suffering servant, dealt with in Voegelin's closing pages (*IR*, 488-515), could be powerfully reinforced and extended. Also in line with an earlier discussion (in connection with Voegelin's "personalism"), emphasizing the sovereignty of grace could help in dealing with the egalitarian and democratic impulse that seems to be present in Voegelin's thought. That impulse is somewhat obscured when Voegelin studies the human "push" involved in the search for transcendence, as in his analysis of Plato. Very few human beings possess the intellectual capacities for striving effectively toward the ground of being. On the other hand, emphasis on the pull of divine grace has a certain egalitarian bias. "The wind blows where it wills" (Jn 3:8), and it may pay little heed to human intellectual powers and attainments. This is why Paul can ask, "Where is the wise man? Where is the scribe? Where is the debater of this age? Has not God made foolish the wisdom of the world?" (1 Cor 1:20) It would be going much too far to say that such questions imply political and social equality. But they do suggest the need for qualifying aristocratic principles such as those present in Plato's political philosophy. It is arguable that qualifications of this kind readily derive from the doctrine that divine grace precedes human initiative, and, moreover, that they would accord with Voegelin's primary intent.

Is it true, however, that divine grace precedes human initiative? *Israel and Revelation* seems to show that Voegelin believes that it does. The question has to be asked, however, if the orthodox conception of Christ is rejected. Should it turn out, contrary to that conception, that Christ was made, not begotten, the sovereignty of grace would be placed in question. A new doctrine of grace would be required. Such are the interconnections of theological and political concepts that even someone whose interests are decidedly political and not theological could not be indifferent to that requirement.

However diverse the avenues of thought that branch out from Voegelin's rejection of orthodox Christianity, however, one avenue is particularly broad and commanding. This is ecclesiology. One institution, the Church, has an intimate connection with every principle of order dealt with in this essay. It provides institutional representation for eschatology, in that the Church, to speak in Augustinian terms, symbolizes a city which attains full reality only with the end of history; it renders institutional pluralism a concrete reality within worldly society; it is a social order open to all nations and races, that is, universal; it is personalist in providing an enclave for individuals—such as slaves in the ancient world—who are threatened or oppressed by the secular order; and finally, as "the body of Christ," or the gathering of those destined to inhabit the City of God, it stands for the meaning of history.

At least these connections obtain within the framework of orthodox Christian thought. If the Church is not strongly affirmed, however, manifest political dangers arise. For example, without a particular institution to represent the spirit there will be a temptation to exaggerate the spiritual significance of society at large; where there is no "second sword" to defend a sphere of life apart from the state, the secure establishment of constitutionalism and personal liberties may prove to be difficult, as it was in the ancient polis, and if there is no society responsible for communicating the deepest spiritual insights to everyone willing to listen, those insights will tend to be confined to a small minority.

I am not sure that Voegelin was fully alert to these dangers. I am confident, however, that the deepest impulse of his thought would not allow him to be indifferent to them. Hence it seems to me that one of the most irresistible imperatives presented by *Israel and Revelation* is that of reflecting on the Church. To what extent is this impulse fulfilled in Voegelin's later work? If the later work does not fully meet the imperative, does it provide materials which could be of use to Voegelinians concerned with the matter? And there are more radical questions. Does Voegelin's theology, and in particular his christology, provide a basis for an ecclesiology? If not, can the dangers specified above be met in some other way than through the Church?

## IV

I have already suggested that political theorists concerned with working out fully the implications of Voegelin's thought might find in Tocqueville ideas enabling them to enlarge and extend the letter of Voegelin's writings in ways fundamentally in harmony with the spirit of those writings. It seems fitting, in concluding this essay, to mention two other writers who might perform a similar service. One of these is Cardinal Newman. A Churchman and a devoted student of the Christian tradition, Newman may at first glance look too different from Voegelin to be of help in developing his thought. Given the ecclesiological problem just discussed, however, it is the difference between the two writers that might generate light. In Voegelin there is radical stress on spiritual experience; there is great wariness, however, of what may happen when experience is translated into doctrine, tradition, and authority. In Newman, by way of contrast, there is great wariness of what may happen when spiritual experience is not effectively embodied in outward social and intellectual forms; Newman showed little concern with the threat of "externalization" which so preoccupied Voegelin. The two writers differed in like fashion in their views of spiritual progress. For Voegelin, spiritual understanding is apt to advance, it seems, primarily through returning periodically to primal spiritual experience. For Newman, on the other hand, spiritual understanding progresses through the development of the outward forms which Voegelin feared, that is, through the development of doctrine, the unfoldment of tradition, and the application of authority such as that vested in the Church. The point I am suggesting is a simple one. To work out the ecclesiological thrust of Voegelin's thought would require intensive analysis of the relations between spiritual experience on the one hand, and doctrine, tradition, and authority on the other; Newman would provide a powerful stimulus in prosecuting that task.

The other writer I shall mention, also a Christian, is of interest, not particularly in connection with ecclesiology, but in relation to the whole range of Voegelin's thought. The writer is Dostoevsky. (I am very conscious as I write this that I am not the first reader of Voegelin to have this thought, for a leading Voegelin scholar, Ellis Sandoz, has written the book, *Dostoevsky: Political Apocalypse: A Study of Dostoevsky's Grand Inquisitor* (Sandoz 1971b). Like Newman, Dostoevsky looks at first glance very different from Voegelin; but while Newman really was very different from Voegelin, Dostoevsky was not. For Dostoevsky and Voegelin alike, it was a difficult and perilous matter for mere human beings to live before a world-transcendent God, and Christ not only brought final truth into the world but also unprecedented dangers of distorted truth (like Gnosticism), and such truth, having the appearance of truth in spite of its falsity, was very appealing in a world that had some acquaintance with Christ. Hence the need for prophets in ancient Israel—a need experienced also during the past century of Western civilization and fulfilled in some measure by Dostoevsky himself. Further, both thinkers were profoundly suspicious of what a follower of Dostoevsky's (Nicolas Berdyaev) referred to as "objectification"—of ways in which truths deeply mysterious in their essence are apt to be translated by spiritually insecure men into doctrines, rules, and institutions which are supposed to preserve, but actually destroy, those truths; the Grand Inquisitor may be seen as a fictional symbol of important Voegelinian themes. Finally, both the novelist and the philosopher found the deepest truths not in theoretical systems or social forms but in concrete human experiences and thus in the dramas of personal and historical life. Both were students of human destiny.

On the other hand, Dostoevsky dramatized Christian themes which are not conspicuous in Voegelin's writings, at least not in *Israel and Revelation*, but which we have already seen to be inherent in the Voegelinian impulse. Thus Dostoevsky depicted human evil (that is, sin) with disturbing dramatic force, as when he wrote in *The Brothers Karamazov* that in every man "a demon lies hidden—the demon of rage, the demon of lustful heat at the screams of the tortured victim, the demon of lawlessness let off the chain." Again, Dostoevsky shows forth with incomparable intensity the infinite value of every individual—even of a sick and malicious old pawnbroker preying on impoverished students. And finally, Dostoevsky realized as fully as any writer who has ever lived that evil cannot be destroyed by action (the illusion that could lay at the source of the tragedies brought about by communism) but only by suffering. It is the profundity with which such truths were apprehended by Dostoevsky, and the power with which he conveyed them, that renders Dostoevsky so promising a resource for Voegelinians.

Admittedly, over a period of years the integrity of Voegelin's thought might be imperiled by efforts to unfold it beyond the letter of his writings. At times, these efforts would be bound to occur in response to an impulse which comes merely from an interpreter and not from Voegelin himself. But a great thinker is never protected by insisting that interpreters say only what the thinker has said. The full stature of a thinker protected in that fashion will never be seen or fully appreciated. Furthermore, the stimulating effect that a great thinker can have is stifled by scholars fearful of venturing beyond his explicit utterances. Thus Plato bore fruit in Western thought not just through Platonists who tried to bring out the conscious ideas of Plato himself but also by those who departed as far from his conscious ideas as did Platonists like Plotinus and Augustine. And one cannot even claim that the integrity of Plato's own doctrine (if, indeed, Plato had a doctrine) suffered as a result of such departures. Hence, if there be "sin" of a kind in misconstruing a thinker whom one is ostensibly interpreting, Voegelinians should act in the spirit of Luther's advice to "sin boldly." Or at least they should be ready to run the risks of "sinning." Voegelin, it seems to me, calls for no less.

# Voegelin's *Israel And Revelation* after Forty Years:
## A Jewish Perspective
# Aaron L. Mackler

According to Rabbinic lore, there are seventy facets to the Torah (Numbers Rabbah 13:16). Torah (or, "Teaching," signifying the Pentateuch, Hebrew Bible, and/or Jewish tradition) is understood as rich enough that no single interpretation can be exhaustive. While some readings may be better than others, multiple readings may coexist and fruitfully complement one another, as different interpretations develop varying dimensions of significance for communities of readers.

In *Israel and Revelation*, Eric Voegelin forcefully and brilliantly develops rich facets of the Hebrew Bible, reading this text as part of a universal drama of being and its symbolization, with special attention to the development of individual spirituality. Voegelin's work is consistently brilliant and thought provoking, his readings of Biblical texts creative and insightful, his comparisons with ancient Near Eastern texts illuminating. Voegelin impressively coordinates close readings of texts with philosophical reflection, molding all into the service of his project. He succeeds in producing a page-turner of philosophy, theology, and history with much to offer. Many of his insights are even more valuable now than they were forty years ago when the work appeared.

At the same time, Voegelin devotes relatively little attention to some other facets of the Hebrew Bible, facets important both to biblical authors (as far as one can make such judgments) and to ongoing dialogue with the text. One such facet that has been typically (though not universally) important for the Judaism of the last two millennia, and that I believe has broader significance as well, concerns ethics and ethical responsibility. Another involves acceptance of human diversity, and respect for the other as other. Common to both is attention to the particular, and a suspicion of great and universalizing projects that risk losing sight of particular persons and communities.

In this paper I hope to acknowledge the impressive strengths of *IR*, but also to note limitations and potential dangers. Voegelin in *IR* fails at times to sufficiently appreciate both particular religions such as Judaism, and particular persons and their ethical responsibilities for particular neighbors. After a glance at Voegelin's methodology, I will examine four biblical sections central to his study (the Covenant Code, Elijah, Deuteronomy, Jeremiah), and two additional passages relevant to his themes (Gen 1-3, Jonah). I will address his treatment of being and concern, and ethical action and the kingdom of God, as well as some of his explicit discussion of Judaism. Finally, I will consider aspects of the scholarly and cultural context of Voegelin's writing that may have influenced his approach, and will offer some reflections on the value of *IR* forty years after its appearance. I will suggest throughout that *IR* is best read not as an exhaustive extraction of value from the Hebrew Bible, but as a partial and perspectival account that develops one of the text's rich dimensions.

Like Voegelin's work, my response will attend to both issues of philosophy and biblical text. My argument will include various strands: a largely internal critique noting limitations with Voegelin's method; alternative views and substantive critique on specific points of his characterization of Israel and the Hebrew Bible; attention to his treatment of Judaism and empirical Israel; and criticism of his slighting of ethical and social concerns. The strands are intertwined and complementary. What might be seen as a comparative phenomenology of Israelite culture on selected points will help to challenge Voegelin's conclusions, or at least qualify them as one particular perspectival reading, thus suggesting limitations of his method. Conversely, the methodological critique will help to blunt the force of Voegelin's substantive claims regarding the Hebrew Bible and Israel, Judaism, and ethics.

## Method

Voegelin's ambitious project is to trace the development of order in history. Because humans are participants in the drama of being, developments in human symbolization and understandings of being themselves represent developments of being (*IR*, 1-5). Central to his approach is the use of theoretical analysis to "extract the experience of order, as well as the symbols" (259) from sources that do not themselves explicitly address such issues. Empirical research and close reading of texts have their role, but must always be in service of theoretical analysis. Phenomenal regularities provide unavoidable starting points, but to focus on these without abstracting to claims about being and human nature is not only superficial, but "reprehensible" (63).

In asking such abstract questions about sometimes uncongenial texts, Voegelin relies on some basic assumptions about human experience and being: the nature of man is constant across human societies, as is the range of human experience; what varies is the structure and clarity with which that experience is understood, which ranges from "compact" simplicity to greater articulation and "differentiation" (*IR*, 60). This basic uniformity of experience warrants the use of terms that might seem anachronistic in analyzing an ancient text, and relying on later interpretations of a biblical passage, for example, to identify elements that are central but unarticulated in the original. Voegelin most clearly addresses this methodological point in connection with his use of the word "history" in analyzing the ancient Israelite experience. "Throughout this part we have spoken of history as the Israelite form of existence . . . while ignoring the fact that the [Biblical] Hebrew language has no word that could be translated as 'history.' This is a serious matter, for apparently we have violated the first principle of hermeneutics—that the meaning of a text must be established through interpretation of the linguistic corpus. It is impermissible to 'put an interpretation on' a literary work through anachronistic use of modern vocabulary without equivalents in the text itself." Having posed the problem clearly, Voegelin argues that his use of such concepts is not only necessary for his project, but valid in light of his understanding of being and its development. The Israelite symbol of covenant has "undergone a process of articulation from which resulted, among others, the idea of history" (162-63). This link legitimates understanding the original in the light of its later developments.

Voegelin acknowledges dangers in this approach. "Extreme caution is necessary in its use, for the idea of history has absorbed experiences beyond the Israelite range, and we run the risk of projecting later, e.g. Christian, meanings into the earlier symbols" (*IR*, 163). Elsewhere, Voegelin articulates a need to "not introduce subjectivity ourselves by arbitrary, ideological surmising," and criticizes others who use categories that are "anachronistic when applied to the prophets' intention" (130, 432). In some places, he warns, the "text is so terse that under pressure it will easily render any meaning desired" (478). In order to avoid these problems, Voegelin states that "the interpretation must be kept as close as possible to the Biblical text" (163).

Voegelin articulates the potential pitfalls of his approach with impressive acuity and candor, and suggests what I take to be good counsel in avoiding them. I will argue below, though, that Voegelin is not always consistent in following his own advice. When examining a particular text, Voegelin often displays remarkable insight, peeling away layers to reveal a striking perception that resonates well with the original.[1] Yet other interpretations, I will suggest, stray excessively from the text, so that they are best understood not as exegesis but as creative (and at times programmatic) appropriation and reworking. Voegelin's work as a whole communicates a picture of the superiority of the universal over the particular, and of the abstract over the concrete. At times Voegelin distorts the text in molding it to fit this perspective: by understating the particular and concrete elements in preferred passages, to create more congenial precursors for his philosophy of being; and by overstating and attacking the concrete particularism of other passages, to better serve as foil.

A final point in this introductory discussion of method is the extent to which the Voegelin of *IR* would be amenable to my suggested reading of this work as perspectival. Voegelin acknowledges that biblical texts and symbols have inspired numerous and varied developments; in his example, covenant has given rise to the idea of history, among others. Accordingly, I think that Voegelin would probably have to agree that the aspects of significance that he brings to the foreground are not exhaustive of the text.[2] Going further, I would argue that the elements that Voegelin highlights do not necessarily represent the central concerns of the biblical authors, nor necessarily the most important points of significance for contemporary readers. To recast my claim in more Voegelinian language, these are not the central aspects of order that the text reflects. Whether Voegelin would go along with these further claims is unclear. Voegelin identifies his task as "relating an ever more comprehensive past of mankind to our own historical form of maximal clarity, which is the Christian" (*IR*, 132)—for, indeed, "each present has its own past" (130). Here an interesting parallel links Voegelin to the ancient historians he presents as having authored much of the biblical corpus. Voegelin presents these historians as utilizing earlier sources, but reworking them to reflect a "shift of interest," and achieving "the desired changes of meaning rather through selection, repression, mutilation, interpolation, and the silent influence of context" (185). Voegelin similarly draws heavily on his sources, here the Hebrew Bible, while using a similar arsenal to introduce his own "shift of interest"; here, from divine-human relationships and interpersonal ethical action, to being and states of participation. This reworking does not make Voegelin's process illegitimate, but it does serve as a cautionary point in evaluating his work.[3] To the extent that Voegelin seeks to present an interesting reading of the text, especially relevant for twentieth century Western Christians but with value for other readers as well, he largely succeeds—although even here, I argue, his position is not without its dangers. To the extent that he seeks to present the definitive reading of the text and its significance, however, he at best overstates his claim.

## THE BOOK OF THE COVENANT AND ELIJAH

Two brief and contrasting examples of Voegelin's interpretations of biblical texts are paired at the end of Chapter 10 of *IR*. First, Voegelin offers a balanced and insightful analysis of the Book of the Covenant (325-34). He presents this text in terms of a model of Elohist development of an earlier core of *debharim*, divine words, or the *mishpatim* decalogue. These are elaborated into more specific rules. Based on a close reading of the text at hand, with some references to outside sources (especially the likely contemporaneous Book of Hosea), Voegelin suggests that "the Elohist text of the Sinaitic legislation is not a code of positive law at all, but rather a complex attempt to weave the meaning of the terse *debharim* into concrete rules of a social order" (333). These elements are intertwined with "counsels of equity and charity," in an attempt to "transform the spirit [of the *debharim*] into concrete social order" (334).[4]

While drawing on outside sources and developing new reflections, Voegelin's analysis of the Book of the Covenant remains centered on the Scriptural text, following his own interpretive counsel. His ensuing discussion of the prophet Elijah, in contrast, does not turn to the biblical narratives of Elijah until page 12 of the 17-page analysis (*IR*, 334-51), after having explored views of Elijah in the prophet Malachi of four centuries later, and in the Gospel of Matthew another five centuries after that. Only then does Voegelin turn to the narratives of I Kings, describing Elijah's confrontations with Ahab and Jezebel, his contest with the prophets of Baal on Mount Carmel, his despair, and his experience of God's word at Horeb. Following this experience, Voegelin states, "the task of Elijah in the world to which he returned was the establishment of the prophetic succession" (350-51). This summary reflects but one part of the task set by God in the text. "Go back by the way you came, and on to the wilderness of Damascus. When you get there, anoint Hazael as king of Aram. Also anoint Jehu son of Nimshi as king of Israel, and anoint Elisha son of Shaphat of Abel-meholah to succeed you as prophet" (1 Kgs

19:15-16).[5] The biblical text suggests concern with the practical and political order of Israelite society, as well as with prophetic succession. Even this quick look at the biblical text suggests Voegelin's activity of "selection" and "repression" in reshaping the material to his new focus of interest.

The biblical account is brief enough that Voegelin is able to refer to almost all of its material, making his omissions doubly significant. A more extensive unit of material omitted (or "repressed") from the Scriptural account is 1 Kings 17:7-24. Elijah encounters a needy widow, and wondrously causes food to be provided for her, food that will continue until the famine is ended. He is told of a child who has died, and prays that the child be returned to life. When the son's life is restored, the mother proclaims, "Now I know that you are a man of God, and that the word of the Lord is truly in your mouth" (1 Kgs 17:24).

While the Elijah narratives are filled with stories of wonder working, the pervasive foci of the prophet's activity are clear. He acts forcefully so that wrong is punished and the social order improved to more fully accord with the divine mandate, and acts with compassion to help specific individuals in need. Elijah's experience of the divine voice at Horeb is an exceptional occurrence; the spiritual serves to renew his strength and orient his activity in the service of concrete people and a concrete society. Even the prophetic succession that Voegelin highlights is less spiritual than the English words might suggest. Elisha follows Elijah's model in proclaiming punishment for wrongdoers and helping particular individuals in need; the biblical account includes no spiritual experience similar to Elijah's at Horeb. The spiritual elements Voegelin emphasizes are present in the text and represent one of its important dimensions. As best as can be judged, however, these are not the central concerns of Elijah or the biblical author/s, nor are they the core of significance of the prophet in the Hebrew Bible.

## DEUTERONOMY AND JEREMIAH

Similar characteristics may be seen in Voegelin's discussion of Deuteronomy and Jeremiah, more extensive sections even more central to his argument. He offers a striking description of Deuteronomy as "a remarkable recovery of Yahwist order," providing for "the preservation of Yahwist order in a concrete community in pragmatic history."

Divine love permeates its order. Before God all men are equal; and the legal order of Deuteronomy stresses, therefore, brotherly aid, the protection of the weak and poor, and the administration of impartial justice with circumstantial detail . . . In their imaginative project of the rule of law (*Rechtsstaat*) the codifiers have successfully translated the divine order of love into an institutional model, counteracting thereby the apotheosis of the state, as well as the conception of a secular order of law and government in isolation against spiritual order (*IR,* 377).

For all this, Voegelin condemns Deuteronomy as a derailment from his preferred direction, that towards abstract, spiritual individualism. The acknowledged successes of Deuteronomy, in shaping the life of a concrete society and helping real people, appear worthless and even a diversion from more important matters. Part of his criticism involves Deuteronomy's presentation as the words of Moses; still, it seems that this element could be attributed to literary convention or mythic recapitulation of the type Voegelin accepts otherwise. It certainly does not account for the vehemence of Voegelin's attack: "The word of God had become the Book of the Torah, written by a Moses who had become a Pharaonic mummy"; "the existence in the present under God has been perverted into existence in the present under Torah" (IR, 365, 364).[6]

The issue of whether and how Torah mediates, strengthens, or interferes with relationship with God is a complex one in biblical and later Jewish thought (Gillman 1990, 1-61; Heschel 1955; Rosenzweig 1955, 109-118; Mackler 1980). Voegelin does not really engage, however, the claim of Deuteronomy that it, and Torah more broadly, provide appropriate forms for Israel's relationship with God and the human response to the divine. For example, Deuteronomy's call to "love the Lord your God with all your heart and with all your soul and with all your might," is followed by a call to keep the words in the listener's heart and mind (*lev*) and to teach them. Repeatedly Voegelin decries the "mortgage" of the practical and concrete on transcendent spirit, inhibiting its free unfolding (*IR,* 367, 369; this image also appears on 164, 180-81). He states that "one can imagine how horrified Jeremiah must have been when he saw conformity to the letter of the law supersede the obedience of the heart to the spirit of God" (367).

Again, Voegelin has focused on one rich dimension of the text, but has neglected others. While he is clearly horrified by the development of excessive conformity to the law, it is unclear that this is what most horrified Jeremiah. For Voegelin, the prophets sought to combat external performance and to come as close as possible to philosophical purity in cataloguing virtues and separating valuable elements of the Decalogue from invidious norms (*IR*, 429, 459). They cared about "the right order of the soul" (440) and above all the preservation of order in history (461, 471, 483). A central task was "reformulating the problem of history in such a manner that the empirical Israel of their time could disappear from the scene without destroying by its disappearance the order of history as created by revelation" (460). Voegelin does acknowledge, however, that "the prophets were concerned with the spiritual order of a concrete people," but he states that "it requires today an effort of imagination to realize that" they could have such interest in a particular, concrete group (356). Read as a perspectival interpretation, *IR* could be seen as perceptively noting that when the prophets speak of ethics, they are at the same time addressing general issues of order. Often, though, Voegelin presents the prophets as concerned primarily or even exclusively with general order, with little care for the actions of their listeners, oppression of the poor, or social harmony. Jeremiah's Temple Address, for example, does not really involve ethics, for Jeremiah was merely using language of the decalogue to "raise problems of order" (432). An interest in ethics and the treatment of concrete individuals is so peripheral to Voegelin's understanding of the prophets that at one point he explains prophetic concern with justice and peace as derivative from terminology of Jebusite hymns (278).

A sharply contrasting view is provided by Abraham Joshua Heschel, a twentieth-century Jewish theologian and biblical scholar.

> A student of philosophy who turns from the discourses of the great metaphysicians to the orations of the prophets may feel as if he were going from the realm of the sublime to an area of trivialities. Instead of dealing with the timeless issues of being and becoming, of matter and form, of definitions and demonstrations, he is thrown into orations about widows and orphans, about the corruption of judges and affairs of the market place. Instead of showing us a way through the elegant mansions of the mind, the prophets take us to the slums (Heschel 1962, 1:3).

For Heschel personally, reading the words of the prophets did not confirm, but powerfully challenged, a life focused on the intellectual and abstract. Heschel finds the prophets urging a claim that might seem surprising, that God is "interested in widows and orphans in

Jerusalem. My Lord, if He were to ask me, I would say, 'It's beneath your dignity. You, God of the Universe, should be concerned about the poor, about the disadvantaged'"? "My Lord, you, God, should worry about spirituality and not about politics and social injustice." But, for Heschel, the prophets teach that God finds humans "terribly important," and justice and peace of utmost value (Heschel 1996, 396, 400). While a full evaluation of Heschel's treatment of the prophets is beyond the scope of this chapter, the contrast on this point of the centrality of ethical and social concerns for the prophets will at least raise the questions for Voegelin's approach; minimally, to show that it does not exhaust the key concerns of the prophets; and further, to suggest that Voegelin in fact misses that which is most central in the biblical account. For Voegelin, it would seem, Heschel mistakes the prophets' central concerns. Not concrete widows and orphans, but spirituality and abstract order are the highest priority; within the Hebrew Bible, this hierarchy is found most clearly in the prophets.

To adjudicate the radically opposing views of Heschel and Voegelin, one might follow Voegelin's counsel of keeping interpretation as close as possible to the biblical text (*IR*, 163). The text of Jeremiah that Voegelin chooses for his most extensive analysis is the Temple Address of Jeremiah 7, presumably because he believes that this passage is one of the more congenial to his interpretation. Because of the intensity of the dispute and the importance of the point, I will quote at some length (Jer 7:2-11):

> Hear the word of the Lord, all you of Judah who enter these gates to worship the Lord! Thus said the Lord of Hosts, the God of Israel: Mend your ways and your actions, and I will let you dwell in this place. Don't put your trust in illusions and say, "The Temple of the Lord, the Temple of the Lord, the Temple of the Lord are these [buildings]." No, if you really mend your ways and your actions; if you execute justice between one man and another; if you do not oppress the stranger, the orphan, and the widow; if you do not shed the blood of the innocent in this place; if you do not follow other gods, to your own hurt—then only will I let you dwell in this place, in the land that I gave to your fathers for all time. See, you are relying on illusions that are of no avail. Will you steal and murder and commit adultery and swear falsely, and sacrifice to Baal, and follow other gods whom you have not experienced, and then come and stand before me in the House which bears my name and say, "We are safe"?—[Safe] to do all these abhorrent things! Do you consider this House, which bears My name, to be a den of thieves? As for Me, I have been watching—declares the Lord.

It seems clear that the prophet is most concerned with the actions of his listeners, especially those concrete actions that harm concrete human persons. For Voegelin, Jeremiah here is "in conflict with the constitution of Israel," opposing "conduct which every Israelite of importance, from the King down, considered legal and constitutional under the Sinaitic Covenant and the Decalogue" (*IR*, 434). Keeping close to the text, however, it would appear that Jeremiah is attacking those who act in ways that violate the norms of the covenant. Some of those he condemns may radically misunderstand what constitutes legal behavior. Many others, however, likely believe that God does not care about their actions, or that the Temple's sacred quality and rituals will magically protect them regardless of their acts. For Voegelin, there is "no doubt" that the prophets believed that "the normative component of the decalogic constitution was a source of evil" (410). For Jeremiah, however, the clearest evil is that people do not act in accord with these norms.

In the Temple Address, Jeremiah attends to additional aspects of the broad relationship between God and the people of Judah. He criticizes the people both for acts of idolatrous worship and for failing to listen to God. Again, the spiritual and intangible elements that Voegelin highlights are to be found in the prophetic addresses of the Hebrew Bible. But the best account for these concerns is not that they were the sole true agenda of the prophets. Rather, what might be termed the spiritual is for the prophets one of the important dimensions of the human person, and intangible qualities are an important aspect of the fabric of relationships among persons, society, and God. Voegelin perceptively attends to these facets of the Hebrew Bible, but neglects other vital aspects, while presenting his favored aspects as the objective and even exclusive truth of the prophets. The prophets' most compelling concerns were with the concrete actions of concrete persons, especially as these actions affected other concrete persons, and the justice and welfare of their concrete society.

Voegelin makes one further claim regarding Jeremiah: that the "omphalos" linking divine and human contracted to Jeremiah as a single individual. "The Chosen People had been replaced by the chosen man" (*IR*, 467). While Voegelin creatively explores developments in the understanding of the importance of the individual in the Hebrew Bible, here he overstates his claim. As a prime indicator of the replacement of the people by one man, Voegelin cites Jeremiah's action, at God's behest, of buying a field in Anathoth (466). The text, however, presents Jeremiah as less like a solitary omphalos than, to use Voegelin's description, "the self-effacing Moses who plays no more than a mediatory role in a drama which is enacted fundamentally between Yahweh and his people" (384). Jeremiah expresses his commitment to his God and his people through a concrete action, buying a piece of land, in accord with detailed legal norms. Although Jeremiah was in prison, he sought to publicize the action and its message. He gathered "all the Judeans who were sitting in the prison compound," and in their presence charged his scribe to place the documents in an earthen jar, "so that they may last a long time. For thus said the Lord of Hosts, the God of Israel: 'Houses, fields and vineyards shall again be purchased in the land'" (Jer 32:12, 15). Jeremiah finds himself amazed by this message that he conveys from God to the people. God replies, "Behold, I am the Lord, the God of all flesh. Is anything too wondrous for Me?" While Jerusalem will be captured and its inhabitants banished, those who were banished will be returned to dwell securely in the land. "For I will restore their fortunes—declares the Lord." "They shall be my people, and I will be their God" (Jer 32:27, 44, 38).[7]

## GENESIS AND JONAH

My analysis to this point has focused on the texts that Voegelin himself has used as central to his argument. I wish briefly to look at two additional sections relevant to his central themes, especially the relation of universal and particular. The intent is to show Voegelin's selectivity in the selection of biblical sources, both suggesting limitations of his methodology, and challenging or qualifying his account of biblical Israel. One is found in the creation narrative/s of Genesis 1-3. Voegelin insightfully notes the resonance of the *toldoth* (generations or story) of heaven and earth with the *toldoth* of Adam. "The authors intended the meanings of creation and procreation to merge in a co-operative process; the order of being is meant to arise from the creative initiative of God and the procreative response of the creation" (*IR*, 169-70; Gen 2:4;5:1). I would agree, and note passages suggesting additional human cooperative activities: filling and exercising dominion over the land, working it and preserving it (Gen 1:28;2:15). More generally, the chapters provide some fundamental understandings of God, humans, and the world. God is other than and prior to the world and humanity; God chose to create the world and humans, found them good, and continues an ongoing relationship of concern. Moreover, God is a personal God, who cares for individual persons.

As Voegelin notes, these chapters and others present a view of humankind as an extended family, "deriving its community bond from a common ancestor." Voegelin finds this model unsatisfactory and insufficiently universal, suggesting that "the idea of mankind as a universal church" is much to be preferred (*IR*, 165-66, 248). I would argue, however, that the model of family has some advantages over the model of church. If humankind is a church, its members would be expected to share certain faith commitments. Those with differing commitments might be viewed as somehow outside the communion. Worse, they might be perceived as heretics who are objects of revulsion and sources of danger, who must be brought into confor- mity, by coercion if necessary. The model of family suggests deep bonds of mutual responsibility that do not depend on uniformity of belief or action.

Together with the concept of God's covenant with Noah and his offspring (Gen 9), the model of the family of humankind reflects the value of and God's relationship with all humans. These concepts received further development in later Judaism. A classic rabbinic interpretation is found in a third century document, Mishnah Sanhedrin 4:5, in the context of an exhortation to witnesses in capital cases to appreciate the weight of their responsibility.

> Therefore was a single man [Adam] created, to teach you that anyone who destroys a single person from the children of man is considered by Scripture as if he destroyed an entire world, and that whoever sustains a single person from the children of man is considered by Scripture as if he sustained an entire world; and for the sake of peace among people, that no one could say to his fellow, my ancestor was greater than your ancestor . . . and to proclaim the greatness of the Holy One, blessed be He, for man stamps many coins with the same die and they are all alike one with the other, but the King of the kings of kings, the Holy One, blessed be He, stamps every man with the die of the first man and not one of them is alike to his fellow.

As Voegelin rightly notes, the tension between universal and particular has not been fully resolved, in the Hebrew Bible or in later Judaism, or, for that matter, in any Western religion. Still, the text suggests that human differences need not be obliterated or ignored to appreciate humanity. The value of each individual person, harmony among people, and respect for and even celebration of differences among humans are at least ideally all dimensions of the same teaching.

Another resource relevant to the relation of God and humans, and the universal and the particular, is found in the Book of Jonah. Voegelin quotes only from the book's first three verses, in order to illustrate that "the tragic dilemma of Israel had acquired a comic touch" (*IR*, 357). Reading further, one discovers not only comedy, but a God who cares very deeply for the people of Nineveh and for Jonah. Having given Jonah a task, God has entered into a relationship with Jonah, and will not let go. God will not let Jonah evade his responsibility and he will not let Jonah die. When Jonah finally delivers the message, the people of Nineveh fast and resolve to turn from their evil ways and injustice. "When God saw their actions, how they turned away from their evil ways," God renounced the punishment that had been threatened. Even after this, God continues his caring relationship with the prophet. Through the lesson of the gourd, God seeks to teach that he cares about the people of Nineveh because he has toiled for and nurtured them (Jon 4:10-11).

For the Book of Jonah, God cares deeply about the concrete persons of Nineveh and their concrete actions. He cares too about Jonah. God cares not only about the message, but also about the messenger; in fact, a crucial part of the message is that God cares about the messenger. The embodied persons of the story are not fungible, but in all their embodied particularity are the objects of God's concern and nurturing efforts. The Book of Jonah reflects and provides the basis for further development of a concern with all humans, or universalism, different in important ways from that emerging from Voegelin. The reader does not find God's presence abstracting from particular individuals to a generic soul, nor moving away from some persons to others, nor diffusing to an abstract humanity. Rather, God is able to care for and expend efforts on behalf of all humans in their concrete particularity.

Both of these biblical sources, and the sketch of later developments in Rabbinic Judaism, contribute to a response to Voegelin in at least two ways. Most clearly, they are relevant to his evaluation of Judaism, which will be discussed below. As well, they go to the heart of Voegelin's presentation of the Hebrew Bible precisely because of the weight he gives to later developments in understanding a passage as key to appreciating elements present but unarticulated in the original text. Such an approach, if it is to avoid being arbitrary retrojection or merely subjective appropriation that may say little about the original (neither of which would suffice for Voegelin), minimally must attend seriously to the range of later developments.[8] Thus, the significance of these sources not only has implications for evaluating Voegelin's views of Judaism, but also for his methodology, and the picture of biblical Israel that emerges.

## BEING AND CONCERN

The quick survey of texts from the Hebrew Bible, mostly those chosen by Voegelin, reveals characteristics that mark his work as a whole. *IR* often reflects a series of dichotomies, in which abstract is valorized over concrete, general over specific, universal over particular, spiritual over practical, individual over community, thought over action, soul over embodied person. Voegelin argues perceptively that one cannot completely eliminate the lesser term of each pair; the practical does have some instrumental value in supporting the spiritual, for example. Still, Voegelin typically urges us to focus on the former or greater term of each dichotomy. To pay much attention to the lesser term (e.g., the particular), or to expend effort to improve it (e.g., the community), is misguided and worse, distracting from the spirit and threatening derailment of the advance of history. Historical developments of increasing focus on the former, more spiritual terms represent advances; historical developments of increasing focus on the latter, more practical terms represent recessions.

For the Hebrew Bible, I would argue, the central task is for whole persons to synthesize all such practical and spiritual elements in service of the one God. For Voegelin, it often seems, the task is for individual souls to get as much as possible beyond the more practical elements to achieve purer attunement with higher orders of being. Voegelin often recasts vivid biblical accounts of actions and relationships to more ethereal and static descriptions of being. As seen above, prophetic outrage against the actions of concrete people harming concrete people is translated to an interest only in abstract order and spirit. Voegelin's reworking of Hosea 12:14 offers another example. "'By a prophet Yahweh brought Israel up from Egypt.' The order of Israel has its origin in Moses; and the order in the soul of Moses has its origin in the leap in being" (*IR*, 402).

Most basically, one might challenge Voegelin's fundamental assertions: that being is ultimate, that "preoccupation with the lasting and passing (i.e., the durability and transiency) of the partners in the community of being" is central to the human condition, and that molding of the transient to accord with the more durable in order to avoid extinction provides a fundamental ordering principle of humanity (*IR*, 3-4). Stasis and durability are the defining characteristics of higher orders of being. An extreme example is provided in his discussion of ancient Egypt: "In the animal species, with its unchanging constancy through the generations, man senses a higher degree of participation in being than his own; the animal species, outlasting the existence of individual man, approaches the lasting of the world and the gods" (73).

Here again, Heschel offers a sharp contrast. For Heschel, concern is more basic than being, and the personal God of the Hebrew Bible most fundamental of all. The being of organic life is characterized not primarily by unchanging constancy, but by concern for its own survival, or reflexive concern, akin to Voegelin's desire to avoid extinction. Human existence is characterized essentially not only by reflexive concern, but also by transitive concern, or concern for others. God is marked by concern that is purely transitive (Heschel 1951, 136-44; 1996, 1:264; Rothschild 1975, 24; Mackler 1991, 294).[9] Thus, higher orders of being, to the extent that one could use the phrase, are characterized not by increased durability, or even by astute promotion of one's own durability, but rather by the extent of active concern for others. Heschel thus presents a contrasting view of being, God, and humanity that emerges from consideration of the Hebrew Bible. Minimally, such a reading should be grappled with in light of Voegelin's program of understanding the original in light of later developments. Further, I would suggest that (as with their differing characterizations of prophetic interests) Heschel's account again is at least as close as Voegelin's to the biblical text, and of at least equal value for the contemporary reader.

## ETHICAL ACTION AND THE KINGDOM OF GOD

Voegelin's and Heschel's divergent understandings of the prophets and of being accord with their analyses of ethics and action. For Heschel, acting to help one's neighbor and to achieve justice in society are central both to biblical faith and to truly human existence. For Voegelin, they are peripheral, and even misguided. The call of Leviticus 19:18, "love your neighbor as yourself," does not appear once among the hundreds of scriptural citations in Voegelin's massive volume. Voegelin criticizes "perverting faith into an instrument of pragmatic action." Human attempts to improve society are inherently futile. "Christian thinkers had to stress that sacramental acceptance into the Mystical Body did not touch the social status of a man—that masters still were masters, and slaves were slaves . . . that the Gospel was no social gospel, redemption no social remedy" (*IR*, 454, 129, 183). Here again, I would argue that Voegelin fails to give sufficient weight to central elements of the Hebrew Scriptures that are his main focus of analysis and his proposed touchstone for authenticity of interpretation.[10]

Voegelin's lack of appreciation for ethical action and the concrete is reflected in his understanding of the kingdom of God. The kingdom of God is purely spiritual, involving one's abstract soul. "The Kingdom of God lives in men who live in the world, but it is not of the world" (*IR*, 114). Accordingly, the prophets sought to disengage the kingdom from the world. Voegelin criticizes "attempts to bring the obstreperous reality of the world, through metastatic imagination and action, to conformity with the demands of the Kingdom" (453). At times he seems to portray such attempts as not only hopeless, but blasphemous: "The will to transform reality into something which by essence it is not is the rebellion against the nature of things as ordained by God" (453). As well, I would argue that Voegelin moves too quickly from arguing that human actions alone are insufficient to realize perfectly God's kingdom in the world, to claiming that actions and the world are irrelevant to the kingdom (343). Bernhard Anderson had argued similarly in previous chapters. This move may be rhetorical. It also may represent a distinct theological position; for example, one similar to positions associated with Paul and Luther according to which, because humans will not obey the "Law" to perfection, all efforts to follow the law are of no value and even detrimental to salvation.[11] A distinct philosophical outlook might be involved as well. Classical categories of logic include "all," "some," and "none," but not "most" or "little"; if real world societies are marked by some justice and some love of neighbor, but will not achieve perfection of no injustice and all love, the situation will not be essentially changed, and so change is not worth worrying about. To radically decrease social exploitation might make a difference to Jeremiah, and certainly would make a difference to those humans who would be freed of oppression, but seems to make little impact on the abstract order of being. This view would explain in part Voegelin's disparagement of the program of Deuteronomy, not as unsuccessful or even worthless, but as detrimental because it distracts attention from an otherworldly kingdom to a concrete society and real people.

For Voegelin, it often seems that the practical and concrete are something that the spirit must endure. Their value is purely instrumental, in keeping the flame of spiritual order burning and advancing. The order of history is like a fanatic's view of the Olympic flame carried to Atlanta for the last games, in which a runner would have value only in keeping the torch lit and moving it on. The experience of other persons would count for nothing, and the disappearance or death of a runner after he or she had passed on the flame would be trivial. True, the Olympic torch needs people to carry it; similarly, it is a perhaps regrettable fact that the order of the spirit needs embodied persons and their institutions for its survival in the world (*IR*, 366-67). One cannot ignore necessary conditions for survival of these people while they are performing the valuable function of carrying the torch, and should do whatever needs to be done in the practical world to keep the flame advancing, but otherwise should not waste attention on the concrete. To care too much about the people carrying spiritual order through history risks the delay or derailment of the project. Accordingly, it would seem, the prophets cared little for the welfare or survival of the people of Israel, or the concrete lives of its individuals, but only about the purification and advance of the flame of order.

Voegelin's claim that the prophets offered a "rejection of the institutional order on principle," and "ontological denial of the conditions of existence in the world" (*IR*, 455) can be understood in light of his frequent philosophical abstraction and devaluation of the concrete. When the prophets complain about tall towers, perfume, and fine clothes, Voegelin sees them "rejecting the order of mundane existence altogether." "If such were the complaints of the prophets, we may say, the people could well have answered that the prophets had no respect for the beauty of God's creation, that they did not permit man to unfold his God-given faculties of mind and body, and that they could not distinguish between pride and joy of life. And the countercharges would have been justified indeed" (443-44). A better reading would be that the prophets utilized rhetorical exaggeration in responding to the practices they encountered. The prophets did not formulate a general or quasi-philosophical position that trees, fine clothes, military action, national identity, worship of God, or even sacrifice are wrong intrinsically or in general. Rather, they conveyed a specific, urgent message to their immediate listeners. In their society in their time, the accumulation of wealth, worship in the Temple, and the rest had become cancerous, becoming obstacles to justice and to the covenantal relation with God, and so had to be attacked (Heschel 1962, 1:9-14).

Voegelin is reluctant to understand the prophets as concerned with the world (or as understanding God to be so concerned) in order to change actions within it. Voegelin's preferred approach, it sometimes seems, would be live and let live; the prophets should concentrate on the abstract and spiritual, and let the generals and politicians do their work. He commends a situation in which "the order of the world regained its autonomy" (*IR*, 454). A differing perspective might argue in response that the prophets do not despise the world, and indeed because they hold the world to have importance they devote attention to the world and to concrete actions. The world does not simply have autonomy, as indeed nothing has absolute autonomy for the Hebrew Bible and later Judaism: all is under the reign of God, the earthly as well as ethereal.[12]

## JUDAISM

With this, I would like briefly to consider Voegelin's discussion of Judaism, and the related issue of the empirical people of Israel.[13] My analysis will be brief, because I believe that these discussions do not approach the depth or sensitivity that characterize Voegelin at his best. Here, his focus on forcefully developing his project overwhelms his qualities of insightful exposition. It would not be simplifying matters much to suggest that Voegelin has two basic assertions with regard to Judaism: one, that Judaism is in some ways like Christianity, and good (e.g., *IR*, 37, 121, 379); two, that Judaism is in some ways distinct from Christianity, and bad, or at best not so good (e.g., 144, 372). The Christian scandal of particularity, the Incarnation, is to be revered as a mystery "that is impenetrable. And its consequences for the substantive order of history are not fully realized as long as history lasts" (345n). The Israelite and Jewish scandal of particularity, of "Israel as the people of God through the Berith" (418) or covenant, is to be dismissed. One need not wait for the end of history, but may simply eliminate the particularity (i.e., Israel) as soon as it seems no longer useful in carrying important ideas.[14]

Perhaps most disturbing in Voegelin's discussion of Judaism is the violence to be found in his language. Israel is appropriately to be the object of revenge (*IR*, 167). When symbols of the Hebrew Bible are reworked by the New Testament, they are not simply reinterpreted, or transcended, or made irrelevant, but "extinguished" (310). Israel must undergo an Exodus from itself, not only in growing spiritually and extending concern to all humans equally, but in obliterating all traces of its particularity and leaving its own existence as definitively as it once left the foreign society of Egypt (491-92, 501, 506). Indeed, Israel must die. "It looks as if it had been the destiny of Israel, during the short five centuries of its pragmatic existence, to create an offspring of living symbols and then to die" (315, similarly 506). The harshness of these passages may reflect resentment against Judaism as the other that will not fit into one's universalizing approach, as the ancient Romans resented Jews (and Christians) who refused to participate in expected rituals of pagan worship, and who failed to appreciate the honor of having their divinity included in the pantheon.[15] It may reflect a degree of insensitivity to real people and their concrete situations. However interpreted, Voegelin's harsh and violent language a decade after the Holocaust suggests a need to examine his work carefully for dangers and deeper flaws. It is an extreme exemplification of broader patterns to which Jewish (and perhaps other minority) readers may be especially attuned, but which should be of concern to all readers committed to values of tolerance and respect for persons. Evaluating the extent to which Voegelin himself was able to grow beyond these faults of this foundational volume in his later writings, and the extent to which correcting these faults remains the responsibility of his disciples and interpreters, is beyond the scope of this paper.

## EVALUATING VOEGELIN IN HIS ENVIRONMENT

In evaluating Voegelin's method and general account of the Hebrew Bible, as well as his treatment of Israel and Judaism in particular, a sense of his cultural and intellectual context is helpful. A central area is biblical theology. Many of the shortcomings of Voegelin's treatment of the Hebrew Bible correlate with characteristics common among biblical theologians, especially those writing before the appearance of *IR*.[16] While a variety of methodological approaches marked biblical theology over the centuries, a common element was a program of getting the Hebrew Bible to cohere with both the New Testament and the author's own religious approach. As with Voegelin, passages from the Hebrew Bible were both studied in their original context and evaluated according to an external standard of what the author took to be true religious values. For example, Johann P. Gabler in his 1787 address argued the need to sort through the Bible to distinguish between timeless and universal truths that were to be valued, and elements that were temporally bound, and so could be relegated to the past or ignored.[17] As historically oriented approaches developed in the nineteenth and twentieth centuries, these presented the Hebrew Bible, or Old Testament, as developing toward the New Testament and the author's own sense of religious truth (Blenkinsopp 1980; Childs 1992, 3-29; Lemke 1992; Reventlow 1992; Levenson 1993; Brooks and Collins 1990).

An especially illustrative parallel with Voegelin is presented by the approach of Hermann Schultz. As summarized by Joseph Blenkinsopp:

> The earlier "natural" phase, with its "simple and joyous existence," is contrasted favorably with the latest period characterized by the

legalism of the scribes. In between is the high point, that of classical prophecy which culminates in the career of the Isaian servant. Beginning with the Persian period we are invited to note how life and worship becomes increasingly artificial and how the letter of the law increasingly takes the place of that inward religious assurance which was the gift of prophecy. In the closing era, beginning with the Ptolemies, "the consciousness of inward emptiness, and the feeling that the Spirit of Jehovah had departed, kept on increasing." Externalism, formalism, and legalism take over, the emergence of sects is seen as symptomatic of the decay of spiritual power and, in general, the "unhealthy" elements predominate over the "healthy." The conclusion is clearly drawn: "The two tendencies at work in Israel since the eighth century . . . are now accentuated and point clearly to their respective goals, to Christianity and to the Talmud" (Blenkinsopp 1980, 107).[18]

A similar schema marks Voegelin's work. The earliest layers of the Hebrew Bible present a natural religion. While one path of development led to static legalism, a more promising path is found in the prophets and finally Isaiah's suffering servant. Adumbrations of the New Testament occur repeatedly throughout *IR*, coming to a culmination in its last pages. The closing lines present the New Testament (Acts 8) narrative in which Philip turned to the Ethiopian eunuch and "he told him the good news about Jesus" (515).

A common program of biblical theologians, that of evaluating the Hebrew Bible by standards of the New Testament and later Christianity, often was accompanied by a devaluation both of the Hebrew Bible relative to the New Testament, and of Judaism relative to Christianity. If the timeless truth or apex of development was the New Testament and ultimately modern (Protestant, especially German Lutheran) Christianity, other views would represent at best a lower level. As Levenson (1993, 9) argues, "The thrust of Christian exegesis, thus, is to present the 'Old Testament' as somehow anticipating the New, but only anticipating it. The 'Old Testament' must be made to appear essential but inadequate." In this schema, the promising aspects of the Old Testament found fulfillment in Christianity. Judaism, in contrast, represents an evolutionary dead end. Lacking the New Testament, it is essentially incomplete. Judaism is marked by stagnation, narrow particularism, alienation from God, and petty legalism. The failure of both the Old Testament in itself and of later Judaism help to demonstrate both the need for and strength of Christianity (Levenson 1993; Blenkinsopp 1980; Rentdorff 1992; S. Heschel 1994; Klein 1978; Barr, 1968).[19]

Rolf Rendtorff traces the concept of "postexilic Israel," and its depreciation, to Wilhelm de Wette in the early nineteenth century. "By this devotion to the letter of the Mosaic law, they became estranged from Moses' spirit." Rendtorff also connects these negative stereotypes to the author's general hermeneutical program. "The main interest in the negative characterization of postexilic Judaism is to build up a dark background for the New Testament, and at the same time to save the 'better' parts of the Old Testament as a precursor of Jesus and the New Testament" (1992, 166). Some of the clearest expressions of this approach are provided by Julius Wellhausen later in that century. "After the spirit of the oldest men of God, Moses at the head of them, had been in a fashion laid to sleep in institutions, it sought and found in the prophets a new outpouring; the old fire burst out like a volcano through the strata which once, too, rose fluid from the deep, but now were fixed and dead." Characteristic of the development of Judaism is that "the Creator of heaven and earth becomes the manager of a petty scheme of salvation; the living God descends from His throne to make way for the law. The law thrusts itself in everywhere; it commands and blocks up the access to heaven; it regulates and sets limits to the understanding of the divine working on earth. As far as it can, it takes the soul out of religion and spoils morality" (Wellhausen 1957, 398, 509).

Such views remained common well into the twentieth century. Walther Eichrodt, for example, claims that in postexilic Judaism "the living fellowship between God and man, which had found expression in the ancient sacrificial concepts of gift, communion and expiation, shrivelled up into a mere correct observance of legal regulations." In rabbinic Judaism "real worship of God is bound to be stifled under the heaping-up of detailed commands, from which the spirit has fled." "The essence of the Jewish religion of the Law may therefore be seen as a regulation of the God-man relationship which exhausts itself in endless casuistry, and leaves the heart empty." Eichrodt explicitly links this depreciation of Judaism to the vindication of the New Testament and Christianity. "This movement [of development within the 'Old Testament'] does not come to rest until the manifestation of Christ, in whom the noblest powers of the OT find their fulfillment. Negative evidence in support of this statement is afforded by the torso-like appearance of Judaism in separation from Christianity" (Eichrodt 1961, 1:168; 2:348n; 2:315; 1:26; Levenson 1993, 16-21; Rendtorff 1992; Blenkinsopp 1980, 109). Similar views were very common through the time of the writing of *IR*, and for some authors have persisted since. As Blenkinsopp summarizes the characteristics of biblical theology well into the twentieth century: "Whatever the model, the possibility of a positive evaluation of Judaism and of its ongoing existence after the rise of Christianity was never seriously entertained" (1980, 103).

Such attitudes fit well with those Christian views, especially powerful through the time of the appearance of *IR*, that are supersessionist, in which Christianity represents the true Israel to the exclusion of Jews and Judaism. As argued by Jon Levenson, modern biblical theology has had additional programmatic reasons to emphasize these views. Biblical theology as it has developed attends to both the historic context of the Hebrew Bible and its sources, and the broader and later context of the Christian biblical canon and ongoing Christian religious life. As argued by Levenson, many biblical theologians portray these contexts not only as largely compatible, but as consistently in agreement, so that the meaning in the historical context is identical to the meaning in the Christian context. As one example:

> The unmistakable implication of Eichrodt's methodological program is that the historical and systematic principles only work in tandem and never at cross purposes. A historical inquiry into the "religious environment" of the Old Testament that casts doubt upon "its essential coherence" with the New must be disallowed. The consequence of this for Judaism is no less clear: the postbiblical Jewish tradition is a denial of the religious message of the Hebrew Bible not only according to the claims of Christian faith, as one would expect, but even according to the results of historical investigation.

In general, "the endurance and vigor of Judaism should always have cast doubt upon the claim of univocality, but, as we have seen, the dominant Christian theological tradition, practiced by ostensible historical critics no less than by fundamentalists, has, in the past, blindfolded itself to that vigor and clung religiously to the old defamations. The aspersions so often cast upon Judaism in the 'Old Testament' theologies and related works are thus not incidental. They are indispensable to the larger hermeneutical purpose of neutralizing historical criticism from within" (1993, 16, 29).[20] Voegelin thus followed well-established patterns in viewing Judaism negatively, not taking it seriously as a source of challenge or dialogue partner, and subordinating biblical interpretations to the needs of his larger project.

Comparisons of Voegelin with the biblical theologian Gerhard von Rad, the writer on which Voegelin most heavily relies in his discussion of the Hebrew Bible and Biblical Israel, are especially illuminating. Voegelin shares much with this author. Like von Rad, Voegelin largely follows a traditio-historical approach, with sensitivity to layers in the development of the Hebrew Bible, in which earlier sources are preserved by and at the same time reworked by later hands. Voegelin's focus on experience as understood by the ancient Israelites is similar to von Rad's attention to ancient Israel's kerygmatic or faith understandings. Both authors emphasize the diversity of voices within the biblical canon, and both articulate the importance of interpreting the Hebrew Bible sympathetically and on its own terms, without imposing foreign categories. Both portray the New Testament and Christianity as the continuation of rather than identical with the Hebrew Bible, thereby giving the Hebrew Bible some room to speak in its own voice (Rad 1962, esp. 1:3-5, 106-28).[21]

While von Rad is attentive to different framings of material in the Hebrew Bible, he is clear that the definitive framework is that provided by the New Testament and Christianity. These represent not only an important continuation of the Hebrew Bible, but the only one of significance and so the only one worth looking at. "The Old Testament is a history book. It portrays a history brought to pass by God's Word, from creation to the coming of the Son of Man" An understanding of the Hebrew Bible in terms of Israelite religion would represent an "insidious reduction." Moreover, the Christian context does not simply represent his confessional appropriation, but the definitive and objective context for its understanding. "We face the undeniable fact that so very often even the best 'historical' exegesis is achieved from a theological point of view—that is to say, in the final analysis, from the side of the Christian faith" (Rad 1963, 25, 24, 38).

Von Rad, like most of the biblical theologians preceding him, did not take Judaism seriously as a source of insight into the Hebrew Bible or as potential dialogue partner. He devotes little attention to Judaism, and what he has to say generally is negative and repeats familiar stereotypes of legalism, alienation from God, and death. The characteristic factor of the emergence of Judaism was that "the law becomes an absolute entity," and with that "the saving history necessarily ceased moving on. This Israel no longer had a history, at least a history with Yahweh." The Judaism of the century before Jesus was accordingly "late Judaism," implying the irrelevance at best of Judaism subsequently (Rad 1962, 91; 1965, 301). As Levenson evaluates von Rad: "Like Hegel, Wellhausen, and Eichrodt, he simply assumed the spiritual necrosis of Judaism after Jesus. After 'the end was reached,' why consider the Jews?" (Levenson 1993, 23; Barr 1968, 211).

Of special relevance to evaluating Voegelin is von Rad's use of typological interpretation. Like Voegelin, von Rad interprets the Hebrew Bible so as to develop meanings of which the biblical authors were not aware, but which are apparent from the vantage point of modern Western Christianity. "Typological interpretation will thus in a fundamental way leave the historical self-understanding of the Old Testament texts in question behind, and go beyond it. It sees in the Old Testament facts something in preparation, something sketching itself out, of which the Old Testament witness is not itself aware, because it lies quite beyond its purview." This approach to interpretation, unlike that found in some other biblical theologians, allows the Hebrew Bible to differ from the New Testament, at least to some extent. Still, differences that emerge are necessarily understood in a way pejorative to the Hebrew Bible. "Typological interpretation is aware of the differences between the redemptive benefits of the Old Testament and those of the New; it is aware of the way in which limitations upon salvation are removed in the new covenant; above all, it is aware of the incompleteness of the old covenant." "Typological interpretation transcends the self-understanding of the Old Testament texts" (Rad 1963, 36-37). More specifically, historical acts as experienced and understood by Old Testament writers provide "the prefiguration of the Christ-event of the New Testament." Also correlating with Voegelin is von Rad's presentation of the general characteristic of typological thinking, which is "to discern the order" that is immanent in the multiplicity of things, and thus "hints at an order that dwells deep within things, in which the smallest as well as the greatest things participate" (17).

As a number of scholars have noted, such a typological approach inhibits full appreciation either of the Hebrew Bible or of later Judaism. Typology often attends to selective aspects of the Hebrew Bible; indeed, proponents such as Eichrodt admit that "(typology) will hardly avoid the blame of being arbitrary, all the more so as it must leave aside a good deal of the Old Testament" (Eichrodt 1955, 109). If Christian typology were to be presented as one perspectival reading of the original, there could be room for other elements of significance, such as Jewish interpretations and developments. Most typically, however, the typological reading is presented as the definitive, historical, and objective reading, as it is by von Rad and similarly by Voegelin.[22]

Voegelin's approach to the Hebrew Bible is similar to von Rad's in many ways. He has a developmental understanding of the work, and is sensitive to multiple contexts, including those of early sources and of later groupings and redactions (*IR*, 121-22). The Hebrew Bible at its best points beyond itself, to the New Testament and ultimately Voegelin's own position in modern Western Christianity. Ultimately, his context is the better, and he understands the text more fully than authors or compilers themselves, since he has the advantage of later developments of differentiation that unfold elements latent in the original. Like von Rad (and earlier biblical theologians), "he simply assume[s] the spiritual necrosis of Judaism after Jesus" (Levenson 1993, 23).

A central point of Voegelin's methodology, his focus on meanings latent in original texts that only become explicit through later developments, fits well with von Rad's typological interpretation. Indeed, in a later work Voegelin explicitly endorses an approach that attends to typology, or prefiguration, and ties this to the methodology found in *IR*.

> For prefiguration, as can now be said with more precision, has its solid basis in the historical process of differentiating experiences and symbols. Christ is indeed prefigured in the Old Testament, especially in Isaiah and Deutero-Isaiah, even though in specific cases zealous interpreters have found more in it than there is to be found. This ebullience of scriptural proof, as well as the controversies in its wake, are caused by the inadequacy of a method which does not distinguish between experience and symbolization. Compact experiences will be expressed by compact symbols; and the full meaning of compact symbols cannot be understood without analysis of the motivating experiences—an analysis which obviously can be conducted only from the historically later position of experiences that have differentiated from the compact complex (HG, 87).

In this passage, Voegelin acknowledges that the later interpreter, even when he articulates aspects latent in the original, may distort and thereby fail to do justice to the original. "The symbols created in the process of differentiation, however, will specifically express only the area of reality newly differentiated. Their creators, absorbed by the importance of their new insight, will rarely shoulder the burden of creating additional symbols for the areas of reality left behind in their passionate search for the specific truth" (HG, 87).

Accordingly, Voegelin at one point criticizes Bultmann for offering only a partial appreciation of the significance of the Old Testament, one that unfairly distorts and disparages the elements of the original that Bultmann finds insignificant. "In the same manner as Comte, Bultmann assumes the reality covered by the differentiated truth of 'eschatological existence' to be coextensive with the reality covered by earlier conceptions of history. The differentiated truth becomes the 'true resolution' of a problem, the earlier conceptions correspondingly the 'untrue resolutions' of the same problem" (HG, 86). Voegelin criticizes Bultmann and Heidegger alike for offering "a subtle blending of truth presented with conviction and untruth through omission." "For the reality of Scripture is much larger than the reality admitted by [Bultmann's] existentialism" (65, 88).

In *OH* II, roughly contemporaneous with *IR*, Voegelin similarly criticizes Paul for distorting the original significance of the Old Testament, even while developing an appropriate insight.

> The Pauline method of historical interpretation is defective because it does not take into account the problems of compactness and differentiation. When St. Paul interprets the spiritual process, and especially the relation between law and sin, his insights are achieved through the experience of faith in Christ. Only in retrospect, from the position of faith achieved, will the old law become visible as the guide to the new law of the spirit; only when the experience of justification through faith has differentiated, will obedience to the law correspondingly acquire the differentiated meaning of a "justification through works" which it has in the letters of St. Paul. However, for the men who live unbroken in the Jewish tradition the problems of this nature do not exist. In the compact order of the Chosen People, the Torah is inseparable from the Berith; and the Berith is the unconditioned act of divine grace (12).

Still, while Voegelin here empathetically reads the Hebrew Bible and Judaism, his empathy has its limits. He is careful to state that "we have no quarrel with the profoundness of this insight" expressed by Paul, and Voegelin emphasizes that he "does not deny the differences in the levels of truth between Judaism and Christianity" (12).

Compared to many of the biblical theologians he read, Voegelin exerts greater effort to attend to the text of the Hebrew Bible, and to understand it through its own categories. His project does not require imposition of a precise message on the Hebrew Bible. Rather, the approach is one in which the Hebrew Bible provides a chapter in a

"chain novel," with subsequent chapters including the New Testament and leading ultimately to Voegelin's own position (Dworkin
1986, 228-38). The Hebrew Bible must be read both to point in the
direction of this development, and to provide the ingredients needed
for Voegelin's project. Still, there is considerable leeway on how this
could occur, and Voegelin is willing to exert impressive effort in
developing a reading that is as close as possible to the original text—
consistent with meeting the requirements of his project.

Accordingly, Voegelin will criticize readers he judges to be less close
to the original of the Hebrew Bible than he is, such as (in his
judgment) Bultmann. Similarly, he attacks Toynbee for failing to do
justice to the diversity of the original material. As presented by
Voegelin, Toynbee understands civilizational cycles to follow a set
pattern, derived from Greco-Roman history, without significant
variation or cumulative development. Voegelin notes Toynbee's
anticipation of a billion civilizational cycles continuing until the
destruction of the earth, each with its analogous "reproductions" of
the Roman Empire and the Catholic Church (*IR*, 53-57, 118-26). For
Voegelin, the forcing of an invariable pattern on the Hebrew Bible is
problematic partly because this may distort the original, so that "we
begin to wonder what has become of the Israel whose history is
preserved in the Old Testament" (120). Even more importantly, such
a repetitious pattern fails to play its role in Voegelin's desired broader
pattern of development.[23]

While Voegelin devotes greater attention to the details of the
Hebrew Bible, its acceptable meaning still is constrained by the
demands of his overall project. Moreover, Voegelin repeatedly insists
that his interpretation not only provides a valid and helpful reading,
but represents the objective truth (e.g., *IR*, 130). In a later work, he
argues that "prefiguration should emerge from the twilight of benevolent acceptance into the full light of a *science* of experience and
symbolization" (HG, 88, emphasis added). He accordingly is reluctant to acknowledge the plausibility of other interpretations, because
they are seen as threats to his claim that his reading is objectively and
univocally supported by the text. If his reading is scientifically
established to be true, theirs must be false. Differing developments,
such as Judaism, must be wrong. To counter these competing
readings, Voegelin argues against and disparages them, or ignores
them. As noted, in this as in other areas he follows broader patterns in
the biblical theology he knew.

Given Voegelin's project of seeking meanings latent in the original
that emerge only with later developments, it would seem important

to examine comprehensively the range of later developments (unless one were to limit one's result to a single confessional perspective, a limit Voegelin denies). This study and perspective would be important to ascertain which elements are truly latent in the original and which are added later, or whether in fact multiple possibilities may be latent in the original. With respect to Judaism, while there are large areas of overlap, Jewish developments on some points contrast both with Voegelin, and with much of Christianity. On these points, where Judaism witnesses to a different truth found in or emerging from the Hebrew Bible, Voegelin has a tendency to avoid taking Judaism seriously, either ignoring or disparaging it, in order to discredit this witness. Similar tendencies in biblical theology have been discussed above. These tendencies both shaped the view of Judaism and the Hebrew Bible Voegelin found in his sources, and provided a model for the development of his own project (Klein 1978, 2-7).

Evaluated against his background, Voegelin's shortcomings are more understandable, and his advances more striking. His failure to engage Judaism seriously continues the often unstated assumption of many of his sources. His developmental schema allows room for variation and leeway for the Hebrew Bible to say something new and important in its context, and to differ from Voegelin's ultimate position. For Voegelin, it needs to be a precursor, or play its assigned role as an earlier stage of development—roles that allow more room for the Hebrew Bible to speak in its own voice than would an approach such as Toynbee's. Still, the interpretation of the Hebrew Bible and evaluation of its significance must ultimately line up within the constraints of Voegelin's project.

A sympathetic evaluation of Voegelin on these issues might follow the lines of his responses to Paul and to Bultmann. From a later developmental standpoint, he accurately perceives elements latent in the original in ways that were not apparent to the original authors. In doing so, he sometimes neglects other elements latent in the more compact original. Voegelin attempted to provide the most comprehensive evaluation he could of the Hebrew Bible, but like any author was limited by his sources and his own interpretive standpoint.[24]

A more sharply critical evaluation might parallel Voegelin's evaluation of Heidegger (and Bultmann), as offering "the subtle blending of truth presented with conviction and untruth through omission" (HG, 65). Voegelin fails to follow his own stated requirements for interpretive caution, and frequently presents his reading as the objective, even the exclusive reading of the text. Voegelin does not merely relegate concerns such as ethics as beyond the scope of his study, but vigorously denies their importance to the Hebrew Bible. He ignores or quickly dismisses differing insights of Judaism, at times with language of mockery and violence.

However sharply or sympathetically expressed, Voegelin's short-comings with regard to the Hebrew Bible and Judaism are evident. While examination of Voegelin's context may help to explain these faults, it also shows the depth of their roots. These failings are intertwined with central elements of Voegelin's project. As such, they must be addressed by any responsible interpretation or development of his work. The potential for such developments has been helped greatly by developments in much of both biblical studies and Christian theology in the decades since the publication of *IR*.[25]

## CONCLUDING REFLECTIONS

In some ways, the value of *Israel and Revelation* is greater in 1998 than it was in 1956. One reason stems from Voegelin's own later work, which at least offers greater potential for a reading of *IR* not as definitive and exhaustive of the value of the Hebrew Bible, but as perspectival and partial, impressively developing some of its facets. As argued above, such a reading is both better warranted, and more valuable, than the more absolute claims sometimes found in *IR*. Some of the more specific elements of Voegelin's project have heightened value for today's readers as well. In a society searching confusedly for both order and spirit, Voegelin provides valuable insights into both and especially their interconnection. While I have argued that Voegelin's account of the Hebrew Bible is partial and at times unbalanced, the spiritual elements he emphasizes remain vital parts of the Hebrew Bible and its heritage. Understood as a partial and perspectival rather than absolute reading, as one powerful voice in conversation, *IR* may serve as a useful corrective, a reminder that the Bible is not only concerned with ethics, that ethics are not only about practical action, and that humans are not characterized only by their behavior and practical attributes.

As well, United States society of the 1990s is in some ways better insulated from what I take to be the most troubling flaws of *IR*, the sometimes lack of concern for particular individuals and their ethical responsibility for others, and sometimes lack of respect for the other as other. The world of 1956 was one in which racial segregation was the rule of law in many places, and patterns of discrimination against blacks, Jews, women, and others were both more common and more socially acceptable than such practices are today. Since 1956, the

United States has experienced successes of the civil rights movement, and increasing tolerance and positive dialogue among faith traditions. Discussion of ethical issues, and exploration of professional ethics, have developed as well.

Still, Voegelin's work will only achieve its potential value if readers attend to dangers of the work, some of which have become more acute with the passing of time. The "collective existence" of United States society has in many ways experienced the "dissolution into the freedom of individual souls" that Voegelin celebrates (*IR*, 359). Many Americans have learned very well to despair of changing society, and to avoid being distracted by the cries of concrete persons. For some of the most spiritually gifted, the devolution of American society may provide an impetus to pursue Voegelinian reflection. For many, though, these changes, as perhaps reinforced by *IR*, are more likely to be spiritually impoverishing and alienating. And for the poor and powerless, our society's analogues of the prophets' widows and orphans, the situation risks becoming increasingly deadly.

Perhaps most clearly, Voegelin's quest itself provides an inspiring model. For an academy marked by increasing specialization but also by awareness of the need to reach across disciplines, Voegelin presents an impressively ambitious model, uniting history and theology, philosophy and biblical scholarship, in a way that combines detailed expertise and grand vision. This example of creative close reading, asking great questions of great texts, has value in its own right. Even those disagreeing with central claims of *IR* may find their views sharpened and deepened through encounter with this work.

## NOTES

[1]To my mind, an impressive example may be found in his exegesis of God's statement to Moses, "Ehyeh-Asher-Ehyeh," drawing on sources ranging from ancient Egyptian hymns to medieval Christian metaphysics (407-14).

[2]Cf. Voegelin's discussion of human experience and philosophical insight as inescapably perspectival in EESH, 120, 126-27. In *OH* IV Voegelin characterizes his approach in *IR* as inappropriately "unilinear," to be superseded by a more nuanced exploration of a "web of meaning with a plurality of nodal points." "Still," he continues, "certain dominant lines of meaning become visible while moving through the web," including "the fundamental advance from compact to differentiated consciousness." He adds that "the analyses contained in the first three volumes [of *OH*] were still valid as far as they went" (7, 57, 2).

[3]Parallel developments in nineteenth and twentieth century biblical theology, described by Levenson (1993, 27) as "reconstructive surgery," are discussed below.

[4]Voegelin does not provide an evaluation of the success of the project. From this passage, it would appear that the combination of *debharim*, *mishpatim*, and

counsels represent an impressive attempt to transform the concrete order in light of the spirit; from later passages, it would appear that the attempt is fundamentally misguided, and only the counsels would have any value. More recently, Greenstein (1984) has written of the significance of biblical law as primarily providing a message for teaching, rather than a code for enforcement .

[5]Biblical sources generally are given in accord with Tanakh 1985, with some modifications to reflect particular points in the Hebrew original.

[6]Similarly, where Deuteronomy speaks of the closeness and relevance of the divine word to common people, Voegelin sees only a negative oversimplification of the human condition before God (373-74; Deut 30). The image of a mummy is used similarly by Schleiermacher (1996, 113-14): "Judaism is long since a dead religion, and those who at present still bear its colors are actually sitting and mourning beside the undecaying mummy and weeping over its demise and its sad legacy." Levenson (1993, 162) connects this passage to Wellhausen's depiction of Judaism as dead.

[7]The analysis is based on the material in the canonical book of Jeremiah. While analysis of the history of the text is beyond the scope of this paper, all of the material quoted is judged by Bright (1984, 235-39, 288-98) to represent core material, as opposed to later insertions that he finds elsewhere in the chapter.

[8]Cf. Levenson's criticism that in much biblical theology, the focus is limited to one particular continuation from the Bible (1993, 96), and further discussion of this issue below.

[9]See also Bernhard W. Anderson's comments on the limitations of Voegelin's philosophy of being for interpreting the Hebrew Bible in chaps. one and two of this book.

[10]Voegelin stands in sharp contrast not only to Heschel, but to Jewish thinkers of diverse inclinations. Some Jewish thinkers, especially many in the medieval period, found models focusing on the spiritual and unchanging being attractive. Even these, however, generally accepted ethical action as central. The concluding chapter of Moses Maimonides' *Guide of the Perplexed* provides one example from a philosopher sharing many of Voegelin's general concerns. Maimonides argues that knowledge of God represents the most desirable human perfection. In support, he cites a verse important also to Voegelin's analysis: "Let not the wise man glory in his wisdom; let not the strong man glory in his strength; let not the rich man glory in his riches; but only in this should one glory: that he understands and knows Me. For I the Lord act with kindness, justice, and righteousness in the world; for in these I delight" (Jer 9:22-23). Maimonides continues:

> When explaining in this verse the noblest ends, [Jeremiah] does not limit them only to the apprehension of Him, may He be exalted. For if this were his purpose, he would have said: "But let him that glorieth glory in this, that he understandeth and knoweth Me," and have stopped there . . . But he says that one should glory in the apprehension of Myself and in the knowledge of My attributes, by which he means His actions, as we have made clear . . . In this verse he makes it clear to us that those actions that ought to be known and imitated are loving-kindness, judgment, and righteousness. He adds another corroborative notion through saying, "in the earth"—this being a pivot of the Law. For matters are not as the overbold opine who think that His providence, may He be exalted, terminates at the

sphere of the moon and that the earth and that which is in it are
neglected: "The Lord hath forsaken the earth." Rather is it as has
been made clear to us by the Master of those who know: "That the
earth is the Lord's" (Maimonides 1963, 637).

Accordingly, a human who has achieved perfections of the contemplative sort
must live by ethical values of loving-kindness, righteousness, and justice, imitat-
ing God's righteous and loving activity with his own actions in the world.
Disputes over Maimonides's intention in his work, and related controversies with
regard to chapter 10 of Aristotle's *Nicomachean Ethics*, are beyond the scope of
this paper. The account presented above strikes me as the most convincing
reading of Maimonides on this point. In any event, the substance of Maimonides's
insistence on ethical concerns, and his incorporation of them into his work,
reflect their centrality in Jewish thought. While Voegelin's focus in his use of the
Jeremiah verses differs markedly from that typical in Jewish thought, his
attention to this passage as significant offers the potential to contribute to a
reconstruction of Voegelin's position that includes greater attention to ethical
concerns; see Baird's chap. in. this book.

[11]Similar is the view that Voegelin elsewhere attributes to Paul: "Not the violation
of the law so much, but the reliance on justification through its fulfillment, is the
sin that leads into death" (*OH* II, 12). Theological and interpretive evaluation of
these views is beyond the scope of this paper. Such views were not uncommon in
the early twentieth-century German-speaking environment in which Voegelin
spent the first decades of his life. See Klein 1978 and discussion below.

[12]For Martin Buber, the Jewish theologian whom Voegelin cites most extensively
and approvingly, all of human and societal life must bear God's imprint. "He who
hears the voice and sets a limit to the areas beyond which its rule shall not extend
is not merely moving away from God . . . he is standing up against him." God
"does not demand . . . for certain spheres of life, but for the whole life of man,
and for the whole life of the people" (1963, 236, 251).

[13]Voegelin's model differs not only from Jewish thinkers, but from other theologians
and approaches as well. Another theological development in interpreting the
Hebrew Bible that serves to qualify and challenge Voegelin's account is offered
by Martin Luther King, Jr. Central points of contrast between the thinkers
include the significance of ethics and societal conditions for the prophets, and the
best contemporary reading of the prophetic message (the latter of which would
shed light on concerns at least latent in the original, following Voegelin's
approach). Some of Voegelin's distinctive qualities could be illustrated by
thinking about what an exchange between him and King would look like. Based
on *IR*, Voegelin might find some value in the work of King, but would find more
to criticize. Most fundamentally, King would stand guilty of perverting faith to
an instrument of action, of trying to improve society, and of acting as if it made
a difference whether one were free or enslaved. If one were to take all of *IR's*
criticisms of Biblical Israel and the Hebrew Bible literally, King's attention to the
mundane needs of the black community would be regretted as a mortgage of
sorts, interfering with free spiritual development. It would seem that King would
have been a more impressive theologian, more in the spirit of the prophets, had
he left behind his experience as a black, not only in expressing concern for other
humans as he did, but in abstracting to general statements about the human soul.
His discourse was too tied to his concrete circumstances and specific religious

tradition, and could have been improved by being recast as a more abstract philosophical analysis.

In turn, King likely would have his criticisms of Voegelin, at least as he expresses himself in much of *IR*. One passage from King's "Letter from Birmingham City Jail" comes to mind.

> In the midst of blatant injustices inflicted upon the Negro, I have watched white churches stand on the sideline and merely mouth pious irrelevancies and sanctimonious trivialities. In the midst of a mighty struggle to rid our nation of racial and economic injustice, I have heard so many ministers say, "Those are social issues with which the gospel has no real concern," and I have watched so many churches commit themselves to a completely otherworldly religion which made a strange distinction between body and soul, the sacred and the secular . . . I have looked at [the South's] beautiful churches with their lofty spires pointing heavenward. I have beheld the impressive outlay of her religious education buildings. Over and over again I have found myself asking: "What kind of people worship here? Who is their God?" (King 1986, 299).

I believe it would not be unfair to suggest that standing on the sideline in order to preserve a focus on the spiritual would be consistent with much of *IR*, and with the understanding of God envisioned in many of its passages.

[14]In his discussion of Isaiah's suffering servant, Voegelin spurns the very possibility that Israel as a people could undertake a laborious task that "will bring ridicule, humiliation, persecution, and suffering to the men who undertake it under such unauspicious circumstances" (507). While the continuity of Israel may be a disputed theological point, the course of Jewish history would suggest minimally that Voegelin is overly hasty in his dismissal of the possibility of the Jewish people's (or empirical Israel's) willingness to undergo and survive persecution.

[15]If the analysis of this study is correct, Judaism would be especially irksome because of bearing witness to the biblical God's concern with ethical action and concrete persons. In his most sustained attack against Judaism, Voegelin criticizes Judaism's cutting itself off from developments of Hellenization, proselytism, and apocalyptic movements (144). All of these developments carry the risk of destruction of the particular other, either physically, or at least as other. While mainstream Judaism came to incorporate elements of all of these developments in moderate form, caution in their appropriation, while troubling for Voegelin, may accord with biblical and other ethical values.

[16]Negative views of Judaism and other characteristics discussed below were especially prevalent among German-language scholars, who dominated the field and were likely to have most strongly influenced Voegelin. Voegelin was born in Germany in 1901, and moved with his family to Vienna in 1910, where he attended and then taught at the University of Vienna until 1938. He thus spent most of his formative years and early professional career in the German-speaking world, before World War II. He was fired from his position and fled Austria because of his opposition to National Socialism (*AR*, ix, 1-56; see also *HGe*).

[17]"When these opinions of the holy men have been carefully collected from Holy Scripture and suitably digested, carefully referred to the universal notions, and cautiously compared among themselves, the question of their dogmatic use may

then be profitably established, and the goals of both biblical and dogmatic theology suitably assigned. Under this heading one should investigate with great diligence which opinions have to do with the unchanging testament of Christian doctrine, and therefore pertain directly to us; and which are said only to men of some particular era or testament" (Gabler 1992, 500).

[18]Citing Schultz 1892. Blenkinsopp argues (106) that for Schultz, "the task of the Old Testament theologian is to discern between 'healthy' and 'unhealthy' developments and this implies, though he does not say it explicitly, that he must evaluate each phase of the history within the Old Testament period as it progresses toward or deviates from the goal."

[19]"While there were perhaps few major Old Testament scholars of the nineteenth century who were explicitly and openly anti-Jewish . . . it is sadly necessary to acknowledge that the discipline was carried on to a considerable extent under presuppositions decidedly unfavorable to a positive theological evaluation of Judaism. This was true whether the dominant influence was the rationalism of the Enlightenment, which dictated a cultured despisal of the miracles and miscellaneous crudities of the Hebrew Scriptures, or a humanism which devalued the Semitic Old Testament in favor of the Greek New Testament (consonant with the Semitic-Aryan dichotomy of the racial theorists), or a Hegelianism which at the very best relegated Judaism to a superseded stage of evolution" (Blenkinsopp 1977, 21).

[20]See similarly Barr 1968, 214. "The brunt of my argument . . . is that the results of the historical-critical study of the Hebrew Bible have rather generally been at odds with the underlying method. The method is historical and therefore privileges the period of composition at the expense of all later recontextualizations. The results have been skewed toward one of those recontextualizations, the Christian church, as Christian categories, preferences, and priorities have been restated and even occasionally reenergized by historical-critical study" (Levenson 1993, 96).

[21]While this work was published in German the year after IR, it offers a convenient statement of the approach found in works that Voegelin cites. See also Rendtorff 1992, 171-73; Levenson 1993, 21-27. Levenson (22) observes: "Von Rad's method allowed the texts of the Hebrew Bible to speak more in their own voices than did the historicism of Wellhausen or the dogmatism of Eichrodt. His ear was more finely attuned to the plurality of notes sounded in the Hebrew Bible, and his mind was, relative to theirs, less inclined to force external schemes onto the texts themselves."

[22]Lacocque argues that typology negates the specificity of the Hebrew Bible, and with that leads to "a total dismissal of meaning from the Old Testament" (1980, 132, quoting Fohrer 1957, 7). Others argue similarly that typology as a method tends to ignore or attack differing Jewish perspectives; e.g., Blenkinsopp 1980, 113, 118 n. Typological interpretation is criticized more generally in Barr 1966, 103-48. Barr argues among other things that, contrary to the claims of thinkers such as von Rad (and Voegelin), typology does not differ sharply from allegory. Allegory has recently received a creative defense in Cahill 1996. Cahill argues for the plausibility of allegory in commentaries of earlier centuries, however, and does not come close to advocating allegory (or typology) as a contemporary hermeneutic, especially not one aimed at discovering the univocal objective truth.

²³In general, Voegelin seeks "descriptions that will determine [civilization's] form for each case of a concrete society by relating it to a supracivilizational process in which the compact experiences of order differentiate" (61). Toynbee's discussion of a billion reproductions is found in Toynbee 1935, 1:163. Later works of Voegelin suggest that later volumes of Toynbee allow for more of a process of development (*OH* II, 20-21; THST).

²⁴Compare his criticism of Bultmann (HG, 88)—"the reality of Scripture is much larger than the reality admitted by existentialism"—with Anderson's view of the limitations of Voegelin's philosophy of being for the Hebrew Bible in chap. one.

²⁵I was heartened by the serious and thoughtful attention given to an earlier version of this study by scholars passionately devoted to Voegelin, at a meeting of the Eric Voegelin Society, American Political Science Association Annual Meeting, San Francisco, CA, August 31, 1996. Developments in Christian theological understandings of Judaism are surveyed in Ochs 1997, 607-25. Still, stereotypes and disparaging views also survive, as discussed by, e.g., Klein 1978.

# THE MOVEMENT TOWARD PERSONALISM
## IN *Israel and Revelation*
## AND EMMANUEL LEVINAS' ETHICS OF
## RESPONSIBILITY:
### TOWARD A POST-HOLOCAUST SPIRITUALITY?

# Marie L. Baird

## INTRODUCTION

Eric Voegelin's understanding of personalism as the attunement to divine being such that the personal soul becomes the principle upon which society will be symbolically ordered is an important, if in his estimation not altogether attained, phenomenon in Israelite experience as recounted in *Israel and Revelation*. Certainly, the theme of personal attunement to divine being is also central to the development of Christian spirituality giving rise, with the passage of the centuries, to many "schools" of spirituality. Such schools constitute, in part, different "styles" by means of which the soul's attunement to and personal love of God is experienced and expressed in and through various forms of apophatic and/or kataphatic spiritual belief and praxis.[1] It has often been remarked in the literature of these schools that one of the most notable outcomes of the sustained praxis within which the personal love of God is expressed will be a merciful and compassionate turning toward the world, culminating in genuine acts of sustenance and care toward one's neighbor.

The relentless recurrence of genocide in this century alone has prompted many scholars in the realm of spiritual theology to examine anew the foundations undergirding the Christian spiritual tradition and praxis. My own efforts in this regard continue to be focused on the possibility of constructing a post-Holocaust Christian spirituality that is rooted in, not merely compatible with, the body's own efforts to stay alive in conditions of extremity. The work of Emmanuel Levinas has been instrumental in helping to provide a philosophical basis for the formulation of such a new Christian spirituality. Specifically, his characterization of an ethics of responsibility as "first philosophy" is a most welcome aid in the advancement of this new project.

The lives and work of Voegelin and Levinas were profoundly influenced by their personal confrontations with totalitarian political systems. To a very real extent, both men devoted their scholarly careers to an "unmasking" of such systems, albeit yielding quite divergent results. Nevertheless, their common commitment to the eradication of the conditions countenancing genocide is rooted in a shared experiential frame of reference that has yielded Voegelin's vision of order in history and Levinas' ethics of responsibility.

Given their shared experience and dedication, the resulting work of both authors is in some degree applicable to the conceptualization of a post-Holocaust spirituality. The present essay will point out, in a provisional manner, specific elements of the thought of each that might be germane to the formulation of such a spirituality. The essay's purpose is threefold. First, it will provide a survey of Voegelin's ontologically-based vision of the movement toward personalism within Israelite experience, thus chronicling the development of the "true" knowledge of, and participation in, (divine) being that is also common to many traditional conceptualizations of spirituality and spiritual theology. This discussion will also point out the secondary ethical thrust discernible in Voegelin's vision of personal attunement to divinity. Next, it will present an overview of selected aspects of Levinas' ethics of responsibility that is particularly helpful in laying the parameters for an ethically, rather than ontologically, based spiritual theology that may be more capable of confronting the realities of bureaucratized and technologized atrocity—a properly millennial concern. Finally, it will show how the challenge Levinas provides to Voegelin's ontologically-based vision of the order of history is helpful in providing further direction to the formulation of a post-Holocaust spiritual theology.

## ISRAEL'S MOVEMENT TOWARD PERSONALISM

Voegelin's all-important introduction to *Israel and Revelation*, "The Symbolization of Order," clearly states the conceptual framework within which his vision of the order of history is situated. Briefly, the transient yet very real participation of humanity in being is characterized by the human effort to symbolize, and thus render intelligible, "the relations and tensions between the distinguishable terms of the [quaternarian] field" (3). The quest for symbolized intelligibility is accomplished through human attunement to those terms of the

field which are more durable than ourselves: society, world, divinity
(4). The actual activity of symbolization entails the attempt to create
symbols which render intelligible the necessarily unknowable order
of being through analogy with that which is already known (5). Successive attempts at symbolization may themselves form the basis for
a history of symbolization which Voegelin characterizes as the movement from compact to more differentiated symbolizing systems (5).
By this means, knowledge is created and, eventually, the "true order
of being" is approached with increasingly adequate degrees of accu-
racy (8).

   In Voegelin's estimation, the movement from compact to more differentiated symbolizing systems has realized itself in a rather decisive
shift from society viewed as a microcosm to society ordered
"macroanthropically" in which the human soul's attunement to a
wholly transcendent divinity has resulted in the generation of symbols that will now order society analogically in the attuned soul's
image (*IR*, 6). The creation of macroanthropic forms of symbolization visible at the societal level thus allows for "the differentiation of
philosophy and religion out of the preceding, more compact forms
of symbolization" (6). Such differentiation also entails the discovery
that increasingly adequate symbolization of the "true order of being"
requires a decisive break with "misleading" forms of symbolization
because "true" participation in the order of being can only be rooted
in an attunement to the revelation of divine being (9-10). Such "true"
participation "becomes emphatically a partnership with God, while
the participation in mundane being recedes to second rank" (10). As
such, a "tension" is inevitably created between the two forms of attuned participation, leading to a "dualistic structure of existence"
that symbolizes itself at the societal level in the forms of "temporal
and spiritual powers" (11). For Voegelin, such a tension is readily
visible in Israel's history and, as shall become clear, plays an influential role in the movement toward personalism with the shift in leadership from the monarchy to the prophets.

   In the case of Israel, the development of macroanthropic forms of
symbolization rooted in a collective attunement to the revelation of
divine being is responsible for the creation of historical form. For
Voegelin, all societal experiences of form, historical or otherwise,
emerge from "the interpenetration of institutions and experiences of
order" (*IR*, 60). The three principles governing the degree of compactness or differentiation of such experiences of order are the constancy of human nature, the always-present fullness of the range of
human experience, and the structure of this range, which is always

located somewhere along the compactness-differentiation gradient (60). Historical regularity is a manifestation of the reality of these three governing principles (63). In Voegelin's estimation, Israel's unique contribution to the "supracivilizational, universal drama of approximation to the right order of existence through increasingly differentiated attunement with the order of being" was the largely collective attunement to divine revelation that enabled the Israelites to symbolize the Exodus (in the overall structural context of Sheol-Desert-Covenant) as the paradigm of historical form that constituted a decisive break with the cosmologically based symbolization of the cyclic nature of consubstantial order (63). Historical form came into existence as the Sheol of cosmological form was abandoned for the "Desert" of the world (113). Yet the fullness of historical form was only realized when Israel was collectively called forth in the Desert by the wholly transcendent God who, through the Covenant, established Israel as the Chosen People "moving through time, on a meaningful course, toward a divinely promised state of perfection" (126). The remainder of Israel's history will recount, in the retrospective work of historiography, the periods of obedience to and/or defection from its status as God's Chosen People as Israel moves through the societal configurations of confederacy, monarchy, empire, divided kingdom and prophetic succession, exile and return from exile with its attendant end of societal existence. Throughout Israel's experience as Chosen People, the struggle for attuned participation in divine being will confront the mundane exigencies of survival in a realm surrounded by the Sheol of cosmologically ordered civilizations. The result will be that the collective nature of attunement to divinity will begin to give way to the rising personalism of the prophets at the same time that the temporal concern with political survival will largely obstruct, or so it seems, the development of personal attunement to God for the vast majority of the collectivity. For Voegelin, the ever more complex symbolization of prophetic personalism must inevitably point beyond the ethnic and parochial boundaries of a "Chosen People" to the universalism of Christianity.

The historiographic work which recounts Israel's existence in historical form is constellated around three great symbols, all of which point to the collectivity of identity and behavior: *toroth*, the "divine instructions that furnish the measure for human conduct and its appraisal" (*IR*, 164); *toldoth*, the genealogies that "chronicle the generative descent from God" (170), thus constituting the legitimacy of the Chosen People as "the main line of mankind" (166); and the *berith* which, according to Voegelin, symbolizes "the relation between

Yahweh and Israel, as it was established at Mount Sinai" (171). These three great symbols, utilized in the historiographic work that constitutes the biblical narrative, have as their primary motivation "the foundation of the Kingdom with whose end the story ends" (176). The historiographic undertaking could commence once "the organized people had emerged of which a history could be written:" "the foundation of the Kingdom became the motivating center of Israelite historiography" (177, 178). It is essential to note that the organization of the Chosen People into a political entity, although necessary from the pragmatic viewpoint of sheer societal survival, set up the problem of two focuses which proved to be uniquely irreconcilable:

> In the situation of the "conquest," under the threat of extinction at the hands of the Philistines, the organization of the people under a monarchy was understood as the fulfillment of the task imposed by the Covenant. But as soon as the monarchy was established, and had adjusted itself to the internal and external exigencies of politics, it became obvious that the new social order did not correspond to the intentions of the Covenant at all. Hence, only with the reaction to the monarchy began the intense interest in Moses and the Instructions which ultimately caused the Kingdom to appear as a great aberration (180).

It is the inevitable clash between paradigmatic and pragmatic orders that will give rise to the prophetic succession, paving the way for the movement toward personalism that in Voegelin's estimation will achieve its fullest expression in Christianity. Before turning to the prophetic experience proper, it is necessary to focus more closely on those aspects of the history of Israelite pragmatic political order that seem to function as prefigurations of the movement toward personalism, thus laying the groundwork, however unconsciously, for the rise of the prophetic succession.

With the shift from clan society to kingship under Gideon, Voegelin notes that "when Israel found its national existence through the creation of a king as its representative, it also found, in Yahweh, the transcendental representative of the nation. Political particularism, therefore, must be recognized as a movement, in Yahwism, of the same rank as the universalist movement of the prophets" (*IR*, 215-16). For Voegelin, such political particularism will have the final word in the matter for Israel, as is evident for him in the rise of Talmudic Judaism. Yet even within the ethnic and parochial boundaries of Israelite political order, Yahweh retained the "latent quality . . . as a nonpolitical, universal God who, because of his universality, could be the spiritual force that formed great individuals" (222). And so, the possibility of the spiritual formation of character becomes a reality for the first time, leading to the conceptualization of history as "a course of actions motivated by the characters of the actors" (222).

Saul is the first "great individual" who struggles unsuccessfully, in the context of Yahwist order, with the "problem" of a life after death, a problem arising when the intimation of a wholly transcendent divine being requires the concomitant development of the personal soul as a "sensorium of transcendence" (*IR*, 235). Voegelin indeed characterizes Saul's struggle as involving "the problems of a personal soul" (235). Yet Saul's suppression of any invocation or worship of the *elohim*[2] resulted in a curious sort of suspension in which the understanding of the personal soul remained hanging; the notions of divine guidance of the soul, its graced perfection in the afterlife, the necessity of assuming personal responsibility for one's actions and their consequences, and so on, only emerged in the late sixth century as recorded in the writings of Ezekiel (236). With Saul's suppression of the *elohim*, the experience of the personal soul remained "diffuse" and therefore very compact, resulting in the preclusion of the development of the personal love of God as the soul's ordering center (240). And because the compact symbolism of Israel as the Chosen People was never decisively broken by the experience of the universal God of all humankind, the fullest flowering of the personal love of God as the soul's ordering center would have to await the development of Christianity, in Voegelin's estimation.

The passage from theopolity to theocracy was inevitably accompanied by the notion that obedience to the Covenant required that Israel have a political structure like its neighboring nations. The result, recounted by Voegelin in the chapters entitled "From Clan Society to Kingship," "The Struggle for Empire," and "The Mundane Climax," was the growing clash between the pragmatic political order under a king and the paradigmatic order of the Chosen People under Yahweh. Tellingly, however, even the compact cosmological symbols borrowed by the Davidic Empire, for example, the Egyptian "Son of God" symbol first used for Israel and then for King David, will eventually be differentiated into the symbol of the Lord's Anointed under the decisive influence of divine revelation as the source of symbolized order: "when the revelation of the transcendent God has become the experiential center of order and symbolization, the transcendental implications of the compact symbols are set free; and correspondingly the volume of meaning in the symbols shrinks until the

ritual renewal of order in time becomes a prefiguration of its ultimate restoration in eternity" (*IR*, 303). The ongoing differentiation
of this compact "Son of God" symbol will thus culminate in the
universalist vision of the Messiah. Indeed, the Israelite movement
toward personalism will, to a certain extent, be constellated around
the differentiation of this symbol, as will become apparent in a discussion of the prophetic succession.

The end of Israel's formal political organization was preceded by
the division of the Empire into the Northern and Southern Kingdoms, an occurrence that was succeeded by the prophetic revolt of
the ninth century. Voegelin notes the burst of literary activity that
accompanied these political events, motivated by "experiences in
search of expression," such experiences "point[ing] toward a communal order under Yahweh beyond the mundane existence of either
Israel or Judah" (*IR*, 312). The political crisis gave rise to such written codifications of the law as the Book of the Covenant (Exod
20:23—23:19). The political crisis also gave rise to the need to clarify
the meaning of Israel's existence under the will of God, whence the
flowering of the historiographic work and prophetic utterance. The
figure of Moses, as the original prophet and lawgiver, became the
center around which historians, prophets, and lawmakers organized
their efforts to constitute Israel as a Chosen People whose existence
would transcend the exigencies of pragmatic political order (328). In
the historiographic reconstruction of a past now become paradigmatic of the Chosen People's existence in the present, Voegelin believes that the historiographic effort "transfers the authority of Israel's
order from the Kingdom to the new carriers of the spirit" (334). The
prophetic succession is thus born, and the movement toward the
personal love of God as the ordering center of the soul may now
develop in greater earnest. The prophet will now become the messenger of the Covenant in whose voice Yahweh may be heard. The
*malakh* of the *berith* is now the one who knows the will of God and
who threatens divine judgment—the terrible Day of Yahweh—in
the face of Israel's ongoing defection (335). An eschatological thrust
now becomes apparent in the development of symbols designed to
re-establish and maintain standards of order in the wake of the division of the Empire and the prophetic revolt (343-45). All in all, the
prophet becomes a permanent installation on the horizon of Israel's
experience as the Chosen People in the present under God; he will
take upon himself the authoritative role of "Chosen Man" when it
becomes apparent that the People itself cannot retain its chosen status. The movement toward personalism will receive a decisive boost,

for example, in the experience of a Jeremiah at the same time that the "fierceness of collective existence" will be largely maintained (359).

Voegelin notes that "the history of prophetism from Amos and Hosea to Deutero-Isaiah furnishes rich evidence for the tendencies to break the parochialism of Israel through the universalism of a mankind under God and its collectivism through the personalism of a *berith* that is written in the heart" (*IR*, 369). This set of tendencies is largely obstructed by the Deuteronomic Torah, in which Israel's historical form of existence in the present under God is "frozen" into "a constitutional doctrine for the people of Judah" (370). In his characterization of the Book of Deuteronomy as textual evidence of the genesis of "religion," Voegelin makes an important, and perhaps somewhat contentious, distinction between existence in the present under God as the essence of Israelite historical form, and its transformation into "the secondary possession of a 'creed' concerning the relation between God and man" (376). On the basis of this distinction, human souls can also be divided into two groups: those who must rely on "religious" institutional support with its attendant creed and symbols, and those rare souls, the "prophets, philosophers, and saints, who can translate the order of the spirit into the practice of conduct without institutional support and pressure" (376). Somewhat ironically, perhaps, Voegelin notes that belief in a creed can be instrumental in destroying the order of the spirit that it is supposed to stabilize and in that sense standardize. At any rate, the paradigmatic figure of the prophet in Israel's experience of historical form, the prototype for the "Son of God" symbolism that will culminate in the figure of Jesus Christ, is Moses, the prophet and lawgiver extraordinaire. He is the one who becomes the focus of ninth century historiographic efforts in the wake of the prophetic revolt, because "the appeal to Moses could provide the background of legitimacy for prophetic action" (384).

The point is to set Moses up as the paradigmatic prophet available for imitation, providing the context in which he becomes the original prophet, lawgiver, and historian of the history he was responsible for making—the Deuteronomic Moses (384). Voegelin notes the singularity of Moses' position between Egypt and Israel, between cosmological and historical order: "On the obscurities surrounding the position of Moses now falls a flood rather than a ray of light, if we recognize in him the man who, in the order of revelation, prefigured, but did not figure himself, the Son of God" (398). The crucially important point to grasp, in relation to Moses' position as a possible model for the movement toward the personalism of the ninth century prophetic experience onwards, is that "the order of Israel has its origin in Moses; and the order in the soul of Moses has its origin in the leap in being, that is, *in his response to a divine revelation* [emphasis added]" (402). The impetus for the rise of historical form takes place, in other words, when Moses becomes aware of the will of God for Israel, a will which now becomes the ordering principle of his soul, enabling his action in history (407). A "new dispensation" is created when the thornbush revelation is completed by that of Mount Sinai (415). Historical form comes into existence as the newly created Israelite theopolity receives the *berith* from Mount Sinai. From now on Israel will make manifest its existence in historical form as it oscillates between obedience to and defection from this *berith*. The establishment of historical form as (collective) existence in the present under God is "an event not in literature but in the souls of men," Voegelin notes (423). The Decalogue functions as "the substance of divine order to be absorbed by those who listen to the call," establishing the parameters of obedience to the will of God and based on the insight that genuine attunement to divinity precludes action on the basis of "human self-assertion," the fundamental motive for defection (426). The establishment, through the Decalogue, of the criteria for obedience to/defection from the divine will forms the indispensable "existential" basis, for Voegelin, without which the rise of prophetic personalism would be unthinkable (439).

The prophetic succession was faced with a number of problems: to reawaken in the Israelites an awareness of their existence in the present under God as an attempt to bring them back from their adherence to other gods, and to convert the Israelites away from excessive reliance on the mere husk of ritual observance and toward "a communal life in the spirit of the Covenant" (*IR*, 429). Most serious in Voegelin's estimation, however, was the problem of deciding just what Israel's existence in historical form really meant: "Had the Kingdom of God, of necessity, to assume the form of a political Israel; and if that question should be answered in the negative, had it, of necessity, to assume the form of a politically organized people at all" (430)? The prophets experienced the inevitable conflict, alluded to throughout *Israel and Revelation*, between the exigencies of pragmatic political order and paradigmatic order as the Chosen People in the present under God. The very identity of that which constituted "Israel" was at stake in that conflict (438).

As we have already seen, the Israel established under the *berith* at Mount Sinai was the Chosen People whose status as such required its obedience to the will of God as revealed in the Decalogue. Yet such obedience could not be fulfilled by an observance of the mere letter of the law, as Voegelin notes: "the prophets judged conduct in terms of its compatibility not with a fundamental law but with the right order of the soul" (*IR*, 439). Yet given the fact that there was as yet no experience of the personal soul attuned to God and ordered in and through such attunement, the prophet's judgment of (mis)conduct could not distinguish the "existential" issues of obedience to/defection from the will of God from the "normative" hortatory form of "Thou shalt not . . ." in which they were couched (439). However that might be, Voegelin is quick to point out the "great achievement" of the prophets in a very useful passage:

> The insight that existence under God means love, humility, and righteousness of action rather than legality of conduct was the great achievement of the prophets in the history of Israelite order. Even though their effort to disengage the existential issue from the decalogic form did not lead to expressions of ultimate, theoretical clarity, the symbols used in their pronouncements leave no doubt about the intended meaning: The normative component of the decalogic constitution was a source of evil in as much as it endowed the institutions and conduct of the people, which derived through interpretation from the Decalogue, with the authority of divinely willed order, however much the actual institutions perverted the will of God. Moreover, the prophets recognized that any letter, as it externalized the spirit, was in danger of becoming a dead letter, and that consequently *the Covenant written on tablets had to give way to the Covenant written in the heart* [emphasis added] (440).

The crucially important insight that constitutes this "great achievement," namely, that the "normative" form of the Decalogic articulation which carries within it an "existential" and perhaps prototypically "spiritual" articulation of the right order of the soul under God, seems to have become the primary motivation for the prophets' eventual separation from a so-called Chosen People who wanted to continue being "a people like the others" in the Sheol of cosmological order (*IR*, 442). The danger inherent in this separation was that the prophets' justified rejection of the Israelites' cosmological tendencies seems to have been made in the assumption that "clarify[ing] the meaning of the Sinaitic revelation" would require a rejection of the mundane order altogether (444). On a more positive note, however, Voegelin quotes Jeremiah 9:24 to demonstrate that the prophets indeed had succeeded in identifying the "desired traits of the soul" such as mercy (*hesed*), justice (*mishpat*), and righteousness (*zedakah*), which could be acquired if we "understand and know" God. And so, "knowledge" (*da'ath*) of God becomes a "comprehensive, formative virtue of the soul" that is awakened, assuming the prior rejection of the externalizing practices of cosmological and Yahwist order: "[The prophets] disengaged the existential issue from the theopolitical merger of divine and human order; they recognized the formation of the soul through knowledge (Hosea) and fear (Isaiah) of God; and they developed a language to articulate their discoveries" (445,446). Their efforts, however, did not lead to institutional expression (446-47). Indeed, for Isaiah the rejection of the mundane order alluded to above transformed "the leap in being" into "a leap out of existence" with his metastatic vision (452). For all the prophets, however, the rejection of the mundane order was motivated by factors such as their insight into true existential order in the present under God, moral sensitivity, defense of Yahwism, and nostalgia for the past (455). And so their mission, if one might call it that, was the clarification and "reordering of human existence through the knowledge (*da'ath*) of God" (456). This was accomplished through the identification of virtues discussed above, leading to the differentiation of the original Covenant (*berith*) symbolism into the new symbol of a covenant written on the heart (459). The new criterion was thus established according to which the conduct of the people could be judged, and the prophets acquired the insight that the Covenant was broken: "For the first time men experienced the clash between divinely willed and humanly realized order of history in its stark brutality, and the souls of the prophets were the battlefield in this war of the spirit" (461).

The prophetic movement toward personalism becomes more readily evident at this point, as it becomes clear that personal responsibility in the sense of a "change of heart" is necessary for the realization of the future that has been prophesied. Voegelin characterizes the issue at stake as "the dialectics of divine foreknown and humanly realized order" requiring an "ontologically real struggle for order conducted in every man's existence" (*IR*, 462). As is evident in the experience of the prophets, "divine foreknown order" may only be realized in the souls of certain individuals who suffer under the weight of the disorder of the community to which they belong (465). In a fascinating discussion of the oracles of Jeremiah (Jer 1:5,6-8,10), Voegelin concludes that "the prophet had to act out the fate of Israel in his own life, because the holy omphalos of history had contracted from the Chosen People into his personal existence . . . The Chosen People had been replaced by the chosen man," whence the problem of the

future identity of "Israel" (466-67, 472). Voegelin identifies this issue as "the Messianic problem" (472).

Voegelin discusses the Messianic problem in terms of the "phases"
in which the prophets themselves were preoccupied with it: the "institutional" phase, the "metastatic" phase, and the "existential" phase
with Jeremiah as its chief representative. The last phase is the object
of our particular concern. Jeremiah's achievement, as already noted,
was to take upon himself the identity of "Israel," arrogating royal
symbolism to himself in the oracles and "enact[ing] the fate of the
people while carrying the burden of the Anointed" (*IR*, 484.) Voegelin
identifies the "greatness" of his achievement in a crucially important
passage:

> What is new in his extant work are the pieces of spiritual autobi-
> ography, in which the problems of prophetic existence, the concen-
> tration of order in the man who speaks the word of God, become
> articulate. The great motive that had animated the prophetic
> criticism of conduct and commendation of the virtues had at last
> been traced to its source in the concern with the order of personal
> existence under God. In Jeremiah the human personality had
> broken the compactness of collective existence and recognized
> itself as the authoritative source of order in society (485).

The "greatness" of Jeremiah's achievement also entails the insight that
"prophetic existence is participation in the suffering of God" (488).
Part of the human experience of this suffering will entail "the Exodus
of Israel from itself" as Jeremiah, in the tradition instituted by Isaiah,
realizes that the "concrete Israel" can no longer function as the holy
omphalos upon which historical form will be established (491). The
stage is now set for the prophetic symbol of the "suffering servant"
found in Deutero-Isaiah, as the "Exodus" mentioned above has already taken place in the soul of the author of Isaiah 40-55 (491-95).

Voegelin notes that the Deutero-Isaianic "salvation" is "a revelation
of God as the Redeemer" (*IR*, 499). With the revelation of the message
of God's salvation, the prior prophetic concern with the (mis)conduct
of the people disappears, and with it the Sinaitic Covenant, to be
replaced with the acceptance of God as Redeemer (500). And only
now does the "true" order of being emerge in all its clarity: the
"mystery of redemption is the flower of suffering" (501). God is also
now revealed as the "God of all mankind" and Israel must now take
its proper place in history as "the people to whom the revelation has
come first to be communicated to the nations" (506). The task of the
suffering servant, the "unknown genius," will be to spread the news of

God's redemption to the world, and thus to become "the light of salvation to mankind" (515).

At this point it is necessary to point out the perhaps somewhat overlooked, yet discernible, ethical thrust of Voegelin's "existential" account of the prophetic movement toward personalism. The human soul's ever more personalized attunement to the wholly transcendent divinity seems to lead, in Voegelin's account, to an increasingly differentiated set of symbols that not only constitute a "knowledge," but become expressed in a particular kind of presence and action that bear a merciful, just, and righteous character. We have seen that the movement toward personalism requires the prior establishment of historical form, in which Israel oscillates collectively between obedience to/defection from the will of God using the Decalogic Constitution as the criterion for judgment. Defection from the will of God occurs when the terms of the *berith* are broken on the basis of human self-assertion: "right order will somehow grow in a community when the attunement to the hidden divine being is not disturbed by human self-assertion" (*IR*, 427). Far from constituting a "moral catechism" for Voegelin, we have seen that the Decalogue functions as the existential basis for the creation of the Chosen People, and hence as the existential basis within which the prophetic movement toward personalism will occur (415). Once this basis is in place the rare soul, the prophet, may make the "leap in being" out of the collectivity of existence into a more personalized attunement to the unknowable divinity, whence the differentiation of symbols that are now capable of describing those personal virtues of the soul that, taken together, constitute knowledge (*da'ath*) of God. Yet as already mentioned, if we examine these symbols we will see that the "knowledge" of God expressed by a Jeremiah, for example, consists of knowledge of a Yahweh who *exercises* those formative virtues of the soul such as mercy (*hesed*), justice (*mishpat*), and righteousness (*zedakah*) (445). Surely it is possible to assert that knowledge of God as an agent of mercy, justice, and righteousness must have included, for the prophets, the call to similar agency on the part of Israel (445). Indeed, although these virtues as recounted in Jeremiah 9: 24 are attributed to Yahweh, Voegelin notes that humans will make manifest their knowledge (*da'ath*) of God when they *exercise* the same virtues—virtues that presuppose some prototypical experience of personal responsibility in relation to God and others. That sense of personal responsibility is going to develop further with the collapse of the Chosen People into the "Chosen Man," as Jeremiah "act[s] out the fate of Israel in his own life," culminating in the Deutero-Isaianic "suffering servant" symbol-

ism with the revelation of the universally redemptive nature of God
(466). Without lapsing into the anachronistic kind of reading that
Voegelin so correctly warns us against, I do believe it to be possible to
ascribe the development of ethical awareness and action—in the form
of personal responsibility rooted in the personal love of God that plays
itself out in acts of mercy, justice, and righteousness—to the prophetic
movement toward personalism. In this regard, I agree with Bernhard
Anderson's characterization of Israel's experience, in chapter one, as
an ethical one. In light of this possibility, and in another essay, it
would be interesting to speculate on whether or not Voegelin's
"existential" account of the prophetic movement toward personalism
constitutes a "perpetual mortgage" on the primacy of its ethical
character (164).

Finally, as will become evident, the "existential" context within
which Voegelin situates his account of the prophetic movement toward personalism makes his account precisely the sort of "totalizing"
system which Emmanuel Levinas' ethics as "first philosophy" will
oppose as being antithetical to the very possibility of ethical practice.
Nevertheless, Voegelin's account provides a fruitful space of encounter with Levinas' ethics because of its discernible ethical thrust.

## EMMANUEL LEVINAS' ETHICS OF RESPONSIBILITY AS "FIRST PHILOSOPHY"

The nakedness of someone forsaken shows in the cracks in the mask
of the personage, or in his wrinkled skin; his being "without
resources" has to be heard like cries not voiced or thematized,
already addressed to God. There the resonance of silence—*Geläut
der Stille*—certainly sounds. We here have come upon an imbro-
glio that has to be taken seriously: a relationship to . . . that is not
represented, without intentionality, not repressed; it is the latent
birth of religion in the other, prior to emotions or voices, prior to
*"religious experience" which speaks of revelation in terms of the
disclosure of being,* when it is a question of an unwonted access, in
the heart of my responsibility, to an unwonted disturbance of
being. Even if one says right away, "It was nothing." "It was
nothing"—it was not being, but otherwise than being [emphasis
added] (Levinas 1989, 181).

This passage goes directly to the heart of the fundamental philosophical differences between Voegelin's vision and Levinas' stance:
Levinas opposes a Voegelinian-type, ontologically based vision of "'religious experience' which speaks of revelation in terms of the disclo-

sure of being" with the ethical relation of responsibility to the other. Such a relation is not an ethical stance that I take in the existential context that is already mine, but instead constitutes the "first philosophy," replacing ontology, as that which is "otherwise than being" because it is *better* than being (Levinas 1985, 8-9).[3]

The replacement of ontology with ethics occurs, for Levinas, in a critique of the "correlation" between knowledge and being as "the very site of intelligibility, the occurrence of meaning" (Levinas 1989, 75-87). This correlation seems to imply a sort of conquest of knowledge over being, as that which is unknown is ever challenged and its frontiers are pushed back in the relentless quest for truth: "the known is understood and so *appropriated* by knowledge, and as it were *freed* of its otherness. In the realm of truth, being, as the *other* of thought becomes the characteristic property of thought as knowledge" [emphasis his] (76). Levinas will thus characterize the pursuit of knowledge as an "act of grasping" that captures "the otherness of the known" and incorporates it into the known in the conquering act of absorption (76). "Knowledge would be the suppression of the other by the grasp, by the hold, or by the vision that grasps before the grasp" (Levinas 1969, 302). More specifically, Levinas identifies the Husserlian notion of intentionality, which for Levinas is a superlative example of the grasping quality of knowledge acquisition, as "a hold on being which equals a constitution of that being" (Levinas 1989, 79).

Far from constituting an achievement that *participates* in the "true" order of being (with greater or lesser degrees of adequacy, as it is for Voegelin), knowledge becomes an "immanence" for Levinas that perpetuates "the *isolation* of being"[emphasis added]: "There is in knowledge, in the final account, an impossibility of escaping the self; hence sociality cannot have the same structure as knowledge . . . The most audacious and remote knowledge does not put us in communion with the truly other; it does not take the place of sociality; it is still and always a solitude" (Levinas 1985, 57, 60). This assertion certainly articulates one of Levinas' most serious challenges to Voegelin's vision of the symbolizations of order and their societal expression. The model of knowledge-as-immanence that for Levinas results in the *isolated* being of the "knowledgeable" subject has encouraged the generation of "totalizing" models of order that constitute Hegelian-type visions of synthesis: "The notion of a subjectivity which coincided with the identity of the Same, and the rationality which went with it entailed the gathering together of the world's diversity within the unity of a single order that left nothing out; an order produced or reproduced by the sovereign act of Synthesis" (Levinas 1989, 208). The only escape from the solitude of knowledge is in the ethical relation: "Onto-logy—that is, the intelligibility of being— only becomes possible when ethics, the origin of all meaning, is taken as the starting point" (231). The only escape from the synthetic vision of order is also in the ethical relation: "The Other is not a particular case, a species of otherness, but the original exception to order. It is not because the Other is novelty that it 'gives room' for a relation of transcendence. It is because the responsibility for the Other is transcendence that there can be something new under the sun" (245). In Levinas' estimation, it is in the ethical relation that humans "dis-inter-est" themselves, thus "loosen[ing] the ties of that unconditional attachment to being" and hence becoming available for relatedness to divinity in and through the ethical relation (233).

At this point it may be legitimate to ask why one would want to replace ontology with ethics in the first place or, in a more properly Levinasian formulation of the question, why it is that ethics is *better* than ontology. One of Levinas' responses, partially implicit in his critique of the correlation between knowledge and being, is that "one cannot think God and being together," or, more specifically, "the relation to the Infinite is not a knowledge but a Desire" (Levinas 1985, 77, 92). Because that which is Infinite is incapable of being captured in the totalizing vision of western philosophy and theology, Levinas embraces an implicitly apophatic stance that seeks to free Infinity from the totalizing constraints within which western ontology has held it:

> transcendence precisely refuses totality, does not lend itself to a view that would encompass it from the outside. Every "comprehension" of transcendence leaves the transcendent outside, and is enacted before its face. If the notions of totality and being are notions that cover one another, the notion of the transcendent places us beyond categories of being. We thus encounter, in our own way, the Platonic idea of the Good beyond Being (Levinas 1969, 293).

Another reason why the breach of totality is desirable for Levinas is to be found in his critique of the absorption of the other into the same that is characteristic of knowledge as a grasping, a sort of ownership. I believe he sees a very real form of violence in such activity which he considers to be constitutive of the ego—the context in which the other becomes absorbed, objectified and thus available, ultimately, to be murdered: "In thought understood as vision, knowledge, and intentionality, intelligibility thus signifies the reduction of the other [*Autre*] to the Same, synchrony as *being* in its egological gathering" (Levinas 1987, 99). Along similar lines and perhaps in light of his own life experience, Levinas vehemently considers any totalizing system of thought, philosophical or otherwise, that would permit the inviolability of the human face to be compromised as impossible for him, as the end result of systems that correlate knowledge and being. As he tirelessly insists, the human face is "that whose meaning consists in saying: 'thou shalt not kill'" (Levinas 1985, 87). The ethical subject is held hostage by the human face and takes up responsibility for the life of the other—before being for itself (Levinas 1989, 108). The subject is "a *sub-jectum*; it is under the weight of the universe, responsible for everything" (105). In making this assertion, Levinas is able to identify the ethical subject in terms that are strongly reminiscent of Jeremiah's "heart of flesh" symbolism as well as the Deutero-Isaianic suffering servant symbol: "[Responsibility] does not allow me to constitute myself into an *I think*, substantial like a stone, or, like a heart of stone, existing in and for oneself. It ends up in substitution for another, in the condition—or the unconditionality—of being a hostage . . . Already the stony core of my substance is dislodged" . . . "The subjectivity of a subject is responsibility of being-in-question in the form of the total exposure to offense in the cheek offered to the smiter" (180, 101). We will return later to Levinas' usage of the prophets in the characterization of the ethical relation.

The ethical relation is structured asymmetrically as responsibility, "without noematic correlation of any thematizable presence" (Levinas 1987, 108). It is "irreducible" to knowledge—Levinas will insist that to know the good is already not to have done it—and decisively decenters the ego's "natural" hegemony over its own being (108). The asymmetrical quality of the ethical relationship resides in the radicality of the responsibility which the ethical subject exerts in relation to the other: "I am responsible for the Other without waiting for reciprocity, were I to die for it. Reciprocity is *his* affair" (Levinas 1985, 98). Responsibility must thus be freed from its moorings in the realm of "logical deliberation summoned by reasoned decision" and must be reconfigured as the response, anterior to the knowledge of being, to the simultaneous transcendence and vulnerability of the face of the other (Levinas 1987, 111):

> The face in its nakedness as a face presents to me the destitution of
> the poor one and the stranger . . . The poor one, the stranger,
> presents himself as an equal. His equality within this essential

poverty consists in referring to the *third party*, thus present at the encounter, whom in the midst of his destitution the Other already serves. He comes to *join* me. But he joins me to himself for service; he commands me as a Master. This command can concern me only inasmuch as I am master myself; consequently this command commands me to command. The *thou* is posited in front of a *we*. To be *we* is not to "jostle" one another or get together around a common task. The presence of the face, the infinity of the other, is a destituteness, a presence of the third party (that is, of the whole of humanity which looks at us), and a command that commands commanding (Levinas 1969, 213).

The appeal for justice which the human face bears in its destitution and vulnerability arises out of its transcendence, whence Levinas' formulation of the face as "a command that commands commanding." The human face, in other words, in both its radical equality and its radical vulnerability, appeals to me from an ethical position of height, of transcendence, as the one for whom I am to be directly responsible, and commands me from the depth of its destitution to take charge, to say "Here I am," and to interpose myself between the face and its would-be murderer as the one who is responsible: "The Other who dominates me in his transcendence is thus the stranger, the widow, and the orphan, to whom I am obligated" (215). The ethical encounter is also the event of a theophany: "in this strange mission that orders the approach to the other, God is drawn out of objectivity, presence and being. He is neither an object nor an interlocutor. His absolute remoteness, his transcendence, turns into my responsibility—non-erotic par excellence—for the other (Levinas 1989, 179). The apophatic quality of the divine-human encounter, in and through the ethical relation, is nevertheless "kataphatized" (at the risk of introducing a neologism) in concrete acts of responsible care. For Levinas asks, "Is divinity possible without relation to a human Other?" (247).

The temporal structure of the ethical relation-as-responsibility is perhaps one of the most striking elements of Levinas' thought. In his estimation, responsibility covers an "immemorial past" in the sense that there has never been a time for which I have not been ethically responsible: ". . . I am thrown back toward what has never been my fault or my deed, toward what has never been in my power or in my freedom, toward what has never been my presence, and has never come into memory . . . The dia-chrony of a past that does not gather into re-presentation is at the bottom of the concreteness of the time that is the time of my responsibility for the Other" (Levinas 1987,

111, 112). This temporal structure also points to the extreme *passivity* of the ethical subject in relation to the other; I am the one who is accused by this "immemorial past" and held hostage by this other to whom I am responsible to the point of death and even beyond death (Levinas 1985, 100; 1987, 115). As such, the future must be understood *not* in terms of the coming to fruition of my own anticipations, but rather in terms of this "imperative" of my responsibility for the other that constitutes a "rupture of the natural order of being" calling forth "the very coming of God to the idea" that, in its turn, is constitutive of revelation: "The futuration of the future is not a 'proof of God's existence,' but 'the fall of God into meaning'" (Levinas 1987, 115). God "comes to the idea" in and through the face of the other (Levinas 1969, 78-79). And so, the "immemorial" quality of the past and the "imperative" quality of the future break through "the natural order of being" and thus "the representable time of immanence and its historical present" in the ethical relation, opening up the possibility for God to "fall into meaning" in revelation (Levinas 1987, 118).

Levinas' characterization of revelation as "the fall of God into meaning" articulates a decisive break with a Voegelinian-type notion of revelation as the disclosure of being. The reader will recall that ethics, for Levinas, supplies the realm of meaning which then enables onto-logy, the intelligibility of being, to emerge (Levinas 1989, 231). Levinas indeed dismisses "'religious experience' which speaks of revelation in terms of the disclosure of being" as remaining "assimilated to philosophical disclosure" and thus dependent upon its conceptualization of God as "being, presence and immanence" (181, 173). But because divinity cannot be contained within totalizing systems of thought, and therefore within categories of being, "the fall of God into meaning" requires a thought that does not find its origins in "the very presence of the thought that thinks it" (174). Instead, the extreme passivity of the ethical subject, faced with the transcendent and destitute face of the other-as-theophany, enables "the putting into us of an unincludable idea [that] overturns that presence to self which consciousness is, forcing its way through the barrier and checkpoint, eluding the obligation to accept or adopt all that enters from the outside" (175). This "unincludable" idea of divinity is an idea that is anterior to being, presence, and immanence, without any origins in consciousness; it is "the trauma of awakening" that is a "devastation" of thought, enabling the "endless desire for what is beyond being [a]s dis-inter*estedness*, transcendence—desire for the Good" (175-77). This "an-archic" desire that is "incommensurate

with consciousness" *is* the ethical relation which Levinas characterizes as an "obsession" that "undoes thematization" (90-91). The trauma
of awakening may also be described as a "shudder of incarnation" in
which "a subject becomes a heart, a sensibility, and hands which give"
(182). And so, God "falls into meaning" or "comes to the idea" in
and through the ethical relationship; the face of the other is the event
of revelation.

The event of revelation also takes place for Levinas as a "saying." In
the ethical relation, I become "open" to the other by means of a "saying" that is anterior to its content, "before the said uttered in this
sincerity forms a screen between me and the other" (Levinas 1989,
183). Saying is thus a stance which is silent, but "not with hands
empty" (183). The radical anteriority of saying establishes its
antecedence to experience, for Levinas, because to say is to stand
accused and held hostage before the transcendence and destitution
of the other—from time immemorial. Levinas characterizes saying
as "[a] pure testimony . . . a martyr's truth which does not depend on
any disclosure or any 'religious' experience; it is an obedience that
precedes the hearing of any order" (183). As "pure testimony," saying never gives witness to experience, but only to the Infinite. *It is the
prophetic voice par excellence:* "Prophesying is pure testimony, pure
because prior to all disclosure; it is subjection to an order before understanding the order" (184). Levinas insists that such testimony is
not born as a kind of knowledge generated in the present. Because
Infinity utterly exceeds all categories of being and thought, the event
of revelation can only occur as an "inspiration" that "constitutes, prior
to the unity of apperception, the very psyche in the soul" (184). Revelation thus "fractures" the totality of rational thought because it
appears as the "trauma of awakening" alluded to earlier, in which
God "comes to the idea" in and through the ethical relation—the
face that commands me to command: "Could we account for intelligibility in terms of a traumatic upheaval in experience, which confronts intelligence with something far beyond its capacity, and thereby
causes it to break? Surely not. Unless, perhaps, we consider the possibility of a command, a 'you must,' which takes no account of what
'you can'" (205). And so, for Levinas, the model of revelation must
always be an ethical one (206).

As already mentioned, the event of revelation as a "saying" is prior
to understanding that which one is commanded to do, and so belongs to the discernibly prophetic stance. Levinas insists that
prophetism is "the fundamental mode of revelation" that belongs to

"the human condition itself," and not just to those individuals who have been traditionally recognized as prophets:

> For every man, assuming responsibility for the Other is a way of testifying to the glory of the Infinite, and of being inspired. There is prophetism and inspiration in the man who answers for the Other, paradoxically, even before knowing what is concretely required of himself. This responsibility prior to the Law is God's revelation. There is a text of the prophet Amos that says: "God has spoken, who would not prophesy?," where prophecy seems posited as the fundamental fact of man's humanity (Levinas 1985, 113-14).

The ethics of responsibility that precedes ontology is thus, finally, the very fact of incarnation that "guarantees" human spirituality; we become "a heart, a sensibility, and hands which give" (97; 1989, 182).

## VOEGELIN, LEVINAS, AND POST-HOLOCAUST SPIRITUALITY

Voegelin's insistence on the centrality of "attunement" to divine being such that the symbolization of order becomes more macroanthropically situated in the personal soul's love of God (as constitutive of societal order) remains wedded to a typically western ontological vision that gives primacy of place to being, presence, intelligibility, and knowledge. As such, his vision of order in history as recounted in *Israel and Revelation* is "existential," with the emphasis on the movement, in the symbolization of order, from collective existence in historical form under the one God to the potential for personal existence in the knowledge (*da'ath*) of God as Redeemer of all humankind. Collectivism and parochialism are thus on the way to being replaced by personalism and universalism as the symbol of the Covenant written on "tablets of stone" gradually gives way to the symbol of the Covenant written on the "heart of flesh," with the attendant "Exodus of Israel from itself."

I have already noted what I consider to be the discernible ethical thrust in Voegelin's "existential" account of the prophetic movement toward personalism. Not only does the personal soul's attunement to divinity lead to the progressive differentiation of symbols constituting knowledge (*da'ath*) of God, such attunement also leads to the *exercise* of such knowledge in the form of merciful, just, and righteous acts in the world. Yet it seems to me that the very symbolizations making ethical action possible in the world, symbolizations whose history of partial differentiation is recounted in *Israel and Revelation* by the prophets' identification of the desired virtues of the

personal soul, remain necessarily contingent upon the prior ontological and existential context—the requisite degree of personalized
attunement to divinity. And so, ethics remains contingent upon ontology for Voegelin. The dependence of ethics upon ontology in *Israel and Revelation* helps clarify Voegelin's insistence upon the "existential" rather than "normative" nature of the Decalogic Constitutions; as noted earlier, the Decalogue was the existential yardstick by
means of which the Chosen People's obedience to/defection from
God could be measured. The normative languaging of the Decalogue
then became the source of "evil" because "it endowed the institutions
and conduct of the people, which derived through interpretation from
the Decalogue, with the authority of divinely willed order, however
much the actual institutions perverted the will of God" (*IR*, 440).
For Voegelin thus, stripping the Decalogic Constitutions of their
"normative" articulation lays bare their "true" *existential* nature. This
is a crucially important distinction in relation to the rise of personalism, as the mere husk of ritual observance becomes recognized as
such, and hence forsaken in favor of the personal soul's attunement
and obedience to the will of God, made manifest in the form of
merciful, just, and righteous action in the world. Nevertheless, ethical action is derived from prior ontological/existential attunement to
divinity.

Levinas' ethics of responsibility, on the other hand, rejects an
ontologically based vision such as Voegelin's because of the "grasping" nature of knowledge acquisition, based on the "totalizing" correlation between knowledge and being, whereby the other becomes
"absorbed" into the same in what can ultimately culminate in murderous acts of violence. Knowledge does not participate in the "true"
order of being, but rather perpetuates the "isolation" of being because knowledge remains immanent to the subject. Also, because "the
relation to the Infinite is not a knowledge but a Desire" (Levinas
1985, 92), ethics becomes the means by which relatedness to divinity is undertaken. Because God "falls into meaning" or "comes to the
idea" in and through the face of the other-as-theophany, the ethical
relation is the event of revelation and thus the source of all meaning.
Because the meaning of the face consists in proclaiming "Thou shalt
not kill," it is surely possible to assert that Levinas posits the primacy
of an ethical interpretation of the Decalogic Constitutions over an
existential one. The extreme passivity of the ethical subject who is
"accused" and "held hostage" by the transcendence and destitution
of the other enables the fall of God into meaning in and through the
"trauma of awakening" that "devastates" thought, engendering the

"endless" desire for the Good that is beyond being and knowledge. Such desire becomes incarnated in "a heart, a sensibility, and hands which give." It is the stance of the prophet.

Eric Voegelin's account of the movement toward personalism within Israelite prophetic experience is a most valuable example of an overall model of order rooted in the existential participation in being, with its concomitant attempts at intelligibility, through symbolization, of the terms of the quaternarian field. His account of the movement toward personalism is also valuable to scholars of Christian spirituality and spiritual theology because it chronicles his vision of the developing insight into and symbolization of those desirable virtues of the soul that are indicative of knowledge (*da'ath*) and personal love of God. Although the exercise of such virtues remains dependent upon prior knowledge as gained in existential attunement to divinity, an ethical thrust is still discernible in that knowledge of God will be made manifest in merciful, just, and righteous acts in the world. For those of us who are concerned with the formulation of a spirituality that is rooted in the body and the body's attempts to survive conditions of extremity, however, the primacy that Voegelin's vision (as limited to his account in *Israel and Revelation*) gives to the symbolization of order, as reflective of the overall primacy given to being, presence, intelligibility, and knowledge, seems to lose sight of the preeminent importance of the safety and well being of individual human life. As such, one suspects that Voegelin's vision of being is a "totalizing" one, in the Levinasian sense of the word; one that is unable to take up, let alone defend, the right to be of the particular, the individual, the "other" as "the original exception to order." Nor should it have to, I might add. But as the dawning of a new millennium approaches, and as the unprecedented events of this century continue to reverberate and threaten to be resumed, it is important to ask oneself whether such a "totalizing" vision, philosophical or otherwise, can still be considered benign in an age in which the extreme vulnerability of the individual, as well as the group, has been made manifest in waves of genocidal atrocity. Although Voegelin's vision is not to be discounted on this score, Levinas' ethics of responsibility provides a crucially needed perspective that tempers the "totality" of existential participation in being with the "infinity" of the ethical relation. A post-Holocaust spirituality and spiritual theology that is capable of confronting the violence done to bodies with something more concrete than promises of otherworldly redemption could hardly do better than to begin by stressing the incarnated transcendence and destitution of the other-as-theophany—the other for whom I am infinitely responsible.

## NOTES

[1] The apophatic/kataphatic distinction in Christian spirituality is important to our discussion. Bernard McGinn clarifies this distinction as follows: "It would be easy to draw up a lengthy list of texts from the mystics . . . that speak of a special consciousness of the divine presence as the goal of all their hopes and efforts. But this would be to tell only half the story. Precisely because of the incommensurability between finite and infinite Subject, Christian mystics over the centuries have never been able to convey their message solely through the positive language of presence. The paradoxical necessity of both presence and absence is one of the most important of all the verbal strategies by means of which mystical transformation has been symbolized. The relationship has been portrayed in many forms. Sometimes, among the more positive, or cataphatic, mystics, it is primarily a successive experience . . . At other times, among the negative or apophatic mystics, presence and absence are more paradoxically and dialectically simultaneous. If the modern consciousness of God is often of an absent God (absent though not forgotten for the religious person), many mystics seem almost to have been prophets of this in their intense realization that the 'real God' becomes a posibility only when the many false gods (even the God of religion) have vanished and the frightening abyss of total nothingness is confronted. If everything we experience as real is in some way present to us, is not a 'present' God just one more *thing*? This is why many mystics from Dionysius on have inisted that it is the consciousness of God as negation, which is a form of the absence of God, that is the core of the mystic's journey" (McGinn 1991, 1:xviii-xix).

[2] See the selections on this episode from *IR*, chap. 8, 234ff., in the anthology of this book.

[3] I am restricting my examination of Levinas' thought to his characterization of ethics as "the infinite obligations and responsibilities of social life" in relation to the radical alterity of the other, and his characterization of the relationship with "the absolute alterity of God" (Levinas 1987, 3).

# THE PROBLEM OF METASTASIS: ERIC VOEGELIN'S READING OF ISAIAH

## David L. Morse

Eric Voegelin is one of the few political philosophers in this century who has given both attention to and positive treatment of the experience of Israel as part of the unfolding search for political order in history. Most contemporary political philosophers make a negative distinction between reason and revelation. They are thus inclined to locate the beginnings of political science with Greek philosophy and, in particular, with Plato and Aristotle. Voegelin, however, rejects this negative distinction between revelation and reason. He interprets both as epochs in the unfolding of the consciousness of order in history.

A basic principle guiding Voegelin's search for order is that "the order of history emerges from the history of order" (*OH* I, ix). Therefore, for Voegelin, the discovery of the life of reason in Greek philosophy and the experience of the revelation of the transcendent God who establishes a covenant with Israel represent two great "leaps in being" that occurred in the history of the western world. *Israel and Revelation* is an effort to analyze Israel's "leap in being." In this volume, Voegelin analyzes the experience of the revelation of the transcendent God to the community of Israel. Voegelin's analysis of this event of revelation includes an appreciation of its contribution to the understanding of order as well as a description of its limits and problems.

This chapter will focus on one aspect of that analysis, Voegelin's interpretation of the work of the prophet Isaiah, and, in particular, Voegelin's claim that Isaiah is "a metastatic thinker" (*OH* I, 452). In the first section, I will summarize Voegelin's analysis of Isaiah and what he meant when he called Isaiah a metastatic thinker. I will also try to show how the problem of "metastasis," as Voegelin understands it, is a political problem not only in Isaiah's thought, but to some extent in the other Hebrew prophets. In the second part I will present, as an alternative to Isaiah, Voegelin's reading of Plato's *Laws*. For Voegelin the *Laws* are a better example of how one can move from spiritual insight to concrete political structures. As such, it is a preferable alternative to metastatic thinking. In part three, I will suggest what I think is the enduring significance of Voegelin's concept of metastasis for contemporary political discussions of the movement from the experience of transcendence to concrete political structures.

## I. Voegelin's "Reading" of Isaiah

Voegelin's analysis of Isaiah is in the context of his understanding of Hebrew prophecy in general. This in turn has its place in the fundamental "leap in being" which occurred historically in the constitution of the people of Israel. Israel's leap in being marked a dramatic turning point in the consciousness of order in history. It represented a break with the cosmological civilizations of the ancient world and introduced a new consciousness of the transcendent ground of being as the constitution of history. For Israel this transcendent ground was represented by Yahweh, the covenanting God of Israel.

> The major theoretical issues arising in a study of Israelite order have their common origin in the status of Israel as a peculiar people. Through the divine choice Israel was enabled to take the leap toward more perfect attunement with transcendent being. The historical consequence was a break in the pattern of civilizational courses (*OH* I, 116).

This break had its particular origins in the historical experience of Moses and the clash between his experience of Yahweh and the cosmological order of Egypt (*OH* I, 388, 392, 402f.). A central symbol of this revelation is preserved in the story of the thorn bush incident (Exod 3) in which the hidden God is revealed to Moses (405-14). This experience prepared the way for the empirical exodus out of Egypt and a symbolic exodus out of the cosmological world. The exodus led Israel to the experience of the covenant revelation at Sinai and their constitution as a peculiar people (415-27). As Voegelin noted,

> What emerged from the alembic of the Desert was not a people like the Egyptians or Babylonians, the Canaanites or Philistines, the Hittites or Arameans, but a new genus of society, set off from the civilizations of the age by the divine choice. It was a people that moved on the historical scene while living toward a goal beyond history (*OH* I, 113).

With this new differentiation of the consciousness of order in history, in particular, the consciousness of divine transcendence, Israel faced a new problem. The consciousness of the revelation of the divine presence and the election of Israel as a chosen people placed Israelite society in the midst of a tension. On the one hand, the goal of its life was beyond history. On the other hand, as a political community it was still constituted in history. Israel was a specific society. It had conquered a particular territory (Canaan) which had to be organized, managed and protected. In this respect, Israel was no different from any other society even if its consciousness of political order was distinctive. Hence, there existed for Israelite society, as for all persons oriented toward the transcendent ground of history, a fundamental tension in its existence. This was the tension between the transcendent political order of the Kingdom of God and the necessities and realities of the earthly kingdom of a particular people who lived in history. Because of this tension and the ambiguity that it produced in Israelite existence, there was always the possibility of a derailment of consciousness into some deformed articulation of that order. This derailment could occur if the goal of life, which is beyond history, became confused with particular situations in history. This problem was present from the founding of the original state and continued through the later, divided kingdoms of Israel and Judah. A political consciousness originally constituted by the exodus from Egypt and the covenant at Sinai and the transcendent insights achieved in this particular leap in being was always wedded to the earthly existence of the empirical state or states. This created what Voegelin called "the mortgage of Canaan" (*OH*, I, 164). This "mortgage" is one of the fundamental motifs in Voegelin's analysis of Israel's political consciousness. One of the best descriptions of this problem can be found in Voegelin's introductory remarks on this situation.

> The derailment, indeed, did occur right in the beginning. It found its expression in the symbol of Canaan, the land of promise. The symbol was ambiguous because, in the spiritual sense, Israel had reached the promised land when it had wandered from the cosmological Sheol to the *mamlakah*, the royal domain, the Kingdom of God. Pragmatically, however, the Exodus from bondage was continued into the conquest of Canaan by rather worldly means; further, to a Solomonic kingdom with the very institutional forms of Egypt or Babylon; and finally, to a political disaster and destruction that befell Israel like any other people in history. On its pragmatic wanderings through the centuries Israel did not escape the realm of the dead. In a symbolic counter movement to the

> Exodus under the leadership of Moses, the last defenders of Jerusalem, carrying Jeremiah with them against his will, returned to the Sheol of Egypt to die. The promised land can be reached only by moving through history, but it cannot be conquered within history. The Kingdom of God lives in men who live in the world but it is not of this world. The ambiguity of Canaan has ever since affected the structure not of Israelite history only but of the course of history in general (114).

This statement summarizes the ongoing struggle in Israel's history. This is the struggle of the differentiated consciousness of the divine, transcendent ground of being with the political realities of the mundane world, the "mortgage of Canaan." That struggle and the efforts to resist the continued possibility of derailment that it was prone to produce was carried on in the work of the Hebrew prophets. The message of the prophets represented an effort to recover the original covenant and the heritage of Moses, a heritage deemed to have been lost by the people in the eyes of the prophets. The real issue for the various prophets, with their distinctions and similarities, was the "effort to regain, for the Chosen People, a presence under God that was on the point of being lost" (*OH* I, 429).

Yet the prophet's efforts to call the people back to the original experience at Sinai and their divine constitution as a chosen people produced a very "strange" situation. Given the current, historical situation of Israel, the prophetic message looked back to the original covenant and its positive political expression in the Decalogue. At the same time, however, the real issue for the prophets in appealing to the Decalogue to criticize the present society was not the observance of particular laws in their external, normative sense for that society. Rather, the real issue was the experience of the divine order in the soul of persons that found symbolic and concrete articulation in the Decalogue. There is, therefore, for Voegelin's reading of the prophets, a distinction to be made between the normative content of the Decalogue (the actual laws, rules, regulations and so forth) and the existential significance of the covenant per se.

This differentiation, however, was a problem for the prophets because, according to Voegelin, the compact form of the Decalogue "did not allow for a distinction between existential and normative issues" (*OH* I, 439). This was a significant disadvantage for the prophets in their proclamation. It is one of the reasons why their message was, to a great degree, negative. It was clear in their pronouncements what they were condemning and why they condemned it. The people had rejected the covenant God. The people were following false gods. The social practices of the society in which the prophets lived and to which they spoke reflected an existential abandonment of the fundamental event of exodus and covenant. Hence, the people, even their religious institutions in many instances, were to be denounced. What was more difficult for the prophets was the articulation of how this divine order in the soul, the existential issue in the consciousness of transcendence, should be articulated in the positive construction of a concrete social order or the criticism of the present social order.

The problem of being unable to translate the content of this existential experience of transcendence into positive political structures represents for Voegelin one very significant difference between the experience of revelation in Israel and the experience of philosophy in Greece. To a greater degree than the Hebrew prophets, the Hellenic experience of order, especially as represented by Plato and Aristotle, was able to develop a vocabulary that could articulate positive political structures.

> In particular, the positive relation between God and man, man and God, was expressed negatively in the injunction not to have other gods in the face of Yahweh. We have previously studied the meaning of this peculiarity when we reflected on the difference between Israelite Revelation and Hellenic Philosophy: A positive articulation of the existential issue would have required the experience of the soul and its right order through orientation toward the invisible God; and that experience never in Israelite history clearly is differentiated from the compact collectivism of the people's existence—not even in the prophetic age, and certainly not in the age that formed the Decalogue. Hence, at a time when a theory of the psyche and theology would have been required to unfold the meanings implied in the Sinaitic legislation, the prophets were badly handicapped by the want of a positive vocabulary (*OH* I, 439).

To be sure, on the one hand, the prophetic message moved in the direction of this differentiation between existential and normative issues. In fact, Voegelin can note, "The insight that existence under God means love, humility, and righteousness of action rather than legality of conduct was the great achievement of the prophets in the history of Israelite order" (*OH* I, 440). On the other hand, the mortgage of Canaan created a problem. Not only did the normative laws and institutions coming out of the basic covenant with the world-transcendent God become an occasion to misunderstand the transcendent source of order, but the very existence of Israel in the world was a temptation to become like other nations. The nation faced a constant temptation to abandon the covenant and find refuge in the intra-cosmic gods of the cosmological order of civilization. The constant "temptation to false God, idols, etc." is but one part of this. Voegelin noted that as the prophets denounced, and even rejected, various aspects of what Israel was doing, it was also difficult to answer the question, "What did the prophets really want of the people in their concrete political life?" (*OH* I, 444f.). The prophets appeared to have lacked clarity about the relationships between spirit and the world. Therefore, as the prophets criticized the defection from the order of Yahweh and the capitulation to the cosmological myth, they ended up rejecting, or at the very least appearing to reject, mundane existence all together. On the one hand, the prophets make concrete demands on the people to be ordered by the existential reality of divine transcendence, and they recognize that this is to be differentiated from sheer external obedience to particular laws. On the other hand, they constantly have to express rejection of the present institutions of Israel because they are a sign of defection from the covenant. According to Voegelin, this puts them in the following difficult situation, a situation which appears to defy common sense.

> The juxtaposition of rejection and demand make it clear that the prophets wanted to overcome the externalization of existence; and the texts reveal the remarkable degree of success their efforts achieved: they disengaged the existential issue from the theopolitical merger of divine and human order; they recognized the formation of the soul through knowledge (Hosea) and fear (Isaiah) of God; and they developed a language to articulate their discoveries. They were handicapped, to be sure, by their inability to break through to philosophy, but the part of their work we are examining at present runs parallel, without a doubt, to the discovery of the *aretai* in Hellas. Nevertheless, the rejection of the mundane order remains an oddity. The prophets apparently were not only unable to see, but not even interested in finding, a way from the formation of the soul to institutions and customs they could consider compatible with the knowledge and fear of God. The attitude of the prophet is tantalizing in that it seems to violate common sense (*OH* I, 446-47).

Voegelin's analysis of the work of Isaiah is set in this particular context of the role of prophecy in general.[1] Isaiah provides a concrete illustration of what Voegelin has identified as the prophetic problem. This problem was a situation that called for the prophet to speak some constructive word to specific circumstances that involved the public order of the nation as it organized itself for pragmatic action in history. There were at least two occasions in his prophetic career when Isaiah was placed in a situation of offering advice to the king concerning specific political realities. The first was the war with Israel and Syria in 734 B.C.E. The city of Jerusalem was threatened by an enemy, and the prophet, under the command of Yahweh, went forth to address the king. The incident is found in Isaiah 7. Isaiah went out to speak to the King of Judah, Ahaz, to proclaim to him the word of the Lord. That word, as articulated by Isaiah, was quite simply, "Take heed: Be quiet, do not fear, let your heart not be faint because of these two smoldering stumps of firebrands" (Isa7:4, *NRSV*). With respect to Isaiah's "advice" to Ahaz in the face of a concrete political crisis, Voegelin simply notes, "That was all" (*OH* I, 448). In other words, all that Isaiah could say to Ahaz was, "Just trust God."

The second instance where Isaiah spoke to a particular political situation was the threatened Assyrian invasion and the alliance that Judah was seeking with Egypt. In Isaiah 30:15 the same advice is repeated by the prophet: "In returning and rest you shall be saved; in quietness and in trust shall be your strength." Voegelin understands this to be a repetition of the same word as given to Ahaz in Isaiah 7. He goes on to note that Isaiah affirms the foolishness of this alliance in 31:3 with a declaration "that Egypt is man, and not God, and his horses are flesh, and not spirit." Once again the prophet's word was simply to trust in God and not trust in human alliances, institutions and plans. At the very best, this is obviously simplistic, even foolish advice, in the face of a real threat in which the very existence of the nation as a political entity was at stake. At the very worst, it appears to be counsel to national suicide.

What is one to make of this rather strange advice that Isaiah gave to Ahaz? Voegelin's answer to that question represents the key to his claim that Isaiah is a "metastatic" thinker. Drawing from von Rad's analysis of the rituals of holy war in Israel and tracing their development through the concept of sympathetic magic represented by Elisha to the utilitarian concept of trust presented in Chronicles, Voegelin places Isaiah midway between these ideas (*OH* I, 448-51). Trust in God coupled with the action of the people led by the charisma of the prophet is what Elisha represented. According to Voegelin, this represents a type of sympathetic magic. In the Chronicles, this same imagery is simply rewritten and presented under the form of the concept of trust in God flattened into a kind of utilitarian affirmation of providence. According to Voegelin, however, in Isaiah's words to Ahaz you have a different form of magic. It is a message based on a trust in God that rejects all human action and at the same time asserts a belief that if you have sufficient trust, you will command some action that will win the battle. Isaiah's advice is rooted in the idea that faith is distinct from human action, and therefore the king was challenged to trust in God. Yet, faith is not a matter of a trust that affirms the presence of God regardless of, even in the face of, adverse circumstances. For Isaiah, the exercise of faith involves a belief that God is going to do something for you to change the circumstance of life, not just give you power to accept it. This word of Isaiah is not simply spiritual advice for coping with history. This is a plan designed to address a specific situation in history and to achieve particular results, namely a change in the circumstances of that history. This is why Voegelin suggests that Isaiah's position between the old concept of the holy war represented by Elisha and the historicized concept in Chronicles represents a type of magic. On the one hand, there is a severe repression of human, political action. This is a sign of a lack of faith. On the other hand, there is reliance on a set formula for specific change, "If you do not trust, you will not last." This formula, for Voegelin, implies the affirmation of the opposite, "if you do trust you will then last or remain established."

> Isaiah's counsel does not originate in an ethics of nonviolence; it is not calculated to lose the war in order to gain something more important than earthly victory but on the contrary to win the war by means more certain than an army. In the counsel of Isaiah, we may say, the element of faith in a transcendent God (which is also contained in the compactness of magic) has differentiated so far that a practice of sympathetic magic, as in the Elisha legend, has become impossible; and the sensitiveness for the gulf between divine plan and human action has even become so acute that all pragmatic assistance in the execution of the plan is considered a display of distrust (*OH* I, 451).

Voegelin's judgment is that "an aura of magic undeniably surrounds the counsel" (*OH* I, 451). For Voegelin, this is the kind of magic that anticipates the later phenomena of gnosticism. At this point for Isaiah his proclamation, and its quasi-magical base, stems from the continuing clash between mundane existence represented by the nation and its political institutions and the overpowering experience of transcendence. Although Isaiah has rejected the cosmological symbol-

ism, the cycle of life associated with cosmic rhythms is transferred to
the cultic presence of the kingdom of God, which, for Isaiah has
become a pragmatically effective presence in the history of Israel.
The leap in being experienced by Israel became for Isaiah a leap out
of being. Isaiah expected that the mundane world in which the nation lives and in which political decisions have to be made in the face
of the enemy will be transfigured into the world beyond history. This
transformation is due to the prophet's "knowledge" of that realm and
its operative force in transforming the world. This is what Voegelin
means by the term "metastasis." It refers to Isaiah's experience of God
and his application of that consciousness to the world.

"Metastasis" is the name Voegelin gives to the form of consciousness in the psyche of a person "in which the experience of cosmic
rhythms in the medium of historical form gives birth to the vision of
a world that will change its nature without ceasing to be the world in
which we live concretely" (*OH* I, 452). "Metastasis" is, however, a
futile dream because it represents a denial of reality as it is constituted. Reality, as given by God, is an order which cannot be changed.
In fact, the effort to project such a change onto reality is a rebellion
against the order of history as constituted by God.

As Voegelin goes on to note, metastatic faith did not originate with
the prophets. It is, as a possibility, inherent in the fundamental experience of transcendence in Israel itself. Its possibility is rooted in the
recognition of a difference between the divine order that is beyond
history and the mundane order of this world. Whenever metastatic
consciousness takes over and seeks to impose itself on the specific
historical order, you have a derailment from reality as constituted in
history. This derailment took several forms in the experience of Israel, which can be organized and analyzed with regard to empirical
time. There was a future dimension which, according to Voegelin,
took two forms. One form viewed Israel as suffering a day of judgment in the future for its sins. This is represented in Amos' proclamation of a terrible Day of Yahweh. Another version, also represented
by Amos, had Israel coming through the time of suffering and entering into the Kingdom of God in which the present age is transformed
into a Golden Age. Metastatic derailment also had a present dimension which likewise took two forms. In the one, the kingdom of God
would be forced onto present reality through myth and constitutional enactment (e.g., the Deuternomic Torah). In the other, it would
be forced on the world through the kind of magical metastatic trust
represented by Isaiah. Finally, this transformation could be projected

back into the past through the rewriting of Israelite history as was seen in the Chronicler.

Isaiah, then, represented only one strain of metastatic thought. Within Israel, as a result of the aforementioned tension, there were various metastatic images and concepts. They all, however, represented a common desire which was the expectation that historical existence would be transformed into something other than what it is. "In the variety of symbolic forms is recognizable the common substance of the metastatic will to transform reality by means of eschatological, mythical, or historiographic phantasy, or by perverting faith into an instrument of pragmatic action" (*OH* I, 454).

Furthermore, this form continued to be influential in Israel long after the political decline of the nation. Through prophetism in the period of later Judaism, it gave raise to apocalyptic symbols and apocalyptic literature. This, in turn, had a profound effect not only on Christianity, but on the course of Western Civilization.

> Moreover, the recognition of the metastatic experience is of importance for the understanding not only of Israelite and Jewish order but of the history of Western Civilization to this day. While in the main development of Christianity, to be sure, the metastatic symbols were transformed into the eschatological events beyond history, so that the order of the world regained its autonomy, the continuum of metastatic movement has never been broken. It massively surrounds, rivals, and penetrates Christianity in Gnosis and Marcionism, and in a host of gnostic and antinomian heresies; and it has been absorbed into the symbolism of Christianity itself through the Old Testament as well as through the Revelation of St. John. Throughout the Middle Ages the Church was occupied with the struggle against heresies of a metastatic complexion; and with the Reformation this underground stream has come to the surface again in a massive flood—first, in the left wing of the sectarian movements and then in the secular political creed movements which purport to exact the metastasis by revolutionary action (*OH* I, 454).

Although Voegelin stated that Isaiah's vision is not nearly as dangerous as modern metastatic thinkers, nevertheless Isaiah's consciousness, as Voegelin understood it, represents a deformation. As such, it discloses the prophetic problem. What can be said concerning the positive ordering of society? How does one translate the profound leap in being that took place in the revelation of the one God into a word that can speak concretely to political, social and institutional concerns without suffering the deformation of metastatic thought? This is Isaiah's problem when it comes to mundane existence. It is, as the circle widens to include the other prophets, part of the continuing problem all of them faced. This problem is itself set in the wider context of Israel's existence and the "mortgage of Canaan." But it is not even unique to Israel. It is a fundamental political problem inherent, as a possibility, in any leap in being that leads to a consciousness of the transcendent ground of history. Every consciousness of transcendence gives rise to a basic question. How is that transcendent ground to be related to mundane existence? To that question we now turn.

## II. The Relationship of Order and History

It must be remembered that Voegelin was not a Biblical exegete or theologian, per se, but rather a political philosopher who analyzed Isaiah and the experience of Israel as a manifestation of one of the great leaps in being in the consciousness of order that occurred in western history. Voegelin's work was begun, and to a great degree motivated, by his response to the crisis of existence that he experienced in his own world. His work is therapeutic. He wanted to analyze the root cause of the disorder he experienced in his own time as the first step toward the recovery of a balanced experience of order. Disorder, according to Voegelin's careful analysis, arises out of the concrete experience of order and the possibilities of derailment that are contained in the experience of order. To recover the consciousness of order, one must both analyze and "deconstruct" the disorder as well as recover sources of order that have been achieved in history. Since disorder is a derailment from the order that has been achieved in history, the path to order is to rediscover at the level of consciousness the vision of order that has been given in the great leaps in being that have taken place in history.[2]

Both of the leaps in being in Israel and in Hellas represent an experience of the transcendent ground of order. This relationship presents one with a new consciousness of the tension of existence, the tension toward the divine ground. In Israel, the emphasis falls on the divine ground and its initiative in relating to history, hence the characterization as "revelation." In Hellas the emphasis is on the human pole and the one who seeks and is drawn into an awareness of the beyond; hence the characterization as "reason." In each leap, however, there is a new consciousness of the transcendent ground of history and a new understanding of existence in tension toward that ground. Voegelin characterizes tension as existence in the *"metaxy,"* the in-between.[3] Following the historical differentiations of consciousness represented by Israel and Hellas, human existence is understood to be located in the tension of the metaxy. We are historical beings. We have existence in the mundane world, but we also have an orientation toward and a consciousness of the transcendent pole of being. As we saw for Israel and for Isaiah, this tension in existence creates the possibility of derailment. For this tension is experienced not simply as ambiguous but also as anxiety-producing. As human beings seek to relieve the tension of existence, a turn from order to disorder may well occur.

Modern ideological movements and systems are manifestations of such disorder which Voegelin, drawing from Schelling, has called pneumopathological consciousness (*SPG*, 101; GUOGS, 6, 30, 35; RCE, 278; QDD, 388; ER). At the close of his lecture on the German University, Voegelin, quoting the prophet Ezekiel, stated what might be thought of as his political mission with respect to this condition.

> Since the heart of the evil is a pneumopathological condition of consciousness, the first step to recovery would involve making people aware of the evil and opening the situation up to public discussion. Making aware of the evil through its diagnosis is the purpose which this lecture has intended to serve. The individual can do no more. In Ezek 33:7-9 we read of the watchman: "So you, son of man, I have made a watchman for the house of Israel; whenever you heard a word from my mouth, you shall give them warning from me. If I say to the wicked, O wicked man, you shall surely die; and you do not speak to warn the wicked to turn from his way, that wicked man shall die in his iniquity, but his blood I will require at your hand. But if you warn the wicked to turn from his way, and he does not turn form his way; he shall die in his iniquity, but you will have saved your soul" (GUOGS, 35).

For Voegelin, "metastasis," as represented in aspects of Isaiah's message, is one of the forms this revolt takes. Like all forms of the disordered consciousness, it is a spiritual revolt against existence in the metaxy. Michael Franz' (1992) introduction to Voegelin's thought and analysis of his views of ideology, not only shows how, for Voegelin, all forms of disorder represent a spiritual pathology, but also presents a very helpful chart that organizes Voegelin's various concepts of pneumopathology (10). Following Voegelin's analysis, as well as citing the works of other interpreters of Voegelin, Franz acknowledges that disorder occurs when consciousness seeks to overcome the tension of existence in the metaxy. "More generally, attempts to artificially relax the tensions associated with the de-divinization of the world tend to assume one or the other of two characteristic forms: disregard for the requirements of existence in the world or a turning-away from transcendent reality to live in this world alone. Both forms of 'escapism' from the tensions of existence in the metaxy can be observed in all periods of history, subsequent to the 'leaps in being' identified by Voegelin in the ancient world" (7).

Franz (1992) provides a further organizational analysis by dividing each of these two forms of revolt into two sub-types. The effort to disregard the world and the requirements for existence in it give rise to two variations, "either a profound disregard for mundane necessities and an all-consuming desire for eternal perfection or a longing for an apocalyptic transformation of the worldly vale of tears" (7). The former represents metastatic faith, while the latter is named "parousiasm." With regard to the second path of spiritual revolt, "to eclipse the transcendent dimension of human experience by establishing man as the measure of all things" (8), this also takes two forms. These revolts "may take the form of hatred of the gods or, among more ambitious moderns, of attempts to usher in an era of human autonomy through a redirection of humanity's energies toward a perfection of the 'estate of Man.'" (8). Franz calls these two ways "Promethean revolt" and "ideological consciousness." The dividing line between each of the two sub-groups for Franz is the coming of Christianity into the world. Thus, he is able to construct the following chart of the various forms that pneumopathological revolt takes (10):

*****************************************************************

|                              | B.C.                  | A.D.                       |
| ---------------------------- | --------------------- | -------------------------- |
| Eclipse of worldly reality   | Metastatic Faith      | Parousiasm                 |
| Closure against transcendence | Promethean revolt    | Ideological Consciousness  |

*****************************************************************

I cite this chart of Franz' not only to show how Voegelin's reading of Isaiah relates to other forms of disorder but also to call attention to the larger political problem that Voegelin's analysis of Isaiah, as well as modernity, has disclosed. That is the problem of how to relate new differentiations of the consciousness of transcendence to mundane existence and its pragmatic requirements without derailing into some deformed consciousness. What all of the above forms of existence have in common is a revolt against the reality of life in the metaxy. Some, as Voegelin noted, are relatively benign for society, while others are positively dangerous, but all represent existence in revolt against reality.[4]

Voegelin's reading of Isaiah has exposed one of the dangers of the differentiation of consciousness known as "revelation." It has a certain tendency toward instability, a tendency to lose the balance of consciousness because of the emphasis placed on the divine pole of the tension. This tendency is less pronounced in the differentiation known as "reason," also (and later) named by Voegelin "noetic differentiation." Both the experience of Isaiah and the experience of philosophy, especially represented by Plato, are rooted in a revelation of the transcendent ground of history. In philosophy, however, the emphasis falls on the human pole, which is the philosopher in his or her own tension toward the divine. This provides a different possibility for relating the truth of transcendence to concrete political order. Unlike the prophets, who were unable to overcome the compact collectivism of Israel's experience, the philosophers, especially Plato and Aristotle, are able to differentiate the soul as the particular sensorium of transcendence (*OH* II, 221). For this reason, when it comes to resisting the tendency toward derailment in the application of transcendent insight to concrete society, Plato is superior to Isaiah. Although for Plato this movement involves a struggle, indeed sometimes a war, he is more able than Isaiah to make modest but real recommendations for the good society.[5]

Since this is not a study of Voegelin's reading of Plato, I will only sketch in broad strokes Voegelin's analysis leading up to Plato's final work, *The Laws*, where some specific recommendations for society find their final form. I will treat Voegelin's analysis of *The Laws* in more detail to draw out the contrast between Voegelin's understanding of Plato and Isaiah on this question. Voegelin develops his interpretation of Plato and his contribution to the consciousness of order following an analysis of those forces in Hellenic culture which preceded Plato and Aristotle and especially those figures in whom the differentiation of philosophy achieved significant articulation. In particular, Voegelin gives attention to Parmenides (*OH* II, 203-19) and Heraclitus (220-40).

Voegelin began his analysis of Plato by challenging a popular assumption that Plato was a philosopher in our modern sense of the
word who taught a set of philosophical doctrines known as
"Platonism." For Voegelin this is a significant historical error (*OH*
III, 5). Rather, Voegelin argues, Plato was engaged in a much more
concrete, historical and existential task. This was the struggle to resist the disorder he experienced in the society of his day and to articulate a true consciousness of order for society. The autobiographical reflections of the Seventh Letter indicate that Plato came to realize that this task was more than just political reform. It involved the
experience of the right order of the cosmos in the philosopher's own
soul and its articulation as a paradigm for the larger society.

> [Plato] had understood that participation in the politics of Athens
> was senseless if the purpose of politics was the establishment of just
> order; he had, furthermore, seen that the situation in the other
> Hellenic poleis was just as bad as in Athens, if not worse; and above
> all he had understood (what modern political reformers and
> revolutionaries seem to be unable to understand) that a reform
> cannot be achieved by a well-intentioned leader who recruits his
> followers from the very people whose moral confusion is the source
> of disorder. When he had gained those insights in the course of
> fifteen years, he did not fall, however, into despair or sullen
> resignation, but resolved on that "effort of an almost miraculous
> kind" to renew the order of Hellenic civilization out of the
> resources of his own love of wisdom, fortified by the paradigmatic
> life and death of the most just man, Socrates (*OH* III, 5).

Voegelin's reading of the dialogues from the *Gorgias* to the *Laws* is
an interpretation of this effort. The best model for Plato is Socrates
and the best means of the articulation of order is the dialogue. Socrates
represents the one in whom the consciousness of order has become
clear in his own soul as opposed to the Sophists of his day. Socrates
becomes a model for society because the good society is modeled on
the good soul. "The polis is man written large" (*Republic* 368 c-d),
characterized by Voegelin in one place as "the anthropological principle" (*NSP*, 61). In addition to regarding the philosopher's soul as
the model, the philosopher seeks to articulate this order in the dialogue form. The philosopher stands in contrast to the Sophist who
delivers speeches and expects the hearers to listen and learn. "The
dialogue is the symbolic form of the order of wisdom, in opposition
to the oration as the symbolic form of the disordered society. It re-

stores the common order of the spirit that has been destroyed through the privatization of rhetoric" (*OH* III, 12).

Plato began the analysis of the disorder in Athenian society by declaring war on that society in the *Gorgias*. Voegelin notes that its opening words are "war and battle," and this is symbolic of the content of the dialogue. Like the Hebrew prophets, Plato declares that the society of which he is a part is disordered. In the *Gorgias*, Plato shows that the present society is under judgment. According to Voegelin, "The Gorgias is the death sentence over Athens" (*OH* III, 39). This prepared the way for a positive statement of Plato's articulation of the rightly ordered society following the paradigm of the rightly ordered soul. This is the theme of the *Republic*. The *Republic* is Plato's articulation of the exodus event of Hellas, the exodus of the philosopher out of the corruption of society into a new vision of transcendence symbolized by the *agathon* (the good).

Again, as with the *Gorgias*, Voegelin calls attention to the *Republic's* opening Greek word, *kateben* (I went down), as a symbol of "the great theme that runs through it to its end" (*OH* III, 52). The *Republic*, as a dialogue, is a descent that reflects the human condition in Hades, and raises the question, "Must man remain in the underworld, or has he the power to ascend from death to life?" (54) The parable of the cave is a symbol of philosophy and of the life of Socrates who "is the savior because he is the philosopher who has traveled the way up from the night of Hades to the light of Truth. This Parmenidean component in Plato's work dominates the center of the *Republic* in the Parable of the Cave with its ascent to the vision of the Agathon" (59).

What happens, however, when society is unwilling to respond to the appeal of the philosopher? What happens when philosophers are not rulers or when society even refuses to learn from them? The answer, on the one hand, is that the philosopher withdraws from society and works at preserving the order of truth in his/her own soul. The philosopher may gather around him/her a group of like-minded persons and seek to instruct them preserving the insights within the small group. Many of the dialogues following the *Republic* concentrate on the differentiation of the truth of existence in the attunement of the soul to the divine order. The Academy that Plato founded reflected this tendency to withdraw from political life and concentrate on the order of the soul. On the other hand, the Academy becomes a means by which the insights discovered in the soul can become a force in society. Hence the withdrawal can become the means of a new influence in society. According to Voegelin, "the Academy is conceived as the institutional instrument by which the Spirit can wedge its way back into the political arena and influence the course of history" (*OH* III, 226). In the end, Plato cannot completely abandon society, for human existence is existence in history. Humans are incurably political creatures and the insights of the transcendent consciousness of order must be made operative in society. The spiritual insight into the transcendent ground of existence must be mediated to society to the greatest extent possible if it is to keep its balance and not disintegrate into a disorder that either tries to leap out of history into transcendence or tries to deny transcendence or swallow it up into some kind of one-dimensional historical existence.

Therefore, Plato does not in the end abandon society but seeks to maximize to the greatest degree possible the insight of the transcendent ground of existence in the society of which he is a part. Plato's final effort to accomplish this is found in the *Laws*. The historical problem which Plato addresses in the *Laws* is the problem of how to institutionalize the spiritual insights achieved in Plato's experience of divine order, especially as that order is articulated by him in the *Republic*.[6] According to Voegelin, "[Plato] wants to persuade, but also to embody the Idea in the community of a polis. And in order to give the visible form of institutions to the invisible flow of the spirit, in order to enlarge the erotic community of the true *philoi* into an organized society in politics, he is willing to temper persuasion with a certain amount of compulsion on the less responsive and to cast out the obstreperous by force. He could not know that he struggled with a problem that had to be solved through the Church" (*OH* III, 226).

Plato's problem is how to achieve in history, in the metaxy, the proper balance between spirit and power, the classical political problem. Spiritual insights, if they are to become socially effective, must be embodied in history. This is one of the roles of social institutions, regulations, norms, laws, etc. Hence, for Plato, concrete politics is the challenge of the relationship between the experience of spirit and the use of institutional power in the organization of a community. Faced with the tension between spirit and power, there are three choices available to a person. One can withdraw from the sphere of power and opt for a life of involvement in spirit. This involves retreating from the world and living either alone or in a community of persons responsive to the spirit. The Platonic expression of this option would be life in the Academy. On the other hand, one can go to the other extreme and opt for the coercive use of power. This option involves the exercise of power politics without any considerations of spiritual grounding or reform. This is the option represented by what is popularly known as "Machiavellianism." Although tendencies toward this solution are represented by speakers in Plato's dialogues, he rejects this option as the final solution to the problem of institutionalization. The third way is to recognize that in the in-between we struggle with both spirit and power. The authentic political philosopher will seek a balance between both of these. According to Voegelin, this is the search that drives Plato's *Laws*. The recognition of the problem of spirit and power and the movement toward its solution represents the particular difference between the *Republic* and the *Laws*. "The peculiar combination of power politics with spiritual reform causes the difficulties which unsettle Plato's earlier position and urge him on toward the position of the *Laws*" (*OH* III, 224).

The specific content of the *Laws* is related to the particular historical situation of Hellenic politics, but underlying that content is the fundamental issue of the institutionalization of spiritual insights in history. For Voegelin, this is also the issue facing the Church. The question before the Church is how to take the "eschatological heroism" of the Sermon on the Mount and translate that into everyday experience. Voegelin suggests that there were three specific ways in which Plato tried to institutionalize in the community the spirit of the laws that undergirded the new city that was being founded. The first of these ways was to communicate to the citizen the true meaning of the laws and the spirit that animated them. The law is a mediation of the spirit for the community, but the law often appears to be coercive. The wise leader of the community will seek to mediate between God and the human soul by persuasion (*OH* III, 225). For Plato, in direct opposition to the Sophists, God, not the human being, is the measure of all things. The place where this measure is operative is in the most divine part of a person, one's soul. The mid-point between God and the soul is persuasion not coercion. The way to promote this persuasion is through the articulation of a prelude or preamble to the law (722d: *prooimia nomon*) (256). Noting the rich symbolism of the dialogue, Voegelin calls attention to the Stranger's speech reaching this critical point in the middle of the longest day, the high noon of revelation.

> In the present interlude on Persuasion, the decisive speech of the Stranger is introduced by the reminder that we have arrived at the middle of this longest day. The conversation has taken such a course "under the guidance of God," from daybreak to noon, that now at the height of the day the means is revealed to the wanderers by which they can achieve the constant persuasion of *nous* in their

polis (722c). The stranger begins his reflections by saying that in this long conversation about the laws the wanderers have hardly begun to talk about the laws themselves; all they have talked about were preludes or preambles to the law (*prooimia nomon*) (722d) (256).

These preludes seek to explain, and foster the appropriation of, the meaning and purpose of the laws. Laws themselves are often short and to the point. They are prescriptions for the health of a community. Drawing on Plato's image of a doctor curing the sick, Voegelin notes that a doctor treating a slave simply issues orders to the slave as to what he or she is to do for the sake of health. "The law deals with the citizen like a physician with an ignorant slave: he tells the slave what to do but he does not discuss with him the nature of the disease, nor does he give him the reasons for the treatment" (255). While this is how some lawgivers often work in a community, a more preferred way to institute laws is to issue them with preludes that endeavor to explain their particular purpose in the life of the community. By setting forth these preludes before instituting the laws, the lawgiver will seek to persuade the citizen to obey the law by giving to him or to her adequate reasons for the law. The lawgiver will seek to maximize the spirit in the community by not simply issuing dictates but will endeavor to appeal to the understanding of persons, the reason (*nous*) that orders their being. In this way, he or she will be like a physician who gives prescriptions to a patient along with an explanation of the reason for the prescription and what it intends to do. "They have developed in fact a 'persuasive' (*peistikon*) for the citizens, like the physician who explains and gives reasons for his treatment to the freeman. Laws should consist in principle of two parts: a coercive part, the 'dictatorial prescription,' and a persuasive part, the expository prooemium (256).

The prooemium, thus, becomes the means whereby the leaders of the community seek to justify and to rationalize, in the best sense of that word, the meaning of the law so as to persuade compliance on the part of the citizens. The prelude appeals to their soul, to their reason and, thus, seeks to move them to comply through a decision on their own part that this law is an institutionalized expression of the measure of God. "The literary form of the Prooemium, thus, becomes the mediator of the nous for the polis of the *nomoi*" (*OH* III, 256).

The second way that Plato tried to institutionalize the spirit in the community was through the phenomenon of play. As Voegelin notes,

"Throughout his lifetime Plato was preoccupied with the problem of play. The dialogues themselves are plays under the aspect of literary form and more than once we had occasion to observe Plato's mastership as a dramatist" (*OH* III, 257). Unlike the Sophists for whom play was just an occasion to show off their supposed rhetorical skills to the public, play for Plato is serious business. Drawing from Huizinga's interpretation of Plato as well as the historical phenomenon of play in general, Voegelin characterizes play for Plato as a means whereby the spirit is recognized in life and mediated to the person and community.

> In this interpretation, play is an "overflow" beyond the "normal" level of existence, a source for the creation of new worlds of meaning beyond the everyday world. By virtue of this quality of transcendence play could become the vehicle of cultural growth through the creation of spiritual worlds in religions, legal institutions, languages, philosophy and art. The history of culture shows indeed that the spiritual world of the high civilizations grows out of archaic forms in which the origin in forms of play is still clearly discernible. In particular, play is the vehicle of religious expression from archaic rites to the subtleties of the liturgical drama and the symbolism of the dogma (258).

The theme of play is constant throughout the *Laws*. "God plays with men as his puppets or as pieces on a board; man conducts his life as a serious play in following the pull of the golden cord; and the dialogue itself is an elaborate play with various symbols" (*OH* III, 259). Play originates in the world of the child but is extended by Plato to cover the "sacred play" of adults that leads on to the appropriation of the experience of transcendence. In Voegelin's view, Plato presents culture (*paideia*) as growing out of the play of children (*paidia*) (260), quoting Plato's statement, "Education (paideia), I say, is the virtue that first comes into being in children" (653b) (260). Plato has the stranger go on to say that the great festivals which contribute to the education of a person are really activities grafted onto the play of children (653e-654a). The play of children leads to the serious play of adults and the great poetic festivals and dramas in which the mystery of the community is constituted, rehearsed and reconstituted. Through the medium of play, the drama of the acts of God are brought into and constitute the life of the community. Play becomes the means whereby humanity is "caught up" in the game and becomes open to the transcendent dimension of life. Play produces a spontaneity and a freedom that overflow into a participation in the divine constitution of life. This emphasis on play finds its parallel in the Church in the great liturgical dramas that constitute communal existence and define life before God. The substance of Christian worship is the dramatic presentation of the grace of God made present in Jesus Christ which, entered into in the Spirit, becomes the play that constitutes life together in Christ.

The third way used by Plato to bridge the gap between God and the community was through the symbolism of dogma proper. Voegelin seems to believe that this is inferior to the vision of the *agathon*, but still necessary given the human condition.

> On the lower existential level, which is presupposed for the citizenry, the divine measure cannot be the living order of the soul; God and man have drawn apart and the distance must now be bridged by the symbols of dogma. From the vision of the Agathon man has fallen to the acceptance of a creed. Plato the savior has withdrawn; his polis cannot be penetrated by the presence of his divine reality; Plato the founder of a religion is faced by the problem of how the substance of his mystical communication with God can be translated into a dogma with obligatory force (*OH* III, 261).

Comparing Plato to Spinoza at this point, Voegelin presents the purpose of these minimal dogmas within the *Laws* as one of providing both structure and freedom in the community.

> [Spinoza] tried to solve his problem through the creation of a minimum set of dogmas that would leave the utmost liberty to individuals who might wish to embellish the bare structure with details of their own, while it would be sufficient as a religious bond for the political community. Moreover, Spinoza the mystic needed the dogma for himself no more than Plato, but created it deliberately, as did Plato, for the mass of men whose spiritual strength is weak, and who can absorb the spirit only in the form of dogmatic symbols (*OH* III, 263-264).

Dogma is then a symbolic form through which the more direct vision of the spirit may be mediated to the community. One has the impression that while Voegelin recognizes the necessity of such a symbolic form, he wishes to keep it to a minimum, like both Plato and Spinoza.

Ranieri's recent book on Voegelin's political philosophy (1995) analyzes Voegelin's work with respect to the question of moving from spiritual insights to concrete political realities. In his chapter, "Is the Good Society possible?," he suggests that Voegelin's work uncovers a recurring tension in society itself that can be expressed in two affirmations that Voegelin would make about any society. "It is this acute consciousness that the truth of order ought to be embodied in society, joined to the belief that human nature and pragmatic exigencies prevent this from happening, that account for the paradoxical combination of fervor and resignation that marks Voegelin's thinking on the good society. In this he once again mirrors Plato" (211).

Perhaps this analysis of both Isaiah and Plato will direct attention to what is Voegelin's most enduring contribution to political philosophy. Voegelin's work articulates the tension between spirit and power. The transcendent realm of spirit ought to shape every exercise of political power. Yet, there is a limit to the effect that this will have in any given moment in history. In this sense then, the work of Voegelin is truly therapeutic, for it reminds us of the necessity of maintaining a balance between the effort to maximize the insights of the consciousness of transcendence without manipulating human nature or social structures. In this respect, Voegelin has shown that not only the good person but the good society exists in a tension between the necessities of its political existence in history and its openness to transcendence. In this sense, of course, society mirrors the person. This is why Voegelin can agree with Plato that society is the person writ large. The best hope for the good society is to fill it with as many good persons as possible. When that begins to fail, then certain minimal efforts at organization, as noted by Plato in the *Laws*, are necessary, but they remain second best.

For Voegelin then, politics in the sense of the ordinary affairs of society is, to use an old adage, "the art of the possible." The philosopher, the one in whom the love of wisdom and the openness to transcendence is present, will seek to do what can be done, given the nature of the situation. Such a one will not seek to flee society, nor will one make recommendations or engage in action that endeavors to force society in certain directions. This places the philosopher in a very difficult situation. He or she is passionate in his/her love of wisdom, but realistic in his/her recognition of what, in any given situation, can be done. In this respect, for Voegelin, we are still in a situation where we are not unlike that greatest of political philosophers, Plato. We therefore can learn much from him, not in terms of what specifically we ought to do, but rather, the kind of persons we ought to be.

### III. A Final Note on Metastasis

In reflecting critically on Voegelin's reading of Isaiah, one could move in at least two directions. There is the historical and textual direction. One could discuss the question of whether or not Voegelin has read Isaiah correctly and fairly. Moving in this direction one might ask the following questions. Did Isaiah really intend his advice to Ahaz to be a political program, a response to a particular situation or, set in the larger context of his thought, is this advice a type of spiritual exhortation to ground or guide certain other forms of political action? If one had more knowledge of the context of this event, even more text about the events, one might be able to answer some of these questions and, therefore, draw different conclusions. The problem is that of the interpretation of any text that is distant from present experience. One can only draw limited conclusions about the situation based on what is in the text. One lacks sufficient information to know what exactly Isaiah intended. Thus, Biblical scholars, political scientists, theologians, philosophers and others bringing different agendas and posing different questions, end up with different readings of Isaiah. Obviously, the text itself exercises some controls on the readings so that interpretation is not an idiosyncratic process, but due to the limitations of the text and knowledge of the context, there is a space created for different readings. Hence, the final answer to the question, "Just what did Isaiah mean in these particular contexts that Voegelin cites?," remains ambiguous.

Biblical scholars remind us, however, that these particular texts need to be placed in the larger context of the work of the prophet. In this perspective, Isaiah's message possesses a certain consistency, not as a political program, but as a message to his people. That message, as von Rad (1965, 147-75) has shown, although wide ranging, is rooted in two basic strains of the Jerualem tradition, namely, that of Zion and of David. The call to calmness in the face of adversity may be seen as a call to faith in the God who had elected Israel in general and Zion in particular. An alliance may well have been an "insult" to God's sovereignty in this perspective, or, in Voegelin's terms, a return to the cosmological order and a reversal of the exodus.

Nevertheless, on the pragmatic level Voegelin is correct about the lack of realism displayed by Isaiah. Still, Voegelin's charge of magic seems less clear. Had the advice led to success, it could then have been interpreted as magic, for Isaiah would have had the "right formula" for effecting change in history. The truth is, however, that on the pragmatic level Isaiah's message was a failure. The fact that the message was preserved by the prophet and his followers would seem to indicate that they viewed this as something more than magic. The message underwent a shift from the present moment to the future, to a confidence that the promise of God will be realized, even if not within one's own lifetime. As von Rad (1965, 167) noted, "This is one of the important differences between Isaiah and Jeremiah, whose relationship with Yahweh was much more critical. Isaiah apparently acquiesced in the failure of his work. This he could do, because for him the word of Yahweh with which he was charged was beyond all criticism. If his own generation had rejected it, then it must be put in writing for a future one."

Voegelin's observations about the mortgage of Canaan are still relevant in this shift. That mortgage still had a hold on Isaiah. The future still represented a restoration of Zion and a restored Davidic line. Here is the real tension which Voegelin has noted in Isaiah and the other prophets: between the mortgage of Canaan and the degree to which spiritual discoveries are linked to a particular people and a particular place, and a God whose word is not simply bound to any such particularity. Isaiah never overcame this tension (perhaps it can never simply be overcome), even if some of his disciples moved his message in a more universal direction. Nevertheless, given his own experience of "failure," his own consciousness underwent an exodus beyond himself. How far he went in that exodus is matter for debate.

A second way to evaluate Voegelin's reading of Isaiah is to focus on the symbolism of "metastasis," and ask what significance it may have for political discussion today. It seems that this is a less contentious direction in which to move. One can suspend for a moment the question of whether or not Voegelin offers a correct reading of Isaiah and ask, "What is the value of the symbolism of 'metastasis' for political philosophy today?" Here in this question one finds perhaps the clearer value of Voegelin's analysis. Voegelin is engaging in political therapy. "Metastasis," as Franz has shown in his insightful book, is one of several technical terms Voegelin uses to analyze the deformations of our political consciousness. These deformations occur when the balance between the experience of transcendence and concrete existence in history is lost to one side or the other. "Metastasis" is the deformation that occurs when one expects a magical transformation in the present state of history. It is a temptation more likely under the pressure of a powerful experience of transcendence, which is what one imagines was the case in the consciousness of the prophet Isaiah. Then, the temptation is to expect that with the right formula one can effect a structural change in historical reality.

While "metastasis" is, for Voegelin, a deformation, it is only one of several kinds of deformations that can take place. In fact, it is not nearly as prevalent today as are the contemporary ideological versions of deformation that actually seek to force upon society various "second realities." This is the common characteristic of the modern ideological movements of both the right and the left against which Voegelin protested in his writings. Certainly, one of the enduring contributions of Voegelin as a philosopher is his reminder of the need for balance in the consciousness of order. Human beings are creatures of the in-between, and this fact must never be lost from view as persons engage in political action. Humanity walks a fine line. There is a need to maintain balance. If balance is not maintained, existence falls prey to those deformations that not only characterize the twentieth century, but which, as Voegelin has shown, are the constants of historical life. This reminder of the constant need for balance, so clearly demonstrated by modern ideological movements, does, however, raise a final question. What can a prophet hope to accomplish? By prophet I mean not just the historical prophets of Israel, but anyone who has a message concerning problems in his or her society, and hopes to see those problems addressed. Prophecy arises out of any differentiation of consciousness that places emphasis on the divine pole of the differentiation. Such prophets still arise today. What can such a prophet do? Is the reformation of society possible?

For Voegelin, the answer would seem to be that there is very little that one can hope for in terms of making the message socially effective. Even though Voegelin is one of the few philosophers in the twentieth century to make a place for the experience of the transcendent ground of order, there is a certain pessimism that hangs over his analysis of the application of that insight to political society. There appears to be very little that the prophet can do or say in any situation other than to resist the evil that is present and seek to persuade individuals to orient their souls toward the good order. The apparent options for the prophet (or even philosopher for that matter) seem to be either to function as a representative of virtue in the face of a corrupt political order, or to try to persuade those in power to share one's insights into the spiritual ground of order. Beyond these options, there is little more that one can do without slipping into some kind of deformed ideology. This limited role for the prophet tends to blunt the value of any prophetic critique in society. Certainly, Voegelin's reading of Isaiah is a warning to any prophetic voice about one of the real dangers in prophetic articulation based on pneumatic differentiation. At the same time, Voegelin's very real doubts about the possibility of change in the historical nature of things may tend to render any political program at best useless, at worst dangerous. This, in turn, seems to call into question the whole value of prophecy for a society. Because of the dangers of pneumatic differentiation, Voegelin favors the kind of political philosophy represented by noetic differentiation exemplified most clearly by Plato. What Voegelin seems to be indicating is that it is important, in the realm of concrete society, to balance pneumatic differentiation by some kind of noetic controls. One might even call this, remembering Reinhold Niebuhr, a form of "political realism." For Voegelin, there is a value in balancing prophecy with "noesis." As Voegelin's analysis has shown, when prophecy endeavors to speak to particular political situations, it has a tendency to move toward either irrelevancy or possible danger for a particular society. Nevertheless, prophets do arise.

Persons do have spiritual insight and are moved by that insight to address concrete problems in society. Voegelin's analysis of Isaiah would seem to suggest that the most a prophet can accomplish is to play a negative role. He or she can resist corruption and deformation by setting over against such deformation a powerful witness to the transcendent ground of order. At the same time, the prophet will be severely limited in what he or she can hope to accomplish in the transformation of real structures in society. Perhaps there is something useful in knowing that limitation, but there is also something very frustrating about that limited role.

In the end, however, the reminder of the limits of participation in the metaxy and the need to maintain balance in our consciousness of order in history may be Voegelin's best gift to a world filled with ideological thinkers.

## NOTES

[1] In this context it should be noted that Voegelin is here referring to the eighth century prophet Isaiah whose work is associated with chapters one through thirty-nine in what is called the book of Isaiah in the Hebrew Bible and Christian Old Testament. This Isaiah is to be differentiated from what Biblical scholars call "second" Isaiah (usually chapters 40-55) and possibly "third Isaiah" (chapters 56-66).

[2] This does not mean simply repeating what others have said, but discovering the underlying experiences of order present in the symbolic articulations given in the great leaps in being that constitute the history of our consciousness of order. Voegelin considers this to be a restoration of a true political science. In his Walgreen Lectures, Voegelin noted, "By restoration of political science is meant a return to the consciousness of principles, not perhaps a return to the specific content of an earlier attempt" (*NSP*, 2; see the entire introduction, 1-26).

³The term *metaxy*, the Greek word for in-between, was first used by Voegelin in his lecture "*Ewiges Sein in der Zeit*," translated as "Eternal Being in Time" (*A*, 254-80; AE, 116-42). The description of existence as a tension toward the divine, however, predates the use of this term and is basic to Voegelin's understanding of human existence in history.

⁴See Voegelin's comments on the difference between Isaiah's "metastatic dreams" and the "metastatic nightmares" of modern ideologists (*OH* I, 465). Voegelin's preference appears to be for Isaiah if given a choice between the two. What they both have in common, however, is their revolt against the historical order in which human existence is constituted and in which humans must live.

⁵For a good comparison of Voegelin's reading of Plato and Isaiah on this very question see Ranieri 1995, esp. chaps. five and six.

⁶In this analysis Voegelin notes a number of what he considers to be historic misunderstandings in the interpretation of the *Laws*.

# Taming Israel:
## Voegelin and the Problem of
## Israelite Order

# John J. Ranieri

Throughout his philosophical career Eric Voegelin wrestled with the meaning of Israel. Indeed, one could argue that the tension between society and the truth of order, as crystallized in Israel's experience, was the central issue in Voegelin's work. Students of Voegelin's thought would be hard pressed to find a more lucid exposition of the concerns that animated his philosophical writing than the preface and introduction to *Israel and Revelation*. Nearly all of the predominant Voegelinian themes are present here; history as the struggle for order, the importance of symbols, the distinction between compactness and differentiation, the notion of ideology as rebellion against transcendent order, and an appreciation that "every myth has its truth" (*OH* I, *ix-xiv*).

There is another reason why the study of Israel assumed the importance it did in Voegelin's thought. It was within Israel that Voegelin located the origins of the metastatic faith that he considered to be a great, if not the greatest, source of disorder in the contemporary world. An ardent foe of utopianism, Voegelin warned that metastasis and the related phenomena of apocalyptic and gnosticism must be identified, analyzed, and exposed as delusion before they destroyed society. His analysis of Israel's development was undertaken, "not as an attempt to explore curiosities of a dead past," but as an inquiry into the present structure and crisis of social order.

Israel's experience had, then, a twofold significance. In the first place, the drama of Israelite history epitomized the problems associated with the tension of existence, as Israel attempted to reconcile the claims of transcendent order with those of mundane existence. Because of the intensity of the Israelite experience of the divine, the tension took on a particularly stark form. Secondly, the very intensity of this experience demanded careful study, so that the tendency toward metastasis and other forms of imbalance could be recognized and their excesses avoided. Of course the question of the relationship between social/political order and transcendent reality had been addressed in Voegelin's work before the publication of *Israel and Revelation*. But because the issue had been posed so strikingly in Israel's history, and because in *Order and History* Voegelin was beginning to discover a language with which to speak adequately about these matters, the case of Israel can be seen as paradigmatic for articulating the problem of the relationship between mundane and transcendent orders. In this sense the example of Israel encapsulates and sets the agenda for Voegelin's overall philosophical project. It also suggests that his treatment of Israel will offer important clues as to how he would confront the more general question of how best to reconcile attunement to transcendent order with the demands of life in the world.

While Israel's experience may have clarified the problem of the tension of existence, it could not, in Voegelin's view, provide an adequate solution. Therein lies the source of the ambivalence that characterized Voegelin's evaluation of Israel's historical role. The case of Israel presented in a striking way the discrepancy between the demands of the truth of order and the exigencies of pragmatic existence. Yet from its very beginning as a people the attempt to master these often conflicting obligations led to an apparently irresolvable impasse. From Voegelin's perspective, Israelite solutions to the tension of existence tended to move in two directions: to follow the way of the "nations" and anoint a king whose pragmatic policies would be identified with the will of God; or to reject the pragmatic compromise and fall into the dangerous path of metastasis. For Voegelin, metastasis was to be avoided at all costs; hence, in addressing the problem epitomized in Israel's struggle he sharply criticized the prophetic solution. As I have attempted to show elsewhere, his philosophy developed in other ways to address the tension of existence in a way that avoids metastatic deformation (Ranieri 1995). This essay will focus on how this development effected his understanding of Israel.

In my view, Voegelin's conception of Israel and its importance changed during the time between the writing of *Israel and Revelation* and his late works. The problem of the relationship between transcendent order and life in the world had been posed in Israel, and as he worked out his own philosophical response to the problem, Voegelin continued his dialogue with Israel, sometimes explicitly and other times more obliquely. Thus the manner in which he eventually came to resolve the problem could not help but have consequences for his understanding of Israel. What were those consequences and how did Voegelin's view of Israel change over time? And what might be the implications of this change for Voegelin's work as a whole? In considering these questions it is not my intention to review *Israel and Revelation* in its entirety. Instead, I will focus on the nature of the Israelite differentiation or "leap in being" as presented in that volume, with some attention to the prophets and other relevant dimensions of Israel's experience. This will be followed by a discussion of how the development of Voegelin's thought resulted in a reevaluation of the contribution of Israel. A concluding section will reflect on some of the implications of this development.

## ISRAEL AND REVELATION

In *Israel and Revelation*, the Israelite "leap in being" is understood as constituting a unique people with history as the inner form of their existence (*OH* I, 139, 355, 412). To exist in historical form means that a society consciously acts and takes its bearings in light of a transcendent reality that has been differentiated through the leap in being. History, for Voegelin, is the form of existence in response to this revelation of the transcendent, and it was in Israel that this manner of existence first emerged (xi, 124, 128, 163, 355, 409).

What further distinguished Israel's experience was the suddenness and intensity of this revelation:

> Here was a people that began its existence in history with a radical leap in being; and only after the people had been constituted by this initial experience did it acquire, in the course of centuries, a mundane body of organization to sustain itself in existence. This sequence, reversing the ordinary course of social evolution, is unique in history . . . A society is supposed to start from primitive rites and myths, and thence to advance gradually, if at all, to the spirituality of transcendent religion; it is not supposed to start where a respectable society has difficulties even ending (*OH* I, 315-16; also 240-41, 409).

In Israel we have "a new type of people, formed by God"; "set off from the civilizations of the age by the divine choice," and moving in the historical arena "while living toward a goal beyond history" 112-13). Voegelin emphasizes the constitutive nature of revelation in forming Israel as a society *sui generis*: "When man is in search of God, as in Hellas, the wisdom gained remains generically human; when God is in search of man, as in Israel, the responsive recipient of revelation becomes historically unique" (496). Throughout *Israel and Revelation*, Voegelin speaks freely of Israel's singular status as a people called into being through an act of God (116, 124, 127-29, 139, 163-64, 240-41, 315, 409, 496); at some points challenging other scholars who doubt whether such an event is possible (315-16, 409).

Israel is further differentiated from other societies by the nature of the originating revelation it has received. The Israelite experience of divine reality is distinguished from that of other societies and civilizations (including those, such as Hellas, in which the differentiation of transcendence also occurs) by its immediacy, intensity, and fullness. Indeed, in relationship to the leap of being as it occurred in Hellas, "the two experiences *differ so profoundly in content* that they become articulate in the two different symbolisms of Revelation and Philosophy" (emphasis added) (*OH* II, 1).

Both Israel and Hellas were conscious of their existence as historical; yet at the level of motivating experiences there were significant differences. Israel was the recipient of divine revelation that made the truth of order blazingly apparent and demanded a response. As a result, Israel emerged as a society oriented toward the future—a future in which the transformative possibilities open to itself (and ultimately to all of humanity) lay hidden in the mystery of the gracious and faithful God who intervened in ways that could effect the desired transformation (*OH* II, 51). By contrast, the Hellenic consciousness of history and the discovery of the truth of order, "the unseen measure," is motivated by the experience of a society in crisis. From the perspective of a social order in decline, Aeschylus can teach wisdom through suffering, while in Plato we witness the poignant process of one who, rather than completely abandoning hope for the city, continues, in the *Laws*, to design paradigms for a second, or even third best polis. The "essential difference" between the historical forms that developed in Israel and Hellas is characterized by Voegelin in the following manner:

> The word, the *dabar*, immediately and fully reveals the spiritual order of existence, as well as its origin in transcendent divine being, but leaves it to the prophet to discover the immutability and recalcitrance of the world-immanent structure of being; the philosopher's love of wisdom slowly dissolves the compactness of cosmic order until it becomes the order of world-immanent being beyond which is sensed, *though never revealed*, the unseen transcendent measure (emphasis added) (*OH* I, 52).

Evidently, at the time of the writing of the first three volumes of *Order and History*, Voegelin found the language of reason/revelation to be useful in distinguishing the leaps in being in Israel and Hellas, which, while parallel in time, were the result of different kinds of experiences. Eventually Voegelin would abandon the distinction between natural reason and revelation; but at this point in his philosophical evolution it is important to note that it is a difference *in experiential content* that separates the two symbolizations.

The soteriological dimension of the revelatory experience is also present (although not emphatically) in *Israel and Revelation.* Israel's experience reveals God as "the Creator, the Lord of Justice, and the Savior" (*OH* I, 139). The Mosaic encounter with the divine presence offers the assurance that one "can fulfill a command he feels beyond his human powers" (417). In the prophecy of Deutero-Isaiah the message of God's redeeming mercy and forgiveness is announced to Israel, and Israel, in turn, is to bring this good news to the nations (499-515). In each of these instances we find the transforming graciousness of God as an essential element in the revelation; a graciousness that would seem to have implications for the realm of human action.

That the experience of revelation opens up transformative possibilities for society seems clear from the introduction to *Israel and Revelation.* There Voegelin states that the leap in being is not simply an increase in knowledge concerning the order of being; rather "it is a change in the order itself." The response to the "act of grace" that is revelation changes the very structure of society's participation in being, "with consequences for the order of existence" (11). In describing the effects of the leap in being as they pertain to Israel, Voegelin commented:

> While nothing happens externally when man beholds God and the leap in being occurs in the soul, a good deal happens afterwards in the practice of conduct. The Hebrew clans who concluded the Covenant with God . . . became a new people in history through their response to revelation. They became Israel, in so far as their existence was now ordered as a theopolity under fundamental rules emanating from their God" (424).

What is notable here is how closely interwoven are the response to revelation and the development of ways in which to order social life in a manner that reflects Israel's constitutive identity as a people oriented to God. To the extent that this new people becomes Israel *in so far* as they structure their lives in a way that reflects the divine goodness, it would seem that response to revelation and its social embodiment, while distinct, are inseparable. I emphasize this point because with the development of the theory of consciousness in Voegelin's later work this relationship between leap in being (or differentiation) and social incarnation becomes more tenuous, with implications for his evaluation of Israel's significance.

Having described what for Voegelin are the characteristic features of Israel's experience, it should be noted that even during the time of the writing of *Israel and Revelation*, Voegelin was critical of certain aspects of the Israelite form of existence. His recognition of Israel's importance did not prevent him from expressing reservations about the direction in which Israel developed.

First of all, Voegelin cautions his readers not to exaggerate the consequences of the differentiation that occurred in the midst of this people. The assertion that the leap in being is an actual change in being with consequences for the order of existence is immediately qualified with a warning that the leap is not a leap out of existence, and that the recipients of revelation must "remain adjusted to the order of mundane existence" (*OH* I, 110-11). This warning occurs within a context in which Voegelin makes it clear that we must be careful to distinguish between the area of existence that is affected by differentiation, and "the much larger area which remains relatively unaffected." Differentiation may be an advance in clarity, but it does not replace the previous symbolism. Noting the enduring presence of cosmological symbolization well after differentiation has taken place, Voegelin goes further to argue that differentiation is "not an unqualified good" (xi, 299, 84). That is, as far as the ordering of mundane existence is concerned, there is much that can be retained from the cosmological model of society. To do otherwise would be to accept as practicable the premises of Covenant/prophetic order; premises that are notable precisely for their disregard of the requirements of life in the world. Acceptance of such premises is "impermissible in a critical philosophy of order and history" (300-301).

Another facet of Voegelin's critique has to do with the role of prophecy in Israel. Those familiar with his thought are aware that some of his sharpest criticism is reserved for the prophets. Without engaging in a detailed exposition of his critique (see Anderson, chaps. 1 and 2 of this book), it is relevant to point out that in Voegelin's view, the tensions inherent in the Israelite struggle for order become most clearly problematic in the prophetic movement; particularly in the Isaian notion of metastasis, in which the world as we know it is transfigured, through an act of faith, into a realm of harmonious and peaceful perfection. The unyielding stance of the prophets when confronted with the seemingly reasonable accommodations of Israelite society to the demands of life in the world is especially perplexing to Voegelin in that it seems to violate the common sense required for survival in a world of aggressive empires (*OH* I, 444-47; 451-53). From Voegelin's perspective, the only way to make sense of the prophetic movement is to understand it as a particularly acute manifestation of the gap that exists and will always exist between experiences of true order and the concrete order of society. One must strenuously resist any inclination to take the prophetic prescriptions seriously as practicable in bringing about the creation of a more just social order. The following commentary on Isaiah is a clear expression of Voegelin's attitude toward the prophets:

> The constitution of being is what it is, and cannot be affected by human fancies. Hence, the metastatic denial of the order of mundane existence is neither a true proposition in philosophy, nor a program of action that could be executed. The will to transform reality into something which by essence it is not is the rebellion against the nature of things as ordained by God . . . This metastatic faith, now, though it became articulate in the prophets, did not originate with them but was inherent, from the very beginnings of the Mosaic foundation . . . (453)

If one recalls that, for Voegelin, philosophy is "the love of being through love of divine Being as the source of its order," then the seriousness of Voegelin's indictment of the prophetic effort becomes clear (xiv). To say that the Isaianic faith is not a true proposition in philosophy would imply that the prophet has seriously misjudged the nature of divine being. This interpretation is supported by Voegelin's further statement that such metastatic faith constitutes "rebellion against the nature of things as ordained by God." Of course this raises the question of the source of Voegelin's own knowledge of the nature of things as ordained by God. What is clear, though, is that in Voegelin's view, Isaiah knows neither God nor the intelligibility of the world as authored by God. Instead, one must look to philosophy rather than to the prophetic word for normative guidance in these matters. And for any who would try to separate Voegelin's critique of the prophets from his overall treatment of Israel, Voegelin blocks the way with his claim that metastatic faith was implicit in Israel's development from the very beginning. What is already present in this relatively early formulation of Voegelin's philosophical horizon is the subordination of biblical revelation to philosophy understood in Voegelinian fashion. I will argue that in the development of

Voegelin's thought, this is precisely what occurs. Before doing so, I would note one other area of Voegelin's criticism of Israelite differentiation.

Unlike Hellas, the emergence of the individual, personalized soul as the locus of response to the divine measure never developed in Israel. The notion of *psyche* could develop in Greek culture because the polytheistic character of its religion allowed for the notion of the "soul as a daimon, that is, as a divine being of lower rank" (*OH* I, 235). This also enabled Greek philosophers to handle the issue of immortality more easily than their Israelite counterparts. If the soul was, in some sense, a divine substance, then it could partake in the immortality characteristic of divine beings. It is not difficult to understand why this development was blocked in the Israelite orbit. The radically transcendent nature of God discovered in Israel's experience did not allow for the conception of the soul as daimon; hence the Greek view of the soul as personal and as somehow sharing in divine immortality did not emerge in the Israelite context:

> The idea of the psyche . . . could not be fully developed in Israel because the problem of immortality remained unsolved. Life eternal was understood as a divine property; afterlife would have elevated man to the rank of the Elohim; and a plurality of elohim was excluded by the radical leap in being of the Mosaic experience. As a consequence, the eroticism of the soul that is the essence of philosophy could not unfold; and the idea of human perfection could not break the idea of a Chosen People in righteous existence under God in history (327).

As in the case of his criticism of prophetic metastasis, Voegelin views the absence of the notion of a personal soul as stemming from the very nature of Israel's experience. Nor is this absence insignificant; Voegelin maintains that without the idea of the soul the prophetic movement was unable to break through to philosophy. It is also the case that he understands this to be a definite handicap (439, 446).

It appears, then, that there is already present in *Israel and Revelation* a tendency on Voegelin's part to criticize the Israelite leap in being from the perspective of philosophy, a philosophy whose basic terms are taken from the Greeks. At the same time, there is much in *Israel and Revelation* that highlights the singular character of Israel's experience and its expression. What seems clear is that Israel's leap in being, however glorious, contains within itself disruptive, destabilizing tendencies that prevent it from serving as a model in the quest to strike a balance between the truth of order and life in the world. Instead, Voegelin turns to philosophy in addressing this perennial problem. The outline of a philosophical critique of the Israelite solution to the problem of order is already present in *Israel and Revelation*. With the emergence of Voegelin's mature philosophy of history and consciousness, the effect of this critique on his understanding of Israel would come more clearly into view.

## The Changing Dimensions of Voegelin's Thought

Commentators on Voegelin's work generally agree that a change occurs in his thinking sometime between the publication of the first three volumes of *Order and History* and the fourth volume, *The Ecumenic Age*. There has been a good deal of discussion concerning the nature of this development; some seeing in it a radical break with Voegelin's previous philosophy while others (including myself) would see in his later thought a drawing out of what was already implicit in his earlier work (Corrington 1987; Douglass 1977; Sandoz 1981; Ranieri 1995, 34-45). The precise dating of the shift is difficult to pinpoint; for my purposes here I would simply note that "History and Gnosis" (1963), in its treatment of Israel, still operates within the horizon of *Israel and Revelation. Anamnesis* (1966) marks a significant advance in Voegelin's philosophy of consciousness. By 1970, in a discussion eventually published (*CEV,* 104-5), the distinction between reason and revelation has been rejected. However one evaluates this shift, there are several important features of this development that bear on his assessment of Israel.

In the work that follows the early volumes of *Order and History*, the notion of a leap in being gives way to the terminology of "differentiation of consciousness." The change is important; for the evolution of Voegelin's theory of consciousness was accompanied, and in some sense, inspired by his attempts to delineate those areas of reality that had been affected by what he had previously referred to as a leap in being. In *The Ecumenic Age*, the fourth volume of *Order and History*, Voegelin carefully delimits the effects of the prophetic and philosophic insights by emphasizing that they "pertain directly only to man's consciousness of his existential tension." If the reader was still in doubt as to what this means, Voegelin offers the following clarification:

> I have circumscribed the structure of the event as strictly as possible, in order to make it clear how narrowly confined the area

of the resulting insights actually is: The new truth pertains to man's consciousness of his humanity in participatory tension toward the divine ground, and to no reality beyond this restricted area (*OH* IV, 8).

John Corrington (1987, 159) remarks on the change that has taken place in Voegelin's approach:

> In the earlier volumes there is no sharp distinction between the pneumatic or noetic insights and the context in which they appear. The manifold of existential reality was taken to be invaded from the divine ground by the new insights . . . What was not present in the previous volumes was the kind of language that required the reader to understand that the subject of *Order and History* was, indeed, the history of order as it emerged in human consciousness—and nothing else.

The leap in being described in *Israel and Revelation*, with its radical consequences for the order of existence, has become a differentiation of consciousness that illuminates human existence in its tension toward the divine ground.

Another significant factor affecting the direction of Voegelin's later philosophy was his realization that his earlier view of the emergence of order and its symbolization as a sequential series of advancing differentiations is not adequate in accounting for the manifold of historical data. To be sure, it is still possible to speak of an advance in differentiation; but there is now a recognition that differentiations are no longer able to be arranged neatly on a time line. Historical intelligibility is far more complicated and refractory than Voegelin had previously imagined, with similar lines of meaning and symbolizations appearing in cultures widely separated by geography and time. This insight led Voegelin to revise some of his earlier views on the nature of history. A notable example of revision is Voegelin's abandonment of the idea that "the conception of history as a meaningful course of events on a straight line of time was the great achievement of Israelites and Christians who were favored in its creation by the revelatory events, while the pagans, deprived as they were of revelation, could never rise above the conception of a cyclical time" (*OH* IV, 7). From his study of the historical materials, it became increasingly clear to Voegelin that the "unilinear construction of history, from a divine-cosmic origin of order to the author's present," had its origins in the empires of the Ancient Near East, well before the advent of the Israelites.

Concomitant with this new understanding of the process of history/ differentiation was a focus on "equivalences of experience." To speak of equivalences is to recognize that while symbols may differ, they may exhibit a notable sameness at the level of the experience they aim to express. For Voegelin, this meant that "not the symbols themselves but the constants of engendering experience are the true subject matter of our studies" (EESH, 115). The theory of equivalences fit nicely into Voegelin's evolving philosophical perspective. With the realization that the intelligible lines of historical order are no longer to be understood primarily in terms of a single, unfolding, process of advancing differentiation, the intelligibility of order is discovered to lie at a level of experiences and symbolization that cuts across historical epochs. Thus, in his later work, Voegelin concentrates on the common configurations and broad structures of humanity's quest for order; the emphasis is now on the commonality of experience, rather than on what is distinctive. In this context, differentiation becomes a matter of greater or lesser clarity and/or balance within the consciousness of experiences that are essentially equivalent.

Another consequence of this evolution in Voegelin's thought is his eventual rejection of the distinction between natural reason and revelation. Given the focus in his later work on equivalences of experience, this is hardly surprising. The notion of equivalence underlines the commonalty of experience among diverse cultures. The symbolic expressions by which these experiences are rendered may differ from society to society and culture to culture, but it is the shared structure of experience that is highlighted. With the differentiation of consciousness one can gain *greater clarity concerning the structure* of these experiences, but on the level of experience itself there is little difference between the experience of an Isaiah and a Plato:

> In Christian theology there is the encrusted conception that revelation is revelation and that classic philosophy is the natural reason of mankind unaided by revelation. That is simply not true empirically. Plato was perfectly clear that what he is doing in the form of a myth is a revelation. He does not invent it by natural reason; the God speaks. The God speaks, just as in the prophet or in Jesus. So the whole conception which is still prevalent today, not only in theological thinking but penetrating our civilization: "on the one hand we have natural reason and on the other hand revelation," is empirically nonsense. It just isn't so (*CEV*, 104-5; GC, 187-88).

For Voegelin the realities referred to by the terms "natural reason" and "supernatural revelation" both fall within what he would understand as experience. To distinguish the two is to fracture the divine and human movements that merge in the "in-between" character of human existence. He goes so far as to state that "there is no such thing as either natural reason or revelation," and attributes the emergence and perdurance of the distinction to an attempt by the Judeo-Christian tradition (as the possessors of revelation) to have its form of the quest for truth take precedence over others (MOPKO, 44).

Before discussing how these developments in Voegelin's philosophy might impinge upon his evaluation of Israel, there is one further tendency in his later philosophy that should be noted. Although already present to some degree in his criticisms in *Israel and Revelation* of the Israelite leap in being, in the later work we find an increasing contrast between the balance characteristic of the noetic differentiation of consciousness (as well as its less differentiated pre-Socratic predecessors) and the unstable, potentially dangerous quality of the pneumatic differentiation. Unlike the prophetic enterprise, "the epochal consciousness of the classic philosophers did not derail into apocalyptic expectations of a final realm to come." In contrast to the prophets, the philosophers "preserve the balance between the experienced lastingness [of the cosmos] and the theophanic events in such a manner that the paradox becomes intelligible as the very structure of existence itself." While Plato was aware of a God beyond the Nous, he declined to elaborate it so as to avoid disturbing the balance of consciousness (*AE*, 90; *OH* IV, 228, 232).

The noetic differentiation exceeds the pneumatic not only in balance but in clarity. Thus, when one wishes to articulate something of the structure and movement of reality, it is to noetic thinkers that one must turn for the appropriate language. Voegelin continued to acknowledge that the pneumatic differentiation surpassed the noetic in terms of expressing the eschatological movement of reality toward the "God beyond the gods." At the same time, Voegelin was quite insistent that the noetic differentiation, if less intense than the pneumatic, is equally theophanic in character. Any claims to superiority based upon the intensity of pneumatic vision, however, are more than offset by the noetic achievement in discovering a suitable language with which to speak of existence in the metaxy. The noetic differentiation is both theophanic in nature and better able to express the divine/human movements and countermovements within reality. Similar to the pneumatic differentiation in its revelation, superior in the precision and clarity of its language, is it any wonder that Voegelin sees the noetic differentiation as taking precedence over the pneumatic in judging and implementing the truth of order? (*AE*, 89-115; *OH* IV, 212-38)

## ISRAEL IN THE LATER THOUGHT

At this point the question to be addressed is whether these developments in Voegelin's thought have any implications for his evaluation of the significance of Israel. It may be helpful to recall briefly Voegelin's views concerning Israel at the time of the writing of *Israel and Revelation*. As noted earlier, Voegelin understood Israel's experience as: (1) constituting a singular people with history as the inner form of their existence; (2) involving a powerful and radical revelation that makes them "historically unique," in contrast to Hellas, where wisdom remains "generically human"; (3) differing so profoundly from Hellas at the level of *content of experience* that the symbolisms of Revelation and Philosophy arise in order to express the essential difference; (4) opening up transformative possibilities for society; (5) soteriological in nature.

It would seem that this earlier view of Israel would be seriously affected by the changes in emphasis that characterize Voegelin's later philosophy. There is in the later work an often implicit, but sometimes explicit, ongoing critique of the Israelite attempt to mediate the tension between divine and human order; a critique that assumes three basic forms. There is, first of all, the absorption of revelation into the noetic differentiation and the consequent abandonment of the reason/revelation distinction. Given Voegelin's earlier understanding of Israel, this would certainly pose a challenge to the previously espoused view of Israel as uniquely constituted by revelation. For if the noetic differentiation is also revelatory, if Plato is just as conscious of revelation as Isaiah, then what becomes of Voegelin's original position that it was revelation that made Israel a people different from all others?

Another form of criticism becomes apparent in Voegelin's insistence on the superior balance to be found in both pre-Socratic and noetically differentiated Greek thinkers. In Anaximander we have a thinker operating within a relatively compact, undifferentiated horizon yet acutely aware of the limits of human striving, while with Plato we have an instance of someone who, by careful use of language, moderates the intensity of revelation in order to protect the balance of consciousness. The wisdom of these philosophers is extolled for having understood human finitude and the boundaries set to human achievement by the structure of reality. By contrast, the dynamism set in motion through Israel's experience must be approached cautiously, with an awareness that no exodus is ever an exodus from the pragmatic constraints that govern life in this world (*OH* IV, 212-16). If one accepts this view, as well as the previously discussed idea that revelation is not peculiar to Israel, then one is confronted with a serious question as to what, if anything, has been gained by Israel's radical leap in being. The observation offered in *Israel and Revelation* that differentiation is "not an unqualified good" when compared to the orderliness emphasized in cosmological symbolization, has developed, in *The Ecumenic Age*, into the overarching principle of the "balance of consciousness" by which all orders are to be judged. In one sense, there is nothing here that was not previously mentioned in *Israel and Revelation*. After all, in the preface to that volume Voegelin had already identified metastatic faith and its attendant destabilizing tendencies as one of the greatest (if not *the* greatest) sources of disorder in the contemporary world. What emerges in his later thought is the development of a philosophy of history and consciousness designed to address the problems of order caused by pneumatic excess. When the principles of this later philosophy are conscientiously applied, Israel does not fare very well.

This leads to a third form of Voegelin's critique that might be appropriately described as "benign neglect" with regard to Israel. It is benign in that there is no overt repudiation of his earlier views, but it is nevertheless neglect, insofar as references to Israel in the later work are few. It is no exaggeration to say that Anaximander, Hesiod, Plato, and Aristotle are the real heroes of *The Ecumenic Age* and *In Search of Order*.[1] This becomes clear in a further benign, yet implicitly critical aspect of Voegelin's treatment of Israel in his later writings—the tendency toward a greater and greater approximation of Israelite experience to a philosophical analysis whose language is largely derived from Greek sources. References to Israel in *The Ecumenic Age* and the writings that follow, when not critical of Israelite tendencies toward imbalance, seem to have been passed through the prism of Voegelin's mature theory of consciousness. As a result, we are left with an Israelite experience that bears little resemblance to the one recognized by Jews and Christians or even to Voegelin's own earlier account in *Israel and Revelation*.

Two examples may illustrate the point. The spiritualization of the Exodus found in *The Ecumenic Age* has already been noted. The pragmatic exodus of Israel from slavery comes to be understood as the backdrop for the more important exodus that takes place at the level of consciousness.[2] An equally striking instance is Voegelin's treatment of the creation account(s) of Genesis in *In Search of Order*. After noting that "theological conceptions of 'revelation' would be of little help" in answering questions concerning the character of the divine word, the identity of those to whom this word is addressed, or the nature of the God who calls, Voegelin argues that the authors of Genesis were attempting to express "the experience and structure of what I have called the It-reality" (*OH* V, 19). In Voegelin's thought, the It-reality refers to the encompassing, dynamic process/whole "that comprehends the partners in being, i.e., God and the world . . ." (16). The biblical writers, then, were trying to describe the tensions of human participation within this encompassing whole, to give an account of existence in the *metaxy* of consciousness. As is characteristic of the later Voegelin, the emphasis here is on the overall structure of reality as a whole, within which there are greater and lesser degrees of differentiation of consciousness. The gracious God who initiates the history of redemption in a free act of creation is scarcely in evidence.

Applying the language of equivalences, the reader is reminded that the language of Genesis is simply a variation on the common experience of participation most clearly articulated in the achievement of the philosophers; for all languages "symbolize the same structures of consciousness which, in a more differentiated mode, are symbolized in the philosophers' quest for truth." In differentiating, within the It-reality, an evocative, spiritually dynamic word and a corresponding formless waste to be formed, Genesis represents a notable advance from compactness to differentiation. Understanding the importance of Genesis in this fashion, one can better appreciate "the equivalences between the symbolization of the Beginning in Genesis and its symbolization as the imposition of form on a formless *chora* in Plato's *Timaeus*" (*OH* V, 23). It would appear that there has been a significant change from the earlier volumes of *Order and History*. The essential difference in content of experience, requiring the distinct symbolizations of Revelation and Philosophy, has given way to the recognition of the essential sameness of experience, differentiated according to varying degrees of clarity. But if this is so, what becomes of Voegelin's earlier understanding of Israel?

Voegelin never attempted to return to *Israel and Revelation* and revise his evaluation of Israel systematically in light of later developments in his thought. There are a few places in the later writings, however, where he does mention Israel directly, and these instances reveal a substantial movement away from his previous understanding.

In the section of the introduction to *The Ecumenic Age*, entitled "The Balance Lost—Gnosticism," Voegelin discusses the Israelite experience in terms of the effects and motivation behind the contraction of divine order into personal existence. This contraction is a disturbance of consciousness involving an ever increasing loss of balance with regard to the structure of reality; a disturbance that has become "most clearly articulate in the Israelite-Judaic case . . . as a series of even more radical variations on the theme of Exodus." What follows in Voegelin's analysis is a brief account of the evolution of this distortion from the Exodus through prophetic metastasis and apocalyptic, to its final culmination in gnosticism. Looking back on the history of these deformations of consciousness, Voegelin concludes that "the revelatory experience of the Israelite type becomes visible as an independent cause of imbalance." While this observation could easily have been taken from the preface to *Israel and Revelation*, there is also something new. To speak of the "revelatory experience of the Israelite type" is to acknowledge that there are other variations of revelatory experience; revelation cannot be considered the hallmark of Israel alone. The revelation to Israel has become one variant among others; and it may be the case that there are other types of revelatory experiences that avoid the unfortunate imbalance inherent in the experience of Israel. In Voegelin's view, this is indeed the case, for the Israelite dilemma "can be historically understood as a consequence of pneumatic differentiation in a tribal society, *wanting in noetic differentiation and conceptual distinctions*"(italics mine) (*OH* IV, 26-27). The roots of Israel's problem can be traced back to its being a tribal society lacking in noetic differentiation. The Israel described in *Israel and Revelation*, whose singular experience of revelation constituted it as one of the two great sources of western civilization, has virtually disappeared from view. In its place we have an Israel whose communal social structure and lack of philosophical vocabulary distort the revelatory experience, and whose chief legacy to the world would seem to be one of the chief breeding grounds for gnosticism.

This interpretation is further reinforced in Voegelin's 1981 essay, "The Meditative Origin of the Philosophical Knowledge of Order." Here, Israel is discussed in the context of a criticism of the distinction between natural reason and revelation. Voegelin argues that this distinction is the result of a misconstruction of the historical unfolding of symbolization in Israelite and Hellenic cultures. A more accurate account would recognize that:

On the one hand we have a so-called philosophical development that, prescinding from the fact that it is philosophical, is also an ethnic development; that is to say, an occurrence that took place within Hellenic culture. It is an ethnically Hellenic cultural event, which has to be understood in its connections, pre-conditions, and results. On the other hand, there is the so-called revelatory culture, which goes back to Israel and the movement of Judaism, which then had its culmination in Christ. Here we have an ethnically Israelite culture. Thus, we have to do with the categories of two ethnic cultures, each of which is concerned with the quest for truth, but in quite different forms.

What distinguishes Israel and Hellas are ethnic differences within a common quest for truth, where "ethnic" is understood as having to do with the particular cultural forms inherited and developed by the society in question. In both cases we are dealing with revelatory cultures; but due to particular cultural factors, the Greek accent "always falls on the search, on the *zetesis*." In an Israelite context, the emphasis is different:

> Here a prophet has express recourse to forms of revelation with a Babylonian and Egyptian provenance. When Jeremiah narrates his experience of revelation, he narrates it in a form that an Egyptian Pharoah would use to tell how he was preborn of God for his office and so on . . . An imperial context of truth is present here, then, and not a scientific-philological investigation concerning the false use of terms which now have to be corrected. In a revelational context of the kind presented in the Israelite-Christian culture, there is always recourse to the divine spirit . . . This spirit—which is the reason why I name the accent on revelation "pneumatic"—ethnically determines the problem of a Christianity that grows out of the Jewish-Israelite contexts. Of course, the word "pneuma" comes up in the Greek context as well. Anaximenes has a "pneuma" theory very similar to that of the Book of Genesis; but in this case it is not a matter of a dominant theory. The dominant theory will be the noetic *zetesis*, the search (MOPKO, 44-46).

To explain the difference between Israel and Hellas in terms of ethnic/cultural characteristics seems to beg the question as to *why* these societies differ at the level of culture. One can readily agree that the Hebrews and the Greeks made use of the cultural and linguistic forms available to them to express their differentiating experiences. At the same time, one must never lose sight of the fact that it is the differentiating experience that, in some sense, forms or constitutes culture. Cultural differences have their origins, to a significant degree, in the experiences that engender them. Cultural form and engendering experience are intimately intertwined. This certainly was Voegelin's view at the time he wrote *Israel and Revelation*. However, the tendency in his later thought to focus on differentiation as differentiation of consciousness has, I believe, led to a movement away from this recognition of an integral connection between experience and cultural form. There is a certain degree of dualism in Voegelin's philosophy, which became more pronounced as his thought evolved (Ranieri 1995, 124-25, 130-35, 188-89, 232-35). The model operative in "Meditative Origins" is that of a common stream of experience clothed in various ethno-cultural forms, with cultures acting like prisms refracting the experience in varying guises. The same approach is evident in *The Ecumenic Age*, where Israel's singularity is said to stem from the salutary coincidence of finding "a suitable ethnic carrier for a spiritual outburst" prior to the rise of ecumenic empires (*OH* IV, 149-50). Israel is unique, not because of the qualitatively distinct nature of the revelation it has received, but because differentiating consciousness has found a proper pragmatic shell in this people escaping from bondage.

While this explanation of the distinctiveness of Israel and Hellas in terms of ethnic difference may be Voegelin's final view of the matter, it does not seem adequate in accounting for some of the peculiar strengths and weaknesses he detects in the Israelite and Greek differentiations. An emphasis on *zetesis* may very well be a characteristic ethnic feature of Greek society, but we are still left with the question as to *why* this is the case. Why is the quest emphasized in Hellas? Why did revelation not lead to destabilizing tendencies toward imbalance in Greek society? What was it about the quality of Israelite experience that did lead in this direction? Why do the Israelite prophets refuse to be reconciled to what most societies would view as a perhaps unfortunate but nevertheless acceptable level of injustice? The truly important differences between Israel and Hellas are not accounted for by attributing them to ethnic differences. The metastatic problem that mars the Israelite struggle for order is not explained by saying that, in this case, revelatory experience has been expressed in language/ cultural forms borrowed from Egypt and Mesopotamia. If what distinguishes Israel from Hellas is that the experience of revelation is expressed in language conditioned by an "imperial context of truth," and if it is also the case that metastasis is a phenomenon found in Israel but not in Hellas, then it would seem that the occurrence of metastasis is somehow linked to the imperial context of truth. We would expect, then, to find evidence of metastasis wherever an imperial context is found. But such is not the case at all. Metastasis is not found in Mesopotamia or Egypt; it is a distinctly Israelite phenomenon. If one were to argue instead that it is not the imperial context of truth, but revelation that is the source of metastasis, then one must explain why this deformation of consciousness emerged in Israel but not in the revelatory culture of Hellas. And if we go on to say that the explanation is to be found in the imperial context of truth, then we have come full circle in search of an explanation. The language of ethnic differences may help in explaining some of the peculiarities of expression and symbolization that mark Greek and Israelite society, but it is inadequate in explaining the fundamentally distinct horizons of Israel and Hellas. Perhaps Voegelin's insight in the second volume of *Order and History* was correct after all: "The two experiences differ so profoundly in content that they become articulate in the two different symbolisms of Revelation and Philosophy" (*OH* II, 10).

Far from accounting for the dissimilarity between Hebrew and Hellenic society, the notion of ethnic differences would appear to be rather a *consequence* of a far more profound difference at the level of experience. However, the emphasis in Voegelin's later work on equivalences of experience, and the corresponding rejection of the natural reason/revelation distinction, prevent him from adequately articulating these differences at the level of experience. As a result, he no longer considers that the reason why Israel developed differently from Hellas may have to do with the fact that there was something qualitatively different about its experience of revelation. Perhaps the intensity of the Mosaic encounter and the uncompromising character of the prophetic critique is due to there being something present in the Israelite experience which was *not* present in that of Hellas. Instead of dismissing the natural/supernatural distinction as an attempt to show the superiority of biblical faith, Voegelin might have considered more carefully that the reason for the distinction may be found in the effort of post-biblical philosophers and theologians to recognize in the experience of Israel a dimension of the encountered mystery that is disproportionate to, yet continuous with, the human capacity for ongoing conversion and, at the same time, capable of effecting the desired transformation. In reacting viscerally to the dangers of metastasis, Voegelin became less capable of appreciating that which was unique in the life of Israel.

## Consequences and Possible Implications

It appears that Israel has been effectively tamed. Nor is this a peripheral matter in Voegelin's philosophy. There is a sense in which the very logic of Voegelin's thought pushes him in this direction. As a clear instance of the tension between the transcendent truth of order and its social implementation, the experience of Israel focuses the issue that is at the heart of Voegelin's enterprise. For Voegelin, Israel's response to this tension is, for the most part, unrealistic, and in some ways positively dangerous. Thus, while the possibilities suggested by the Israelite "solution" to the tension of existence are to be rejected, the tension cannot be ignored; especially if one is attempting to formulate a philosophy of order. In a sense, this is the key to understanding Voegelin's interpretation of Israel. His is a philosophy of order, and Israel, from his perspective, was a society whose response to transcendent mystery tended to undermine the balance needed to sustain order in the world. As Voegelin's entire philosophy is an attempt to strike the proper balance between transcendent order and pragmatic existence, it is no exaggeration to say that the problem at the heart of Voegelin's philosophy is the problem of what to do with Israel.

In responding to this problem Voegelin develops a highly original theory of consciousness; one, however, that draws upon Greek wisdom for its fundamental language. More specifically, in addressing the difficulty of incarnating the truth of order in society, Voegelin's approach is essentially Platonic in inspiration. Like the Plato of *The Republic* and *The Laws*, what matters is the proper ordering of one's soul in light of the divine measure. Truly philosophical persons may be pained, evenly deeply pained, by the failure of society to embody the truth of order; but they must adapt their expectations to the limitations of human nature, serene in the confidence that they, the lovers of wisdom, live in accordance with the pattern of the city laid up in heaven. This was not the solution of the Hebrew Bible, for whom human nature itself was something to be transcended through the loving action of God. Because this biblical faith could not fit comfortably within a Platonically inspired approach to the problem of order, the Israelite solution had to be either explicitly rejected, effectively ignored, or somehow approximated to the more adequate noetic account. This is precisely what happens in the evolution of Voegelin's thought.

As a consequence, an appreciation for the particular genius of Israel virtually disappears from Voegelin's later writings. One is forced to ask whether the philosophical framework employed by Voegelin in his later work is capable of doing justice to biblical experience. When the idea of a singular revelation constituting a new kind of society (rather than a differentiation of consciousness in search of a pragmatic carrier) is abandoned, it seems that the meaning of Israel has been lost. It would be hard to reconcile Voegelin's later views on Israel with what many biblical scholars would see as part of Israel's essential identity, or even with Voegelin's own position in *Israel and Revelation*. For Paul Hanson

> There was . . . an organic connection between the exodus event and the communal structures that were true to Israel's origins in God's gracious act of deliverance. That connection . . . demanded a quality of life relating inextricably to systems of justice, land distribution, use of capital, treatment of vulnerable classes within society, and the like. These institutions are not formal accidents, but essential structures already implicit in the nature of the God revealed in the exodus (Hanson 1986, 23).

Along these same lines Walter Brueggemann has written:

> The appearance of a new social reality is unprecedented. Israel in the thirteenth century is indeed ex nihilo. And that new social reality drives us to the category of revelation. Israel can only be understood in terms of the new call of God and his assertion of an alternative social reality. Prophecy is born precisely in that moment when the emergence of social political reality is so radical and inexplicable that it has nothing less than a theological cause (Brueggemann 1978, 16).

Both authors, in addition to underlining the integral connection between revelation and social incarnation, also bring out the concern for social justice that animates so much of the Hebrew Bible. Voegelin's analysis of Israel is particularly weak in this regard; any hints in *Israel and Revelation* concerning the social implications of revelation are completely absent from the later work. The cautionary reminder in *The Ecumenic Age* that the differentiating truth pertains to consciousness "and to no reality beyond this restricted area" has been rigorously applied in the case of Israel.

A related consequence of Voegelin's "noeticization" of Israel is a lack of attention to the soteriological dimension in this people's experience. Biblical salvation is not the same as philosophical illumination; and there is more than a verbal difference between Platonic "vision" and prophetic "hearkening." The language of sin, faith, repentance, and grace is scarcely present in Voegelin's later work; nor do we find much appreciation for the dialogical and personal relationship between the biblical God and his people. Bruce Douglass, commenting on Voegelin's treatment of Christianity, offers insights that are just as easily extended to Israel. Noting that what is missing from Voegelin's interpretation is "a sense of the Gospel as salvation," he adds further:

> What is principally at issue . . . is the notion that God is actively present in the world, transforming it in anticipation of the consummation of His kingdom. This idea . . . is problematic for Voegelin because of its vulnerability to Gnostic corruption. His answer to the problem is, if not to eliminate the idea altogether, to transform its meaning beyond recognition. In place of the biblical image of a God whose presence and purposes in history are made manifest we are given a divine flux whose direction is a mystery (Douglass 1987, 146, 149; see Kroeker 1993).

Finally, Robert Doran observes how Voegelin consistently misjudges the role of Israelite symbols. Rather than displacing the tension of existence between transcendent and mundane orders, "The genuine anagogic symbol serves not to displace the tension of consciousness . . . but, *precisely as symbol*, to heighten the tension and release the psyche for cooperation with the divinely originated solution to the mystery of evil" (Doran 1990, 272-73).

If these insights are accurate, then the implications of Voegelin's interpretation of Israel extend well beyond an analysis of this particular society. Rather, they raise the serious question as to whether Voegelin's philosophy can serve as an adequate foundation for a philosophical/theological method within the Jewish or Christian tradition. This has become a matter of some debate among Voegelin scholars;[3] my own view would be that while Voegelin's method can be useful in certain areas affecting theology (e. g., his avoidance of subject/object language when speaking of God, his nuanced analysis of religious experience, his careful analysis of compact and differentiated symbolisms), it remains a bit too Platonic in orientation to serve as the basis for a fundamental theology that takes seriously the "scandal of particularity" that is so much a part of the biblical tradition. Without necessarily asserting any superiority, it seems that the claims made by Jews and Christians concerning the singular status of Israel's revelation go beyond what Voegelin is willing to accept; just as his philosophical rendering of Israel's experience falls short of what believers would affirm about this people and its historical/theological importance.

Recently John Caputo (1993) has written of the need to demythologize Heidegger. This involves a critique of Heidegger's tendency to accord a privileged position to a primordial Greek beginning with its corresponding myth of Being. The positive countermovement to such a critique would entail a recovery of the biblical horizon and its myth of Justice. Caputo believes this critique/recovery can be accomplished with Heidegger's thought in a way that preserves his greatest contributions to philosophy, while simultaneously avoiding the mythologizing tendencies that contributed to his embrace of National Socialism. Of course there are important differences between Heidegger and Voegelin in these areas. Most obviously, Voegelin never succumbed to the illusions of National Socialism; in fact his philosophical orientation led him away from the movement rather than toward it, as in the case of Heidegger. In addition, despite his profound admiration for the Greeks and a tendency to look to Plato when considering problems of order, Voegelin remained far more sensitive to the truth of order as manifest in various cultures throughout history. As a result, there is no "freezing" of any historical epoch in Voegelin's thought, and the myth of a Greek beginning never assumed as dominant a place in his work as it did in that of Heidegger. Nonetheless, perhaps the time has come for a demythologization of Voegelin as well. For Voegelin has allowed the biblical voice to become muffled, and in so doing he may have overlooked what is unique in the voice of the biblical writings—that the "kingdom of God" is "a kingdom of flesh, of banquets and of hunger, of cripples made whole, dead men made to live again, a realm of bodies in pleasure and pain, of flesh and blood" (65). Certainly, if the good society envisioned by Voegelin is to come into existence, this voice must be heard as well; the luminous vision of a Plato must be complemented by the prophetic witness of Israel. This may mean "disrupting the myth of Being with the myth of Justice, of disturbing the power, glory, and prestige of Being with the poverty, invisibility, and humility of justice" (3). Far from doing violence to Voegelin's thought, such a critique would be very much in keeping with his lifelong commitment to personal and social authenticity.

## NOTES

[1]The index to *The Ecumenic Age* contains a combined total of 61 references to Anaximander, Hesiod, Plato, and Aristotle. By contrast, there is 1 reference to Jeremiah, 2 to Isaiah, 7 to Moses, and 4 to Deutero-Isaiah. There are 9 references to the Book of Daniel, 6 of which are critical of the metastatic tendencies of apocalyptic thought. In *OH* 5, the absence of Israel is even more apparent: 25 references to Hesiod, Plato, and Aristotle; 1 reference to Isaiah, 1 to Deutero-Isaiah, and 4 to Genesis.

[2]See Ranieri 1995, chap. 7, for a more extended discussion of this tendency in Voegelin's later thought.

[3]For widely diverging interpretations concerning the appropriateness of Voegelin's method for Christian theology consult Morrissey 1994 or Wilhelmsen 1975, 32-35; 1978, 193-208.

# CHRIST AND CHRISTIANITY IN
## *Israel and Revelation*
# William M. Thompson

## A PRÉCIS OF THE TEXTS

In the presiding introduction, "The Symbolization of Order," Christianity emerges with the breakdown of the "cosmologically symbolized empires." With the philosophers and other religious sages throughout the world, it helps along a movement toward symbolizing the order of society as a "macroanthropos." The soul that experiences and understands itself as in attunement to the unseen divine being gains a new awareness of itself as a reality in movement toward the divine. This, then, "becomes the model of order that will furnish symbols for ordering society analogically in its image" (*IR*, 6). The world-transcendent God is experienced "in its absolute transcendence" (9) in Israel and Christianity. And there are varying manifestations of macroanthropic symbolization among the Greek thinkers and the religions (see *OH* IV). As the "gulf" between divine and mundane is emphatically sensed, we have a decisive "leap upward in being" which brings about "a change in being" even if not "a leap out of existence." Tensions and frictions between the newly differentiated *civitas Dei* and "being in mundane existence" inevitably emerge (10-11). An early tolerance for differing symbolizations of order becomes increasingly troubled and is finally replaced by intolerance as earlier symbolizations are found to be inadequate "to their purpose of making the true order of being transparent" (7-9). Eventually, however, some sort of compromise and new tolerance emerges, as there develops "a respect for the tortuous ways on which man moves historically closer to the true order of being." In the Christian sphere, besides the friction there can also be balance. In Hellas, there is the old but tolerant Plato of the *Laws* (11).

## PART ONE

While only two references to our theme explicitly surface in Part One, "The Cosmological Order of the Ancient Near East," still

Voegelin's imagination poignantly captures something of the novelty of the Incarnation of Christ by way of a contrast, which his exploration of the cosmological symbolism provides. In reference to the Egyptian order, he suggests that we can "get an inkling of the scandal which Christianity must have been for men emerging from cosmological civilizations, if we consider that not a king [as in Egypt] was the god incarnate but an ordinary man of low social status who represented nobody but nevertheless was claimed by his followers to be the representative mediator and sufferer for mankind" (*IR*, 74). Similarly, one can grant some truth to the notion that the "word of Ptah" which "creates the world" is similar to the Logos of the Prologue of the Gospel of John, provided one does so on a scale moving from compactness to differentiation. The symbolism of Ptah remains only compact, while the Johannine Logos represents "an experiential break with the cosmological form and an opening of the soul toward transcendence." If you want, the "Logos of the Memphite Theology created a world that was consubstantial with Egypt; but the Logos of John created a world with a mankind immediate under God" (94-95).

## Part Two

Explicit references to our theme surface rather regularly throughout Part Two, "The Historical Order of Israel," numbering some nine in all (*IR*, 114, 130-32, 133, 139, 144, 163, 167, 173-74, 182-83). Some attention is given to the continuity between Israel and Christianity. For example, Israel's articulation of God as Creator, Lord of Justice, and Savior remains fundamental for Christianity as well (139). Likewise, then, its articulation of the "idea of History" is the origin of our own modern vocabulary (163). Along these lines, Matthew's use of the *Toldoth* symbolism in 1:2-16 (*biblos geneseos*) manifests how the "great problem of the periodization of history" is an issue shared by both Israel and Christianity, as well as modernity (173-74).

The overwhelming sense one gains from this part, however, is that while Israel "noticeably began" the differentiation between the transcendent and the mundane, still, it was "never quite achieved." Christianity would later differentiate these into "sacred and profane history, into Church and State" (*IR*, 180). Was this later Christian differentiation a fully adequate achievement? At this point in *IR* Voegelin does not clearly say. The clearest stress seems to fall upon Israel's incomplete differentiation, at least in those passages where it is a matter of comparing it with Christianity. Page 144 (see anthology) is a particularly forceful and clearly contentious statement of the issue.

In terms of contemporary Jewish and Christian relations, this page is possibly the most quarrelsome of the entire book, for it argues that, in terms of achieving the differentiation in question in such a way that the transcendent in its proper universality is articulated and so freed from territorial and ethnic restrictions, Israel in its "branch of Talmudic Judaism" was the unsuccessful and Christianity the apparently successful "Jewish movement." This would seem to be what Voegelin means by the "historical revenge" of the *am-ha-aretz* through Jesus and Christianity. The former had been "excommunicated" by the returning Jewish exiles (cf. Ezr 4:1-4), and now, in Christianity, they have found themselves included (167).

Let us return to the question of how successful was Christianity. We come upon a fascinating passage in which Voegelin argues that the problem of the early Christians was exactly the "inverse" of the "Israelite difficulty" with regard to coming to an understanding of the "exigencies of world-immanent social and political order" in the light of the differentiation of the world-transcendent God. "In Christianity the *logia* of Jesus, and especially the Sermon on the Mount, had effectively disengaged the meaning of faith, as well as of the life of the spirit, from the conditions of a particular civilizational order. The separation was so effective indeed that loss of understanding for the importance of civilizational order was a serious danger to many Christians." Here we are at the Augustinian *saeculum senescens* theme (Augustine is mentioned, along with St. Paul, as struggling for a right understanding of the matter here in this passage), which Voegelin will more explicitly emphasize elsewhere (*NSP*, 109; *OH*, III, 156; IV, 268).[1]

Voegelin's point is that Christianity's greater differentiation could be "no substitute for organized government," while the prophets had to make it clear that Israel's political success "was no substitute for a life in obedience to divine instructions." The manner in which Voegelin concludes this issue is haunting, given current discussions about political and liberation theologies. "The Prophets had to explain that social success was not a proof of righteousness before God; the Christian thinkers had to explain that the Gospel was no social gospel, redemption no social remedy, and Christianity in general no insurance for individual or collective prosperity." In the light of the earlier statement, Voegelin does not seem to mean that Christianity can be purely apolitical. Rather, we need balances "between life of the spirit and life in the world." These "balances . . . work for a while," but eventually the finiteness of such arrangements leads to a degeneration and consequent need "for the spirit to break a

balance that has become demonic imprisonment." "Hence, no criticism is implied when the problem is characterized as unresolved. But
precisely because the problem is unsolvable in principle, an inesti-
mable importance attaches to its historically specific states of irresolution" (*IR*, 182-83). How successful, then, was Christianity? In
terms of differentiating the transcendent, decisive, it seems; in terms
of the realm of the politically mundane and its relationship to the
former? At this point, Voegelin leaves it with early Christianity's
problem.

Voegelin's desire to be hermeneutically "fair" with respect to both
Israel and Christianity seems to surface in these observations. History
is more complex than a simple "dualism" between an allegedly more
primitive Israel and a more sophisticated Christianity might lead one
to believe. In a related way, Voegelin is explicitly aware of the
hermeneutical dangers of approaching Israel from the perspective of
the later Christian differentiation. In fact, he writes of the "risk of
projecting later, e.g. Christian, meanings into the earlier symbols" of
Israel. And he formulates a hermeneutical guide to help in avoiding
this: keeping interpretation "as close as possible to the Biblical text"
(*IR*, 163[2]).

## Part Three

Part Three, "History and the Trail of Symbols," as we know, traces
the gradual emergence of the "paradigmatic" dimension of history
under God in Israel, covering the history of Israel from Abraham to
the exiles. What Voegelin has more formally articulated about Christianity and Jesus, and its relationship to Israel, finds its narrative
expression in this part, in some nine references in all (*IR*, 232, 239-40,
247-48, 299, 309-10, 314, 338-40, 343, 345, 345 n. 19). In a
fascinating codicil-like section on the witch of Endor story (1 Sam
28:3-25), in the larger narrative context of Saul's rise to kingship and
its meaning (see the anthology), Voegelin has occasion to argue that
the awareness of the soul in Israel was sufficiently differentiated to
foster historical realism, but too inadequately to bring about the
development of philosophy (237). By the time we reach Trito-Isaiah
(63:16ff.), we certainly come upon "enough . . . to suggest the spiritual
mood in which men were receptive for the appearance of God on earth
and to become the followers of Christ." Even the dimension of scandal
in Christianity—"the return of the world-transcendent God into a
cosmos which had become nondivine, and into a history which had
become human"—is found here in Trito-Isaiah. Nonetheless, "the

spiritual life of the soul . . . can be experienced only compactly, through the mediation of tribes and clans . . ." We are not yet at the "personal love of God . . . present as the ordering force in the soul of every man, as the Nous of the mystic-philosophers or the Logos of Christ is present in every member of the Mystical Body, creating by its presence the *homonoia*, the likemindedness of the community" (239-40).

Operative here is Voegelin's view that the differentiation of God and the differentiation of the person in relation to God mutually coimplicate one another (*IR*, 235). If Israel must struggle with its differentiation of God, then it is not surprising that its articulation of the soul in relation to that God undergoes a similar period of struggle. God has been "sensed" as world-transcendent, but the soul has not yet discovered itself as fully sharing in that transcendence and "eternity." Apparently, Voegelin suggests, Saul's awareness of his soul was still somewhat obscure, for even though he had banished the ghost-consulters (Yahweh, the transcendent, has no rivals!), still at a time of difficulty he would capitulate to this more archaic belief (witch of Endor). At the same time, Saul's banishment of the ghosts, but with nothing to take their place other than a place of being forgotten, illustrates the lack of a development of a view of the full range of the nature of the soul.

This pattern of analysis remains constant throughout this part: Israel's decisive but partial differentiation of the divine-human realities, and Christianity's dependent but greater clarification, along with Hellas (with respect to the soul). The imperial psalms, for example, in some ways become a last flicker of the imperial symbolism, and yet they bring us "one step closer to a humanity in the historical present under Christ" (*IR*, 309-10). The resolution of what Voegelin calls the "eschatological problems"—the precise relationship between God's kingdom and mundane kingdoms—had to wait for Christianity for its greater clarification, although from the ninth century to the postexilic fifth of the time of Malachi, decisive contributions are made to an eventual resolution (338-46).

The narrative context, of course, is always the mysterious interplay between Israel's representative mission as the carrier of the truth about the world-transcendent God and the exigencies imposed by the conditions of mundane existence. The movement on the pragmatic level from tribal confederacy, to kingdom and empire, and then to civil war and divided kingdoms and the catastrophes of the exiles provides the battlefield, so to speak, on which Israel must articulate the meaning of its order. Voegelin emphasizes the struggle of Israel to remain faithful to its leap in being and the ever-pressing tendency to derail back to the standards of cosmological existence, particularly as it must adjust to the pressures of reality by forming itself into a kingdom. The pattern of the cosmological kingdoms and empires of the day, as Voegelin reads Israel's history, all too frequently provides the norm for Israel's institutional experiments in kingdom-formation. This pressure "backward" to an earlier standard is one of the key factors holding Israel back from the greater differentiations achieved by Christianity and Hellas.

But it is only one of the factors, and not the greater factor at that, it seems. For Voegelin is very far from basing his analysis on a simple relation of cause and effect between historical circumstance and human action. That there is some kind of relation is clear enough. But it is embraced within a larger mystery. Here it is helpful to recall the solemn words of the overture "Introduction": Existence is "an adventure of decision on the edge of freedom and necessity," and so "we act our role in the greater play of the divine being that enters passing existence in order to redeem precarious being for eternity" (*IR*, 1, 5). Israel is not Christ, and that is not Israel's fault. For Voegelin, it is part of the mystery that Israel does what it does, and nothing more. In fact, in the final chapter of this part, Voegelin offers us an Augustinian-like reflection on "the mysteries attaching to the destiny of Israel," mysteries which are "profound beyond penetration and at the same time flat on the surface of facts" (315). Underlying this is particularly the mystery that, uniquely in history, Israel has reversed the "ordinary course of social evolution." "Here was a people that began its existence in history with a radical leap in being; and only after the people had been constituted by that initial experience did it acquire, in the course of centuries, a mundane body of organization to sustain itself in existence." As a result, it was given to Israel to enact "something in the nature of a model experiment in the creation of symbols of mundane existence under the conditions of an already enacted leap in being" (315-16).

Perhaps the most emphatic expression of Christianity's representative mission in this part comes toward the end of its final chapter, "The End of Israel's Worldly Existence," in the context of a discussion of the eschatological problems. Together with the earlier page 144, this may well be the "christological summit" of *IR*. Voegelin credits the book of Malachi with achieving "something like a balance" of eschatological symbols, inasmuch as "historical events and figures . . . are clearly symbols for the experienced presence of defection, voice of the spirit, judgment, and restoration," although the concreteness of the symbols keeps the restorative element somewhat submerged (*IR*, 345, 338). Nonetheless, in Malachi we find "the eternal present in which the divine-human drama of history was enacted" (345). Voegelin immediately adds a christological appendix: "With the appearance of Jesus, God himself entered into the eternal present of history. The Kingdom of God was now within history, though not of it." But the immediate qualification in the text and the clarifying footnote are surely crucial for an adequate appreciation of Voegelin's views on Christ and Christianity:

> The consequences of the Incarnation for the historical order of mankind were not realized at once; and it took some time to find even moderately suitable forms of expression (345).
> This sentence refers strictly to the problems of adequate symbolization. The mystery of the Incarnation itself, of the consubstantiality of God and man, is impenetrable. And its consequences for the substantive order of history are not fully realized as long as history lasts. Even in reference to adequate symbolization the sentence must be taken with proper qualification, for the meaning of history under the Christian dispensation is as far from satisfactory positive expression today as it was at the time of Jesus and his generation. The sentence, thus, means only that it took some time to overcome even the most obvious inadequacies of traditional symbols of historical order (345 n. 19).

## Part Four

The final Part Four, "Moses and the Prophets," contains the greatest number of references to Christ and Christianity in the entire work, some twelve in all (*IR*, 356, 372-73, 398, 408-14, 423, 431, 467, 472, 494 n., 495-96, 501, 515). This section of the work concentrates, in the light of the Deuteronomic Torah, upon "the clarification of right order in the light of the Sinaitic revelation." If Part Three probed the emergence of Israel's paradigmatic history through a study of pragmatic events as those events "acquired symbolic meaning," so this concluding part will dwell more fully upon the probing of that paradigmatic meaning by studying the biblical Moses and Prophets (187). Late Israel's probing and articulation of the meaning of Moses and the Prophets is something like an x-ray of the meaning of its own revelatory substance. Not surprisingly, then, this also seems to provide Voegelin with an opportunity to think through, x-raylike, some of the substantive issues pertinent to Christ and Christianity.

First, and not surprisingly, since it falls within the initial chapter on the nature of the Deuteronomic Torah, Voegelin mentions the issue of the canonization of the scriptures. He had referred to this earlier, and readers of *OH* IV, 48-57 will note how Voegelin's concerns and cautions with regard to canonization are a persistent theme.[3] It is an issue touching Christianity, for the Hebrew Scriptures have become part of its own canon as the Old Testament and the rabbinic determination of the Hebrew canon provided something of a model of the Christian canonical process itself. His concern was poignantly but still compactly expressed earlier in the initial chapter of Part Two, in a rehearsal of some of the difficulties in assessing Israel's "creation of history" (*IR*, 115). For there he had already written of "the deformations of meaning caused by rabbinical and Christian canonization and interpretations" (114). Accordingly, now in this final part, Voegelin cautions that we are not first concerned with a book: "The fundamental fact that the Bible was never the book of Israel lies so deeply below the historians' consciousness that today it is practically forgotten" (373). Consequently, "it requires today an effort of imagination to realize that the prophets were concerned with the spiritual order of a concrete people, of the people with whom Yahweh had entered into the Berith" (357). Thus he will distinguish two strata in the Deuteronomic Torah: one which swims in the continuity of Israel's traditions, for it attempts to reconstruct "the concrete order in the spirit of the decalogic words"; a second, which rather more problematically confuses the "historical contingencies" of revelation with the revelation itself (369). Voegelin has in mind certain concrete notions regarding "the king, the priests, the prophets, and Moses" (cf. Deut 17:14-18:22), and particularly the new conception of war, not as defensive actions as at the time of the confederacy, but as offensive means of "exterminating" non-believers in Yahweh (cf. Deut 11:23ff.; 19:1; 20:16ff.) (376).

It is not difficult to grasp the implications for Christianity coming from this kind of analysis of the Deuteronomic Torah. Here, too, we perhaps glimpse something of the different sensitivities of the political philosopher from those of a rather more "doctrinal" theologian. It is precisely what the latter is liable to submerge beneath consciousness that the former intensifies to paradigmatic significance. When Voegelin writes that "exegetes and historians of religion are interested in the Torah not as the entombment of Israel, but as the transmitter of its spirit to Judaism and Christianity" (*IR*, 373), he shows something of his hermeneutics of suspicion. He is attempting to bring out something of the entombing qualities as well, and the forces which foster such qualities.

> The prophets, philosophers, and saints, who can translate the order of the spirit into the practice of conduct without institutional support and pressure, are rare. For its survival in the world, therefore, the order of the spirit has to rely on a fanatical belief in the symbols of a creed more often than on the *fides caritate formata*—though such reliance, if it becomes socially predominant, is apt to kill the order it is supposed to preserve (377).

Secondly, the chapter on Moses introduces us to the important notion of prefiguration. So far as I can tell, this is *IR*'s only mention of this principle, although it is intrinsically connected with its fundamental and often-expressed principle of the dynamics of the interrelation between compactness and differentiation.[4] The passage in question concerns Moses, who "prefigured, but did not figurate himself, the Son of God." This Moses "stands between the compactness of the Egyptian order and the lucidity of the Christian order" (*IR*, 398). This peculiar status indicates that "the presence of God has become historical" through Moses. He is "not God," but he "is something more than man," writes Voegelin in an exegesis of Exodus 4:14-16 and 7:1 (399).

The dynamics between prefiguration and figuration would seem to be another way of thinking of aspects of the dynamics between compactness and differentiation. Certainly the whole context of *IR*, with its frequent appeal to the latter principle, inclines one to that view. But we really do not need to lose ourselves in endless debates on the matter, for Voegelin has made the matter rather clear in his discussion with Bultmann on the significance of the Old Testament for Christianity. "When reflection turns to the continuity of the historical process and when, in order to demonstrate the continuity, the later position [that has been differentiated] is confronted with the earlier one on the level of symbols (and that is what scriptural proof does), the peculiar problems of prefiguration will arise." The creators of newly differentiated insights are "absorbed by the importance of their new insight," and so they "will rarely shoulder the burden of creating additional symbols for the areas of reality left behind in their passionate search for the specific truth."

Such is what Voegelin is concerned with here in the section on Moses. He is, so to speak, shouldering the burden of articulating the significance of Moses in the wake of the greater lucidity of the Christ.

In the debate with Bultmann, Voegelin dwells on the Isaianic materials, but the transfer to the Moses materials is easily made by the
reader. "Symbolisms like the Isaianic Prince of Peace or the
Deutero-Isaianic Suffering Servant can, according to the interpreter's
preference, either be locked up in the history of Israel as an autonomous entity, if the reflection is addressed to their compact surface, or
be drawn into the continuous history issuing in Christ and Christianity, if the reflection recognizes behind the compact surface the
differentiated area of truth which they also embrace in their compactness" (HG, 87).[5] That Moses shall be as a god both to Aaron and to
Pharaoh (Exod 4:16; 7:1) seems to Voegelin to be not yet the
Incarnation, but surely more emphatically an intimation of God's
historical and personal presence than what we find in the pre-personal
cosmological symbolizations.

This mode of interpretation illustrates, I think, something of
Voegelin's "figural" imagination. It is rather close in some ways to
what is known as a typological form of exegesis, and of course it
touches upon the deep question of the entire validity of Voegelin's
(and indeed Christianity's) "Christian-reading" of the Hebrew Scriptures. What is it that keeps a figural imagination from simply
projecting later meanings onto earlier symbolisms? At this point
Voegelin is guided partly by an attentiveness to the compact surface
of earlier symbolisms. He disciplines his interpretation, not allowing
himself to be simply blinded by what he regards as the greater lucidity
of a later differentiation. Here is something of the differentiated soul
of the philosopher exercising a certain balance. But of course on a
deeper level what underlies and even demands this kind of figural
exegesis is the universal Logos of the world-transcendent God, who
ultimately grounds the discontinuity and continuity of the historical
process (OH IV, 186).

A third feature with important implications for any assessment of
Christ and Christianity surfaces in the course of Voegelin's study of
the revelation of the divine name, "I Am Who I Am" (Exod 3:14),
again in the Moses chapter. In response to those who refuse to accord
any significant advance in humanity's understanding of the "metaphysics of being" to the divine name, Voegelin not surprisingly
appeals to his principle of compactness. "While the Exodus passage is
not a metaphysical proposition, it contains in its compactness the
meaning differentiated by the Christian philosophers" (IR, 410).
Voegelin's exegesis is quite worthwhile and compelling, I think,
although Voegelin scholars would want to introduce certain (likely

contentious!) nuances with respect to his developing views on
metaphysic's tendencies toward hypostatization.

I want to emphasize an observation made somewhat in passing,
because I think it carries enormously significant implications for
Christianity. In reference to the authors in question with whom he is
taking issue Voegelin argues that they "take it for granted that nothing
extraordinary can happen in history; no unique personality, even if
God so wills it, can break the 'stage of development.'" This in turn fails
to understand that "revelation creates history as the inner form of
human existence in the present under God." Analysis, then, has to
move to a much more profound level than simply tracking terms in
a philological manner (*IR*, 409-10). This sense of the historically
unique, of course, points ahead to Christianity. This more clearly
surfaces in the final chapter in the course of an analysis of Israel's
Suffering Servant (Isa 40-55). When man is in search of God, as in
Hellas, the wisdom gained remains generically human; when God is
in search of man, as in Israel, the responsive recipient of revelation
becomes historically unique. Since the human experience of revelation is an event in the history constituted by revelation, historicity
attaches to the recipient of revelation, to the very historicity of Christ
(496).

Such attention to the unique—rather than to the generic—created
by history does not seem to me to be common in *IR*, although such
can plausibly be argued to be implied in the emergence of historical
order as Voegelin understands that. I have come across only two other
references. Fascinatingly they are both in reference to Moses (*IR*, 388,
425 n.). It is as if the historical materials on Moses force Voegelin to
surface this dimension: Moses, we recall, is in that peculiar space
between cosmological pre-personalism and Christian personalism.
Jeremiah's autobiographical sections are perhaps similar, for Voegelin
will say that they articulate the fact that in "Jeremiah the human
personality had broken the compactness of collective existence and
recognized itself as the authoritative source of order in society" (485).
In any case, this sensitivity to the uniquely personal is rather critical
in appreciating how Voegelin views the "Christian distinctive."

In these texts just referred to, the focus is on the human side of the
divine-human relationship. The encounter with the world-transcendent God tends in the direction of the emergence of the uniquely
personal historical "carrier" of revelation. We have seen, in earlier
parts, how Voegelin will accord the greater and even decisive differentiation of the human side of historical order to Christianity, and to
some extent to Hellas. We are in something of an obscure region,

however, when we come to Moses, to Jeremiah, and to the Suffering Servant, it seems, for apparently something of a decisive break from the collective to the personal has clearly occurred.

But perhaps Voegelin means that the other and more decisive side of the relation—the divine side—was the factor inhibiting Israel's full breakthrough to historical personalism. A continual theme, even in this final part, is the cultural mortgage of Israel's inability to break through fully to God's universality (*IR*, 423). Even "the Suffering Servant stands on the borderline between Prophetism and Christianity" (431). To some extent, the cultural mortgage is our human problem. But we have also seen that the greater mystery is that of God's freedom, and the divine choice of when and how to reveal. In a certain sense, this would seem to imply that God is uniquely personal, along with humans. And in fact, thinking it through, one would have to say that God's "unique personality" is the ground and source of human personality. Voegelin does not exactly say this, but his thought clearly implies and more than implies it, particularly his principle that the relation to God determines the quality of human self-understanding and action (235).

In this regard, two statements stand out with particular force. In commenting upon Jeremiah's intensive sense of humanity, as he transfers Israel's vocation as God's son to himself (Jer 1:5), Voegelin adds: "While this is by far not yet the Christian revelation that only God can be the Son of God—the mystery expressed in Trinitarian theology and the Christology—it is a long step toward the insight that the order from eternity is not incarnate in a people and its rulers in pragmatic history" (*IR*, 467). The second text comes in the course of the analysis of Deutero-Isaiah, where Voegelin powerfully writes of "the Exodus of Israel from itself." In one sense, he will characterize this as a "completion," inasmuch as "the order of being has revealed its mystery of redemption as the flower of suffering." But he follows this with an immediate qualification which clearly has reference to Christianity, given the way the book ends with the citations from the *Nunc dimittis* of Lk 2 and Acts 8 (515). That completion "does not mean . . . that the vision of the mystery is the reality of redemption in history: The participation of man in divine suffering has yet to encounter the participation of God in human suffering" (501).

What does all of this mean: only God can be God's Son, and it is this God who participates in suffering? Here it seems to me that Voegelin is "bordering," to use his word, on the beliefs (which also became doctrines) of the Trinity, Incarnation, and salvation, beliefs/doctrines to which the Church Fathers seemed inevitably to come as they pondered through participation in the mystery of Christ and redemptive suffering. *IR* appropriately ends here, on the border. It is after all the prefiguration that is mainly in question throughout.[6]

## CHRISTIAN TYPOLOGY AND PHILOSOPHY OF
## ORDER AND HISTORY

The way the Christian dimension surfaces in Voegelin's interpretation of Israel's history throughout *IR* can be, and to some extent has been, challenged from at least two sides. On the one hand, it can be read as a projection of Christian meanings into texts which, in themselves, are not thought to legitimate such references. Here one might imagine, for example, that a faithful member of Talmudic Judaism, out of a desire to preserve the "integrity" of Hebrew Scipture, would raise such a challenge. In this case the matter is somewhat complicated, because Talmudic Judaism does hold to a long rabbinic tradition of typological exegesis, in which the later beliefs of rabbinic Judaism are in some way prefigured in the Torah. Thus, from this quarter, biblical interpretation of a typological kind is not in all cases ruled out. It is a particular kind of typology that is challenged. Perhaps more commonly a more historicist or simply positivist conception of history would raise such a challenge. Here the contentious point would be the latter's unacceptance of transcendental meanings and truths in history, and so an a priori rejection of Christian messianism in any significant, revelatory sense.

On the other hand, *IR* could be, and to some extent has been, viewed as inadequately Christian. So far as I can tell, the charge has not arisen, or at least not commonly arisen, until the appearance of some of Voegelin's later works, especially perhaps *OH* IV. Before that, perhaps, the Christian "loading" of *IR* seemed much more secure. In any case, one might imagine certain Christians being uneasy with Voegelin's "historical" interpretation of revelation, which gives the impression that the self-communication of God, which is after all supposed to be supernatural, somehow becomes all too natural on this account. Revelation might be thought to be much more dialectical vis-à-vis humanity and history, not so "wedded" to the structures and contingencies of human history. Voegelin's hesitancies with respect to the canonization of Scripture, noted above, might be related, it could seem, to this inability to give full weight to the supernatural dimension of Hebrew revelation. Certain interpreters in the tradition of Leo Strauss as well have argued against Voegelin's seemingly historicist interpretation of revelation, and so they would interestingly join arms with the "dialectical supernaturalists" on this issue.

However, a rather common objection to Voegelin's interpretation of Christianity is just the opposite of its seemingly historicist bent; namely, that it seems insufficiently historical in its estimation of revelation and especially of Christ and the Church. Christ seems more generic rather than historically unique: a kind of example of every man or woman, at least potentially. "Representative" is Voegelin's common term in some of his writings, although its use in *IR* but not its equivalent meaning is rare to the point of near nonexistence (for example, 240, 507).[7] Again, to return to the canon of Scripture, one might from this perspective argue that it is precisely the inadequate attention to revelation's necessary historicity and embodiment that causes Voegelin's difficulties. This charge, so far as I know, emerges rather commonly only after the appearance of *OH* IV, however. This is connected to concerns noted in previous chapters (concerns of Anderson and Ranieri mainly, but also Mackler and Baird) as well, although those chapters are directly focusing upon the historicity of revelation in the case of Judaism itself. Nonetheless, the general issue is whether Voegelin gives due regard to revelation's historicity, a feature shared in common by both Judaism and Christianity.

Which is it to be, then? Is *IR* too Christian or not Christian enough? The work itself manifests an attentiveness to the problem, for we recall the assertion of "the risk of projecting later, e.g. Christian, meanings into the earlier symbols" (163). And there are, of course, hermeneutical guidelines that one must follow in order to minimize the dangers of such Christian over- or under-interpretation. Hence, Voegelin's attempt to remain "as close as possible to the Biblical text" and his important dialogue with the modern history of Old Testament interpretation (163, and chap. 6 as a whole). But guiding and grounding the project as a whole is Voegelin's deep down view of the interpreter's participation in the partnership of being. I believe it is this more fundamental perspective—as expressed in the important preface as well as overture introduction—that, in the end, leads Voegelin to his key interpretive proposals.

God and human beings, society and world form a primordial community of being. We humans are not spectators looking at this community but already actors within it, whose knowledge emerges only from participation within the whole. The quality of our participation, our attunement or not to the multiple dimensions of this whole, determines the quality of our knowledge, which is itself expressed in symbols which exegete or differentiate our experience of participation. The always compact whole undergoes a history of differentiating exegesis. The great symbols of the cosmological civilizations, and the Scriptures of Israel, are varying forms of this "history of exegesis," and it is the interpreter's burden to participate in this history, the quality of one's participation in turn determining the quality of the interpretation. Deficiencies in interpretation will arise from inadequate or nonexistent attention to one or more of the partners in the community of being.

Voegelin, it seems to me, is always moving in an alert way through participation within this primordial partnership in being, on its more compact as well as varyingly differentiated levels, as his own exegesis in *IR* unfolds. This kind of interpretation, while in some way imposed on all of us by reality, is enormously challenging and difficult, given its multistructured nature in combination with our own level of attunement. Keeping this in mind, then, what would Voegelin's response be to the possible charges of over- or under-emphasis of the possible Christian dimension of the biblical text? There can be no simple answer, it seems, other than to search for some inadequacy in the level of attunement to the partners in the community of being. Voegelin's "hermeneutics" is quite hopeful, however, in the sense that he resolutely holds that all of us are within this community; no one is excluded. In principle, there is no purely esoteric knowledge reserved for the few, for all are invited to participate by the appeal of being itself. On the other hand, Voegelin is no dreamy utopian. History is a mystery entailing "the greater play of the divine being" along with the quality of our own action within this (*IR*, 5). The quality of the latter is woefully abysmal all too often, and the play of the former is a light exceeding bright (*OH* IV, 184, 187, 228).

Have we made some progress? Let us return for a moment to the charge of an over-Christian interpretation of Israel. On Voegelin's account, the historicist or positivist argument fails because it ignores the divine partner in being and in varying ways is based upon a truncated, reductionistic view of the other partners in being. Voegelin's entire *Werk* is in some ways a sustained *nein* to such reductionism, both through a direct confrontation with the inadequate epistemological foundations of such thinking, and through a more indirect "display" of the manifold richness of the partners in being as disclosed in the drama of history itself. As I indicated a moment ago, the difficulties that might be raised by a Talmudic Jew would seem more complicated, and it would also seem that the kind of hermeneutics Voegelin practises would be much more congenial to our hypothetical

Talmudic Jew. For here there is a mutual attunement to the divine partner and the consequences of this for our order in existence.

How can Voegelin respond? The issue needs to be sharpened. Voegelin argues that Israel's revelation "prefigures" the Christ and Christianity in certain specified senses. The notion of prefiguration would not seem to be an insurmountable obstacle to agreement, for Talmudic Judaism is well acquainted with typological forms of exegesis. The way Voegelin clarifies the hermeneutical problems of prefiguration-figuration (or typology, one can say) through his notion of the movement from compactness to differentiation is perhaps a promising way of working through the issue. The precise nature of what is prefigured—namely, the *Figura* (Christ and Christianity)— or the what rather than the how of prefiguration—now becomes the central issue.[8] If by Christ and Christianity Voegelin means the traditional beliefs/doctrines of Trinity and Incarnation, as he seems to indicate at one point (*IR*, 467), then surely the Talmudic Jew would demur. On the other hand, should Voegelin mean only that the universality of God was too compactly understood in Israel (too tied to the kingdom), or that the human person under God was likewise too compactly understood, then it is not inconceivable that our hypothetical Talmudic Jew might find this plausible, and might even be willing to grant that these aspects of the community of being achieve a clearer differentiation in the Christian doctrines. On the other hand, I suspect that the Talmudic Jew would argue that it has been one of the achievements of Talmudic Judaism itself to attempt to articulate these differentiations as well, but to do so in a way that is also attentive to the important role of the ethnic and cultural dimensions of revelation. Think, for example, of the work of Martin Buber, so highly regarded by Voegelin himself, or of Abraham Heschel. What of Moses Maimonides, for example? Thus the contentious page 144 would be directly countered! Like Voegelin, the Talmudic Jew is also participating in the community of being through a profound attunement to the divine ground. From his or her own retrospective point in the flow of history (ix), what was known only more compactly by one's ancestors can now be rendered more differentiated. In certain ways, the complex hermeneutical relationship between Scripture and Talmud might be likened to the complex relationship between the compact and the differentiated.

However, if Voegelin means something more along the lines of the traditional beliefs/doctrines of Trinity and Incarnation, as above indicated, then clearly we are at one of those conflicts of interpretation which will necessarily push us to a deeper level. We will return to this, but for now let us move to the other charge against *IR*, that of its being too little Christian. Let us take the issue from the viewpoint of the dialectical supernaturalist, who in the interests of protecting the properly supernatural character of revelation questions Voegelin's seemingly historicist interpretation of the same. We also noted that some from within the Straussian "School" would also question Voegelin's interpretation on the same score (Emberley and Cooper 1993, passim). Here the charge might be that there is an undercutting of the ability of God to reveal himself in a truly absolute, transhistorical manner on historicist assumptions. Ultimately this leads to Voegelin's problems with the notion of a canonical scripture (and doctrine) as possessing transhistorical normativity. It also leads to a calling into question of the supernatural and even miraculous elements of revelation.

How might Voegelin respond? We could point to his notion of the partnership in the community of being. True ontological partnership presupposes a unity in difference appropriate to the partners in question. Partnership is not simple identity of equality, as if God were reduced to the level of the finite partners in the community or as if those latter were somehow transmuted alchemically to divine status. The form of historicism which would reduce the world-transcendent God to the world-historical presupposes not partnership with God but a kind of pantheistic identity. Such is not what Voegelin holds.

There can be no doubt that Voegelin holds a rather strong view of the historical nature, not only of revelation, but of all partners in the community of being. Such is implied by the solemn opening of the preface: "The order of history emerges from the history of order" (*IR*, ix). But this would seem to be a notion of historicity rather than historicism as normally understood. The latter seems to entail an historical determinism, while Voegelin's project entails a rather more modest historical conditionedness. Not all forms of the latter are deterministic, and Voegelin's is emphatically not. This is so, both from the Godward side, as well as from that of the free human subject who possesses not absolute but still real freedom of response within reality.

Because partnership exists, God can "reveal" and the human person through listening attunement can respond. Voegelin nowhere writes that God must reveal, but rather that history's symbols witness to a history of revelation in which God has mysteriously chosen to reveal. Revelation is, in other words, mediated through the partnership. What Voegelin writes of Abraham, in certain respects, might easily be generalized: "Religious personalities who have [revelatory] experi-

ences, and are able to submit to their authority, do not grow on trees."
Required is the "spiritual sensitiveness of the man who opened his soul
to the word of Yahweh," accompanied as well by "the trust and
fortitude required to make this word the order of existence in
opposition to the world" (*IR*, 195[9]). Yahweh's word can elicit a
response from a sensitive soul only because there is a partnership in
being. Here is the source of Voegelin's difficulties with the dialectical
supernaturalist. It would not be their emphasis upon God's
world-transcendent nature, nor upon God's grace and freedom, that
Voegelin would in any way deny, but rather their seeming separation
between God and creature. There would seem to be a chasm with no
bridge between the two. Voegelin opts for a primordial *community* in
being; the dialectical supernaturalists, for a primordial *chasm*. If I
might put it this way, Voegelin's imagination is primarily analogical,
and subordinately dialectical. That is, because God is in partnership
with creation and present within it, God may employ created realities
as analogues of the divine presence. Inasmuch as God remains
world-transcendent, there is a valid sense in which God is dialectically
over-against creation, as its uncontrollable source and ground and as
the source of moral opposition to evil and sin. But God, so to speak,
transcends even a simple no or even yes to creation. God is more than
and inclusive of both a yes and a no to creation; analogical in other
words.

Questions about Voegelin's Christianity, however, can emerge and
have emerged from interpreters arguing that his work exhibits an
inadequate stress upon the historical dimension of revelation. As with
the dialectical supernaturalists, the claimed end result is an inadequate
view of Christ and Christianity, but unlike them and in fact in precise
opposition to them, the claimed source is too little a stress upon
historicity rather than too much. While this is a charge which
generally surfaces in response to Voegelin's later work, especially *OH*
IV, it might be possible to find intimations of such already in *IR*
(Morrissey 1994, 227ff.). As noted above, this is related to the view
of some of this book's interlocutors that intimations of a lack of
attunement to Israel's historicity are already present within *IR*.

One might argue, for example, that the role of a canonical scripture
is precisely an example of the "divine use" of the historical for the sake
of mediating revelation and fostering obedience to it. Voegelin's
tendency to associate deforming qualities with the canon, along with
a constant negativism toward doctrine, for the same reasons, can be
brought forward as examples of a kind of spiritualistic view of
revelation, too divorced from history (*IR*, 94-95, 247, 370, 376-77,

454, 481, 483, 494). Some later interpreters have seen in this the influence of Plato or at least Platonism in Voegelin's view of Christ and Christianity (Ranieri in this book brings a similar charge with respect to Voegelin's view of Judaism). Does the negative view of the kingdoms in Israel's history not imply an excessively spiritualistic view of revelation as well? Does revelation not almost become an affair between the isolated soul and a world-transcendent God, a soul too detached from the body and from a larger insertion into a physical and social world? Does all of this hint at what seems to some like the relative inattention to the Church as a mediating structure of revelation in Voegelin's later work (noted especially by Tinder in an earlier chapter)? And does the negative view of the Jewish kingdoms hint at Voegelin's own seeming lack of attention to political forms in society in his own later thinking? And, of course, all of this would hint at a deficiently *incarnational* view of revelation, meaning by *incarnational* the way God "accomodates" himself to the human condition by becoming incarnate. Is there something of a hint of a semi-docetism here, which in a sense is also a form of the kind of pathology Voegelin most intensively attacked, that is, gnosticism? Surely, such a deficiency would almost inevitably make it impossible for Voegelin to arrive at an adequate Christology, at least from the viewpoint of Nicene and Chalcedonian orthodoxy. And, of course, if the Christology is inadequate, then the soteriology would be as well, on the traditional grounds that "[what] he has not assumed he has not healed; but that which is united to his Godhead is also saved" (Nazianzen 1989, 440).

What do the texts of *IR* indicate by way of response? Certainly on the most general level the overture introduction would seem to indicate that right order follows from listening attunement to *all* the partners in the community of being. An inattention to dimensions belonging to any of the partners, or worse, simply an ignoring of any of the partners (for example, society or world), would, on these terms, be pathological. But has Voegelin now done precisely this in his interpretation of Israel? A particularly disclosive text will have to serve us as our representative example of how Voegelin deals with many of the issues in question. It occurs in the context of the emergence of the Deuteronomic Torah, aspects of which are similar, claims Voegelin, to the transition from "existence under God to acceptance of the Torah." That is, "in Deuteronomy we were touching the genesis of 'religion,' defined as the transformation of existence in historical form into the secondary possession of a 'creed' concerning the relation between God and man." His assessment is that we must not understand this in a "depreciatory" way, for the spirit lives in the world as an ordering force in the souls of human beings. And the human *anima naturalis* has an amplitude of characterological variety that breaks the ordering spirit in a broad spectrum of phenomena. Plato and Aristotle, in the construction of their paradigms of the best polis, which must accomodate the variety of characters, have made this fundamental problem of social order explicit. The prophets, philosophers, and saints, who can translate the order of the spirit into the practice of conduct without institutional support and pressure, are rare. For its survival in the world, therefore, the order of the spirit has to rely on a fanatical belief in the symbols of a creed more often than on the *fides caritate formata*—though such reliance, if it becomes socially predominant, is apt to kill the order it is supposed to preserve (376-77).

The text is a difficult one. It is not yet the more mature formulation on doctrine that I had cited earlier from *OH* IV. Still, it gives a significant place to institution and creed in religion, and realistically even acknowledges both the positive and negative aspects of even a *fanatic* clinging to these supports. Noteworthy as well is something of a subtle but significant distinction between institutional support and pressure, on the one hand, and social order, on the other. Society is more than its institutional structures, it would seem.

It seems clear throughout *IR* that Voegelin avoids a solipsistic view of the human person. The human person is always a partner in the community of being. Note, for example, how quickly Voegelin moves to the social dimension in his exegesis of Jeremiah: "In Jeremiah the human personality had broken the compactness of collective existence and recognized itself as the authoritative source of order in society" (485). In other words, institutional structures are ways in which social order is achieved, but the latter is not simply reducible to the former. Jeremiah's new sense of order is not a flight from society, but a new formative force within and for society which will foster the development of new institutional forms.

This attunement in *IR* to social order, and to its articulation in a variety of concrete, institutional ways, is further emphasized by Voegelin's criticism that the "prophets apparently were not only unable to see, but not even interested in finding, a way from the formation of the soul to institutions and customs they could consider compatible with the knowledge and fear of God" (446-47). And we should recall his warning that this was to be early Christianity's danger as well (182-83). It would appear, then, that Voegelin's understanding of revelation, certainly in *IR*, is not burdened by the kind of spiritualism with which his thought—at least his later thought—has been charged. It is not social order, nor institutions and customs, in a generalized sense that Voegelin suppresses or resists in his analysis of revelation. Rather, as the helpful sentence just quoted suggests, the struggle is one of finding a way from the formed soul to a social order compatibly formative of souls. For example, Voegelin writes of "the spirit of God" that is "present as the ordering force in the soul of very man, as the Nous of the mystic-philosophers or the Logos of Christ is present in every member of the Mystical Body, creating by its presence the *homonoia*, the likemindedness of the community." And he continues by describing the more differentiated human personality of Plato's philosophy as the "man, [who] while living with his fellow man in the community of the spirit, has a personal destiny in relation to God . . ." (240).

In fact, Voegelin's focus upon a philosophy of order, in which he explores the dynamics between formed soul and formative order in society and history, seems to lead him to generalize features of the Christ, so that he might be able to surface the consequences for social order of the Incarnation. For example, from the Godward side now, he writes that "with the appearance of Jesus, God himself entered into the eternal present of history" (*IR*, 345). And, from the humanward side: "the Logos of John created a world with a mankind immediate under God" (95). A formulation putting both sides together would be the one in which he describes "the mystery of the Incarnation itself [as] . . . the consubstantiality of God and man . . ." (345 n. 19).

The difficulty with such formulas is that they might cause the individual Jesus himself to vanish into every human person. Incarnation would then be generalized into a general structure of humanity. Inasmuch as Voegelin is not a dualist or spiritualist, but someone holding to the somatic and social nature of human beings, we could not call this universalizing of the Christ a sort of simple spiritualism. But without certain correctives, it is in danger of deindividualizing Jesus, and if him, then by implication everyone. In other words, what has happened to the individual Jesus Christ? And how more precisely is he to be distinguished from other human beings? One of the ways in which Paul, for example, tries to handle this problem is through his distinction between Jesus' natural sonship and our adopted sonship (Rom 8:12-17). The Gospel of John similarly will speak only of Jesus as the son of God, while the rest of us are "children" (Jn 1:18, 12). Later ecclesial tradition will speak of Jesus' hypostatic union, a union of divinity and humanity uniquely and in a nonpareil way his. At least two issues are involved here. First, if Jesus is not to vanish into a generalized structure of humanity at large, he must be a truly historical and individual person. Further, what if any difference is there between this Jesus in his relation to God and all other human beings?

*IR* remains largely "prefigurational" in its articulation of Christ and Christianity, fittingly. We can only expect hints at this point in the project of Voegelin's philosophy of order. But there are some significant, if few, references, we might recall. From the humanward side, there is the statement that humans remain generically human in Hellas, where "man is in search of God," whereas they become "historically unique" in Israel, where "God is in search of man." And Voegelin goes on to say that this feature of historical uniqueness is one of the meanings of historicity, attaching "to the very historicity of Christ" (496). When one keeps in mind the theme of the emergence of the human personality throughout *IR*, with its characterological features of body, emotions, intellect and will, along with cultural formation; and when one recalls that Voegelin claims this to be an especially prominent feature of Christ and Christianity; then it seems clear that the uniquely individual personality of Jesus is explicitly and implicitly expressed.

We can amplify this somewhat through a few other texts. One occurs on the occasion of a contrast between the Egyptian Pharaoh and the Christ: "We get an inkling of the scandal which Christianity must have been for men emerging from cosmological civilizations, if we consider that not a king was the god incarnate but an ordinary man of low social status who represented nobody but nevertheless was claimed by his followers to be the representative mediator and sufferer for mankind" (*IR*, 74). This comment upon Jesus' ordinariness would at least seem to endow him with the uniqueness enjoyed by other ordinary mortals, only now accompanied by a consciousness of the same and the consequent ontological alteration therein implied attendant upon the Christian differentiation. The earlier statement, in the course of his analysis of the Moses experience, that extraordinary personalities can emerge in history, would also seem to imply that Jesus not only enjoys the uniqueness of ordinary mortals, but a rather extraordinary—greater than Moses and the prophets—uniqueness.

From the Godward side, it would seem that with the Incarnation God reveals himself as not simply (no. 1) world-transcendent, but also as (no. 2) universal in welcoming outreach and (no. 3) personally loving (*IR*, 239-40) through participating in our suffering (501). Israel, it would seem, largely differentiated the first divine "attribute," while the latter two were only somewhat inchoately differentiated, having to wait for the Incarnation for their decisive disclosure, although the Suffering Servant is on the border of differentiating attribute number two.

This, I think, is about as far as the analysis of *IR* goes with respect to our topic. The focus tends to be upon the Incarnation's consequences for social order, when the theme of Christ emerges, and only in a somewhat more muted way upon the uniqueness of Jesus himself as the "bearer" and disclosure of revelation. If you will, the christological analysis remains prefigurationally compact, but is quite compatible— as far as it goes—with a more traditionally orthodox view of the Christian beliefs and doctrines, and in fact might be said to lean in that direction. Let me end with a few observations on the direction of Voegelin's later christological views.

## Voegelin's Later Views of Christ and Christianity

First, there is a trajectory of later texts in which Voegelin does seem clearly to profess the uniqueness of Jesus in a manner quite traditionally orthodox. For example, in his major study of the Gospel symbolism, he comments on "the experience of an extraordinary divine irruption in the existence of Jesus":

> This irruption, through which Jesus becomes the Christ, is expressed by the author of Colossians in the words: "For in him the whole fullness of divine reality (*theotes*) dwells bodily" (2:9). In its whole fullness (*pan to pleroma*), divine reality is present only in Christ who, by virtue of this fullness, "is the image (*eikon*) of the unseen God, the first of all creation" (1:15). All other men have no more than their ordinary share of this fullness (*pepleromenoi*) through accepting the truth of its full presence in the Christ who, by his iconic existence, is "the head of all rule (*arche*) and authority (*exousia*)" (2:10). Something about Jesus must have impressed his contemporaries as an existence in the *metaxy* of such intensity that his bodily presence, the *somatikos* of the passage, appeared to be fully permeated by divine presence (GC, 192-93).

This text preserves the typically Voegelinian interest in the consequences of the Incarnation for social order, for it occurs within a study of how the Gospel relates to human culture, and even in this passage one can note the attempt to relate Jesus to others, by attending to their "share" in the "fullness" (the play between *pepleromenoi* and *pleroma*). But the text is a particularly precious one in the Voegelinian corpus, because it rather more emphatically articulates the difference between Jesus as the Christ and others who share in this. Here something of the extraordinariness of Jesus' personality, hinted at in *IR*, breaks through. There are, of course, some other, similar texts as well: "The *pneuma* [Spirit of God] . . . is pleromatically present in Christ and less fully in the men who can see the Christ . . ." (WME, 370, in reference to 1 Cor 2:10-11); and, while the prophets and apostles bring insights into the dynamics of transfiguration, it is "above all Jesus" who does so (*OH* IV, 270).

The Church Fathers struggled mightily over these questions, as Voegelin explicitly attests, and the decisive resolution was the articulation of the trinitarian belief and doctrine. This is where the Fathers ended up, so to speak, as they grappled with Incarnation and salvation, and it would therefore not be too surprising if Voegelin "ended up" in the same place. This would be an exemplification of Voegelin's principle that the way we think of human persons is intrinsically related to the way in which we think of God. That is, the way we think of Jesus and ourselves must reflect something in the very reality of God. The extraordinary distinctiveness of Jesus would be reflected, then, in the Christian transformation of monotheism into trinitarianism. It seems to me that Voegelin, at least occasionally, explores the trinitarian symbols in a way that evidences a desire to appropriate the work of the Fathers in trinitarian theology (see endnote 6). But matters seem to remain somewhat blurry and (deliberately ?) undifferentiated.

At the risk of oversimplification, on our own we can suggest that the distinction between the Son and the Spirit enabled the Church to draw the important distinction between Jesus (who is Son and Logos) and ourselves (who participate in the Son in our "ordinary" way). If we remain binitarian or ditheistic, with only a Father and no clear differentiation between Son and Spirit, we inevitably end up collapsing the distinction between Jesus the Son and ourselves. It is not easy to simplify what this means, but in a shorthand way we might suggest that the Incarnation (Christological doctrine) reveals God as a personal Thou in and as Jesus, while pneumatology (Paracletic doctrine) reveals God as bringing us into participation with this personally loving mystery. Ditheism would inevitably fail to differentiate the divine personality from our own, and land us in a sort of insufficiently differentiated view of both God's "personality" and our own, not unlike Hinduism.[10]

*The Ecumenic Age* has a fascinating passage (*OH* IV, 259-61) in which Voegelin approvingly writes of the "generous openness" in doctrinal matters of the pre-Nicene Church. This has to do with his hesitations about the deforming possibilities of doctrinalization, his

sensitivity to the "openness of the theophanic field," and his attraction
to the kind of "tolerance in dogmatic matters" typified by the mystics.
This pre-Nicene period knew a ditheistic strand of thought, Voegelin
knows, and he seems to give a somewhat positive interpretation to its
subordinationist constructions inasmuch as the Fathers were attempting to articulate the relation between the Logos incarnate in Jesus and
the Father without lapsing into polytheism.

There seems to be a touch of wistfulness in Voegelin's presentation
as he admits the need for the doctrines of Nicea and even Chalcedon.
They are "a protective device that will shield the oneness of the
Unknown God against confusion with the experiences of divine
presence in the myths of the intracosmic gods, in mytho-speculation,
and in the noetic and pneumatic luminosity of consciousness." The
God become incarnate is not the same as the intracosmic gods of
pre-Christian cultures, but the world-transcendent God who is also
Logos. This God is indeed luminously present to us in consciousness,
but not to be reduced to our consciousness, after the fashion of a
Feuerbach and others who transformed "man into God-man" in the
nineteenth century. In the Christian symbol system, it is precisely the
relation of the Holy Spirit to the incarnate Son which protects our
sense of participation (through the Spirit) in the God become man
without reducing this incarnate God to our own being and consciousness. I would suggest that the consequences of ditheism for social
order are precisely the kinds of ideologies typified by Feuerbach.

In any case, this passage is exceedingly difficult to interpret. It seems
more celebratory of the transcendence of God than of God's
incarnational presence in Jesus. But interestingly, one might argue
that there is a trinitarian implication to the three confusions Voegelin
says the trinitarian and christological doctines protect against. The
doctrine of the Father could be said to protect against confusing God
with the intracosmic gods; the doctrine of the Son, against confusing
the incarnate God Logos with the subordinate *logoi* of
mytho-speculation, as one meets with that in, for example,
Neoplatonism, or Arianism, or in the gnostic speculation. The
doctrine of the Holy Spirit could be said to protect against confusing
our own noetic and pneumatic consciousness with the reality of God,
even while indicating why it is that we do in fact participate in the
divine Beyond. In his later writing, Voegelin seems to deliberately
place in tension assertions of appreciation for Christianity's orthodox
trinitarian and christological beliefs and doctrines, on the one hand,
and assertions of the need to relink those beliefs and doctrines with
their engendering experiences and symbols within the metaxy, on the

other. That is perhaps a modestly fruitful and non-utopian way of both recognizing the limits of each and maximizing the benefits of each.

## NOTES

[1]Cf. Augustine, *Serm.* 81:8, and chap. 25, "Senectus Mundi," in Brown 1969. Voegelin uses the phrase *saeculum senescens*, probably as a shorthand way of referring to the theme of the world growing old and Christians simply waiting out its days, as they expect the coming of the parousia. So far as I can tell, the words do not exactly occur in Augustine but see Ambrose, *De bono mortis*, 10:46. Augustine's *Serm.* 81:8, for example, uses *senescit mundus.* Cf. Augustine, *Enarr. in Ps.* 26:2:18 and 103:3:19. (Special thanks to James J. O'Donnell and Allan Fitzgerald for these references and for their scholarly advice.)

[2]"Hermeneutics"/"hermeneutical" are terms used by Voegelin in *IR*; cf. 96, n. 66; 162.

[3]Earlier references in *IR*: 114, 143, 154; the issue surfaces again, after the initial discussion here (356-57), at 366-73, and 515. The important discussion in *OH*, IV, 48-57, is something like a crescendo in Voegelin's long attention to the theme. His judgment still seems mixed: Canonization is a way of protecting revelatory symbols ("the protective stratum of Scripture"), and yet "the original symbols suffer the same kind of deformation into doctrine as the Platonic mythopoesis through the Stoic hypostases" (55). Is this deformation intrinsically necessary, or rather an ever-present danger? Voegelin seems to mean the latter at least at 56: "The In-Between of experience has a dead point from which the symbols emerge as the exegesis of its truth, but which cannot become itself an object of propositional knowledge. If the metaleptic symbol which is the word of both god and man is hypostatized into a doctrinal Word of God, the device can protect the insight gained against disintegration in society, but it also can impair the sensitivity for the source of truth in the flux of divine presence in time which constitutes history. Unless precautions of meditative practice are taken, the doctrinization of symbols is liable to interrupt the process of experiential reactivation and linguistic renewal. When the symbol separates from its source in the experiential Metaxy, the Word of God can degenerate into a word of man that one can believe or not."

[4]See, for example, the overture announcement of this principle: "Thus, the history of symbolization is a progression from compact to differentiated experiences and symbols" (5). For examples of how Voegelin puts this to work throughout *IR*, cf. 60-63, 94-95, 127, 163, 194-95, 299-303, 410.

[5]Voegelin's later use of the notion of equivalence seems to stress the element of continuity within the historical process more emphatically than prefiguration, naturally. Although, inasmuch as equivalence is not identity, there is still an expressed hint of the dimension of discontinuity. It is not entirely clear to me that the notion of equivalence is meant to replace prefiguration language in Voegelin's lexicon. In any case, cf. Voegelin's EESH, first published in 1970. HG was likely written at about the same time, it would seem.

[6]Particularly crucial, then, would be the issue of the Trinity, a topic to which Voegelin rarely, although insightfully, devotes himself. Cf., for example, the letter to Alfred Schütz, "On Christianity" (Opitz and Sebba 1981, 454-55), or a letter to Leo Strauss (Emberley and Cooper 1993, 83). In the midst of his fine

study of Anselm's meditative *Proslogion*, we find some rich insights into trinitarian theology, culminating with this helpful observation: "The Prayer [of the *Proslogion*] is a movement of the soul. Anselm moves from the first person of the Trinity to the second and third persons, from the Creator to the Christ and the paracletic Spirit, from the mortal imperfection of the creature to its immortal perfection in the beatific vision, from existence in the time of creation to existence in the eternity of the Beyond. For Anselm, thus, the trinitarian Creed is more than the letter of a doctrine to be believed, it has to be lived through as the true symbolization of a reality that moves from creation to salvation; and Anselm can live it through, and can enact the drama of the Trinity in the drama of the Prayer, because the quest of his reason is the proper response to the intelligible movement in the *fides*. There is reason in the Creed" (BB, 195-96). From the references given, I have the impression that Voegelin thinks of the Father as symbolizing transcendence; the Son, the transcendent as personal *Logos*; the Spirit, the transcendent as personally participable.

[7] Typically Voegelin writes that the revelatory experience of an individual (Abraham, Moses, etc.) somehow expands into the social body (194; cf. 199). Representation is esp. treated in *NSP*, chapters 1-3.

[8] Traditional typology would distinguish between "type" and "antitype," or equivalently (and somewhat confusingly) between "figure" and "reality"; "prefigure" and "figure" would be another equivalent set of terms. Thus, for example, as Voegelin exegetes Exod 4:14-16 and 7:1, the person of Moses would be, using Voegelin's terminology, the prefigure (or type, or figure, using other terminological forms encountered in the literature), while Christ would be the figure (or antitype, or reality, in the equivalent lexicons). See Thompson 1996, 51-53, 57-59, 99, 272 n. 70, 286 n. 29, for more on typology.

[9] In the case of Abraham, of course, we also have "the creative imagination used in transforming the symbol of civilizational bondage into the symbol of divine liberation . . ." (195).

[10] Hinduism knows many "incarnations" (better: "manifestations") only because the personality of God and human beings remains insufficiently differentiated. If God is personal, God is not generic, if I might employ a Voegelinian distinction; it is that personal, non-generic disclosure of God which the Incarnation attests. Interestingly, see *OH* IV, 320-21: "There is no doctrine in Hinduism that attaches itself to an historic theophany like the Christian dogma to the epiphany of Christ." Brahmanic Hinduism is "an incipient breakthrough . . . which does not quite reach its goal . . ." (321) "As a consequence, the historical dimension of humanity cannot become articulate" (321-22). "Incarnation" in the Christian sense is precisely not generic but uniquely a one-time event witnessing to a non-generic God as well.

# Exodus and Statecraft: A Postlude

# William M. Thompson

## Reading Voegelin with the Help of

## Heidegger and Levinas

Heidegger writes of the quadrate (*das Geviert*) of earth and sky, mortals and gods, evoking the density of relationships constituting every "thing." He also writes of the *Es gibt*, the German phrase for "There is . . . ," but with a typically etymological stress on the sense of "gift," following a literal translation: "It gives." Heidegger interpreter John Macquarrie describes this "It gives" as "the ultimate in Heidegger's philosophy," the source of his thinking, about which we might be able to say some things, but which as itself we cannot say. The relationship between the quadrate and the "It gives" is unclear, but one has to go against the grain not to view the quadrate as somehow grounded in a mysterious gifting. Levinas writes of the *il y a* (it is), but gives it a decidedly impersonal interpretation, without the Heideggerian sense of joy accompanying the *Es gibt*. Levinas seems to place the accent upon the *il*, the "it," rather than the "is," as if to stress the distance rather than the presence, the darkness instead of the light, which inhibits any pretense to totalization in our thinking and acting. He refers to his childhood memory of silence when sleeping alone. There is a rumbling, so to speak. There it is! "Not that there is this or that; but the very scene of being is open: there is." "It" is impersonal, unspecified, but inescapable. In a somewhat confusing and paradoxical way he even calls it "the phenomenon of impersonal being" on the one hand, and yet "neither nothingness nor being" on the other (Macquarrie 1994, 65ff., 98ff.; Levinas 1985, chap. 3). Levinas certainly shocks customary thinking.

"God and man [sic], world and society form a primordial community of being," constituting a "quaternarian structure," writes Eric Voegelin in the introduction which presides over all five volumes of his *Order and History*. We are not spectators but participators, albeit in varying modes of intensity and attunement, and so knowledge of this primordial community arises only from the perspective of participation within it. Like Heidegger, Voegelin here articulates the primordial source of his work in process in a quaternity which evokes a sense of the whole and our connectedness with it. In fact, Voegelin, borrowing the language employed in Egyptology to explain the experience of reality displayed in early Egyptian myths, writes of the experience of "consubstantiality" between the partners in the community of being. "Connectedness" might be misread as evoking an isolated subject over against isolated objects of inquiry. Voegelin maintains that such isolation is a "second reality" deforming but not eliminating the primary experience of reality. If Voegelin's project is anything, it is a constant protest against deformations of reality. At the same time, it is marked by a cognitive humility and modesty, for the fact that there is no vantage point outside the primordial community from which one knows precludes a totalistic knowledge of the whole.[1]

Intriguingly like both Heidegger and Levinas, Voegelin also wrote of the "It-reality" in his last work, *In Search of Order*, to express this mysterious community of being in its comprehensiveness. "I notice that philosophers, when they run into this structure incidentally . . . have a habit of referring to it by a neutral 'it'" (*OH* V, 16). This evokes the "comprehending reality" within which consciousness participates. Because "It" is comprehending, "It" is mysterious and clearly not available to a totalizing, grasping captivity. We are in its midst, and truth in the comprehensive sense must therefore be an experience of luminosity from within the It-reality. Yet "It" does not disallow our experience of "thing-reality" either, in which our consciousness does reach out to objects. "Consciousness . . . is a subject intending reality as its object [= thing-reality] but at the same time a something in a comprehending reality [= It-reality]" (16, 26).

Does it help to suggest these affinities between Heidegger, Levinas, and Voegelin? Perhaps some of the readers of this volume will be more familiar with Heidegger or Levinas, or both, than with Voegelin, and so this familiarity might function as a bridge for crossing over into Voegelin territory. Moreover, if Voegelin is correct, these three are partners in the community of being, and the partnership ought to be mutually illuminating through being expressive of the actual community of being. With this, we hit upon the deeper reason for suggesting these affinities. For this mutual partnership would be expressive of the It-reality and would bear testimony to the comprehending partnership in the community of being in which Heidegger, Levinas, and Voegelin participate. Such is what Voegelin at times calls the *homonoia* or likemindedness reflecting the common spirit of God known to Israel, or reflecting the common Nous of the mystic-philosophers, or the Logos of Christ known to Christianity (*OH* I, 240). Hopefully, then, the suggestion of these affinities helps. They are expressive of a principle which Voegelin says "lies at the basis of all my later work: *the reality of experience is self-interpretive*" (*AR*, 80). That self-interpretation is coming to articulation in Heidegger, Levinas, and Voegelin.

But the differences between the three remain significant, and perhaps in their own way bear testimony as well to features in the community of being noted by our three actors in the drama of existence. Levinas' forceful protest against all projects of totalization, pointed to in his emphasis upon the impersonality of the "it," can at least raise the question for us of the possibility of coming upon totalistic elements in *Israel and Revelation*, and perhaps even in the entire project of *Order and History*. Baird's paper is greatly concerned with this. In turn, this can stimulate in us the counter-question: How would Voegelin's work form the basis for a response, and would it be a series of distinct responses, given the "in process" nature of his project, which "ended" with the unfinished *In Search of Order*?

A similar back and forth would apply to Voegelin and Heidegger, and between the three as a whole (Heidegger, Levinas, and Voegelin). The note of joy in Heidegger's *Es gibt* evokes a primordial intuition of being's presence. The quadrate indicates the complex interrelations constituting the site for a possible disclosure of being. One gains the sense that the forgetfulness of being has much to do with distortions in the quadrate, on Heidegger's account. One senses much affinity on these points between Voegelin and Heidegger, and it is precisely this affinity which seems to create a profound chasm between them and Levinas. A philosophy of being and presence, if only by intimation, needs decentering by the ethical relationship truly open to the other, who can only be other by being neither nothing nor being, Levinas seems to argue. Without such decentering, an ontology inevitably becomes totalistic and hubristic. Where Heidegger and Voegelin seem to agree, they seem to disagree with Levinas.

But the agreement between Heidegger and Voegelin would seem to be only partial. Voegelin vigorously noted gnostic elements in at least some of Heidegger's writings (*SPG*, 46-48), although he also had some sympathy for him as a "victim" of the deformation of the It-reality into thing-reality by the orthodox philosophy of his time (*OH* V, 63-64). He also seems to credit Heidegger with regaining, albeit laboriously, the agreement between the orders of mind and being as a basic philosophical problem, through a critique of modern objectivist thought (*AE*, 79). Voegelin vigorously (but critically, especially in the later volumes) affirms a philosophy of being, of course, throughout *Order and History*, but distances himself from Heidegger's view of the matter. The latter's view, at least in *An*

*Introduction to Metaphysics*, and by implication throughout his work, offers us a closed construct of being, emptied of all content, "shutting off immanent from world-transcendent being" (*SPG*, 47-48). Is Voegelin being fair to Heidegger? Certainly a submitting to the revelatory experiences of Israel and Christianity is missing in Heidegger. Voegelin would seem to regard this as an eclipsing of the historical field, a gnostic refusal to submit to history (*AR*, 72). One of the reasons for Voegelin's beginning his magnum opus in political philosophy with Israel was precisely to signal a break with gnostic eclipses of the historical field. Voegelin claims that history teaches us that being is open rather than closed, an able-to-be-questioned because an intelligible mystery (a *logos*). History discloses our participation in being through experiences of faith and hope and the willingness of at least some to submit to the authority of those experiences.

On the face of it, the Heideggerian "anticipation of being" seems modest and non-hubristic. Anything but gnostic. And an appreciation of his project can perhaps foster the search for an ontology which avoids objectivistic thought and remains rather modest and chastened by the lessons of history. This is certainly a sensitivity we should bring to our reading of Voegelin. But Voegelin demurs to some extent. He does not find the humility in Heidegger that a chastening from history's lessons offers. Instead, he finds something of the gnostic's alternative construction of history (the "second reality"). One thinks of Augustine's confession that he could not accept Christ because he lacked the humility. Christ the Logos came in the humility of the crucified Jesus, and Augustine the philosopher was too proud (Augustine 1972, 10:29). Well, what if the Logos speaks in a way we are unwilling to anticipate? (*OH* I, 409) What if we are too proud because being is too humble? When Voegelin writes of a willingness to submit to the authority of revelatory experiences (195), he seems to evoke something of this Augustinian humility. Perhaps it is this philosophy of being's humility that creates something of a bridge to the concerns of Levinas, without going all the way in the direction of Levinas. The (pseudo)being that is the projection of the gnostic's desire for a totalizing presence that can be manipulated, while surely a "second reality" on the historical field that has inflicted much misery upon humanity and world, is not the being of the *logos* disclosed within history. Such, at least, would seem to be Voegelin's reasoning faith, or his form of what he describes rather appealingly at one point as "the conspiracy of faith and reason" (461).

Hopefully this will be sufficient to evoke the originary experiences and symbols of Voegelin's thought, especially in *Israel and Revelation*, but also in his project as a whole with its varied shades of nuance. Hopefully, too, this will be sufficient to evoke the non-hagiographical approach of our volume. Our goal is not to erect a Voegelinian canon of thought, but to participate in reality as fully and as critically as possible. Allowing Heidegger and Levinas to interrogate our reading of Voegelin is meant to symbolize, and tutor us in, this kind of participation. At the same time, as we proceed it will perhaps become clear that the concerns adumbrated in this three-way discusssion lie behind the essays of this volume and can serve as a helpful point of reference in this postlude.

## HISTORY, ORDER, AND THE
## PRIMORDIAL COMMUNITY OF BEING

The presiding principle guiding all five volumes of *Order and History* was announced in the preface to *Israel and Revelation*, the first volume of the magnum opus: "The order of history emerges from the history of order" (ix). It is true that Voegelin announced a "break" between this first volume of the series and the fourth, *The Ecumenic Age*, but the break had to do, not with the validity of the guiding principle, but with the manner of its application (*OH* IV, 1-2). So far as I can tell, this estimation by Voegelin of his own principle might apply to the interlocutors in this volume of essays as well. For no one seems to contest the validity of the principle, although the manner of its application is repeatedly, at least by implication, a subject of discussion and even debate. At least no one seems to contest this principle in an unambiguous way.[2] There has already been occasion in this book to note the break in Voegelin's own application of the principle, and we will make reference to it again. For now it will be helpful to indicate the relationship between the primordial community of being, just adumbrated above, and the symbols of order and history noted in the guiding principle. Somewhat roughly we can say that "history" in one of its meanings is the human struggle to become successfully attuned to the partners in the community of being, while "order" expresses the transparency of the partners for one another achieved on the level of society, which in turn reflects the more comprehensive order of being itself. For society's order forms a part of being's order (*OH* I, ix). Voegelin writes of the "truth of order," suggesting by that phrase that being's own transparency constitutes truth, the "Logos of being" as he puts it (xiv). If we look at it this way, history becomes a struggle for truth. In what way does Israel exemplify this struggle (history)? How is it transparent for the partners in the community of being (the truth of order or the untruth of disorder)? Such are the central issues of *Israel and Revelation*. Inasmuch as this study exposes the truth of order, it is a study which does not "explore curiosities of a dead past, but [is] an inquiry into the structure of the order in which we live presently." In this way, following Plato, the study becomes both diagnosis and therapy (xiv). The first, because it exposes the fall into the untruth of disorder; the second, because it attests being's truthful transparency.

While Voegelin compellingly writes of the partners in the primordial community of being, he does so from the perspective of a participant rather than a spectator. It may seem like he is only a subject looking at objects, such as society or nature, or even God. But in a strict sense he, as ourselves, is rather in the midst of these partners. We have seen how he stresses a participatory form of knowing. At the same time, this helps explain his focus upon the human participant within the social and historical fields. There is no romantic tendency to pretend that one can take the perspective of the non-human participants, whether of nature or of God, in Voegelin. There is a rich sense of connectedness in Voegelin's philosophy, one which invites those who would continue his work to explore reality further, on the levels of the human person, nature, of society, and of divinity. He did some of this in varying ways, now being led by the historical materials to this partner, now to the other, and so on. But always there is the "modesty," so to speak, of happily admitting that he operates from his perspective within society, not from nature's, and not from God's. In this way, Voegelin's philosophy is political and historical in the profoundly philosophical sense of society and history as the site within which the human participant knowingly participates in the reality of existence. We will locate, now, some of the suggestions flowing from this books' interdisciplinary discussion under the heading of the presiding principle on history and order just sketched.

## The *History* of Order

"The order of history emerges from the history of order." History as order's source will occupy our focus in this section. Voegelin's work is characteristically historical through and through, as readers of all of his works will attest. His typical manner of procedure is to locate himself and the issues under concern, through a philosopher's reflective distance, within an historical field. He seeks to display the relevant story of history through its events and the narrative(s) articulated by

the human actors within that story as they attempt to express an
unfolding intelligibility, such as it is. The last volume of *Order and
History* appropriately reflected upon "story" as the typical symbolic
form of history as a struggling interaction between events and narrative (*OH* V, 24). Concentrating upon history in this section of our
postlude offers us an opportunity to underline the typically narrative,
expositional quality of Voegelin's work. The more "theoretically"
oriented are apt to pass too quickly over this narrative, dramatic
dimension of Voegelin's work, concentrating on the "order," so to
speak, at the expense of the "history." But if we follow him, it is the
interaction between the two that is critical and fruitful. There is no
escaping the historical, storied nature of our existence. Somewhat like
Hans-Georg Gadamer, Voegelin seeks to overcome the prejudices
against the prejudices ("prejudgments") offered us by history.[3] But
unlike Gadamer, he is himself more of an historian as well, actually
practicing the art of writing the story of history. As he seeks to display
the history of order, he must participate in that history and struggle
through to the intelligible narrative offered through the unfolding
events. Much of the evocative power and persuasiveness of *Israel and
Revelation* and of the entire *Order and History* comes from this sense
of historical participation. Perhaps one of the reasons Voegelin
regularly refers to great literary masters, as well as his constant
attentiveness to symbolic forms, is his appreciation for humanity's
storied nature. The realities of participation, of movement and
countermovement, of struggle, of openness and regression, of questing and of closure, of being drawn, and more, the *pathos* and *eros* of
history—all of these are more evident in the symbolic form of the
story. The "order" which the philosopher discovers, if it is to be
discovered at all, comes through the historical struggle. It is true that
Voegelin seems to place the primacy upon "order" and its "truth." In
this sense, he would partly resonate with Tinder's cautions about
today's stress on narrative. Voegelin is historical, but he is not an
historicist. The narrative discloses a world of truth, and in that sense
is open to transcendence and even broken by it.[4] He is a political
philosopher, after all, and indeed the very title of his magnum opus
places "order" first. This seems as it should be, for surely the untruth
of history is not on the same level as its truth. Still there is the modesty
of the need to remain within history and to refuse to pretend to a
perspective beyond it. Keeping this in mind, it is hard to see how the
charge of totalization really fits what Voegelin is up to.

*Israel and Revelation* would seem to possess a special significance
from the perspective of what we are calling the "guiding principle," for

it makes the claim that "without Israel there would be no history, but only the eternal recurrence of societies in cosmological form" (126). Part of the work's compellingness is the contrast drawn between the cosmological order of the Ancient Near East, constituting part one, and the remaining parts two, three, and four, which explore various features of the historical form of existence brought about through Israel. What does *Israel and Revelation* say about each of these, the cosmological and the historical forms of existence? A number of this book's essays (e.g., Anderson, Baird, Sandoz, Thompson) have touched on the cosmological form, for in *Israel and Revelation* Voegelin maintained that there were continual conflicts between these two forms of existence in Israel itself. One of the most controversial aspects of *Israel and Revelation*, in fact, is Voegelin's proposal that "the cosmological symbolism pours back into the order of Israel with the establishment of a permanent government under kings" (xi). With this, the openness to an historical form of existence constituted by attunement to a world-transcendent God runs the danger of sliding back into the cyclic recurrence characteristic of world-immanent existence, and in fact does so at a number of crucial points. For in the cosmological mode, nature supplies the chief analogue in the light of which the human partner in the community of being understands himself or herself. The fragile differentiation of the divine partner's world-transcendence, as experienced, for example, in Abraham and Moses, is overtaken, so to speak, by the earlier, cosmological experience of consubstantiality.

Israel's experience of a world-transcendent God was indeed a "leap upward in being" (*OH* I, 10), beyond the cosmological mode's "charmed community . . . where animals and plants can be men and gods, where men can be divine and gods are kings . . . where things are the same and not the same, and can change into each other" (3).[5] Voegelin stressed this leap upward, emphasizing that from then on the divine partner would occupy the first rank; "participation in mundane being recedes to second rank." And, in fact, the leap is a conversion "experienced, not as the result of human action, but as a passion, as a response to a revelation of divine being, to an act of grace" (10). Voegelin's argument is that historical form and the experience and symbolization of the world-transcendent God imply each other. In fact, in a shorthand way, he will simply write that "historical form [can be] understood as the experience of the present under God" (130). Why? "When the order of the soul and society is oriented toward the will of God, and consequently the actions of the society and its members are experienced as fulfillment or defection, a historical present is created, radiating its form over a past that was not consciously historical in its own present" (128). When Voegelin writes that "without Israel there would be no history," he means there would be no historical *form* of existence, no differentiated consciousness of history as a form of existence, not that cultures existing in the cosmological form are not historically real (127). Within the cosmological form, experience and symbolization is simply too compact and undifferentiated for the consciousness of an historical present under God to emerge. Voegelin thus recognizes that the term "history" can be used equivocally. On the level of "objective time," the cosmological civilizations are genuine history as much as Israel. But on the level of "inner form," in which there is a sufficiently differentiated understanding of the present under God, history is a peculiarity at first of Israel. Voegelin does not want to simply accept an equivocal use of the word "history," and so he puts Israel's more differentiated understanding to work, so to speak, to resolve the equivocation.

We have thus come across a number of linguistic practices significant for a proper reading of *Israel and Revelation*: "history" as objective time and as inner form. That "history as the present under God was the inner form of Israel's existence" (*OH* I, 355) was the key thesis argued by *Israel and Revelation*. The term "inner form" may remind some readers of H. Richard Niebuhr's distinction between "inner and outer history," or history from the perspectives of the participant and the observer, respectively. Voegelin referred appreciatively to a work of Niebuhr's in which there is a discussion of this distinction (*NSP*, 78), and so there may have been some influence from Niebuhr's side on Voegelin with regard to the notion of historical form (Niebuhr 1941, 47, 59-66). Voegelin wants to discriminate in some way between more surface, spatial and temporal features on the historical plane (history as objective time) and the psychospiritual plane of experience (history as inner form). Doubtlessly Voegelin's terminology here is the result of his own creative thinking through of the historical materials in the light of the contemporary continental philosophy of his time, especially neo-Kantian and Romantic philosophy. The distinctions between history on the "pragmatic" and "paradigmatic," as well as on the "pragmatic" and "spiritual," level—all occurring in *Israel and Revelation* (114, 121, 121f., 147f., 161)— would seem to be further expressions of Voegelin's attempt to discriminate between the spatial-temporal surface and the depth of consciousness within history.[6]

It seems clear that these are distinctions, not separations. "Paradigmatic and pragmatic histories are not rivals." "It begins to dawn on us that history is a complicated fabric of which two strands become visible . . ." (*OH* I, 123). Interestingly a nearly identical distinction between the "pragmatic" and the "spiritual," or between a "pragmatic shell" and a "transcendent substance," plays a prominent role in Voegelin's *The Ecumenic Age* (*OH* IV, 116, 133f., 142, 149, etc.), thus indicating a continuity in his understanding of history in this regard.

Bernhard Anderson in chapter one found no compelling reason from the biblical side to disagree with Voegelin's view of Israel's role in the emergence of historical form. He thought that Voegelin was correct in his view that Israel brought about a novel sense of history through its experience of a present under the world-transcendent God. His later study in chapter two adds observations on the debate between various approaches to biblical history current at the time of the writing of *Israel and Revelation*, namely, that between the tradition of the German school dominated chiefly by Gerhard von Rad, and that of the U. S. American tradition represented by W. F. Albright. If you will, von Rad emphasizes the paradigmatic level of history, while the American emphasizes the pragmatic. Anderson writes that Voegelin relied on the approach of the Germans. Indeed, the many references to von Rad throughout *Israel and Revelation* simply confirm Voegelin's own statement that in matters having to do with views of Israelite historiography he is "closest to those of von Rad" (*OH* I, 162 n. 20). Voegelin had found in von Rad a willingness to go beyond the earlier tendency represented by Wellhausen, who searched for sources behind the final text, and to treat the text of Scripture in its final form. It is the final form which mediates to us the paradigmatic level of history in its varied shades of compactness and differentiation. The over-attentiveness to hypothetical sources "behind" the text (e.g., J, E, D, P) runs the danger of eliminating the paradigmatic plane of history.[7] Voegelin had also found the work of the Uppsala school, especially as represented by Ivan Engnell, moving in a direction similar to his own with its respect for how tradition aids in the emergence of meaning and with its respect for the final text as well. The recovery of the positive role of tradition goes along with Voegelin's view of tradition as, in part, a movement within history from compactness to differentiation.

Voegelin, by self-admittance, is "closest" to von Rad, as just noted. Perhaps von Rad's willingness to attend to the properly theological (paradigmatic) dimensions of Israel's history in his emphasis upon the significance of the creedal centers of meaning (Exodus, Sinai, and Shechem) appeals to the philosophical sensitivities of Voegelin (*OH* I, 137). At one point Voegelin had sarcastically written of the sausage view of history which simply grinds out more and more material, only to crumble under the accumulating weight (*OH* IV, 332). The lack of theoretical penetration was all too glaring. Voegelin had found in von Rad's work something greatly superior to such "sausagesis." Still, Voegelin is a philosopher rather than a creedal theologian, and so, while he may rely on von Rad, he goes his own way. Perhaps this is why, pace Anderson, one also comes across a significant number of positive references to Engnell and even to the American Albright, along with a continual attempt to interrogate the Old Testament from a properly philosophical perspective. "The basic philosophical weaknesses" of the kind of biblical source analysis common at the time of writing of *Israel and Revelation*, Voegelin suggested, was "the attempt to treat the Biblical narrative as if it were 'literature' in the modern sense and the disregard for its nature as a symbolism which articulates the experience of a people's order—of the ontologically real order of Israel's existence in historical form" (*OH* I, 156).

Voegelin's philosophy of symbolic forms may yet possess significant potential in mediating between the conflicting schools of biblical interpretation today. For one of the great strengths of *Israel and Revelation* is its sensitivity to "the difference between empirical, philological work and the interpretations put on its results" (*OH* I, 153). Von Rad, for example, has been criticized for insufficiently attending to the empirical materials "grounding" the biblical narrative, resting content with the text in its final form (Hayes and Prussner 1985, 233-39). This could result in a biblical and confessional positivism. Voegelin greatly appreciates von Rad's theological desire to transcend historical positivism through an attentiveness to Israel's confessions of faith, but he wants to avoid a confessional positivism as well. Hence his dialogue with other traditions of interpretation, as noted above, as well as his philosopher's attempt to work out the dynamics of the movement from compactness to differentiation in the emergence of meaning and symbolic forms. Some, perhaps even all, arguments over actual cases of interpretation of biblical texts in this book (e.g., Mackler) may have to do with differences over what is compact, what is differentiated, in the text. At a minimum, Voegelin's hermeneutics allows us a way of discriminating between the two. In my chapter on Christ and Christianity in *IR*, I endeavored to articulate somewhat more fully *IR*'s typological imagination. Strictly speaking, if I understand it correctly, the text is a witness to, as a result of participation in, the Logos, in Voegelin's hermeneutics. The various texts of Holy Writ articulate dimensions of this Logos on a range between simple compactness and complete differentiation.

When Voegelin strives to express the "experience and symbolization" mediated by the text, one must attend to these along that range, and not simply on the differentiated level. Obviously there will be arguments over interpretation, which depend, it seems, upon the quality of participation in reality of the interpreter.[8]

Anderson in chapter two states that "the view of God's revelation in history, whether understood as ordinary history or a history of traditions, was tried in the balance and found wanting," listing various reasons of differing compellingness for this state of affairs. At the same time, he finds Voegelin's emphasis upon revelation in the consciousness or psyche of inspired individuals, as well as upon the transcendent dimension of history and its symbolization, still fundamentally valid and even "a breath of fresh air." Anderson refers to the two extremes of literalism (or fundamentalism) and historicism, and suggests that Voegelin avoids either. However, I wonder whether Voegelin would fully agree to Anderson's judgment that he (i.e., Voegelin) "is not really interested in revelation *in history*, that is, a process of events, or even in a sacred history (*Heilsgeschichte*), a sequence of crucial historical events charged with revelatory meaning." Or at least I wonder whether Voegelin would want to express it that way. In the terms of *Israel and Revelation*, this would run the danger of turning pragmatic and paradigmatic history into rivals, or this would be a separation rather than a distinction within a unity. Voegelin's philosophy of symbolic forms avoids both a positivistic view of pragmatic history and a fundamentalisic view of paradigmatic history.[9] If you will, the first removes the world-transcendent God from the primordial community of being, while the second removes the world-immanent members of the community of being from God. History is always a struggle for attunement between *all* the partners in the community of being, but the attunement varies in hard-to-categorize ways between compactness and differentiation. It does not seem that Voegelin separates the psyches or consciounsesses of inspired persons from the community of being. In his later thought he would argue that a theory of consciousness is the *center* of a philosophy of politics, but a center is not the whole (*AE*, 3).[10]

As if confirming von Rad's view that the Old Testament offers us more than one theological "center," the field of biblical interpretation today is even more widely pluralistic than it was at the time of *OH* I. Indeed, it would seem that it is in search of a philosophy of history such as Voegelin offers, although it might likely decline the offer. This pluralism in the field, one might argue, represents an intensification and even radicalization at times, of our modern historical awareness.

For example, the so-called linguistic turn is a further awareness of the historical and cultural conditioning of human experience, personally and collectively. The application of literary forms of analysis, now not in the older sense of source analysis (as with Wellhausen, for example), which sought sources behind the text, but in the sense of probing how the symbols and genres of the final text itself work, expresses this awarness of the cultural forms of historical mediation. Voegelin's attentiveness to the final form of the text, and its symbolic forms, seems quite congenial to today's new interest in appropriating the linguistic mediation of human experience. In this respect, *Israel and Revelation* already represented an advance over the attempt to bypass the text and hypothetically reconstruct the "historical past." Such was a part of the legacy of ignoring the "emergence of meaning" in history. The later attention to story, narrative, and event in *OH* V represents a further refinement of this linguistic sensitivity. At the same time, Voegelin's philosophy of history seeks to avoid a mere literary aestheticism, which locks the text up in an ideal world apart from history.[11]

Somewhat paradoxically, a heightened historical awareness can even call into question the very hegemony of the category of the "historical" in biblical studies, and in philosophy in general. For example, the historian's insight that the field of Old Testament theology is intensely pluralistic has led to a vigorous discussion of the implications of biblical scholarship's ignoring the wisdom literature, with its stress upon creation rather than historical events. This is something of a special challenge to *OH* I, which lacks a treatment of the wisdom literature, as Anderson noted. This is an important lacuna, to be sure. Interestingly its inclusion by Voegelin could have strengthened the case for his philosophical ontology, which does not radically separate Israel's revelatory history from the primordial community of being, among which is nature or creation.[12] At the same time, Voegelin's understanding of Israel's historical form would lead him to suggest that Israel's more differentiated undertanding of history as a present under God would necessarily lead to a more differentiated view of creation itself as "under God." And in his *The Ecumenic Age* he takes up this "unfinished" study of wisdom and credits it with contributing "a further differentiation of pneumatic consciousness" (*OH* IV, 51).

Still, I think it must be said that Voegelin's project grants a certain "hegemony" to the notion of history. The guiding principle is, after all, that the order of history emerges from the history of order. One would not even be concerned with creation as a competing center of meaning were it not for the historically aware human partner in the community of being finding meaning in creation. At the same time, the human partner always exists in history, although his or her historical awareness may be more or less compact or differentiated. Cultures governed more by creation or the cosmological symbolism as the center of meaning have not yet undergone the differentiation of the world-transcendent God, a differentiation creating the sense of a present under God's will, a will one might either fulfill or from which one might defect. But those cultures still exist in history, even if not in historical *form*, to use the terminology of *Israel and Revelation*.

Several of this book's essays (e.g., Anderson, Mackler, Ranieri) make reference to Voegelin's "break" with *IR*, a break announced in *OH* IV, but hinted at in earlier works, and perhaps even in *IR* itself, if Ranieri is correct. Chiefly at issue here, it seems, was Voegelin's later view that "the unilinear construction of history" as "the great achievement of Israelites and Christians"—"history as a meaningful course of events on a straight line of time"—was a "conventional belief" that simply did not measure up to the historical materials. He himself had found evidence of the tendency to construct history from a "divine-cosmic origin of order to the author's present" as far back as the Near Eastern empires of the third millennium B.C. He considered this a form of "cosmological symbolism," for it does not represent an adequate awareness of the Divine which is beyond the cosmos. A differentiated awareness of the Divine Beyond would be attuned to the eschatological direction of history, and not seek to close the historical process by having it come to its climax in the author's present within the cosmos. Such unilinear constructions he now named "historiogenesis" (*OH* IV, 7ff., 300ff.). *The Ecumenic Age* (i.e, *OH* IV) is an exceedingly difficult work, for its very form, in following along with the historical materials, breaks with unilinearism. There are advances in consciousness, to be sure, but they do not seem to move on a straight line, nor do they ever really, nor should they, "abolish the cosmos" in which they occur (9). Accordingly, the studies in *OH* IV "move backward and forward and sideways," following a "movement through a web of meaning with a plurality of nodal points" (57). By the way, note how Voegelin does write of a certain movement "forward." History does attest, as noted, to advances in differentiation, advances of consciousness and symbolization transfiguring reality itself (314, 316, 326). This suggests a certain linearity, although it is not a unilinearity, but a plurilinearity, it seems. The term "postmodern" would probably bring more lack of clarity than clarity here, because it is so undefined and too limiting, but in some of its meanings it would seem to capture something of the nonunilinearity of *OH* IV. At the same time, *OH* IV's emphasis upon the cosmos as the site of differentiating consciousness leads to a corresponding emphasis upon the recurring need for cosmogonic myth which gives expression in story form to the "divine-cosmic beginning." And Voegelin adds: "Any attempt to overcome, or to dispose of, the myth is suspect as a magic operation, motivated by an apocalyptic desire to destroy the cosmos itself" (10).

There is a touch of irony in Voegelin's assertion that he had thought that the unilinear construction was the "great achievement" of Israel- ites and Christians. For *OH* IV clearly does not consider it "great." For it is not unique to Israelites and Christians, it turns out, nor is such unilinearism something positive to be sought after in any case. For it is not really an adequate differentiation of the process of history. In terms of the grid from compactness to differentiation, historiogenesis would seem to be rather compact in its articulation of the eschatological, open thrust of the historical process. It is clearly not "fully historically conscious," and indeed *OH* IV makes the claim that "the transfiguring exodus within reality achieves the full consciousness of itself when it becomes historically conscious as the Incarnation of God in Man" (302). This assertion would seem to give greater weight to the epochal role of Jesus and Christianity, rather than of Israel, in forming historical consciousness. This is perhaps true in principle, but a great part of the thrust of *OH* IV would seem to be an argument that Christianity, at least in its Pauline and Johannine forms, along with Israel and others, has also fallen into historiogenesis (7, 13-20, 258).

What, then, according to *OH* IV, is the contribution of Israel to the emergence, not of historiogenesis, but of truly formative historical awareness? Certainly this work argues that the truth of existence comes from a plurality of spiritual events occurring in Persia and India, Israel, Hellas, and China, but that none of these has developed a "fully balanced symbolization of order that would cover the whole area of man's existence in society and history." Rather, "different aspects of the one truth of man's existence under God" tend to be accentuated by the various spiritual irruptions (*OH* IV, 301). So, might we say at least that the historical dimension of human existence receives the greater accentuation in Israel and Christianity according to Voegelin's later thought? Taken as a whole, *OH* IV gives this impression, although Christianity rather than Judaism is explicitly credited with bringing "the historicity of existential truth into sharper focus" (251). This seems to have to do with the sharper differentiation of God's transcendence beyond the cosmos in Christianity (250). But, of course, this is clearly dependent upon the Israelite pneumatic differentiations (12-13). Historical form in the sense of the emergence of a sharp differentiation of living in a moving present under a world-transcendent God is the contribution of Israel. But one has the impression that "historical form," if that is the correct category, has widened in the "later" Voegelin to the view that historical awareness embraces the noetic and pneumatic differentiations which bring various facets of the process of history into visibility (306-9).

## THE *Order* OF HISTORY

So far as I can tell, one will search in vain for a definitive definition of the category of "order" in Voegelin's writings. The final volume of the magnum opus is titled *In Search of Order*, and that is something to keep in mind as we turn now to a consideration of the question of order and Israel. "Order" was the goal of Voegelin's quest, and because its truth emerges from history, like history it has an eschatological, open-ended character to it. The actual term "order" is a key symbolism which Voegelin seems to have greatly derived from the Greek term *kosmos*, which can mean in a highly formal way "an ordered process" (*OH* II, 233-34 [on Heraclitus]). The actual meaning and articulation of this ordered process, however, is in movement, the result of the quality of the participation of the human partners in the community of being. The term "order" should not really be set in opposition to "freedom," as is sometimes done in some treatments of political theory and theology. For freedom in a genuinely human sense is a dimension of the truth of order in Voegelin's understanding of the term. It seems best to return to the preface of *OH* I for one's bearings on this topic of "order." There it refers to "the order of being of which the order of society is a part" (ix). As the insight into the order of being (i.e., the primordial quaternity) develops, so too does the insight into the order of society. Voegelin uses the term, then, much as he uses the category "history": as an instrument for critical analysis and interpretation (163). The actual term may or may not be present in the materials under consideration, but unless we are to regress into nominalism, the realities evoked by the term are present.[13] "Every society is burdened with the task, under its concrete conditions, of creating an order that will endow the fact of its existence with meaning in terms of ends divine and human" (ix). This social struggle for order reflects the quality of a society's participation in the order of being.

It will be helpful to condense our concluding observations under the headings of God, human beings, society, and nature, the four partners in the community of being. The struggle for order is really the struggle for the truth of these partners. Tutoring us in the art and discipline of attunement to *all* of these partners may be one of Voegelin's most significant legacies in the field of political thought. The stress upon the reality of struggle, along with the sensitivity to the concrete conditions under which all societies labor, gives a realistic, modest, non-utopian shape to Voegelin's work. At the same time, this epistemological modesty goes along with an intellectual daringness which attempts to be holistic in its search. The field is not narrowed or eclipsed. We do not out-comprehend it. "It" comprehends us.

Perhaps the dimension of Voegelin's work least developed by his students is that of our partnership with nature. It is probably the dimension least developed by himself as well, although this is still a case of the teacher being ahead of his pupils. Today's ecological awareness brings our relationship with nature into increasing importance. At the same time, there is a need to avoid apocalyptic exaggerations, and so here is a case in which Voegelin's well known attack on metastatic and apocalyptic speculation can be quite useful (*OH* I, xiii; V, 33). *IR* is relevant to this issue of our partnership with nature in at least two ways. The book's part one on the cosmological order of the Ancient Near East is a treasury of insight into how the natural cosmos supplies the chief analogue for the organization of social order within the myths of the Ancient Near East. Voegelin clearly treats these myths seriously, and refuses to eclipse their contribution to social order by dismissing them as prescientific or simply false. They represent a legitimate mode of awareness of the partners in the community of being, albeit a mode of awareness that is less differentiated than that of philosophy and revelation in certain, qualified respects. Their compactness is their virtue, for myth "provides the symbols which adequately express a balanced manifold of experiences" (*OH* I, 84). Coming to expression in the "primary experience of the cosmos" is "the whole, *to pan*, of an earth below and a heaven above—of celestial bodies and their movements; of seasonal changes; of fertility rhythms in plant and animal life; of human life, birth, and death; and above all, as Thales still knew, it is a cosmos full of gods." Voegelin stresses this last, because he teaches that the divine reality was known in the world of the myth, but known as intracosmic rather than as world-transcendent (*OH* I, index, s.v., "primary experiences"; IV, 68ff.) Voegelin nuanced his treatment of myth throughout the magnum opus, and what emerges with increasing force is his view, noted earlier, that any attempt to do away with myth is suspect, for it remains the symbolic form of our cosmic grounding. In that sense it remains true that "to establish a government is an essay in world creation" (*OH* I, 16).[14]

There is clearly a difference between the way myth is understood in the cultures and civilizations before or different from philosophy (the noetic differentiation) and revelation (the pneumatic differentiation) and those which have undergone those epochal experiences. *OH* is aware of this, and with increasing nuance notes the manner in which, for example, a Plato or an Aristotle engage in a philosophical use of myth, or in which mythical elements are absorbed into the worlds of Jewish and Christian revelation.[15] This brings us to the second area of relevance of *IR* to the question of our partnership with nature, namely, this absorption of the cosmological symbolism in Israel itself. The book surfaces for us something of the dynamics of this process of absorption, and in that respect throws critical light upon how well other attempts at establishing government have been "essays in world creation."[16]

We have already noted how *IR* lacks any sustained treatment of the wisdom literature, something pointed out by Anderson. Much of this, of course, would be relevant to a consideration of how Israel absorbed the cosmological, creation-centered perspective of the Ancient Near East, and, as noted, *OH* IV (51ff.) is something of a redressing of the imbalance here when it credits Proverbs 1-9 with a "further differentiation of pneumatic consciousness." Anderson, Baird, Mackler, and Ranieri also stress the theme within *IR* of the tension between the "regression" to an earlier cosmological symbolism, particularly in the period of the monarchy, and the need to "break" with the cosmos brought about by the differentiation of the world-transcendent God. Voegelin argued that the implications of the "break" (which is not to be thought of as complete discontinuity, it seems) were badly thought through and lived through in the monarchy especially, although elsewhere within Israel as well. Anderson, Mackler, and perhaps Ranieri, are inclined to disagree. Each seems to concentrate more on the level of governmental-social relations rather than on Israel's theology of ecology and the land. Helpful in any future thinking through of the matter are *IR*, 298-303, pages which argue that the cosmological and the historical forms of order should not be conceived of as "mutually exclusive." Clearly each "has an organizing center of its own," and grasping this and thinking through its implications would seem to be the great struggle of sociopolitical order. As elements of the cosmological form are received into the historical form, tensions are bound to develop, if there is a "transmission without transformation." But they are also "parts of a continuum in so far as they are linked by the identity of the order of being and existence which man experiences, on the scale of compactness and differentiation, in the course of history." After all, Israel's differentiation of the world-transcendent God does not lift it out of the world. Its own "conditions of existence in the world, such as the celestial and vegetational cycles, birth and death, the rhythm of the generations, the work to sustain life, the necessity of governmental organization, remain what they were and do not require new symbolization."

Human persons and society—perhaps we can condense these into the one phrase of "human partnership"—occupy much of the focus of our book's essays. With the "break" from cosmological to historical form, not nature but the human self as ordered to God "becomes the model of order that will furnish symbols for ordering society analogically in its image." Voegelin names this "macroanthropic symbolization" (*OH* I, 6). One can sense the influence of Plato rather strongly—society is the soul writ large of *Republic* 434e (*OH* III, 86)—but Voegelin applies the dynamics of this process to Israel only *mutatis mutandis*. If you will, the order of Israel is the experience of an Abraham, a Deborah, or a Moses, for example, writ large (*OH* I, 188ff., 201ff., 380ff.).[17] This is the aspect of *IR* which many political scientists will find at least somewhat familiar, for it surfaces themes commonly discussed in the literature. The dignity of the human person, with its implication of human rights; the quest for a social form of togetherness which fosters those rights; the struggle between freedom and law; the difference between legitimate and illegitimate exercises of freedom; the nature of the common good; the kinds of virtues requisite for social togetherness; the relationship between society and government; etc.—all these questions and concerns break into more differentiated clarity with the emergence of historical form. But while this is familiar terrain, what was somewhat decentering for the political guild was Voegelin's stress upon the role of Israel and revelation in the emergence of these matters into clarity. Crucial in this regard was Voegelin's contention that "the leap in being, the experience of divine being as world-transcendent, is inseparable from the understanding of man [sic] as human" (235). They represent interpenetrating, although not necessarily completely simultaneous, processes of differentiation. So far as I can tell, none of this book's essays contests these proposals of Voegelin.

Recently Wolfhart Pannenberg (1977, 100) has praised Voegelin for avoiding the "excessively individualistic" tendency of modern thinking, which makes the struggle for individual freedom the great struggle in history. Pannenberg claims that Voegelin more soberly sees the great struggle as one for "the true order of society," although Voegelin also places the concern for freedom within the context of this social struggle. As we have noted, freedom and social order are not rivals in Voegelin's thought. Nonetheless, our essayists would seem to rather sharply divide on the nuances of the relationship between self and society in *IR*. In the interests of analysis, we may distinguish at least three questions, always bearing in mind that within the community of being influence always moves back and forth among the partners in mutual yet exceedingly complex ways. What, according to *IR*, is Israel's contribution to the differentiation of the human self? What is its contribution to the differentiation of human partnership in society? And what, thirdly, is the differentiation of the dynamics of the relationship between human selves and society?

A key passage regarding the self's differentiation within Israel occurs on the occasion of Voegelin's exegesis of the witch of Endor story (1 Sam 28:3-25). As we have noted, the reader will find this in our selections from *IR*. Saul's banishment of the ghost-masters is viewed as an expression of the new awareness of the world-transcendent God's radical difference from all created beings. There are not even to be any "ghosts" to share dignity of status with this God. But this banishment impeded a further consideration of the personal soul's "perfection through grace in death," relegating it to a kind of "public unconscious." And in fact, this state of public unconscious of the soul or human self runs throughout the period of the Kingdom. Reflection on the soul's destiny even eludes the prophets, at least until Ezekiel takes some steps toward recognizing personal responsibility and merit (Ezek 14;18;33). This represents a "break with the principle of collective responsibility," but the "idea of immortality" would enter Israel only under Persian influence in the third century. This public unconscious of the soul promoted "the advance of historical realism" in the sense that Israel, in the public sphere, developed historical narratives of the patriarchs rather than ancestor myths. On the other hand, it hindered "the development of philosophy," for this requires that "the soul must have disengaged itself sufficiently from the substance of particular human groups to experience its community with other men [sic] as established through the common participation in the divine Nous" (*OH* I, 232-42).

Still, those passages on the soul's public unconscious need to be balanced by some few others which credit a certain degree of differentiation of human personality to the prophets, and a great degree of differentiation indeed to Jeremiah. Sandoz notes the acclaimable observation by Voegelin as he seeks to describe the prophet's vocation:

"There are times, when the divinely willed order is humanly realized nowhere but in the faith of solitary sufferers" (*OH* I, 465). Apparently it is in the prophet's solitary suffering that we come upon a site for both soul-making and soul-differentiation. Voegelin's intriguing interpretation of the "phases" of the prophetic movement—from an institutional phase represented by Amos and Hosea, to Isaiah's metastatic phase, and on to Jeremiah's existential phase—presents the prophetic movement as an advance in the differentiation of personality (474ff.). Finally as he comes to an exegesis of the pieces of Jeremiah's spiritual autobiography, he observes that here we have something new. "In Jeremiah the human personality had broken the compactness of collective existence and recognized itself as the authoritative source of order in society." For Jeremiah had traced the prophets' social criticism and fostering of virtues "to its source in the concern with the order of personal existence under God" (485).

These are the kinds of passages that lead Baird to speak of Voegelin's personalism, following Voegelin himself (*OH* I, 369), a personalism whose ethical thrust is at least an inchoate bridge to Levinas' concern for ethics as first philosophy. Baird interprets this personalism more positively, it seems, while Anderson seems to view it more negatively, for it seems to lead Voegelin to devalue Israel's more social features. As we have seen, Anderson says of Voegelin that he "consistently stands by an ontology that is primarily personal (being of the soul) and only secondarily social (being in community)." Hence Voegelin's "dismissal of royal covenant theology . . . as a 'derailment.'" This personalism may also have something to do with Voegelin's tendency to largely ignore the priestly tradition of symbolization, a tendency also noted by Anderson. Tinder's essay, like Anderson's, also registers hesitancies about the manner in which *IR* relates the personal to the institutional. *IR* expresses, like Tocqueville, a more aristocratic attitude, and seems to leave the institutional undeveloped, suggests Tinder. With this we pass over to Voegelin's view of Israel's contribution to the differentiation of the social, a matter of some contention among this book's essayists. The force of Ranieri's paper might incline us to see Voegelin's (alleged) primarily personalist ontology as a legacy of his favoring of Greek philosophy, but Ranieri might likely not name Voegelin's ontology "personalist," as does Anderson, but rather "spiritualist," perhaps. It might be relevant to recall the observation of Sandoz that *IR* was written *after* the portions of *OH* dealing with the Greeks (e.g., II and III), even if it was published first. Voegelin's largely Greek philosophy of being supplies the interpretive categories for much of the analysis of *IR*.

By way of response, I offer the following as perhaps giving us a path upon which to pursue further the issues raised. Much of *IR* is directly concerned with the right ordering of society. The great issue of the kingdom is precisely that of whether the monarchy got it right, so to speak. Did it primarily move in the direction of a reordering of society in the light of divine revelation, or did it primarily regress back to a form of social relationships more typical of the cosmological forms of civilization? The issue for *IR* is not whether Israel should enjoy a social order, but whether that social order is to be characterized mainly as a relationship between "pre-personal," collectivist partners in consubstantiality, or rather as a partnership between persons who enjoy a more personal form of likemindedness because they have broken, like Jeremiah, the compact collectivism of the cosmological form. *IR* largely seems to argue that the monarchy was unsuccessful, and that this greatly explains the path pursued by the prophets. Their existence and "ideology critique" (Anderson), the latter stressed by Voegelin, might be argued to represent something of a vindication of *IR*'s interpretation of the monarchy. On the other hand, *IR* argues that the prophets failed to adequately concern themselves with the mundane issues of constitutional order in society, tending rather toward a metastatic otherworldly spiritualism. Passages in Isaiah are especially noted for this, argues Voegelin, but as Morse reminds us in chapter seven, this is a critique given of the prophets in general. Still, *IR* praises the prophets on the main issue, it seems to me: "The insight that existence under God means love, humility, and righteousness of action rather than legality of conduct was the great achievement of the prophets in the history of Israelite order" (*OH* I, 440). Voegelin's praise extends to the prophets' deepened awareness of personal guilt and sin as well as to the suffering servant's insight into forms of suffering that are salvific as Israel learns that redemption finally comes from a divine source beyond itself (236, 457, 488ff.). The still insufficiently developed understanding of the soul kept the prophets from articulating the human virtues with "ultimate, theoretical clarity" (439-40). But if it was not "ultimate," the prophetic trajectory was in this direction. The attempt by the prophets "to clarify the meaning of the Sinaitic revelation was therefore as right in rejecting the mythical form of the people's order as it was wrong in rejecting the order of mundane existence together with the mythical form" (444).

Does *IR*, then, favor an ontology that is primarily personal and only secondarily social? The introduction to *OH* I, we have seen, articulated a quaternarian ontology, one that is neither simply personal, nor simply social, nor simply ecological, but all of these in partnership

264                                           William M. Thompson

with God. *IR* can fairly be said to argue the case that Israel made
enormous advances in the articulating of dimensions of this vast
partnership, but that, on Voegelin's view, it did not articulate with full
clarity a social order between persons who had sufficiently differentiated their own personalities. But such likemindedness (*homonoia*),
which would be community in the deepest sense, was surely the goal
(*OH* I, 240). If you will, Voegelin seems to be arguing, not for the
primacy of a personalism as such nor, even worse, for an individualism, but for a form of personal and interpersonal community which
has "broken" out of cosmological collectivism and is truly a relationship between persons in the differentiated sense. One could call this
an "aristocracy" in the original sense of the rule of virtuous people. But
such virtuous types relate to others in a virtuous way, and, in principle,
such a moral aristocracy is inclusive of others rather than exclusive, in
the sense that it invites all to the fullest possible realization of a
virtuous life. Tinder insightfully suggests that a Tocquevillean reading of Voegelin might further develop such inclusivist implications in
*IR*. For Tocqueville was quite laudatory of the emergence of the
democratic element and yet he, like Voegelin, feared its tendency to
reduce freedom to radical egalitarianism.[18]

A third area needing some discussion, however briefly, is that of the
dynamics of the relationship *between* persons as they are in the process
of forming community. How does the soul *formed* by the encounter
with God, such as an Abraham, a Deborah, a Moses, a Jeremiah, *form*
a community which will truly be *formative* of persons in existence
under God? This "space" between persons is prone to disappear from
sight at times, but in a philosophy of order it is rather crucial. Partly
this space is filled by what Tinder names the "institutional" dimension. Several of this book's interlocutors seem to have this more
precisely in mind as they query whether *IR* does sufficient justice to
the social dimension of revelation (Anderson, Mackler, Tinder,
perhaps Ranieri). For Voegelin can advance an adequately social view
of revelation, reflecting the social dimension of his ontology, and I
have just suggested that he does, and yet not sufficiently surface the
institutional embodiments of this social dimension. I tried to indicate
in chapter nine that Voegelin would refuse to reduce society to
institutions. This needs to be emphasized. Interpersonal likemindedness (*homonoia*) can never be reduced to institutional structures. It is
not too surprising that a thinker like Voegelin, who endured the Nazi
scourge and barely escaped the Gestapo, would be rather sensitive to
this. Society in the deepest sense of *homonoia* is always more than its
institutions, and therefore more than its governmental structures also.

One senses that when Voegelin writes that at times the order willed by God is found only in solitary sufferers, he means someone like a Bonhoeffer. True community glows there, rather than in the institutions that should be its "carriers." This distinction between true community and its institutional embodiment—each being necessary, although the first holds the primacy—runs through *IR*, but perhaps too subtlely at times. When Voegelin writes of "the prophets' struggle with the variegated phenomena of externalization," he has in mind the problem of institutions that have derailed into mere legalistic externality and do not foster the "covenant written in the heart" (*OH* I, 440).

Still, it is a legitimate question whether *IR* always does sufficient justice to the institutional embodiments necessary for the covenant. Anderson's querying the lack of attention to the priestly symbolization would be a case in point. Allied with this would be *IR*'s strident criticisms of the canonization of the Scriptures and of the role of doctrines in Israel, as well as of the institutionalization of belief into "religion" in general. *IR* would be guilty of at least a touch of social utopianism, not unlike its accusation against Isaiah especially, were it to be wrongheaded on this matter of institutional embodiments. Perhaps the most positive treatment of institutional embodiment in religion occurs in Voegelin's study of the decalogue (*OH* I, 418ff.). It is described as a "magnificent construction, with a firm grip on the essentials of human existence in society under God." True, it remains compact, and so does not develop a "philosophy of order." Nonetheless, through it Moses "has given Israel its constitution as the people under God in historical existence." Voegelin even credits it with a high degree of the personal, despite its compactness. He retains the "Thou shalt" in his translation to bring this out: "The commands are not general rules of conduct but the substance of divine order to be absorbed by the souls of those who listen to the call" (426-27). Voegelin seems to find, in the construction of the decalogue as we have it, a balance not unlike that found in Plato's *Laws*, and in this respect the section of Morse's study on this topic in chapter seven could profitably be revisited. As Plato treats the "laws" in the context of the prooemia and play (not unlike liturgy), so the decalogue is placed in the context of the Exodus drama and derives its meaning from that (425). It cannot simply be reduced, in other words, to a set of doctrinal propositions, although such propositions would seem to have their subordinate role (376). Perhaps because Voegelin stresses so intensively the experiential, event character of revelation, he recognizes that doctrine is somewhat removed from the experiential center and so quite liable to derailment into legalism unless proper precautions are taken. This does not seem like utopianism, which is not to say that one necessarily needs to agree with every instance of Voegelin's interpretation of when and where doctrine and institutional mediations derail.

To return to our topic of the "space" (metaphorically understood, of course) between the soul and its social order, Voegelin intriguingly writes of the formed soul becoming "a force in community life" (*OH* I, 436). This "force" is something of a key issue, but it is clear that it opens out onto something much more complex than institutions, important as these may be. Here we touch upon one of Voegelin's greatest challenges to all forms of political theory and advocacy which locate the source of social well-being in institutions. What is this "force" which is truly formative of community and never fully reducible to institutions? It would seem to be an even deeper nexus between the self and social relations than institutions. *OH* II will refer to this as "the problem of communal growth through response to solitary individuals," noting that this is a problem treated by Henri Bergson as that of the "transition from the closed to the open society" (241 n. 1).[19] In Bergson's work, if we follow up Voegelin's hint, it falls to the mystic to keep society dynamic and in a state of openness. Bergson holds that the mystic's primary mission is "that of an intensifier of religious faith," who effects "a radical transformation of humanity by setting an example" (Bergson 1963, 239). As we can see, this is an exemplary cause, to use the traditional language, a sign which transforms, rather than a moral example in the weaker sense of someone we may simply choose to follow or not. There is much of this causal exemplarism in Voegelin's understanding of the epochal figures, whether prophets, philosophers, or saints (*AE*, 72-73), but he certainly integrates his understanding of the mystic into his philosophy of being, and in the process widens and deepens the notion. Voegelin's mystic prophets and philosophers are representative of humanity, to use the typical language of *NSP* (27ff.), because the Logos intensively at work in them is also present in others and able, then, to arouse a resonating response in them (*OH* V, 26). Without this, societies would turn into mere shells, devoid of spiritual substance. They would either degenerate into anarchy, or they would become victims of various forms of brute power. Law would degenerate into mere legalism, ethics into relativism and the rule of the mighty.

Here is the place to think hard about Sandoz' observation, likely in response to Levinas as presented by Baird, that if ethics rather than ontology is first philosophy, then ethics would become legalism. Voegelin's thought, by its critique of ontotheological "objectivism" and its historical grounding, goes a long way toward meeting Levinas' objections to a totalistic ontology. A totalistic ontology would not form community, because it would artificially restrict the world-transcendent Logos to a closed system. In place of a partnership in the community of being, we would have an attempted seizure of that community. But then that would not be true community.

But without the Logos present in all, at least as appeal, how could social life be anything more than legalistic detente? Without the Logos, how in fact could the face of the other actually issue an appeal to us and not remain simply an empty stare? Are not the eyes a "window" onto a depth? As usual, Voegelin would seem to be in the "In-Between" (*OH* IV, 184-85): an historically chastened ontological ethics or ethical ontology (196). When Voegelin writes of the "existential" (*OH* I, 440ff., 445ff.), it is this kind of historically and ethically chastened ontology that he has in mind. If you will, it seems as if Voegelin has been about the business of recovering a vision of reality and being which refuses to separate the true from the good. And the attentiveness to symbolic forms discloses a sensitivity to the beautiful as well, the media through which truth and goodness make their appeal (*OH* I, 339, 343; III, 64ff., 96, 138; WME, 361).

What happens to the true, the good, and the beautiful, when their interrelations are ignored, understressed, or denied? The "true" isolated thus would become abstractly severed from the drama of history (the good), and lose its attractive, transcendental appeal (the beautiful). It would become a form of abstract rationalism, in other words, or what Voegelin castigates as hypostatization. And the good apart from the true becomes relativism or nihilism, while it becomes a despotic and arbitrary restraint apart from the attractiveness of the beautiful which arouses a resonating response. And the beautiful apart from the good would become an abstract aestheticism, while severed from the true it would degenerate into mere emotionalism and narcissism. Levinas, it seems, desires to regain the rights of the good over against a decadent form of the true, but he runs the danger of a suppression of the legitimate "rights" of the true, I suspect. And I would like to see more fully addressed to what degree the beautiful is significant in Levinas' thought.[20]

The nexus between selves which is formative of community is the common Logos, then. *IR* teaches that this reality under its equivalent symbolism in Israel, "the spirit of God, the *ruach* of Yahweh, is present with the community and with individuals in their capacity as repre-

sentatives of the community," although its universal scope had not yet
fully differentiated (*OH* I, 240). Nonetheless, this common *ruach*
would seem to be the deepest basis of social formation, and with this
we have already made the transition to the final and ultimate partner
in the community of being, God. *IR* maintains that "a truth about the
order of being, seen only dimly through the compact symbols of
Mesopotamian, Canaanite, and Egyptian societies, becomes articulate, in the formation of Israel, to the point of clarity where the
world-transcendent God reveals himself as the original and ultimate
source of order in world and man, society and history, that is, in all
world-immanent being" (xi). And in fact we need to remind ourselves
of the principle in *IR* enunciated earlier that the differentiation of the
world-transcendent God and the differentiation of the human partner
are mutually influencing realities. Consequently, the macroanthropic
symbol pattern we have just detailed has had the divine partner as its
"silent" presupposition all along the way. Strictly speaking it is a
"macrotheoanthropic" symbol pattern.

    *IR* holds that this truth of God as the original and ultimate source
of order comes to clarity in Israel. *IR* does not say that it comes to
perfect clarity. Of course, on Voegelinian principles, such would not
be possible in any case, for it would require an Archimedean standpoint outside the community of being. But clarity on this most
important of truths is achieved, sufficient to bring the leap in being
beyond the cosmological symbolism, even if the further implications
entailed by this remain an unfinished work in progress.

    Does *IR* have it right on this supremely important issue? The role
which the existential virtues play in coming to know God; the place
of social and institutional mediations in symbolic forms; the notion
of a history which is open to the extraordinary (*OH* I, 195, 409); the
development of a model of experience as embracing more than sense
perception (395); the placing of all of this within the rich narrative
context of history—these are some of the more significant features of
*IR* relevant to the question of God which our book's essayists do not
seem to contest, and which some greatly praise. A further, most
significant issue which should be noted at this point is the constant
need of societies that have undergone the differentiation of the
world-transcendent God to work out an adequate level of adjustment
to "mundane existence," for the "leap upward in being is not a leap out
of existence." This problem, more or less explicit in our earlier section
on the struggle for *homonoia*, has become known in the Christian
West and East as the Church and State question. From Israel onward
"there develop the tensions, frictions, and balances between the two

levels of attunement, a dualistic structure of existence which expresses itself in pairs of symbols . . . of temporal and spiritual powers, of secular state and church" (11).[21] Beyond this, perhaps at least three questions have emerged from our essays. Does Voegelin give sufficient credit to the full texture of Israel's differentiation of the world-transcendent God? Does he allow a certain "Greek bias" to diminish the significance of Israel's contribution to the truth of order? Does he victimize Israel by a certain "Christian bias" in his intepretation? Clearly these three questions implicate each other.

A key tension prominent in *IR* is that between the divine universality and the divine immanence. A world-transcendent God would seem to enjoy the attribute of universality, and yet if this God is not to vanish into an absolute absence, there must be immanence as well. Did Israel localize this presence too much because of "a perpetual mortgage of the world-immanent, concrete event on the transcendent truth that on its occasion was revealed"? (*OH* I, 164) The answer of *IR* would seem to be "yes," although its interpretation as a kind of finale of the suffering servant songs of Isaiah speaks of the articulation of Israel's "exodus from itself," its "going beyond itself and [becoming] the light of salvation to mankind" (512, 515). Perhaps this means that at least "in words" the sensitive, suffering poet of the songs went very far indeed toward differentiating Yahweh's universal transcendence. Anderson had suggested that the wisdom literature also achieves an articulation of divine universality. Voegelin, we noted, briefly takes this up only in *OH* IV. There he credits Proverbs 1-9 with achieving "a further differentiation of pneumatic consciousness," and he also writes of its "remarkable and charming appearance [as] a Judaic female divinity." However, while he thinks of this differentiation as "ecumenic," he does not think of the wisdom literature as an adequate articulation of "universality," for Sirach's indentification of wisdom with Torah does not adequately articulate the reality of divine universality beyond Israel (*OH* IV, 51-53).

The terms "ecumenic" and "universal" are part of Voegelin's later technical lexicon. "Universality" is an eschatological index, a symbol, of universal humankind's participation in the divine-human mystery of reality. It is not a society concretely existing in the world, but a symbolism articulating our consciousness of this participation.[22] The "ecumene" gives expression to "the contemporaneously living," on the other hand. Communities can derail quite badly when they do not properly distinguish one from the other. Communities, even those with ecumenic ambitions (churches or empires), are liable to confuse "the universality of spiritual order" with the concrete ecumene of any given society at any given time (*OH* IV, 137, 305). This would be to reduce the world-transcendent to the world-immanent. What underlies Voegelin's insistence on these matters is not only the divinity of God's universality (hence, its eschatological nature), but also its inclusivity. "The process of history" is one in which "all men [sic] past, present, and future participate" (315).[23] This does not seem so unlike Levinas' worry about totalization (i.e., totalitarianism). One of *OH's* greatest contributions to political thought is its relativization of all concrete governments and societies, it seems.

Interpreting *IR* through the lens of *OH* IV, but also from the perspective suggested by all that has preceded in this postlude, when Voegelin writes of Israel's "exodus from itself" as an apparently laudatory goal, this would seem to be something which he would say is the goal of all concrete societies. *IR* already named this "the terrible truth" (491). If my argument, helped on by this book's essayists, has merit, *IR* does not push toward a Manichean a-socialism, but toward societies of true *homonoia* which are truly inclusive of all (dead, living, and to come) because they do not confuse their concreteness with God's universal transcendence. Sandoz stresses this meaning of the Exodus symbol in Voegelin, I believe. All are called upon to undergo this exodus, referring to "Voegelin's fondness for a passage in [Augustine's] *Enarrationes in Psalmos* 64.2": "He begins to leave who begins to love" (IES, 12, 78; *OH* IV, 172).

This reference can serve as a natural bridge to our two final questions about the Greek and Christian aspects of *IR*. Ranieri refers to Voegelin's tendency to spiritualize the Old Testament, and the exegesis of Psalm 64:2 would be a case in point. Augustine, too, like many of the Church Fathers, has been accused of such spiritual allegorizing. (Voegelin himself has criticized Augustine for his inattentiveness, in fact, to the world and history [*OH* IV, 268], which would be a form of spiritual allegorizing on the political and cosmic planes.) This would then be an example of a Greek bias: the tendency to favor a Greek preference for the spiritual over the Hebraic sensitivity to the corporeal, the concrete, the historical.[24] On the other hand, were *IR* guilty of this, how is it that the charge arises of its excessively Christian loading and bias, as my study sought to describe the matter? For does not Christianity celebrate the enfleshment of the Logos, rather than its spiritualization? My own recommendation follows along the path of our interpretation of Voegelin's view of the social dimension of existence. Just as *IR* is arguing for a view of the self in true community with others—in interpersonal, postcollectivist likemindedness—, so it is arguing for a view of the divine reality which is both universally transcendent and fully immanent. God is not only the reality toward which we "ascend"—out of the world, so to speak—but the reality who descends toward us all in grace—within the world and society. The "ascent" and the "descent" are in varying degrees of differentiated tension in Israel according to *IR*. Now one, now the other, seems more fully differentiated within Israel. I believe these insights are sound, although we must continue to discuss and even argue somewhat over whether they are always accurately or well exemplified in each concrete instance of interpretation, as our book's essayists have challengingly reminded us. The differentiation, under grace, of God's descent would seem to be especially Israel's insight, which changed radically its understanding of its ascent as well. Voegelin later came to emphasize, certainly from *OH* IV on, that both the ascent and the descent are present worldwide. This was always implicit in his view of the primordial community of being, I think. Was this an abandonment of the distinction between reason and revelation, as Ranieri is inclined to hold? So far as I can tell, Voegelin nowhere abandoned the view that the greater differentiation of the descent occurred in Israel and then definitively in the gospel movement of Christianity.[25] This can be interpreted as meaning that the realities of revelation (and grace) are surely not abandoned in Voegelin's thought, but that they are subject to the grid of variance from compactness to differentiation. (What Voegelin seems to have argued against is a particular view of the "natural/supernatural" distinction, namely, one in which a "purely" natural world apart from grace is thought to exist.) Revelation, even as a technical term, seems widened rather than abandoned (*OH* IV, 270; passim), and it also seems to remain a transfiguring process, rather than simply a matter of cognition, for it "happens to be the movement of reality" itself, according to the "later" Voegelin (314). Concrete history does not seem to have evaporated into a mere ghost of itself. But questions and tensions enough remain, as this book's essays have endeavored to indicate.

## Notes

[1] See *OH* I, 84, where Voegelin refers to J. A. Wilson in Frankfort et al. 1946, 65ff., for the notion of consubstantiality in Egyptology. "Second reality" is, of course, Voegelin's term for "imaginative constructs of ideological thinkers who want to eclipse the reality of existential consciousness"; the term is borrowed from Robert Musil and Heimitio von Doderer (*OH* V, 46-47).

[2] Some observations by Bernhard Anderson in his revisiting of *Israel and Revelation* in chap. two prompt this qualification, as we shall see.

[3]"And there is one prejudice of the Enlightenment that defines its essence: . . . the prejudice against prejudice itself, which denies tradition its power" (Gadamer 1989, 270).

[4]Perhaps this will help: Narrative belongs to thing-reality; luminosity, to It-reality. Keeping this in mind may help us avoid reducing the latter to the former, for the It-reality is the more comprehensive one.

[5]As empires living under cosmological symbolism experience a breakdown, a shift toward macroanthropic societies, in which the soul in its attunement to a more lasting source of order begins to supply the symbols for a new ordering of society, takes place (*OH* I, 6; 111ff.). The multiplicity of empires, their rivalries and defeats or victories, obviously generate questions as to the validity of their claims to truth. Simply raising these questions breaks the spell of the cosmological symbolism (*NSP*, 59-60).

[6]Voegelin's notion of the pragmatic dimension of history seems influenced by Polybius' *Histories* which employs a nearly-identical category. See Voegelin's interpretation of Polybius, with references, in *OH* IV, 117-33. See also Polybius, 1979.

[7] For these source theories, as well as for fine overviews of Old Testament study by biblical scholars, see Anderson 1975 and Bandstra 1995.

[8]The actual term "hermeneutics" occurs occasionally in *IR* (96 n. 66, 162). One might also make the case for a trinitarian structure to Voegelin's hermeneutics, although this remains largely implicit in his work. The interpreter is drawn (Spirit) to the world of meaning and truth disclosed through the text (Logos), a truth which is finally transcendent and divine (God the Father). See Thompson 1996, 25-31, for some of the philosophical and theological implications of trinitarian thought which are relevant to interpretation.

[9]Much of the debate over the ways "history" was understood, both among the Germans, and in the so-called Biblical Theology Movement, with its attempt to wed the latest findings of archaeology with a defense of the biblical narratives, has to do with an almost hopeless labyrinth of dead-ends based on the rival view of the pragmatic and the paradigmatic levels of history. Voegelin's approach will surely not satisfy all, but it does help us disentangle some or even many of the crucial philosophical issues implicit in the debate. Take, for example, the use of archaeological evidence, referred to by both Anderson in chap. two and in Hayes and Prussner 1985, 239-45. Suppose one uncovers evidence from excavations that does not seem to corroborate biblical narratives. Does this invalidate the historicity of the Old Testament? In *Israel and Revelation* Voegelin suggests that "the paradigmatic meaning is not directly imposed by a historian on events but grows through the stages of the events as experienced by the participants." The process is complex, and sometimes the original context can no longer be reconstructed (161). One has to work on both levels of history, the pragmatic and the paradigmatic. A biblical fundamentalist will try to use archaeology to prove literal historical details, underappreciating the paradigmatic dimensions of the text. The historicist will underappreciate the paradigmatic dimensions as well, but argue from that to the historical untrustworthiness of the Old Testament. Voegelin's approach is a mediating one. He argues for the objectivity of faith, and says that we would have to distort the biblical text by subjectively introducing "arbitrary, ideological surmising," if we were to ignore the fact that the "men to whom [revelation] happens explicate the meaning of the events through symbols" and that this casts "an ordering ray of objective truth over the field of history

in which the event objectively occurred" (130). To "extract the historical substance," one must "first ascertain the characteristics and motivations of the form, and then reconstruct the essence of the situations and experiences which lent themselves to the literary formation. That task, while it is not simple, is not as hopeless as it may look at first sight, because it receives variegated support from the source itself. Above all, historical substance has been formed by the Biblical narrative quite frequently for the purpose of heightening paradigmatically its essential meaning . . ." (382).

[10] *Israel and Revelation* occasionally speaks of "consciousness" (2, 4), but one will have to wait for *Anamnesis* for a stress upon the centrality of consciousness in Voegelin's work. The terms "soul" and "psyche" are the relevant categories in *Israel and Revelation* (see index, s.v., "soul").

[11] Voegelin would share with today's new interest in canonical criticism as represented in, for example, Childs 1992, an attentiveness to the final form of the text, but Voegelin would stress even more the literary features of the symbols and genres, he would not so radically separate the revelation occurring in Israel from that of history in general, and he would be quite critical of the potentially deforming features of a canon as well.

[12] See BB, 197-98, for Voegelin's cautions about ontology.

[13] As it turns out, curiously, the actual term "history" does not really show up in the (biblical) Hebrew language, according to Voegelin (*OH* I, 162). The actual term "order" does occur, however, although Voegelin does not seem to make note of it.

[14] An excellent, brief treatment of Voegelin's developing view of myth is supplied by Germino 1982, 33-40.

[15] *OH* IV, 10-11, argues that "cosmogony" or "cosmogonic myth" is now the "general concept," rather than the cosmological myth, which is only one of the forms of the first.

[16] I borrow the term "absorption" from Voegelin's creative use of it in his vol. 4, 136ff., of the *History of Political Ideas* (*CW* 22).

[17] Voegelin's analysis of Deborah's Song (*OH* I, 201-12), as well as his attention to goddesses in the cosmological myth (73, 76, 78f., 91, 93), are fine examples of his attunement to women's religious experiences. Voegelin can also speak of Abraham as one who "appears in the pathetic role of a husband who discards his mistress [viz., Hagar] and exposes her to misery in order to have his peace at home" (182 n. 23). There is sympathy here for Abraham, surely, but one senses the plight of Hagar as well in the way Voegelin explains the matter. I have discovered only one text in *IR* which seems questionable from the perspective of "women's criticism": "When reading the story of Jeremiah's squabbles with the Judaite refugees in Egypt (Jer 44), one wonders whether the Israelite common man, and even more so the common women, had ever really understood why they should have no other gods besides Yahweh . . ." (439). "Common sense" in Voegelin's sense (*AE*, 210-13) might well lead one to think that the common woman might understand such things quite as well if not often better than men. For misogynism and misanthropy as soul sicknesses, see *OH* V, 46.

[18] For Voegelin's views on the relationship between equality, properly understood, and freedom (we are not in all respects equal), see *OH* III, 106f., 110f., 234, 248f., 338f. See also Tocqueville 1969, part 2, chap. 1, 503-6. See *AR*, 29-30, for the importance of U. S. American thinkers in helping Voegelin to become aware of the notion of "likemindedness" (*homonoia*).

[19]Voegelin refers to Bergson 1932. See Germino's interpretation (1982, chap. 9).

[20]The work of Hans Urs von Balthasar (McGregor and Norris 1994) has aided me in this paragraph.

[21]". . . the universal order of mankind can become historically concrete only through symbolic representation by a community of the spirit with ecumenic intentions—that is the problem of the Church." Such a project is clearly "fraught with complications through the possibility that several such communities will be founded historically and pursue their ecumenic ambitions with means not altogether spiritual" (*OH* IV, 137; cf. 116, and *NSP*, 158). I have discovered in Voegelin's writings (published and unpublished) a consistent attention to the irreplaceable role of the Church in forming *homonoia* as well as to its capacity for deforming such likemindedness. This would seem to be an area of thought in Voegelin not adequately appreciated, and one that cries out for a more complete treatment.

[22]See *OH* III, 91-92, for Voegelin's interpretation of the city only described in words and found perhaps in heaven, not on earth (*Republic* 592a-b). As Germino (1982, 101) indicated, Bergson's "open society" in the strict sense actually does not exist anywhere in the world, on Voegelin's view. Polybius' *Histories* would seem to be an important source of Voegelin's notion of the "ecumenic." See *OH* IV, 117-33.

[23]It is hard not to be reminded of Edmund Burke (1993, 96, 97): "Society is . . . a partnership between those who are living, those who are dead, and those who are to be born."

[24]Voegelin has also been accused of a Christian bias in his interpretation of the Greeks, for he does not typically find the excessive spiritualism in them that others do, although there are some cases of this which he notes here and there. It seems forgotten at times that Voegelin could criticize even Plato for tendencies toward hypostatization (*OH* III, 11, 275ff.). Voegelin is not a Tertullianesque "either Jerusalem or Athens" thinker. He finds much of Athens in Jerusalem and much of Jerusalem in Athens.

[25]The thrust of MOPKO, 44ff., as I read it, is that Voegelin holds that there is always a divine side which "moves" and a human side which "responds" in concrete human experience. In other words, there is no experience in which only a divine side is "moving" (= "revelation" in a sort of pure sense), nor is there an experience in which only a human "responding" is taking place (= "natural reason"). Both occur together in a "complex" admitting of differing degrees of differentiation or accent. Admittedly in this essay Voegelin stresses the ethnic differences between the Greeks and the Jewish-Christian orbits as factors contributing to the later medieval distinction between a so-called "natural reason" and a "revelation" which seems to be thought of as severed from the former. But I do not read him as reducing the difference between the two traditions to merely an ethnic misunderstanding, as Ranieri seems to do (chap. 8, section "Israel in the Later Thought"). Ethnic factors play their part, but Voegelin notes that "tension arises between the being moved from the divine side and the questing from the human side" (47). He consistently held that the Greek orbit accented the human questing, while the Jewish-Christian orbits accented the divine moving, as for example in the late *OH* V which wrote of the "differentiated types of consciousness through the experiential accents on either the divine irruption of the *pneuma* or on the noetic quest in response to a divine movement" (32).

# SELECTIONS FROM
## *Israel and Revelation*

(The preface and introduction, given here in full, "preside" over all five volumes of *OH*. The six volumes originally projected in the preface eventually became the five volumes of the completed opus, although the fifth, published posthumously, remained unfinished. Voegelin's "break" with a unilinear view of history, announced in *OH* IV, caused this alteration of the original project. Page numbers of the original 1956 text are given in brackets.—Eds.)

## [IX] PREFACE

The order of history emerges from the history of order. Every society is burdened with the task, under its concrete conditions, of creating an order that will endow the fact of its existence with meaning in terms of ends divine and human. And the attempts to find the symbolic forms that will adequately express the meaning, while imperfect, do not form a senseless series of failures. For the great societies, beginning with the civilizations of the Ancient Near East, have created a sequence of orders, intelligibly connected with one another as advances toward, or recessions from, an adequate symbolization of truth concerning the order of being of which the order of society is a part. That is not to say that every succeeding order is unequivocally marked as progressive or recessive in relation to the preceding ones. For new insights into the truth of order may be achieved in some respects, while the very enthusiasm and passion of the advance will cast a shroud of oblivion over discoveries of the past. Amnesia with regard to past achievement is one of the most important social phenomena. Still, while there is no simple pattern of progress or cycles running through history, its process is intelligible as a struggle for true order. This intelligible structure of history, however, is not to be found within the order of any one of the concrete societies participating in the process. It is not a project for human or social action, but a reality to be discerned retrospectively in a flow of events that extends, through the present of the observer, indefinitely into the future. Philosophers of history have spoken of this reality as providence, when they still lived within the orbit of Christianity, or as *List der Vernunft*, when they were affected by the trauma of enlightenment. In either case they referred to a reality beyond the plans of concrete human beings—a reality of which the origin and end is unknown and which for that reason cannot be brought within the grasp of finite action. What is knowable is only that part of the process that has unfolded in the past; and that part to the extent only to which it [x] is accessible to the instruments of cognition that have emerged from the process itself.

The study on *Order and History*, of which the first volume is here presented to the public, is an inquiry into the order of man, society, and history to the extent to which it has become accessible to science. The principal types of order, together with their self-expression in symbols, will be studied as they succeed one another in history. These types of order and symbolic form are the following:

(1) The imperial organizations of the Ancient Near East, and their existence in the form of the cosmological myth;

(2) the Chosen People, and its existence in historical form;

(3) the polis and its myth, and the development of philosophy as the symbolic form of order;

(4) the multicivilizational empires since Alexander, and the development of Christianity;

(5) the modern national states, and the development of Gnosis as the symbolic form of order.

The subject matter will be distributed over six volumes. One volume will deal with the orders of myth and history; two further volumes will be devoted to the polis and the form of philosophy; a fourth volume will deal with the multicivilizational empires and Christianity; and the remaining two volumes will deal with the national states and the symbolic form of Gnosis. The six volumes will bear the titles:

I. Israel and Revelation

II. The World of the Polis

III. Plato and Aristotle

IV. Empire and Christianity

V. The Protestant Centuries

VI. The Crisis of Western Civilization

The inquiry into the types of order and their symbolic forms will be, at the same time, an inquiry into the order of history that emerges from their succession. The first volume, the present one on "Israel and Revelation," will explore not only the forms of cosmological and historical order, but also the emergence of the Chosen People from the ambiance of cosmological empires. A truth about the order of being, seen only dimly through the compact symbols of Mesopotamian, Canaanite, and Egyptian societies, becomes articulate, in the formation of Israel, to [xi] the point of clarity where the world-transcendent God reveals himself as the original and ultimate source of order in world and man, society and history, that is, in all world-immanent being. Under this aspect of the dynamics of history, the otherwise autonomous study of cosmological order acquires the character of a background for the emergence of history, as the form of existence in response to Revelation, gained by Israel's exodus from civilization in cosmological form. The volumes on polis and philosophy, then, will not only deal with the philosophical form of order as developed by Plato and Aristotle, but also explore the process in which this form disengages itself from the matrix of the Hellenic variant of the myth, and farther back from the Minoan and Mycenaean background of cosmological order.

The older symbolic forms are furthermore not simply superseded by a new truth about order, but retain their validity with regard to the areas not covered by the more recently achieved insights even though their symbols have to suffer changes of meaning when they move into the orbit of the more recent and now dominant form. The historical order of Israel, for instance, approaches a crisis, both spiritual and pragmatic, when it becomes obvious that the exigencies of existence in the world are neglected in an order dominated by the Sinaitic Revelation. The cosmological symbolism pours back into the order of Israel with the establishment of a permanent government under kings, not provided by the word of God from Sinai; and the conflicts between the two experiences of order and their symbolisms occupy the major part of Israel's history. The inquiry must, therefore, extend to a sizable class of further phenomena, i.e., to the interactions between symbolic forms. This part of the study will assume considerable proportions, beginning with the fourth volume, when the multicivilizational empires provide the arena for the struggle between Babylonian and Egyptian cosmological forms, the Roman myth of the polis, the Hellenic form of philosophy, the earlier Israelite historical and the later Jewish apocalyptic symbols; when all of the enumerated types of order enter into the great struggle with the new order of

Christianity; and when from this welter of mutual invalidations and limitations emerges the compound of Western medieval order. And the whole of two volumes, finally, will be necessary to describe the dissolution of the medieval compound through a Gnosis that had been reduced to a thin trickle of sectarian movements during the early Middle Ages, as well as the consequences of the dissolution.

[xii] The reader who is faced with the prospect of six volumes will justly expect a prefatory word about the intellectual situation which, in the author's opinion, makes an enterprise of this nature both possible and necessary. This expectation can be fulfilled only within certain limits—for the size of the work is caused by the complexity of the situation, and the answers to the questions that impose themselves can be given only through the unfolding of the study itself. Still, a few orienting remarks are possible in brief form.

The work could be undertaken in our time, in the first place, because the advance of the historical disciplines in the first half of this century has provided the basis of materials. The enormous enlargement of our historical horizon through archaeological discoveries, critical editions of texts, and a flood of monographic interpretation is so well known a fact that elaboration is superfluous. The sources are ready at hand; and the convergent interpretations by orientalists and semitologists, by classical philologists and historians of antiquity, by theologians and medievalists, facilitate and invite the attempt to use the primary sources as the basis for a philosophical study of order. The state of science in the various disciplines, as well as my own position with regard to fundamental questions, will be set forth in the course of the study. As far as the present volume on "Israel and Revelation" is concerned, I should like to refer the reader to the digressions on the state of Bible criticism (Chap. 6, § I) and of the interpretation of the Psalms (Chap. 9, § 5).

The second reason why the study could be undertaken in our time is less tangible than the first one, inasmuch as it can be described only negatively as the disappearance of the ideological mortgages on the work of science. I am speaking of the pervasive climate of opinion in which a critical study of society and history was practically impossible because the varieties of nationalism, of progressivist and positivist, of liberal and socialist, of Marxian and Freudian ideologies, the neoKantian methodologies in imitation of the natural sciences, scientistic ideologies such as biologism and psychologism, the Victorian fashion of agnosticism and the more recent fashions of existentialism and theologism prevented with social effectiveness not only the use of critical standards but even the acquisition of the knowledge necessary for their formation. The assertion that this incubus on the life of the spirit and intellect has disappeared, must be qualified, however, by the awareness that the forces of the [xiii] Gnostic age are still social and political powers on the world scene, and will remain formidable powers for a long time to come. The "disappearance" must be understood as the fact that in the course of the wars and revolutions of our time their authority has seeped out of them. Their conceptions of man, society, and history are too obviously incongruent with the reality that is within the range of our empirical knowledge. Hence, while they still are powers, they wield power only over those who do not turn their back to them and look for greener pastures. We have gained a new freedom in science, and it is a joy to use it.

The reflections on the ideological incubus have led us from the possibility to the necessity of the study on *Order and History*. It is man's obligation to understand his condition; part of this condition is the social order in which he lives; and this order has today become worldwide. This worldwide order is furthermore neither recent nor simple, but contains as socially effective forces the sediments of the millennial struggle for the truth of order. This is a question, not of theory but of empirical fact. One could draw for proof on such obvious facts as the relevance for our own affairs of a China or India that is struggling with the necessary adjustments of a basically cosmological order to political and technological conditions that are of Western making. I prefer, however, to draw the reader's attention to the analysis of the metastatic problem in the present volume on "Israel and Revelation" (Chap. 13, § 2.2), and he will see immediately that the prophetic conception of a change in the constitution of being lies at the root of our contemporary beliefs in the perfection of society, either through progress or through a communist revolution. Not only are the apparent antagonists revealed as brothers under the skin, as the late Gnostic descendants of the prophetic faith in a transfiguration of the world; it obviously is also of importance to understand the nature of the experience that will express itself in beliefs of this type, as well as the circumstances under which it has arisen in the past and from which it derives its strength in the present. Metastatic faith is one of the great sources of disorder, if not the principal one, in the contemporary world; and it is a matter of life and death for all of us to understand the phenomenon and to find remedies against it before it destroys us. If today the state of science permits the critical analysis of such phenomena, it is clearly a scholar's duty to undertake it for his own sake as a man and to make the results accessible [xiv] to his fellow men. *Order and History* should be read, not as an attempt to explore curiosities of a dead past, but as an inquiry into the structure of the order in which we live presently.

I have spoken of remedies against the disorder of the time. One of these remedies is philosophical inquiry itself.

Ideology is existence in rebellion against God and man. It is the violation of the First and Tenth Commandments, if we want to use the language of Israelite order; it is the *nosos*, the disease of the spirit, if we want to use the language of Aeschylus and Plato. Philosophy is the love of being through love of divine Being as the source of its order. The Logos of being is the object proper of philosophical inquiry; and the search for truth concerning the order of being cannot be conducted without diagnosing the modes of existence in untruth. The truth of order has to be gained and regained in the perpetual struggle against the fall from it; and the movement toward truth starts from a man's awareness of his existence in untruth. The diagnostic and therapeutic functions are inseparable in philosophy as a form of existence. And ever since Plato, in the disorder of his time, discovered the connection, philosophical inquiry has been one of the means of establishing islands of order in the disorder of the age. *Order and History* is a philosophical inquiry concerning the order of human existence in society and history. Perhaps it will have its remedial effect—in the modest measure that, in the passionate course of events, is allowed to Philosophy.

## [1] INTRODUCTION

### The Symbolization of Order

God and man, world and society form a primordial community of being. The community with its quaternarian structure is, and is not, a datum of human experience. It is a datum of experience in so far as it is known to man by virtue of his participation in the mystery of its being. It is not a datum of experience in so far as it is not given in the manner of an object of the external world but is knowable only from the perspective of participation in it.

The perspective of participation must be understood in the fullness of its disturbing quality. It does not mean that man, more or less comfortably located in the landscape of being, can look around and take stock of what he sees as far as he can see it. Such a metaphor, or comparable variations on the theme of the limitations of human knowledge, would destroy the paradoxical character of the situation. It would suggest a self-contained spectator, in possession of and with knowledge of his faculties, at the center of a horizon of being, even though the horizon were restricted. But man is not a self-contained spectator. He is an actor, playing a part in the drama of being and, through the brute fact of his existence, committed to play it without knowing what it is. It is disconcerting even when accidentally a man finds himself in the situation of feeling not quite sure what the game is and how he should conduct himself in order not to spoil it; but with luck and skill he will extricate himself from the embarrassment and return to the less bewildering routine of his life. Participation in being, however, is not a partial involvement of man; he is engaged with the whole of his existence, for participation is existence itself. There is no vantage point outside existence from which its meaning can be viewed and a course of action charted according to a plan, nor is there a blessed island to which man can withdraw in order to recapture his self. The role of existence must be played in uncertainty of its meaning, as an adventure of decision on the edge of freedom and necessity.

[2] Both the play and the role are unknown. But even worse, the actor does not know with certainty who he is himself. At this point the metaphor of the play may lead astray unless it is used with caution. To be sure the metaphor is justified, and perhaps even necessary, for it conveys the insight that man's participation in being is not blind but is illuminated by consciousness. There is an experience of participation, a reflective tension in existence, radiating sense over the proposition: Man, in his existence, participates in being. This sense, however, will turn into nonsense if one forgets that subject and predicate in the proposition are terms which explicate a tension of existence, and are not concepts denoting objects. There is no such thing as a "man" who participates in "being" as if it were an enterprise that he could as well leave alone; there is, rather, a "something," a part of being, capable of experiencing itself as such, and furthermore capable of using language and calling this experiencing consciousness by the name of "man." The calling by a name certainly is a fundamental act of evocation, of calling forth, of constituting that part of being as a distinguishable partner in the community of being. Nevertheless, fundamental as the act of evocation is—for it forms the basis for all that man will learn about himself in the course of history—it is not itself an act of cognition. The Socratic irony of ignorance has become the paradigmatic instance of awareness for this blind spot at the center of all human knowledge about man. At the center of his existence man is unknown to himself and must remain so, for the part of being that calls itself man could be known fully only if the community of being and its drama in time were known as a whole. Man's partnership in

being is the essence of his existence, and this essence depends on the whole, of which existence is a part. Knowledge of the whole, however, is precluded by the identity of the knower with the partner, and ignorance of the whole precludes essential knowledge of the part. This situation of ignorance with regard to the decisive core of existence is more than disconcerting: it is profoundly disturbing, for from the depth of this ignorance wells up the anxiety of existence.

The ultimate, essential ignorance is not complete ignorance. Man can achieve considerable knowledge about the order of being, and not the least part of that knowledge is the distinction between the knowable and the unknowable. Such achievement, however, comes late in the long-[3] drawn-out process of experience and symbolization that forms the subject matter of the present study. The concern of man about the meaning of his existence in the field of being does not remain pent up in the tortures of anxiety, but can vent itself in the creation of symbols purporting to render intelligible the relations and tensions between the distinguishable terms of the field. In the early phases of the creative process the acts of symbolization are still badly handicapped by the bewildering multitude of unexplored facts and unsolved problems. Not much is really clear beyond the experience of participation and the quaternarian structure of the field of being, and such partial clearness tends to generate confusion rather than order, as is bound to happen when variegated materials are classified under too few heads. Nevertheless, even in the confusion of these early stages there is enough method to allow the distinction of typical features in the process of symbolization.

The first of these typical features is the predominance of the experience of participation. Whatever man may be, he knows himself a part of being. The great stream of being, in which he flows while it flows through him, is the same stream to which belongs everything else that drifts into his perspective. The community of being is experienced with such intimacy that the consubstantiality of the partners will override the separateness of substance. We move in a charmed community where everything that meets us has force and will and feelings, where animals and plants can be men and gods, where men can be divine and gods are kings, where the feathery morning sky is the falcon Horus and the Sun and Moon are his eyes, where the underground sameness of being is a conductor for magic currents of good or evil force that will subterraneously reach the superficially unreachable partner, where things are the same and not the same, and can change into each other.

The second typical feature is the preoccupation with the lasting and passing (i.e., the durability and transiency) of the partners in the community of being. Consubstantiality notwithstanding, there is the experience of separate existence in the stream of being, and the various existences are distinguished by their degrees of durability. One man lasts while others pass away, and he passes away while others last on. All human beings are outlasted by the society of which they are members, and societies pass while the world lasts. And the world not only is outlasted by the gods, but is perhaps even created by them. Under this aspect, being exhibits the lineaments of a hierarchy of existence, from [4] the ephemeral lowliness of man to the everlasting-ness of the gods. The experience of hierarchy furnishes an important piece of knowledge about order in being, and this knowledge in its turn can, and does, become a force in ordering the existence of man. For the more lasting existences, being the more comprehensive ones, provide by their structure the frame into which the lesser existence must fit, unless it is willing to pay the price of extinction. A first ray of meaning fails on the role of man in the drama of being in so far as the success of the actor depends upon his attunement to the more lasting and comprehensive orders of society, the world, and God. This attunement, however, is more than an external adjustment to the exigencies of existence, more than a planned fitting into an order "about" which we know. "Attunement" suggests the penetration of the adjustment to the level of participation in being. What lasts and passes, to be sure, is existence, but since existence is partnership in being, lasting and passing reveal something of being. Human exist-ence is of short duration, but the being of which it partakes does not cease with existence. In existing we experience mortality; in being we experience what can be symbolized only by the negative metaphor of immortality. In our distinguishable separateness as existence we experience death; in our partnership in being we experience life. But here again we reach the limits that are set by the perspective of participation, for lasting and passing are properties of being and existence as they appear to us in the perspective of our existence; as soon as we try to objectify them we lose even what we have. If we try to explore the mystery of lasting as if death were a thing, we shall not find anything but the nothing that makes us shudder with anxiety from the bottom of existence. If we try to explore the mystery of lasting as if life were a thing, we shall not find life eternal but lose ourselves in the imagery of immortal gods, of paradisiacal or Olympian exist-ence. From the attempts at exploration we are thrown back into the consciousness of essential ignorance. Still, we "know" something. We experience our own lasting in existence, passing as it is, as well as the hierarchy of lasting; and in these experiences experience becomes transparent, revealing something of the mystery of being, of the mystery in which it participates though it does not know what it is. Attunement, therefore, will be the state of existence when it hearkens to that which is lasting in being, when it maintains a tension of awareness for its partial revelations in the order of society and the world, when it listens attentively to the silent voices of conscience and grace in [5] human existence itself. We are thrown into and out of existence without knowing the Why or the How, but while in it we know that we are of the being to which we return. From this knowledge flows the experience of obligation, for though this being, entrusted to our partial management in existence while it lasts and passes, may be gained by attunement, it may also be lost by default. Hence the anxiety of existence is more than a fear of death in the sense of biological extinction; it is the profounder horror of losing, with the passing of existence, the slender foothold in the partnership of being that we experience as ours while existence lasts. In existence we act our role in the greater play of the divine being that enters passing existence in order to redeem precarious being for eternity.

The third typical feature in the process of symbolization is the attempt at making the essentially unknowable order of being intelligible as far as possible through the creation of symbols which interpret the unknown by analogy with the really, or supposedly, known. These attempts have a history in so far as reflective analysis, responding to the pressure of experience, will render symbols increasingly more adequate to their task. Compact blocks of the knowable will be differentiated into their component parts and the knowable itself will gradually come to be distinguished from the essentially unknowable. Thus the history of symbolization is a progression from compact to differentiated experiences and symbols. Since this process is the subject matter of the whole subsequent study we shall at present mention only two basic forms of symbolization which characterize great periods of history. The one is the symbolization of society and its order as an analogue of the cosmos and its order; the other is the symbolization of social order by analogy with the order of a human existence that is well attuned to being. Under the first form society will be symbolized as a microcosmos; under the second form as a macroanthropos.

The first-mentioned form is also chronologically the first one. Why this should be hardly requires elaborate explanations, for earth and heaven are so impressively the embracing order into which human existence must fit itself, if it wants to survive, that the overwhelmingly powerful and visible partner in the community of being inevitably suggests its order as the model of all order, including that of man and society. At any rate, the civilizations of the ancient Near East that will be treated in Part I of this study symbolized politically organized society as a cosmic [6] analogue, as a cosmion, by letting vegetative rhythms and celestial revolutions function as models for the structural and procedural order of society.

The second symbol or form—society as macroanthropos—tends to appear when cosmologically symbolized empires break down and in their disaster engulf the trust in cosmic order. Society, in spite of its ritual integration into cosmic order, has broken down; if the cosmos is not the source of lasting order in human existence, where is the source of order to be found? At this juncture symbolization tends to shift toward what is more lasting than the visibly existing world—that is, toward the invisibly existing being beyond all being in tangible existence. This invisible divine being, transcending all being in the world and of the world itself, can be experienced only as a movement in the soul of man; and hence the soul, when ordered by attunement to the unseen god, becomes the model of order that will furnish symbols for ordering society analogically in its image. The shift toward macroanthropic symbolization becomes manifest in the differentiation of philosophy and religion out of the preceding, more compact forms of symbolization, and it can be empirically observed, indeed, as an occurrence in the phase of history which Toynbee has classified as the Time of Troubles. In Egypt the social breakdown between the Old and the Middle Kingdom witnessed the rise of the Osiris religiousness. In the feudal disintegration of China appeared the philosophical schools, especially those of Lao-tse and Confucius. The war period before the foundation of the Maurya Empire was marked by the appearance of the Buddha and of Jainism. When the world of the Hellenic polis disintegrated, the philosophers appeared, and the further troubles of the Hellenistic world were marked by the rise of Christianity. It would be unwise, however, to generalize this typical occurrence into a historical "law," for there are complications in detail. The absence of such a shift in the breakdown of Babylonian society (as far as the scantiness of sources allows the negative judgment) suggests that the "law" would have "exceptions," while Israel seems to have arrived at the second form without any noticeable connection with a specific institutional breakdown and subsequent period of trouble.

A further feature in the early stages of the process of symbolization is man's awareness of the analogical character of his symbols. The awareness manifests itself in various ways, corresponding to the various problems of cognition through symbols. The order of being, while [7] remaining in the area of essential ignorance, can be symbolized analogically by using more than one experience of partial order in existence. The rhythms of plant and animal life, the sequence of the seasons, the revolutions of sun, moon, and constellations may serve as models for analogical symbolization of social order. The order of society may serve as a model for symbolizing celestial order. All these orders may serve as models for symbolizing the order in the realm of divine forces. And the symbolizations of divine order in their turn may be used for analogical interpretation of existential orders within the world.

In this network of mutual elucidation inevitably concurrent and conflicting symbols will occur. Such concurrences and conflicts are borne, over long periods, with equanimity by the men who produce them; contradictions do not engender distrust in the truth of the symbols. If anything is characteristic of the early history of symbolization, it is the pluralism in expressing truth, the generous recognition and tolerance extended to rival symbolizations of the same truth. The self-interpretation of an early empire as the one and only true representative of the cosmic order on earth is not in the least shaken by the existence of neighboring empires who indulge in the same type of interpretation. The representation of a supreme divinity under a special form and name in one Mesopotamian city-state is not shaken by a different representation in the neighboring city-state. And the merger of various representations when an empire unifies several formerly independent city-states, the change from one representation to another when the dynasties change, the transfer of cosmogonic myths from one god to another, and so forth, show that the variety of symbolization is accompanied by a vivid consciousness of the sameness of truth at which man aims by means of his various symbols. This early tolerance reaches far into the Greco-Roman period and has found its great expression in the attack of Celsus on Christianity as the disturber of the peace among the gods.

This early tolerance reflects the awareness that the order of being can be represented analogically in more than one way. Every concrete symbol is true in so far as it envisages the truth, but none is completely true in so far as the truth about being is essentially beyond human reach. In this twilight of truth grows the rich flora—luxuriant, bewildering, frightening, and charming—of the tales about gods and demons and their ordering and disordering influences on the life of man and society. There is a magnificent freedom of variation on, and elaboration of, fundamental themes, each new growth and supergrowth adding a facet to the great [8] work of analogy surrounding the unseen truth; it is the freedom of which, on the level of artistic creation, still can partake the epics of Homer, the tragedy of the fifth century, and the mythopoeia of Plato. This tolerance however, will reach its limit when the awareness of the analogical character of symbolization is attracted by the problem of the greater or lesser adequacy of symbols to their purpose of making the true order of being transparent. The symbols are many, while being is one. The very multiplicity of symbols can, therefore, be experienced as an inadequacy, and attempts may be undertaken to bring a manifold of symbols into a rational, hierarchical order. In the cosmological empires these attempts typically assume the form of interpreting a manifold of highest local divinities as aspects of the one highest empire god. But political summodeism is not the only method of rationalization. The attempts can assume the more technical form of theogonic speculation, letting the other gods originate through creation by the one truly highest god, as we find it for instance in the Memphite Theology, to be dated in the early third millennium B.C. Such early speculative outbreaks in the direction of monotheism will appear anachronistic to historians who want to find a clear progress from polytheism to monotheism, and since the facts cannot be denied, the early instances must at least be considered "forerunners" of the later, more legitimate appearance of monotheism, unless, as a still further effort at rationalization, a search is undertaken to prove a historical continuity between Israelitic monotheism and Ikhnaton, or the philosophy of the Logos and the Memphite Theology. The early outbreaks, however, will appear less surprising, and a search for continuities will become less pressing, if we realize that the rigid difference between polytheism and monotheism, suggested by the logical mutual exclusion of the one and the many, does in fact not exist. For the free, imaginative play with a plurality of symbols is possible only because the choice of analogies is understood as more or less irrelevant compared with the reality of being at which they aim. In all polytheism there is latent a monotheism which can be activated at any time, with or without "forerunners," if the pressure of a historical situation meets with a sensitive and active mind.

In political summodeism and theogonic speculation we reach the limit of tolerance of rival symbolizations. Nevertheless, no serious break need yet occur. The theogonic speculation of a Hesiod was not the [9] beginning of a new religious movement in opposition to the polytheistic culture of Hellas, and the Roman summodeism, through Constantine, could even draw Christianity into its system of symbolization. The break with early tolerance results not from rational reflection on the inadequacy of pluralistic symbolization (though such reflection may experientially be a first step toward more radical ventures), but from the profounder insight that no symbolization through analogues of existential order in the world can even faintly be adequate to the divine partner on whom the community of being and its order depend. Only when the gulf in the hierarchy of being that separates divine from mundane existence is sensed, only when the originating, ordering, and preserving source of being is experienced in its absolute transcendence beyond being in tangible existence, will all symbolization by analogy be understood in its essential inadequacy and even impropriety. The seemliness of symbols—if we may borrow the term from Xenophanes—then will become a pressing concern, and a hitherto tolerable freedom of symbolization will become intolerable because it is an unseemly indulgence betraying a confusion about the order of being and, more deeply, a betrayal of being itself through lack of proper attunement. The horror of a fall from being into nothingness motivates an intolerance which no longer is willing to distinguish between stronger and weaker gods, but opposes the true god to the false gods. This horror induced Plato to create the term theology, to distinguish between true and false types of theology, and to make the true order of society dependent on the rule of men whose proper attunement to divine being manifests itself in their true theology.

When the unseemliness of symbols moves into the focus of attention, it seems at first glance that there has not been much change in human understanding of the order of being and existence. To be sure, something is gained by the differentiating emphasis on the area of essential ignorance as well as by the consequent distinction between knowable immanent and unknowable transcendent reality, between mundane and divine existence, and a certain zeal in guarding the new insight against backsliding into renewed acceptance of symbols that in retrospect appear as an illusion of truth may seem pardonable. Nevertheless, man cannot escape essential ignorance through intolerance of unseemly symbolization; nor can he overcome the perspectivism of participation by understanding its nature. The profound insight into the unseemliness of symbols seems to dissolve into an emphasis, perhaps exaggerated, on [10] something that was known all the time and did not receive more attention precisely because nothing would be changed by becoming emphatic about it.

And yet, something has changed, not only in the methods of symbolization, but in the order of being and existence itself. Existence is partnership in the community of being; and the discovery of imperfect participation, of a mismanagement of existence through lack of proper attunement to the order of being, of the danger of a fall from being, is a horror indeed, compelling a radical reorientation of existence. Not only will the symbols lose the magic of their transparency for the unseen order and become opaque, but a pallor will fall over the partial orders of mundane existence that hitherto furnished the analogies for the comprehensive order of being. Not only will the unseemly symbols be rejected, but man will turn away from world and society as the sources of misleading analogy. He will experience a turning around, the Platonic *periagogé*, an inversion or conversion toward the true source of order. And this turning around, this conversion, results in more than an increase of knowledge concerning the order of being; it is a change in the order itself. For the participation in being changes its structure when it becomes emphatically a partnership with God, while the participation in mundane being recedes to second rank. The more perfect attunement to being through conversion is not an increase on the same scale but a qualitative leap. And when this conversion befalls a society, the converted community will experience itself as qualitatively different from all other societies that have not taken the leap. Moreover, the conversion is experienced, not as the result of human action, but as a passion, as a response to a revelation of divine being, to an act of grace, to a selection for emphatic partnership with God. The community, as in the case of Israel, will be a chosen people, a peculiar people, a people of God. The new community thus creates a special symbolism to express its peculiarity, and this symbolism can from then on be used for distinguishing the new structural element in the field of societies in historical existence. When the distinctions are more fully developed, as they were by St. Augustine, the history of Israel will then become a phase in the *historia sacra*, in church history, as distinguished from the profane history in which empires rise and fall. Hence, the emphatic partnership with God removes a society from the rank of profane existence and constitutes it as the representative of the *civitas Dei* in historical existence.

[11] Thus, a change in being actually has occurred, with consequences for the order of existence. Nevertheless, the leap upward in being is not a leap out of existence. The emphatic partnership with

God does not abolish partnership in the community of being at large, which includes being in mundane existence. Man and society, if they want to retain their foothold in being that makes the leap into emphatic partnership possible, must remain adjusted to the order of mundane existence. Hence, there is no age of the church that would succeed an age of society on the level of more compact attunement to being. Instead there develop the tensions, frictions, and balances between the two levels of attunement, a dualistic structure of existence which expresses itself in pairs of symbols, of *theologia civilis* and *theologia supranaturalis*, of temporal and spiritual powers, of secular state and church.

Intolerance of unseemly symbolization does not resolve this new problem, and the love of being which inspires intolerance must compromise with the conditions of existence. This attitude of compromise can be discerned in the work of the old Plato, when his intolerance of unseemly symbolization, strong in his early and middle years, undergoes a remarkable transformation. To be sure, the insight of conversion, the principle that God is the measure of man, far from being compromised, is asserted even more forcefully, but its communication has become more cautious, withdrawing deeper behind the veils of the myth. There is an awareness that the new truth about being is not a substitute for, but an addition to the old truth. The *Laws* envisage a polis that is constructed as a cosmic analogue, perhaps betraying influences of Oriental political culture; and of the new truth there will be infiltrated only as much as the existential vessel can hold without breaking. Moreover, there is a new awareness that an attack on the unseemly symbolization of order may destroy order itself with the faith in its analogies, that it is better to see the truth obscurely than not at all, that imperfect attunement to the order of being is preferable to disorder. The intolerance inspired by the love of being is balanced by a new tolerance, inspired by the love of existence and a respect for the tortuous ways on which man moves historically closer to the true order of being. In the *Epinomis* Plato speaks the last word of his wisdom—that every myth has its truth.

(The selections from part one introduce the cosmological myth, in which political order is experienced and symbolized through cosmic analogies. In *OH* IV Voegelin somewhat nuanced his treatment of myth, suggesting even more variations than originally noted in *IR* and proposing that the constant form is that of the cosmogonic myth, of which the cosmological is a variant. The three chapters of this part explore Mesopotamia, the Achaemenian Empire, and Egypt, respectively.—Eds.)

## [13] PART ONE

### THE COSMOLOGICAL ORDER OF THE ANCIENT NEAR EAST

The societies of the ancient Near East were ordered in the form of the cosmological myth. By the time of Alexander, however, mankind had moved, through Israel, to existence in the present under God and, through Hellas, to existence in love of the unseen measure of all being. And this movement beyond existence in an embracing cosmic order entailed a progress from the compact form of the myth to the differentiated forms of history and philosophy. From the beginning, therefore, a study of order and its symbolization is burdened with the problem of a mankind which unfolds an order of its own in time, though it is not itself a concrete society.

The order of mankind beyond the order of society furthermore unfolds in space insofar as the same type of symbolic form occurs simultaneously in several societies. The very title of this first part of the study, "The Cosmological Order of the Ancient Near East," raises the question: Whose order is supposed to be the subject of inquiry? For the ancient Near East is not a single organized society with a continuous history, but comprises a number of civilizations with parallel histories. Moreover, while in the civilization of the Nile Valley one can legitimately speak of a continuity of "Egypt" in spite of the interruptions of imperial order through domestic troubles and foreign invasions, in Mesopotamia the mere names of the Sumerian, Babylonian, and Assyrian empires indicate a plurality of political organizations by different peoples. And yet we have spoken, not only of the "Ancient Near East" as the subject of cosmological order, but even of a "mankind" that expressed its mode of existence by means of the cosmological myth. Such language implies that a group of societies with separate histories can be treated for our purposes as if they were a single unit in history, and even that the symbols [14] developed to express a concrete order can be abstracted from the society of their origin and attributed to mankind at large.

The problem of mankind has not been raised in order to be resolved on this occasion of its first appearance. It will be with us throughout the course of the study. For the present, the awareness of its existence is sufficient as a basis for the following empirical observation which has a direct bearing on the organization of materials in Part I.

It is a matter of empirical knowledge that the cosmological myth arises in a certain number of civilizations without apparent mutual influences. The question, to be sure, has been raised whether the Mesopotamian and Egyptian civilizations, neighbors in time and space, did not influence one another, or have a common origin that would explain the parallel features in their political culture. Whatever the outcome of a hitherto inconclusive debate will be, the question itself will appear less pressing, if one considers that the same type of symbols occurs in the China of the Chou dynasty, as well as in the Andean civilizations, where Babylonian or Egyptian influences are improbable. The state of empirical knowledge makes it advisable, therefore, to treat the cosmological myth as a typical phenomenon in the history of mankind rather than as a symbolic form peculiar to the order of Babylon, or Egypt, or China. Still less is it advisable to indulge in speculations about "cultural diffusion" of the cosmological myth from a hypothetical center of its first creation.

The cosmological myth, as far as we know, is generally the first symbolic form created by societies when they rise above the level of tribal organization. Nevertheless, the several instances of its appearance are sufficiently variegated to allow the distinction of unmistakably Mesopotamian, Egyptian, and Chinese styles of the myth. Moreover, it is highly probable, though not conclusively demonstrable, that the differences of style have something to do with the potentiality of the various civilizations for the unfolding of experiences which ultimately result in the leap in being. In the area of the ancient Near East, the Mesopotamian empires proved most barren in this respect, while the sequence of Egyptian empires showed a remarkable but abortive development. The break-through was achieved only among the peoples of the Syriac civilization, through Israel. Hence, the varieties within the general type of cosmological myth must not be neglected.

In order to do justice to the various aspects of the problem, the [15] historical materials will be organized in Part I in the following manner: Chapter I will deal with the Mesopotamian empires, because the rigidity of Mesopotamian symbols, with their negligible traces of differentiating experiences, is most suitable to the elaboration of the typical elements in the cosmological myth. Chapter 2, on the Achaemenian Empire, will deal with the modifications of the type under the impact of Zoroastrianism. Egypt will be treated in Chapter 3, because its indigenous development of experiences and symbols tended to break the form of the cosmological myth. This arrangement will provide for the type as well as for the varieties, and it will illuminate the progress of man through the sequence of civilizations.

## [Chapter i: Mesopotamia]

### [38] . . . § 3. The Symbolization of Cosmic Order

Cosmological symbolization in a strict sense may be defined as the symbolization of political order by means of cosmic analogies. The life of man and society is experienced as ordered by the same forces of being which order the cosmos, and cosmic analogies both express this knowledge and integrate social into cosmic order. The rhythms of the seasons and of fertility in plant and animal life, as well as the celestial revolutions on which these rhythms depend, must be understood as the order that furnishes the analogies. The knowledge of cosmic order in this sense, especially as regards astronomy, was highly developed in Sumero-Babylonian civilization.

The preceding sections, however, have revealed a much more complex structure of the problem. Mesopotamian political culture went far beyond cosmological symbolization in the strict sense and even reversed the direction of symbolization. To be sure, political order was under- [39] stood cosmologically, but cosmic order was also understood politically. Not only was the empire an analogue of the cosmos, but political events took place in the celestial sphere. The establishment or change of imperial rule was preceded by political upheavals among the gods who would depose an Enlil of Nippur and transfer his jurisdiction to a Marduk of Babylon. Moreover, the relations between heaven and earth were so intimate that the separateness of their existences was all but blurred. The empire was part of the cosmos, but the cosmos was an empire of which the dominion of man was a subdivision. There was *one* order embracing the world and society that could be understood either cosmologically or politically.

The mutuality of analogical illumination, and especially the conception of the world as a political order, is peculiar to Mesopotamia; it is not characteristic of all the cosmological civilizations. In Chinese civilization, for instance, the rule of a dynasty depends on its possession of a specific virtue, the *teh*. Like all things under the heavens, the *teh* is exhaustible; and when it has weakened to the point of causing suffering to the people and revolutionary unrest, a new possessor of the *teh* with his family will succeed in overthrowing the declining dynasty. This rise and fall of dynasties, then, is integrated into the order of the cosmos in so far as a heavenly decree, the *ming*, ordains the rule of a family that possesses the *teh* and also ordains its overthrow when it has lost the *teh*. The attunement of society to the cosmos depends on the son of heaven and his dynastic *teh*, while the power of heaven, the *t'ien*, will provide for the rise and fall of dynasties. Hence political events, though partaking of the nature of cosmic forces, remain strictly in the sphere of a human struggle for power; heaven preserves its majesty of undisturbed order, while society is engaged in its struggle for attunement. In Chinese civilization political order is symbolized as due to the operation of impersonal cosmic forces.

Further light will be shed on the peculiarity of the Mesopotamian symbolic form by a brief glance at the late Mycenaean civilization as reflected in the Homeric epics. In Homer, as in Mesopotamia, the society of men is duplicated by a society of gods; to the order of aristocratic warriors under a king corresponds the aristocratic order of Olympian gods under a powerful but limited monarch. The relation between the two orders is even more intimate than in Mesopotamia, for the gods direct the destinies of men not only from afar by their decrees, but descend [40] into the human arena invisibly or in various disguises and even participate in battle. Moreover, they find pleasure not only in the daughters of men, as did the Elohim, but also in the sons, and the armies before Troy, on both sides, contain a liberal sprinkling of semidivine offspring. Gods and men form one great society, and the battle lines between mortals also divide the immortals. Nevertheless, important as these parallels between Mycenaean and Mesopotamian symbolic forms are, they must be considered secondary to a decisive difference. The Homeric gods have all but lost their character as cosmic forces and celestial powers; they are humanized as far as it is possible to conceive gods anthropomorphically without destroying their divinity. In Homer, to be sure, there is present the experience of participation in the community of being, but this participation is not symbolized by analogy with cosmic order; the symbolization rather brings into its grasp, without mediation, the divine forces of being themselves. The order of society depends not on the attunement to the cosmos, but directly to the anthropomorphically conceived gods and especially, in the Hellenic period, to the Dike of Zeus. In the transition from Mycenaean to Hellenic civilization we meet with an early flowering of anthropological symbolization.

In comparing the three cases—the Mesopotamian, the Chinese, and the Mycenaean—we can perhaps touch (though certainly not solve) one of the obscurest problems in the intellectual history of mankind; that is, the aptitude of various civilizations for development in the direction of the "leap of being." In the Mesopotamian case we find the early interpenetration of symbolisms, the cosmological symbolization of political order together with the political symbolization of cosmic order. It seems possible that the mutual reinforcement of the two orders made the symbolism particularly inflexible and resistant to dissolution by differentiating experiences. The simpler cosmological symbolism in China left sufficient freedom in the human sphere to allow, in the breakdown of the Chou dynasty, for a conception of social order as dependent, not on the son of heaven alone, but on councillors and an administration formed by the spirit of Confucius. This was a step in the anthropological direction, but not a complete breakthrough. The intermediate position of Confucianism is reflected in the debate on the question whether Confucianism was a "religion." It was not a "religion" because it did not go beyond the conception of the Confucian sage as a man who was so well attuned to the *tao* of the cosmos that he could be an ordering force in [41] society, supporting, if not supplanting, the dynastic *teh*. But since Confucianism was a discovery of the order of the soul, in its autonomy and immediacy under divine order it was a revolutionary break with cosmological collectivism and contained the seeds of a "religion" that might have flowered under more favorable circumstances. In the Homeric case the cosmological symbolism did break down, probably because the Doric invasion and the geographical dislocation of populations caused a much deeper disturbance than the ordinary Times of Trouble in other civilizations. The gods were no longer bound to the structure of the cosmos, and when the discovery of the soul occurred in Hellenic civilization, man found himself in his immediacy under a transcendent God. The preconditions were given for the blending of Greek philosophy with the religious insights achieved on the historical paths of Israel and Christianity.

[Voegelin's Interpretation of the *Enuma elish*—Eds.]

While the political symbolization of the cosmos is presupposed in the Mesopotamian sources even in the third millennium B.C., a coherent exposition of the symbolism is preserved only in the form of a cosmogonic epic of the first half of the second millennium named the *Enuma elish* after its opening words "When Above." The hero of the epic is Marduk of Babylon, who establishes the present world order. His characteristics in the story, however, belong to Enlil of Nippur; hence the epic, in its original form, must have been a much earlier Sumerian creation. Moreover, there is preserved a later version, from the Assyrian period, in which Marduk has been replaced by Ashur. The epic is thus representative of Mesopotamian symbolism from the Sumerians to the Assyrians.

The nature of the *Enuma elish* cannot easily be described because our differentiated vocabulary is not adequate to its compactness. It is a cosmogony in as much as it tells the story of the creation of the world. But a comparison with the Biblical Genesis would create an entirely false impression because in the *Enuma elish* it is not God who creates the world. The gods *are* the world and the progressive structural differentiation of the universe is, therefore, a story of the creation of the gods. The cosmogony is at the same time a theogony. The struggle of the gods for a proper organization of the universe, furthermore, requires new forms of social organization among the younger gods, culminating in [42] the kingship of Marduk. Since the creation of the cosmos is at the same time a political enterprise, the *Enuma elish* is also a political epic. The three factors of cosmogony, theogony, and politics are inseparably blended into one. Hence, the nature of the epic can be determined in a first approach only by weighing these factors quantitatively. The whole poem consists of seven tablets: the first contains the cosmogony and theogony proper, Tablet V describes the creative work of Marduk, and the other five deal with the emergence of Marduk as the savior of the gods, his great battle against Tiamat, and his glorification. Thus the epic as a whole is preponderantly political; it symbolizes cosmic order as political order.

The interpretation of the poem is complicated by the same fusion of component factors that causes the difficulty in determining its nature. However, it is possible to distinguish three stages in the cosmogony. In the first stage only the watery elements are present: Tiamat (the sea), Apsu (the sweet water), and Mummu (probably cloud banks and mist). In the second stage silt is deposited at the border of sea and sweet water, represented by the pair Lahmu and Lahamu, and land is banking up; with the land begin to form the horizons of heaven and earth, represented by the pair Anshar and Kishar; with the rings of the double horizon grow into existence heaven and earth, represented by Anu and Ea (Mummud); and from Ea, finally, is born the god who in the Babylonian version bears the name of Marduk, but in the Sumerian original must have been Enlil, the god of the storm who by its blowing holds heaven and earth apart. The third stage brings the reorganization of power relations between the gods, the elevation of Marduk to kingship, and his completion of the cosmic structure. From the cosmogonic account emerges the cosmos with the structure experienced by man. The cosmogony, however, is not a "creation" but a growth of the cosmos through procreation of gods and struggles between their generations. The gods themselves are bodily the structural parts of the cosmos. And this peculiarity leads to the further problem of aeons of cosmic order.

The cosmos of the *Enuma elish* is a completed order at the end of the story. If the cosmos is understood as the finished product resulting from the growth, there are no aeons of cosmic order because there is no order before its completion. And historians have, indeed, interpreted the first stage of the watery elements as the chaos that brings forth the cosmos. This interpretation, however, puts too much emphasis on the [43] cosmogonic factor in the epic, to the detriment of its political and even historical components. The stage of the watery elements is not a chaos but a self-contained order of the primordial trinity, and the pairs of gods who go forth from it belong to a new, incompatible psychological type that soon arouses the wrath of the powers that be. The new gods are a lively lot:

> The divine brothers gathered together.
> They disturbed Tiamat and assaulted their keeper;
> They disturbed the inner parts of Tiamat,
> Moving and running about in the divine abode.
> Apsu could not diminish their clamor,
> And Tiamat was silent in regard to their behavior.
> Yet their doing was painful to her.
> Their way was not good . . .

The older generation at last takes action. They meet in council and Apsu declares:

> Their way has become painful to me,
> By day I cannot rest, by night I cannot sleep;
> I will destroy them and put an end to their way,
> That silence be established, and then let us sleep!

In the resulting clash the younger vanquish the older gods, and with their victory they have become a permanent part of the new cosmic order which they dominate. This is more than a cosmogonic myth, and certainly it is not the story of a victory of order over chaos. The order is already in existence, cherished by a conservative older type, and the conflict arises from the liveliness of a younger generation that disturbs the order by its activities. Certain details of the story even suggest the nature of the conflict. The leader of the younger gods is Ea, the earth, "the one of supreme understanding, the skillful and wise," the Promethean figure that we have already met in the context of the Adapa myth. By his magic he defeats Apsu, the sweet waters, and on his defeated body he erects his abode—which, if anything at all, can only mean the securing of land against the dangers from the waters. In this conflict can be recognized faint memories of a civilizational crisis from which emerged communities under the authority of wise chieftains, as well as their efforts to secure settlements and lands by dike-building and irrigation.

The main part of the epic is concerned with the transition from the [44] second to the third stage of order. The new order is threatened by a revolt of the older gods who are thirsting for revenge. The revolt is well prepared and this time the magic of Ea is of no avail. In their despair the gods turn to the brilliant young Marduk. He is willing to undertake the defense, but only on the condition that he will be recognized as the supreme god in place of Anu. The gods meet in assembly and the kingship of the universe is conferred on Marduk, who then defeats Tiamat in battle and reorders the universe:

> He created stations for the great gods;
> The stars their likenesses, the signs of the zodiac, he set up.
> He determined the year, defined the divisions;
> For each of the twelve months he set up three constellations.
> In the very center thereof he fixed the zenith,
> The moon he caused to shine forth; the night he entrusted to her.
> He appointed her, the ornament of the night, to make known the days.

The cosmos then is completed by the creation of man out of one of the dismembered enemies. On mankind is incumbent the service of the gods so that they will be free from work. Grateful for this last feat of creation the gods then assemble and resolve to build a sanctuary for Marduk, their last labor before men take over the work:

> So shall Babylon be, whose construction you have desired;
> Let its brickwork be fashioned, and call it a sanctuary.

The epic concludes with the enumeration of the fifty names of Marduk. About the meaning of the Marduk story there can hardly be a doubt: it is the establishment of a Mesopotamian kingship with its center in Babylon. If the first crisis could be understood as the transition from primitive communities to the organized villages which grew into the city-states, the second crisis is the establishment of a Mesopotamian empire.

From the analysis it should have become clear that the three component strands are, indeed, inextricably interwoven. Any attempt to pull out one of them and to interpret the epic either as a cosmogony, or a theogony, or a myth of Mesopotamian history would destroy the meaning of the epic, which rests in its compactness. This compactness is the Mesopotamian peculiarity that we discussed in the opening pages of the present section. The world is not created by the gods, but the gods are massively the world itself. And even mankind participates in this mas- [45] sivity, for it is the dismembered body of one of the gods who in this form goes on to exist. The cosmos is, furthermore, the result of a historical struggle that now has settled down into a fixed and final order, an organized state of the world in the political sense of which mankind is a part. And, finally, the omphalos of this world-state is Babylon itself, where the *Enuma elish* was annually recited at the New Year's festival. Considering such compactness the durability of the symbolism should perhaps not be surprising. It outlasted Babylon through its survival in the Hellenistic idea of the cosmos as a polis.

## [CHAPTER 3: EGYPT]

### [63] . . . § 2. THE COSMOLOGICAL FORM

The Egyptians experienced the order of their society as part of cosmic order. The expression of the experience in symbols belongs, therefore, to the same general type as the Mesopotamian. Nevertheless, from the interpenetration of experiences and institutions there resulted a civilizational form, unique in all of its principal aspects. The form is peculiar because of its sudden birth, which must be considered a flashlike outburst of creativity even if we generously accord a century or more to this "flash" for bringing the form into definitely recognizable existence. Furthermore, the form is peculiar because of several elements of structure which distinguish it from the Mesopotamian, and for that matter from the form of any other cosmological civilization. And, finally, it is peculiar because within it occurs a rich differentiation of experiences which point beyond the limits of cosmology and are interpreted, there- [64] fore, by progressivist historians as anticipations of Hebrew and Greek achievements. The last characteristic is especially noteworthy because, with regard to major literary expressions of the cosmological experience itself, Egyptian civilization proved singularly barren. Egypt has produced neither epics like the Mesopotamian *Gilgamesh* or *Enuma elish*, nor a codification of its law comparable to Hammurabi's . . .

## [Pharaoh's Divinity—Eds.]

[72] . . . When the god chooses Egypt, he does not reveal himself directly to the people, or enter into a covenant with them, but is present with the people through his manifestation in their ruler. We must now approach the most puzzling aspect of Pharaonic symbolism, the divinity of the king. Divine kingship is a rare phenomenon. It occurs in Egypt, but, except in scattered instances, occurs neither in Mesopotamia nor in any of the major cosmological civilizations. Before an interpretation can be attempted, the phenomenon itself must be clearly understood. A divine king is not a god who has assumed human form, but a man in whom a god manifests himself. The god remains distinctly in his own sphere of existence and only extends his substance into the ruler, as it were . . .

## [Consubstantiality—Eds.]

### [§ 3. THE DYNAMICS OF EXPERIENCE]

## [1. The Egyptian Type of Differentiation]

[83] . . . today it is no longer permissible to regard the myth as having no other purpose in the history of mankind than to provide a stepping stone for more rational forms of symbolization; and by the same token, it no longer makes sense to search for the meaning of the myth in its partial anticipation of future accomplishments. We must recognize that the myth has a life and a virtue of its own. While Egyptian thought does not advance from myth to speculation, it is devoid neither of truth nor of intellectual movement. And the very comparison that reveals the limitations of the myth also points toward the source of its strength. For the fact that the speculation on being has differentiated out of the larger complex of cosmogonies suggests that the myth is much richer in content than any of the partial symbolizations derived from it. This richer content may conveniently be subdivided in two classes: The myth, first, contains the various experiential blocs which separate in the course of differentiation; and it, second, contains an experience that welds the [84] blocs into a living whole. That binding factor in the Egyptian cosmogonies is the experience of consubstantiality.

From the interaction of these various parts of the myth results its peculiar flavor of compactness. The previously mentioned "elements," for instance, are not yet distinguished as substances, as the stuff of which the world in the immanent sense is made, but are seen as the creative forces in their most impressive cosmic manifestations—in the sun, the earth, the wind. Moreover, the gods are recognized as manifest in the same cosmic phenomena. And the manner in which the gods are present again defies distinction by a Greek or modern vocabulary. One can hardly speak of their immanence in the world, for "immanence" presupposes an understanding of "transcendence" that is not yet achieved, though certainly from an experience of divine manifestation can develop an ultimate understanding of divine transcendence. The myth in its compact form thus contains both the experiential bloc that was developed by the Ionians and their successors into a metaphysics of world-immanent being and the other bloc, disregarded in such speculation, that developed into the faith in a world-transcendent being.

In a compactness that can not be translated but only dissected by our modern vocabulary, the myth holds together the blocs which in later history not only will be distinguished, but also are liable to fall apart. If we follow the two lines of differentiation as they emerge from the myth, if we consider that they will be pursued to the extremes of a radically other-worldly faith and of an agnostic metaphysics, and if we contemplate the inevitably resultant disorder in the soul of man and society, the relative merits of compactness and differentiation will appear in a new light. Differentiation, one would have to say, is not an unqualified good; it is fraught with the dangers of radically dissociating the experiential blocs held together by the myth, as well as of losing the experience of consubstantiality in the process. The virtue of the cosmogonic myth, on the contrary, lies in its compactness: It originates in an integral understanding of the order of being, provides the symbols which adequately express a balanced manifold of experiences, and is a living force, preserving the balanced order in the soul of believers.

The burden of these virtues is carried by the experience of consub-[85] stantiality. It is, within the economy of the myth, not a mechanical clasp for the various experiential blocs but a principle that establishes the order among the realms of being. The community of being, to be sure, is experienced as a community of substance; but it is divine substance that becomes manifest in the world, not cosmic substance that becomes manifest in the gods. The partners in the community of being are linked in a dynamic order in so far as divine substance pervades the world, society, and man, and not human or social substance the world and the gods. The order of consubstantiality thus is hierarchical; the flow of substance goes from the divine into the mundane, social, and human existences.

In the light of this analysis it will now be possible to characterize the nature and direction of the differentiations which actually occur within the Egyptian mythical form. The differentiation goes neither in the direction of Ionian speculation nor in the direction of a genuine opening of the soul toward transcendent being; it is rather a speculative exploration within the range of consubstantiality. The nature of the divine substance that is manifest in the existentially lower ranks of being becomes the object of inquiry, and the exploration leads—we are inclined to say inevitably—to a determination of the substances as "one" and as "spiritual." Considering that result, it is legitimate to speak of an Egyptian evolution toward monotheism as long as one remains aware that the pluralism of divine manifestations in the world is not really broken by an experience of transcendence . . . [Voegelin refers to John A. Wilson in Frankfort et al. 1946, for the notion of consubstantiality.]

(These selections from chapters 4 to 6, which comprise part two, introduce the reader to Voegelin's view of Israel's contribution to historical consciousness, as well as to his own hermeneutical approach to the Old Testament, in dialogue with biblical scholars, historians, and philosophers. *OH* IV introduced a much noted "break," inasmuch as Voegelin maintained that he had viewed history in too unilinear a way in the earlier volumes. This initiated an ongoing discussion as to how this should impact his earlier interpretation of Israel's contribution to history in *IR*.—Eds.)

## [3] Part Two

### The Historical Order of Israel

The compact experience of cosmological order proved to be tenacious. Neither the rise and fall of Mesopotamian empires nor the repeated crises of imperial Egypt could break the faith in a divine-cosmic order of which society was a part. To be sure, the contrast between the lasting of cosmic and the passing of social order did not remain unobserved, but the observation did not penetrate the soul decisively and, consequently, did not lead to new insights concerning the true order of being and existence. Political catastrophes continued to be understood as cosmic events decreed by the gods. In the Sumerian Lamentations over the destruction of Ur by the Elamites, for instance, the Elamitic attack was experienced as the storm of Enlil:

> Enlil called the storm—the people groan.
> The storm that annihilates the land he called—the people groan.
> The great storm of heaven he called—the people groan.
> The great storm howls above—the people groan.
> The storm ordered by Enlil in hate, the storm which wears away the land,
> Covered Ur like a garment, enveloped it like a linen sheet.

A cosmic shroud, as it were, was thrown by the god over the city and its streets filled with corpses. [From the "Lamentations over the Destruction of Ur" in Pritchard 1950, 455-63.] In Egypt, it is true, institutional breakdowns caused the variety of responses studied in the preceding chapter. The experience of order, more deeply shaken than in Mesopotamia, moved toward the limits that became visible in the Amon Hymns in the wake of the Amarna Revolution. Man, in his desire for a new freedom, seemed on the verge of opening his soul toward a transcendent God; and the new religiousness, indeed, achieved a surprising feat of monotheistic speculation. Nevertheless, even in the Amon Hymns, the attraction of the divine [112] magnet was not strong enough to orient the soul toward transcendent being. The Egyptian poets could not break the bond of the Pharaonic order and become the founders of a new community under God.

And yet, it was their age in which the bond was broken. The Amon Hymns were created under Dynasty XIX, ca. 1320-1205 B.C. And this was the dynasty under which, according to recent trends of conjecture, occurred the Exodus of Israel from Egypt. Ramses II is supposed to be the Pharaoh of the oppression, his successor Merneptah (1225-1215) the Pharaoh of the Exodus. While such precise suppositions may be doubtful, the thirteenth century B.C. in general was probably the age of Moses. At the time when the Egyptians themselves strained their cosmological symbolism to the limits without being able to break the bonds of its compactness, Moses led his people from bondage under Pharaoh to freedom under God.

In pragmatic history the event was too unimportant to be registered in the Egyptian records. The people who followed Moses consisted of a number of Hebrew clans which had been employed by the Egyptian government on public works, probably in the region east of the Delta.

They fled eastward into the desert and settled, for at least a generation, in the neighborhood of Kadesh before advancing to Canaan. In the centralized welfare state from which they fled they had probably not been treated worse than the native population of the same social status. Nevertheless, Egypt had been a house of bondage to a people whose nomadic soul thirsted for the freedom of the desert. When the freedom was gained, however, it proved of dubious value to men who had become accustomed to a different way of life. On the material level, perhaps there was not much to choose between nomadic existence and public works in a welfare state. The frugality of desert life aroused nostalgic memories of the Egyptian cuisine; and for all we know, the house of bondage might have become a home to which the tribes ruefully returned. Even without such an anticlimax the Exodus still would hardly have been worth remembering. If nothing had happened but a lucky escape from the range of Egyptian power, there only would have been a few more nomadic tribes roaming the border zone between the Fertile Crescent and the desert proper, eking out a meager living with the aid of part-time agriculture. But the desert was only a station on the way, not the goal; for in the desert the tribes found their God. They entered into a covenant with him, and thereby became his people. As a new type of people, formed [113] by God, Israel conquered the promised land. The memory of Israel preserved the otherwise unimportant story, because the irruption of the spirit transfigured the pragmatic event into a drama of the soul and the acts of the drama into symbols of divine liberation.

The events of the Exodus, the sojourn at Kadesh, and the conquest of Canaan became symbols because they were animated by a new spirit. Through the illumination by the spirit the house of institutional bondage became a house of spiritual death. Egypt was the realm of the dead, the Sheol, in more than one sense. From death and its cult man had to wrest the life of the spirit. And this adventure was hazardous, for the Exodus from Sheol at first led nowhere but into the desert of indecision, between the equally unpalatable forms of nomad existence and life in a high civilization. Hence, to Sheol and Exodus must be added the Desert as the symbol of the historical impasse. It was not a specific but the eternal impasse of historical existence in the "world," that is, in the cosmos in which empires rise and fall with no more meaning than a tree growing and dying, as waves in the stream of eternal recurrence. By attunement with cosmic order the fugitives from the house of bondage could not find the life that they sought. When the spirit bloweth, society in cosmological form becomes Sheol, the realm of death; but when we undertake the Exodus and wander into the world, in order to found a new society elsewhere, we discover the world as the Desert. The flight leads nowhere, until we stop in order to find our bearings beyond the world. When the world has become Desert, man is at last in the solitude in which he can hear thunderingly the voice of the spirit that with its urgent whispering has already driven and rescued him from Sheol. In the Desert God spoke to the leader and his tribes; in the Desert, by listening to the voice, by accepting its offer, and by submitting to its command, they at last reached life and became the people chosen by God.

What emerged from the alembic of the Desert was not a people like the Egyptians or Babylonians, the Canaanites or Philistines, the Hittites or Arameans, but a new genus of society, set off from the civilizations of the age by the divine choice. It was a people that moved on the historical scene while living toward a goal beyond history. This mode of existence was ambiguous and fraught with dangers of derailment, for all too easily the goal beyond history could merge with goals to be attained within [114] history. The derailment, indeed, did occur, right in the beginning. It found its expression in the symbol of Canaan, the land of promise. The symbol was ambiguous because, in the spiritual sense, Israel had reached the promised land when it had wandered from the cosmological Sheol to the *mamlakah*, the royal domain, the Kingdom of God. Pragmatically, however, the Exodus from bondage was continued into the conquest of Canaan by rather worldly means; further, to a Solomonic kingdom with the very institutional forms of Egypt or Babylon; and, finally, to political disaster and destruction that befell Israel like any other people in history. On its pragmatic wandering through the centuries Israel did not escape the realm of the dead. In a symbolic countermovement to the Exodus under the leadership of Moses, the last defenders of Jerusalem, carrying Jeremiah with them against his will, returned to the Sheol of Egypt to die. The promised land can be reached only by moving through history, but it cannot be conquered within history. The Kingdom of God lives in men who live in the world, but it is not of this world. The ambiguity of Canaan has ever since affected the structure not of Israelite history only but of the course of history in general.

The brief sketch of the issues raised by the appearance of Israel in history suggests a considerable amount of complications in the detail. There are difficulties of chronology; there is the relation between Hebrews, Israel, Judah, and the Jews; the relation between Israel and the surrounding Syriac society, whose importance has been revealed to us by recent archaeological discoveries; the relation between the

Biblical narrative and the history that can be reconstructed from external evidence; and, finally, the relation between pragmatic and spiritual history that issued into the Christian problem of profane and sacred history. These questions should be hurdles enough for a study of the peculiar order of Israel. But they are further complicated by the state and history of our literary sources. There must be taken into account the transformations which the early traditions of Israel have undergone through the postexilic redaction; the deformations of meaning caused by rabbinical and Christian canonization and interpretations; the further subtle changes of meaning imposed on the Hebrew text of the Bible by the English translations since the sixteenth century A.D., changes which have hardened into conventions to such a degree that even contemporary translations of the Bible do not dare to deviate from them; and, finally, the cloud of debate thrown up by a century of lower and higher criticism that settles in thick layers of con- [115] troversy on every problem. We have today reached a state in which competent scholars write volumes on the "Theology of the Old Testament" or the "Religion of Israel," while other, equally competent scholars raise the questions whether a theology can be found in the Old Testament at all or whether Israel had a religion.

It is dangerously easy to be swallowed up by the Sheol of history and philology. In order to avoid such a fate, we shall skirt the controversy and cut straight to the great issue that lies at its root, that is, to the creation of history by Israel. Once the great, embracing issue of history is clarified, the method that must be used in treating the secondary problems will also be clear.

## [116] Chapter 4: Israel and History

The major theoretical issues arising in a study of Israelite order have their common origin in the status of Israel as a peculiar people. Through the divine choice Israel was enabled to take the leap toward more perfect attunement with transcendent being. The historical consequence was a break in the pattern of civilizational courses. With Israel there appears a new agent of history that is neither a civilization nor a people within a civilization like others. Hence, we can speak of an Egyptian or a Mesopotamian but not of an Israelite civilization. In the Egyptian case, people and civilization roughly coincide. In the Mesopotamian case, we can distinguish major ethnic units, such as the Sumerian, Babylonian, Elamitic, and Assyrian, within the civilization. In the Israelite case, we encounter difficulties. Following Toynbee one can speak of a Syriac civilization to which belonged such peoples as the Israelites, the Phoenicians, the Philistines, and the Arameans of Damascus. But the mere enumeration of the ethnic subdivisions makes it unnecessary to argue further that Israel's position was peculiar; for the people that produced the literature of the Old Testament without a doubt stood apart from the others. Moreover, the course of Israelite history did not coincide chronologically with the course of Syriac civilization. It began before the Syriac civilization crystallized in history, and it took an independent, rather surprising development when the Syriac area was conquered successively by Assyrians, Babylonians, Persians, Greeks, and finally Romans . . .

## [123] [1. Israel and the Civilizational Courses] . . .

We shall start from the observation previously made, that Israelite sacred history cannot be discarded as unimportant even in pragmatic history, since by virtue of its possession Israel became the peculiar people, a new type of political society on the pragmatic plane. The men who lived the symbolism of Sheol, Desert, and Canaan, who understood their wanderings as the fulfillment of a divine plan, were formed by this experience into the Chosen People. Through the leap in being, that is, through the discovery of transcendent being as the source of order in man and society, Israel constituted itself the carrier of a new truth in history. If this be accepted as the essence of the problem, the paradigmatic narrative, with all its complications, gains a new dimension of meaning through its role in the constitution of Israel. For the truth which Israel carried would have died with the generation of discoverers, unless it had been expressed in communicable symbols. The constitution of Israel as a carrier of truth, as an identifiable and enduring social body in history, could be achieved only through the creation of a paradigmatic record which narrated (1) the events surrounding the discovery of the truth, and (2) the course of Israelite history, with repeated revisions, as a confirmation of the truth. This record is the Old Testament. Precisely when its dubiousness as a pragmatic record is recognized, the narrative reveals its function in creating a people in politics and history . . .

## [126] . . . 2. The Meaning of History

The Israelite conception of history, being the more comprehensive one, must be preferred to the defective Spengler-Toynbee theory of civilizational cycles . . . Such preference, however, does not abolish the difficulties inherent in the Israelite conception. For, if the idea of history as a form of existence be accepted, the term "history" becomes equivocal. "History," then, could mean either the dimension of objective time in which civilizations run their course or the inner form which constitutes a society. The equivocation could easily be removed, of course, by using the term in only one of the two meanings; but the result would be unsatisfactory. If the first meaning be eliminated, so that only "existence in time" could be predicated of cosmological societies, Egypt or Babylon would have no history. If the second meaning be eliminated, as is done by Spengler and Toynbee, there would be no word for what is history in the just-established preeminent sense of a society's moving through time, on a meaningful course, toward a divinely promised state of perfection. And it would be most inconvenient to use it in both senses, because in that case some societies would be more historical than other historical societies. If the Israelite conception be preferred, it must now be put to work to resolve the problems of its own making.

The trouble originates in the following proposition: Without Israel there would be no history, but only the eternal recurrence of societies in [127] cosmological form. At a first glance, to be sure, the proposition looks absurd, for it leads to the baffling equivocations, and ultimately, perhaps, to the escape, of Spengler and Toynbee. But it will lose its absurdity if it be understood in its methodical strictness as a statement about the inner form of societies. It does not mean that before a future historian there would unfold an interminable succession of Platos, Christs, Roman Empires, and so forth, as Toynbee imagines in his flight of fancy. For "eternal recurrence" is the symbol by means of which a cosmological civilization expresses (or rather, can express, if it be so minded) the experience of its own existence, its lasting and passing, in the order of the cosmos. "Eternal recurrence" is part of the cosmological form itself—it is not a category of historiography, nor will it ever have a historian. A political society which understands its order as participation in divine-cosmic order for that reason does not exist in historical form. But, if it does not have historical form, does it have history at all? Are we not back to the absurdity that Egypt and Babylon have no history? Again the absurdity will dissolve, if intellect intervenes before imagination runs away. Cosmological civilizations, though not in historical form, are not at all devoid of history. Remembering our principles of the constancy of human nature, as well as of compactness and differentiation, we may expect history to be present in them quite as much as metaphysical and theological speculation, but to be bound by the compactness of cosmological form, not yet differentiated. And this presence will be revealed as soon as, through Israel, history is differentiated as a form of existence. We began our history of order not with Israel, but with the Mesopotamian and Egyptian empires, because in retrospect the struggle for order in the medium of cosmological symbols appeared to be the first phase in the search for the true order of being that was carried one step further by Israel. In particular, the Egyptian dynamics of experience proved of absorbing interest because it revealed the movement of the soul toward an understanding, never quite achieved, of the world-transcendent God.

The equivocation of "history," thus, dissolves into the problem of compactness and differentiation. Egyptian history, or for that matter Mesopotamian or Chinese history, though transacted in cosmological form, is genuine history. Nevertheless, the knowledge is not articulated in the compact symbolism of the cosmological civilizations themselves; the presence of history is discovered only in retrospect from a position in which history as the form of existence has already been differentiated. For [128] the first time we encounter the problem that will occupy us repeatedly—that is, the genesis of history through retrospective interpretation. When the order of the soul and society is oriented toward the will of God, and consequently the actions of the society and its members are experienced as fulfillment or defection, a historical present is created, radiating its form over a past that was not consciously historical in its own present. Whether through the radiation of historical form the past receives negative accents as the Sheol from which man must escape, or positive accents as the *praeparatio evangelica* through which man must pass in order to emerge into the freedom of the spirit, the past has become incorporated into a stream of events that has its center of meaning in the historical present. History as the form in which a society exists has the tendency to expand its realm of meaning so as to include all mankind—as inevitably it must, if history is the revelation of the way of God with man. History tends to become world-history, as it did on this first occasion in the Old Testament, with its magnificent sweep of the historical narrative from the creation of the world to the fall of Jerusalem.

The tendency of historical form to expand its realm of meaning beyond the present into the past implies a number of problems that will be elaborated in their proper places in later sections of this study. In the present context only the three most important ones will be briefly suggested. They are (1) the ontological reality of mankind, (2) the origin of history in a historically moving present, and (3) the loss of historical substance.

(1) In the first place, history creates mankind as the community of men who, through the ages, approach the true order of being that has its origin in God; but at the same time, mankind creates this history through its real approach to existence under God. It is an intricate dialectical process whose beginnings, as we have seen, reach deep into the cosmological civilizations—and even deeper into a human past beyond the scope of the present study. The expansion of empire over foreign peoples, for instance, brought into view the humanity of the conquered subjects. In the texts from Thutmose III to Akhenaton the god who created Egypt was transformed into the god who also created the other peoples who now had come into the imperial fold. The course of pragmatic history itself, thus, provided situations in which a truth about God and man was seen—[129] though yet so dimly that the cosmological form of the society would not break. The realm of pragmatic conquest became transparent for the truth that the society of man is larger than the nuclear society of a cosmological empire. This observation should illuminate both the causal mechanism of differentiation and the objective reality of history. The inclusion of the past in history through retrospective interpretation is not an "arbitrary" or "subjective" construction but the genuine discovery of a process which, though its goal is unknown to the generations of the past, leads in continuity into the historical present. The historical present is differentiated in a process that is itself historical in so far as the compact symbolism gradually loosens up until the historical truth contained in it emerges in articulate form. From the articulate present, then, the inarticulate process of the past can be recognized as truly historical. The process of human history is ontologically real.

Nevertheless, there remains the ambiguity of a meaning created by men who do not know what they are creating; and this ambiguity quite frequently engenders the complacency that comes with supposedly superior knowledge, and in particular the all-too-well-known phenomenon of spiritual pride, in later generations. Such complacency and pride certainly are unfounded. For the ray of light that penetrates from a historical present into its past does not produce a "meaning of history" that could be stored away as a piece of information once for all, nor does it gather in a "legacy" or "heritage" on which the present could sit contentedly. It rather reveals a mankind striving for its order of existence within the world while attuning itself with the truth of being beyond the world, and gaining in the process not a substantially better order within the world but an increased understanding of the gulf that lies between immanent existence and the transcendent truth of being. Canaan is as far away today as it has always been in the past. Anybody who has ever sensed this increase of dramatic tension in the historical present will be cured of complacency, for the light that falls over the past deepens the darkness that surrounds the future. He will shudder before the abysmal mystery of history as the instrument of divine revelation for ultimate purposes that are unknown equally to the men of all ages.

(2) The retrospective expansion of history over the past originates in a present that has historical form. There arises, second, therefore, the whole complex of problems connected with the multiplicity of historical [130] presents. Each present has its own past; and there are, furthermore, the relations between the various presents, as well as between the histories created by them. Israelite was a first, but not the last, history; it was followed by the Christian, which extended its own form over the Israelite past and integrated it, through St. Augustine, into the symbolism of its *historia sacra*. Moreover, parallel with the Israelite occurred the Hellenic break with cosmological form, resulting in philosophy as the new form of existence under God; and the stream of Hellenic philosophy (whose relation to historical form will occupy us at considerable length) entered, and mingled with, the Judaeo-Christian stream of history. This manifold of successive, simultaneous, and mingling presents has a suspicious color of arbitrariness. The question arises whether anything like an objective, true history can result from such subjective, fictional constructions?

The question is legitimate; and the suspicion that history is a subjective interpretation of past events cannot be overcome by any amount of "exactness" in ascertaining the events. If there is such a thing as historical objectivity at all, its source must be sought in historical form itself; and conversely, if there is a suspicion of subjectivity, it must attach again to the form. Now, historical form, understood as the experience of the present under God, will appear as subjective only, if faith is misinterpreted as a "subjective" experience. If, however, it is understood as the leap in being, as the entering of the soul into divine reality through the entering of divine reality into the soul, the historical form, far from being a subjective point of view, is an ontologically real event in history. And it must be understood as an event of this nature, as long as we base our conception of history on a critical analysis of the literary sources which report the event and do not introduce subjectivity ourselves by arbitrary, ideological surmising. If now the men to whom it happens explicate the meaning of the event through symbols, the explication will cast an ordering ray of objective truth over the field of history in which the event objectively occurred.

Moreover, since the event is not fictional but real and the symbolic explication, therefore, bound by the nature of the event, we can expect the various symbolizations of historical order, in spite of their profound individual differences, to conform to a general type. And this expectation is, indeed, fulfilled by the manifold of historical presents and their symbolizations. Moses led Israel from the death of bondage to the life of freedom under God. Plato discovered life eternal for the erotic souls and pun- [131] ishment for the dead souls. Christianity discovered the faith that saves man from the death of sin and lets him enter, as a new man, into the life of the spirit. In every instance of a present in historical form, the Either-Or of life and death divides the stream of time into the Before-and-After of the great discovery.

The content of the event, furthermore, provides the principle for the classification of men and societies, past, present, and future, according to the measure in which they approach historical form, remain distant, or recede from it. This principle, while remaining the same in every instance, will inevitably render different results according to the empirical horizon in which it is applied. There will always be the division of time into the Before-and-After, as well as the classification of contemporaries into those who join the Exodus, and thereby become the Chosen People, and those who remain in Sheol. The expansion of historical order beyond this center, however, will depend on the nature of the past that is experienced as socially effective in the present. The model for treating the effective past in relation to the historical present was set by St. Paul in Romans. The historical present was understood by St. Paul as the life under the divine revelation through Christ, while the effective past surrounding the new society was furnished by Jews and Gentiles. All three of the communities—Christians, Jews, and Gentiles—belonged to one mankind as they all participated in divine order; but the order had been revealed to them in different degrees of clarity, increasing in chronological succession. To the Gentiles the law was revealed through the spectacle of the divine creation; to the Jews through the Covenant and the issuing of a divine, positive command; to the Christians through Christ and the law of the heart. History and its order, thus, were established by the measure in which various societies approached to the maximal clarity of divine revelation. This was a masterful creation of historical order, centering in the present of St. Paul and covering the high points of his empirical horizon. Obviously, the construction could not be ultimate but would have to be amended with changes and enlargements of the empirical horizon; but, at least, it remained "true" for the better part of two millenniums.

When we reflect on this long span of time, we are reminded again of the cataclysmic events which, on the pragmatic level of history, formed a horizon like the Pauline and now are changing it. The Israelite and Christian historical forms have arisen in the pragmatic situation created by the multicivilizational empires since Thutmose III, and we have noted [132] how the conquests, even within Egyptian civilization, induced and clarified the idea of a more-than-Egyptian mankind under one creator-god. A similar pragmatic situation, only on a much larger scale, has been created by the earth-wide, imperial expansion of Western civilization since the sixteenth century A.D. Civilizations which formerly were to us only dimly known, or entirely unknown, now fill the horizon massively; and archaeological discoveries have added to their number a past of mankind that had been lost to memory. This enormous expansion of the spatial and temporal horizon has burdened our age with the task of relating an ever more comprehensive past of mankind to our own historical form of maximal clarity, which is the Christian. It is a work that has barely begun.

(3) A society in existence under God is in historical form. From its present falls the ray of meaning over the past of mankind from which it has emerged; and the history written in this spirit is part of the symbolism by which the society constitutes itself. If the story of mankind is understood as a symbol in this sense, we realize that it is exposed, as is every symbol, to loss of substance. Long after the meaning has seeped out of it, the symbol may still be used, as for instance when the past of mankind is not related to a present under God but to the opinions of an agnostic or nationalist historian. It is not necessary, however, to dwell on instances of this type in order to see that the symbol is threatened with grave dangers. For the mass of materials that have a bearing on the meaningful history of mankind tends, by its sheer weight, to disintegrate the meaning which it is supposed to serve . . .

These hints should be sufficient to suggest the problem. We shall now [133] once more consider the Spengler-Toynbee theory, under the aspect that it dissolves history into a sequence of civilizational courses. The theory will appear odd, if one considers that a historian supposedly relates the past of mankind to a meaningful present. Why should a thinker be concerned about history at all, if apparently it is his purpose to show that there are no meaningful presents but only typical, recurrent situations and responses. This apparent oddity will now become intelligible as an expression of the tension between the Judaeo-Christian historical form, in which Western civilization still exists, and the loss of substance which it has suffered. The theory of civilizational cycles should not be taken at its face value; for if its authors were serious about it, they would no longer live in historical form and consequently not worry about history. The theory is of absorbing interest not only to its authors but also to their numerous readers because it reveals to our age history on the verge of being swallowed up by the civilizational cycles. The concern about civilizational decline has its roots in the anxiety stirred up by the possibility that historical form, as it was gained, might also be lost when men and society reverse the leap in being and reject existence under God. The form, to be sure, is not lost—at least not completely—as long as the concern inspires gigantic enterprises of historiography; but it certainly is badly damaged when the mechanics of civilizations occupies the foreground with massive brutality, while the originating present of history is pushed out of sight. The shift of accents is so radical that it practically makes nonsense of history, for history is the Exodus from civilizations. And the great historical forms created by Israel, the Hellenic philosophers, and Christianity did not constitute societies of the civilizational type—even though the communities thus established, which still are the carriers of history, must wind their way through the rise and fall of civilizations.

## [134] CHAPTER 5: THE EMERGENCE OF MEANING

The present chapter will deal with the meaning of history in the Israelite sense. That meaning did not appear at a definite point of time to be preserved once for all, but emerged gradually and was frequently revised under the pressure of pragmatic events. As a consequence, the historical corpus of the Old Testament, reaching from Genesis through Kings, displays the rich stratification previously indicated. All the substrata, however, are overlaid by the meaning imposed by the final redaction, as well as by the arrangement of the books so that they will deliver the continuous narrative from the creation of the world to the fall of Jerusalem.

The intention of the postexilic authors to create a world-history must be accepted as the basis for any critical understanding of Israelite history. The Biblical narrative, as previously suggested, was not written in order to be disintegrated by exploring the Babylonian origin of certain mythologemes or by studying Bedouin customs that illuminate the Age of the Patriarchs, but in order to be read according to the intentions of their authors. A first approach to these intentions is given through Psalm 136.

Organized in three distinct parts the liturgical Psalm 136 gives something like a commentary on the governing principle of Israelite history. It opens with a preamble:

> Give thanks to Yahweh, for he is good,
> Give thanks to the God of gods,
> Give thanks to the Lord of lords.

And then follow the appositions, describing the feats of Yahweh for which thanks are due. First, the creation of the world:

> To him who did great wonders alone,
> To him who made the heavens with skill,
> To him who spread out the earth upon the waters,
> To him who made the great lights,
> The sun to rule by day,
> The moon and the stars to rule by night.

## [135] Second, the rescue from Egypt:

> To him who smote the Egyptians in their first-born,
> And brought forth Israel from the midst of them,
> With a strong hand and an outstretched arm,
> To him who divided the Sea of Sedge into two parts,
> And led Israel over through the midst of it,
> And shook Pharaoh and his army into the Sea of Sedge.

Third, the conquest of Canaan:

> To him who led his people through the wilderness,
> To him who smote great kings,
> And slew mighty kings,
> Sihon, the king of the Amorites,
> And Og, the king of Bashan,
> And gave their land as a possession,
> A possession to Israel, his servant.

The Psalm concludes with a summary invocation of the god who created both world and history:

> Who remembered us in our abasement,
> And rescued us from our foes,
> Who gives food to all flesh,
> Give thanks to the God of the heavens.

The drama of divine creation moves through the three great acts: the creation of the world, the rescue from Egypt, and the conquest of Canaan. Each of the three acts wrests meaning from the meaningless: the world emerges from Nothing, Israel from the Sheol of Egypt, and the promised land from the Desert. The acts thus interpret one another as works of divine creation, and as the historical stages in which a realm of meaning grows: In history God continues his work of creation, and the creation of the world is the first event in history. To this conception the term "world-history" can be applied in the pregnant sense of a process that is world-creation and history at the same time. In its sweep the Old Testament narrative surveys the process from the creative solitude of God to its completion through the establishment of the servants of Yahweh in the land of promise. As in the Amon Hymns one could discern speculative structures which in later history would be differentiated, so one can discern in the compactness of the Israelite historical symbolism the outlines of the three great blocks of Thomistic speculation: God, the creation, and the return of the creation to God. That Israelite history contains this specula- [136] tive structure, though yet in undifferentiated form, is the secret of its dramatic perfection.

While Psalm 136 reveals the speculative sweep of the construction, further texts must be considered in order to understand the richness of motivations in detail. The problems of this nature have received careful attention by Gerhard von Rad in his studies on the Hexateuchal form. The following examples are chosen, therefore, from the materials assembled in his work, though they will have to be moved into a somewhat different light, in accordance with the purposes of the present study.

The oldest of the several motives that have formed the Israelite meaning of history is probably to be found in the famous prayer formula of Deuteronomy 26:4b-9:

A wandering Aramean was my father;
and he went down into Egypt, and sojourned there, few in
    number;
and he became there a nation, great, mighty, and populous.
And the Egyptians dealt ill with us, and afflicted us, and laid
    upon us hard bondage.
And we cried unto Yahweh, thc God of our fathers;
and Yahweh heard our voice, and saw our affliction, and our
    toil, and our oppression.
And Yahweh brought us forth out of Egypt,
with a mighty hand and with an outstretched arm,
with great terror, and with signs, and with wonders.
And he has brought us into this place,
and has given us this land,
a land flowing with milk and honey.

This obviously is not the great construction of Psalm 136. The prayer,
concentrates, rather, on the concrete historical experience of Israel's
salvation from the bondage of Egypt; and since it is a ritual prayer, to
be offered with the first fruits of the land, it properly concludes on
the motif of the Canaan that has produced them. Nevertheless, it has
an importance of its own in so far as it shows how the meanings of
history ramify from an experiential nucleus. In order to be brought
out of Egypt, Israel first had to come into it. If God reveals himself as
the savior in a concrete [137] historical situation, the prehistory of
the situation comes into view. The Exodus expands into Patriarchal
history.

Once the pattern of the expanding nucleus has been set, it can be
elaborated to suit further concrete situations. On the occasion of the
Diet of Shechem, for instance, the tradition attributes to Joshua a
speech which elaborates the prayer formula of Deuteronomy 26. The
reference to the "wandering Aramaean" expands into a succinct recall
of Patriarchal history, mentioning Abraham, Isaac, and Jacob (Josh
24:2b-4). The miracles of the Exodus are then recalled with specific
details (5-7). And the gap between Egypt and Canaan, finally, is filled
with an enumeration of the principal events of the Transjordanian
Wars, as well as of the Conquest itself, down to the present meeting
at Shechem (8-13). On a similar solemn occasion, when Saul was
instituted as king at Gilgal, Samuel's recall of events begins with the
Exodus and brings them down through the period of the Judges to the
Ammonite War, which had aroused the irresistible desire of the
people for a king like Ammon (1 Sam 12:8-l3). In the liturgical

literature, the variations of the theme can achieve considerable length, as in Psalms 78, 105, and 135.

Not all Israelite history grows, however, through expansion from the experience of the Exodus. There are rival centers of meaning. The prayer formula of Deuteronomy 26, for instance, appears with a slight variation in a different ritual context in Deuteronomy 6:20-25. This time it is not the offering of Canaanite first fruits but the question why Yahweh's statutes and ordinances should be obeyed that occasions the recall of God's work of salvation (6:20). Exodus and Canaan together (6:21-23) now become a course of providential history which serves the ulterior purpose of establishing a Chosen People in obedience to the ordinance of God (6:24-25). While the experiential center of the Exodus is not abolished, it has become subordinate to the meaning emanating from the Sinaitic Covenant. A further complication is introduced by the speech of Joshua at the Diet of Shechem (Josh 24:2b-13), in so far as the speech is the prelude to a ritual (24:14-27) by which the assembled tribes enter into a berith with Yahweh that presupposes, but is not identical with, the Sinaitic Berith. A third experiential center seems to have found expression in a festival and ritual of its own. Gerhard von Rad calls it the Covenant Festival of Shechem; and in the reconstruction of its ritual distinguishes:

[138]   (a) Joshua's Paraenesis (24:14 ff.)
        (b) The Assent of the People (24:16 ff.)
        (c) The Reading of the Law (24:25)
        (d) Conclusion of the Covenant (24:27)
        (e) Blessing and Curse (Josh 8:34)

The Law that was read as part of the ritual was presumably closely related to the Sinaitic legislation, so that the Shechem festival would furnish an example of a rite that has absorbed the meaning of another rite originating in a different experiential situation. Of an independent Sinai festival traces are still to be found in Psalms 50 and 81.

The rites and liturgies, thus, are the key to the process in which the meaning of Israelite history grows into its complex form. They reveal above all their own motivation through the experiences of concrete historical events; they show, furthermore, the possibilities of expanding a nucleus of historical experience into the past and the future; and the cases of interlocking rites, finally, foreshadow the method of welding traditions of different experiential motivation into a whole of meaning on the level of historiography. Before that level is reached, however, the rite gives further proof of the strength of its experiential charge in so far as it motivates the creation of cult legends as the literary form in which the historical events that have motivated the cult are presented. As such cult legends are recognizable the Passah legend, which has become the form of the Exodus traditions, and the New Year legend, which has become the form of the Sinai traditions. Only beyond the traditions formed by cult legends begins the historiographic construction proper, in the ninth century B.C., when the motive for writing history is furnished by the Davidic [139] monarchy. On that level it is, then, possible to combine the traditions of variegated origin into a coherent prehistory of the monarchy and to expand the narrative into the past, beyond the Patriarchs, into the prepatriarchal Genesis. A stream of motivations, thus, rises from the primary experiences, through the festivals, rites, and cult legends, into the speculative construction of the narrative. And since the stream rises without losing its identity of substance, the speculative form of the unfolded meaning can revert to the liturgical level, as in the great prayer of Nehemiah 9:6-37 that praises God in his works from the Creation, through the history of the Patriarchs, of Exodus, Sinai, and Canaan, of Kingdom, Exile, and Return, down to the postexilic rite of the new Covenant with Yahweh.

The construction of world history unfolds the meaning that radiates from the motivating centers of experience. And since it is the will of God, and his way with man that is experienced in the concrete situation, world-history is meaningful in so far as it reveals the ordering will of God in every stage of the process, including the creation of the world itself. Beyond the construction of the world-history rises, therefore, a vision of the God who by his word called into existence the world and Israel. He is one God, to be sure, but he bears as many aspects as he has modes of revealing his ordering will to man—through the order of the world that embraces man and history, through the revelation of right order to the Fathers and the Chosen People, and through the aid that he brings to his people in adversity. He is the Creator, the Lord of Justice, and the Savior. These are the three fundamental aspects of divine being as they become the Israelite construction of world-history. They become something like a "theology" when they are brought into focus in the work of Deutero-Isaiah; and they remain the fundamental modes in which God is experienced in Christianity.

The experience of existence under God unfolds into the meaning of world-history; and the emergence of meaningful order from an ambiance of lesser meaning supplies the subject matter for the Biblical narrative. The term "emergence" in the present context is meant to denote the process in which any type of meaningful order is brought forth from an environment with a lesser charge of meaning. It will apply to the three main instances evoked in Psalm 136, as well [as] to all other instances interspersed between them or following them. The Biblical narrative is built around the great cases of emergence, and gains its dramatic movement in detail as [140] the story of recessions from, and returns to, levels of meaning already achieved.

Genesis establishes the dramatic pattern of emergence and recession of meaningful order. It opens with the creation of the world, culminating in the creation of man; and it follows the account of the original emergence of order with the story of the great recession from the Fall to the Tower of Babel. A second level of meaning emerges with Abraham's migration from the Chaldaean city of Ur, with a way station in Haran, to Canaan. That is the first Exodus by which the imperial civilizations of the Near East in general receive their stigma as environments of lesser meaning. Canaan, indeed, is reached in that first venture, but the foothold in the land of promise is still precarious. Repeated famines drive first Abraham to a temporary settlement in Egypt and later the Jacob clans to a more permanent one. Genesis closes the account of this second recession with the return of Jacob's body to Canaan, to be buried in the field that Abraham had bought from Ephron the Hittite, and the oath of the sons of Israel to take the bones of Joseph with them, when they will all return to the promised land. Creation and Exodus, thus, are successive phases in the unfolding of the order of being; but the rhythm of emergence and recession was to be beaten twice in Genesis, and the order of being is not yet completed. Genesis is clearly the prelude to the main event whose story is told in Exodus, Numbers, and Joshua—that is, to the second Exodus, the wandering in the Desert, and the conquest of Canaan. Only with the main event, with the constitution of Israel as a people through the Covenant and its settlement in the promised land, the historical present is reached from which the ray of meaning falls over Genesis. At this point, at the complete emergence of meaning, the guidance offered by Psalm 136 properly stops, for it is the historical present in which the postexilic redactors still live—in spite of the course of pragmatic events which necessitated serious revisions of the original conception. Before turning to the disturbing events under the established present, however, a further aspect of the emergence of meaning must be considered.

The world-history is the history of all created being, not of Israel alone. As far as meaning emerges beyond the creation of the world in the history of mankind proper, the Biblical narrative is therefore fraught with the problem of understanding Israelite as the representative history of mankind. In Genesis 18:18 Yahweh asks himself:

> [141] Shall I hide what I am about to do from Abraham,
> seeing that Abraham is bound to become a great and powerful nation,
> and through him all the nations of the earth will invoke blessings on one another?

In Galatians 3:7-9, St. Paul could interpret his apostolate among the nations outside Israel as the fulfillment of Yahweh's promise to Abraham; and contemporary with St. Paul, Philo Judaeus interpreted the prayer of the Jewish High Priest as the representative prayer for mankind to God. The ability or inability of the various branches of the Jewish community to cope with the problem of its own representative character has affected the course of history to our time, as will be seen presently. For the moment it must be observed that Genesis, as a survey of the past from which emerges the Israelite historical present, fulfills two important tasks. On the one hand, it separates the sacred line of the godly carriers of meaning from the rest of mankind. That is the line of Adam, Seth, Noah, Shem, Abraham, Isaac, Jacob, and the twelve ancestors of the tribes of Israel. On the other hand, it must pay some attention to the mankind from which the sacred line has separated. That task is discharged in Genesis 10, in form of a survey of the nations that have descended from Noah after the Flood and peopled the earth. Not all of the nations mentioned can be identified with certainty. But at least the sons of Japhet are recognizable as the northern peoples, and among them the sons of Javan (the Ionians) as the peoples of Cyprus, Rhodes, and other islands. Under the sons of Ham the populations of Canaan are ranged by the side of the Egyptians, probably because the country was under Egyptian suzerainty. The sons of Shem, finally, comprise the Elamites, Assyrians, and Arameans by the side of Eber, the ancestor of the Hebrews. Certain details, such as the display of violent animosity in Genesis 9 against the Canaanites, suggest that the body of traditions incorporated in this geopolitical survey, was formed not very long after the Conquest.

The problem of emergence can now be further pursued into the course of events under the historical present created by Covenant and Conquest. As far as the course of paradigmatic history is concerned, the pattern established by Genesis simply runs on with its alternate recessions from, and recapturings of, the level of meaning achieved by the Conquest. The book of Judges is a model of this type of historiography, with its partly monotonous, partly amusing, repetition of the formula: "So the Israelites [142] did what was evil in the sight of Yahweh in that they forgot Yahweh their God, and served the Baals and Ashtarts," followed by accounts of prompt punishment through military defeat at the hands of Midianites, Amorites, or some other neighbor, by the repentance of Israel, and by the rise of a major judge who restores independence.

The formal rhythm of the ups and downs of meaning was further formalized by using twelve judges to cover the period; and this pattern of the rhythm, with dozens of judges for punctuation, might have run on indefinitely, unless the exigencies of power politics had persuaded the confederate tribes of Israel that a more effective, centralized government under a king was needed in order to endow the conquest of Canaan with some measure of stability. It was this establishment of a kingdom which inevitably produced the conflict between the Israel that was a peculiar people under the kingship of God, and the Israel that had a king like the other nations. Whether the kingship was pragmatically successful, through assimilation to the prevalent style of governmental organization, foreign politics, and cultural relations with the neighbors, as it was under Solomon and the Omride dynasty in the Northern Kingdom; or whether it was unsuccessful, and ultimately brought disaster on Israel through hopeless resistance against stronger empires, the Prophets were always right in their opposition. For Israel had reversed the Exodus and re-entered the Sheol of civilizations. Hence, the pattern of recession and repentant return still runs through Samuel and Kings but no longer with the ease of Judges, for it is increasingly overshadowed by the awareness that the Kingdom on principle is a recession, while the carriership of meaning, running parallel with it, is being transferred to the Prophets. Moreover, the literary organization of the great historical work can no longer cope successfully with the problem of crisis. To be sure, the story is continued in a formal sense beyond Judges through Samuel and Kings; but for the period of the Kingdom the prophetic books must be read by the side of the historical if one wants to gain an adequate understanding of the spiritual struggle of Israel with the issue of the Kingdom. And with the Exile the leadership of meaning plainly passes to the Prophets.

The construction of paradigmatic history in the light of a present that had been constituted by the Covenant was obviously cracking up—even in the hands of the postexilic redactors, who apparently accepted this present still as valid. The source of the difficulties will perhaps become clearer, if we step back of the redactors and assume the more detached [143] view of the rabbinical canonizers. For the division of the books in the rabbinical canon offers a valuable clue to the disturbance in the emergence of meaning. The sacred writings were subdivided by the canon into (1) The Law, (2) The Prophets, and (3) The Writings. The Law comprised the Pentateuch; the Prophets comprised Joshua-Kings, Isaiah, Jeremiah, Ezekiel, and the twelve minor Prophets; and the Writings comprised roughly the postexilic literature, discarding, however, the Apocrypha and Pseudepigrapha. Looking back on the great political disaster from the vantage point of the synod of Jamnia (*ca.* A.D. 100), the emergence of meaning seemed to have occurred in three main phases. The first phase reached from the creation of the world to the historical constitution of Israel under the Covenant, and the Law made in pursuance thereof, as might be expected. The second phase, however, brought a new development, not yet envisaged by the redactors of the historical writings, in so far as the conquest of Canaan, as well as the whole confederate and royal history of Israel, were subordinated with regard to their meaning to the emergent Yahwism of the Prophets. The third group, finally, under the nondescript title of "Writings," had no more than a firm core of meaning in the books connected with the foundation of the Second Temple (Chronicles, Ezra, Nehemiah), as well as in the hymnbook of the new community, while for the rest it was character-ized rather negatively by the elimination of the Maccabaean history, the larger part of the Hellenizing wisdom-literature, and the almost complete elimination of the apocalyptic literature, the one exception being Daniel. The canonization, thus, formalized a situation that had been sensed to exist in fact already by the author of the Prologue to Ecclesiasticus (*ca.* 130 B.C.), when he wrote: "Many and great things have been delivered unto us by the law and the prophets, and by others that have followed their steps, for the which things Israel ought to be commended for learning [*paideia*] and wisdom [*sophia*]." Israel with its *paideia* and *sophia* belonged to the past. The Law and the Prophets were closed chapters of history. What finally emerged from the double spurt of meaning was no Canaan, but the community of Jews who would preserve their past as an eternal present for all future.

The retrospective interpretation from the rabbinical position makes it clear that the disturbing factor in the Israelite historical form had been the ambiguity of Canaan, that is, the translation of transcendent aim [144] into a historical *fait accompli*. With the conquest of Canaan, Israelite history, according to its own original conception, had come to its end; and the aftermath could only be the repetitious, indefinite ripple of defection and repentance that filled the pages of Judges. From this rippling rhythm the historical form was regained, not by the Kingdom, but through the elaboration of the universalist potentialities of Yahwism by the Prophets. The separation of the sacred line from the rest of mankind—an enterprise that had run into the impasse of a nation among others—would have ended ignominiously with the political catastrophy, unless the Yahwism of the Prophets had made possible the genesis of a community under God that no longer had to reside in Canaan at all cost. Still, the new Jewish community, which succeeded to the Hebrews of the Patriarchal Age and the Israel of the Confederacy and the Kingdom, had to travel a hard way until it could rejoin the mankind from which it had separated, so that the divine promise to Abraham would be fulfilled. And not the whole of the community was successful in ascending to this further level of meaning. For, from the postexilic community there emerged, surviving historically to this day, the branch of Talmudic Judaism—at the terrific price of cutting itself off, not only from the abortive Maccabaean nationalism, but also from its own rich potentialities that had become visible in Hellenization, the proselytizing expansion, and the apocalyptic movements. The representative separation of the sacred line through divine choice petered out into a communal separatism, which induced the intellectuals of the Roman Empire to attribute to the community an *odium generis humani*. What had begun as the carriership of truth for mankind, ended with a charge of hatred of mankind. As the other and, indeed, successful branch, emerged the Jewish movement that could divest itself not only of the territorial aspirations for a Canaan, but also of the ethnic heritage of Judaism. It became able, as a consequence, to absorb Hellenistic culture, as well as the proselytizing movement and the apocalyptic fervor, and to merge it with the Law and the Prophets. With the emergence of the Jewish movement that is called Christianity, Jews and Greeks, Syrians and Egyptians, Romans and Africans could fuse in one mankind under God. In Christianity the separation bore its fruit when the sacred line rejoined mankind.

[CHAPTER 6: THE HISTORIOGRAPHIC WORK]

[§1. The Sources of the Narrative]

[154] ... the unanalyzed conception of authorship facilitated the belief, in the Wellhausen school, that one knew what the presumed authors had written if one called their product a "narrative" or

"history," even though behind such vocabulary lurked the formidable questions of the symbolic form not only of the narrative itself but of the canonical collection of the Old Testament as a whole. Questions of this nature, however, can not be approached through dissection of a text into sources, by literary criteria, but only through an analysis of the contents; and by contents are meant the units of meaning that can be found in the text as it stands, through the application of a theory of symbolic forms. This postulate does not imply, to be sure, that the component strands discerned by Wellhausian analysis are senseless. On the contrary, it is quite possible that the units discerned by an analysis of symbols will fall in their entirety within the range of one or the other "source"; and the sources discerned by literary criticism should by all means be examined closely, for if separated from the context they may reveal units of meaning that otherwise might have escaped attention. Such coincidences, however, are a question of fact, not the consequence of a prestabilized harmony between the sources and symbolic forms. Source analysis, thus, can be of assistance if used with circumspection, in the search for units of symbolic form; but it can become utterly destructive if it pretends that the integral text contains no units of meaning which cut across the sources.

The last reflections lead to the first and second propositions advanced [155] above. The question whether a unit of symbolic form falls within the range of one of the sources of literary criticism, or cuts across several of them, is a question of fact. And our analysis will show on several occasions, especially in Chapter 12 in the study of Moses, that very important units of text, with a distinct form and meaning of their own, as a matter of fact, cut across the sources. But this is not the place to dwell on specific instances. For the Biblical narrative abounds, of course, with an infinity of meanings beyond the component sources, for the commonsense reason that it was composed for that very purpose, or as we should rather say, that it grew into its final form through the compositorial labors, over centuries, of a great number of men who selected and combined traditions in order to bring to paradigmatic perfection meanings which had not been articulated with the same degree of clarity in the component materials. If the compositorial labors had not added new strata of articulated meaning, the Biblical narrative in its final form would be the *Glasperlenspiel* of unemployed intellectuals who had better have left their sources alone. Faced with the alternatives that either the compositors of the Biblical narrative have ruined the meaning of their sources or that the literary critics have ruined the meaning of the compositorial work, we prefer the second one . . .

[158] . . . A comparative evaluation of the new tradition-historical and the older source-critical results must start from the understanding that two sets of assumptions must be weighed against one another. Neither the new nor the old method can draw on independent sources for information about genesis and authorship of the narrative; both have to base their argument on the contents of the narrative itself. If therefore the conception of Engnell be considered a distinct advance over the Wellhausen school, as we believe it must, the reason is that the tradition- [159] historical view is based on a much more thorough understanding of the contents of the narrative than the source-critical conception. What characterizes the work of Engnell, and of the Uppsala school in general, is remarkable respect for the Masoretic Text as it stands, a reluctance to operate with conjectures and emendations (especially a disinclination to use the Septuagint as an easy way out when the Hebrew text is difficult), an excellent philological equipment for dealing with the text, and a vast knowledge of comparative materials for the elucidation of symbols and cult patterns. These technical virtues are the outer bulwark of a will, not always clearly articulated, to return to the meanings intended by the narrative and its subunits, which the Wellhausen school had replaced by the meanings of the J, E, P, and D narratives. And the tradition-historical assumption obviously fits the intended meaning of the narrative very much better than the source-critical assumption. If, for instance, the Tetrateuch is conceived as a work that has received its meaning, together with its final form, through a traditionist circle, the body of text has regained the meaning which it had lost under the assumption of a mechanical combination of sources; and, at the same time, the embarrassing redactor, who combined sources which he had better have left alone, has disappeared. Moreover, the assumption of traditionist circles is sufficiently elastic to accommodate the various genera of traditions clearly to be discerned in the Old Testament in general. There may be assumed circles of scribes and learned men for the wisdom literature, of singer groups in the temple for the psalm literature, of colleges of priests for the law collections, of groups of disciples around a master for the prophetic literature, of bards or poets (the *moshlim* of Numbers 21:27) for proverbs, and finally of storytellers or traditionists in the narrower sense for the various types of patriarchal, heroic, and prophetic legends. A splendid vista opens on the culture of Israel, as well as on the variegated circles of men who preserved and enlarged it . . .

## [162] . . . § 2. The Symbols of Historiography

Throughout this part we have spoken of history as the Israelite form of existence, of a historical present created by the Covenant, and of an Israelite historiography, while ignoring the fact that the Hebrew language has no word that could be translated as "history." This is a serious matter, for apparently we have violated the first principle of hermeneutics—that the meaning of a text must be established through interpretation of the linguistic corpus. It is impermissible to "put an interpretation on" a literary work through anachronistic use of modern vocab- [163] ulary without equivalents in the text itself. Hence, two questions will demand an answer: (1) How can the use of the term "history" be justified in an analysis of Israelite symbols? and (2) what did the Israelite authors do, expressed in their own language, when they wrote what we call "history"?

The justification demanded by the first question will rely on the principle of compactness and differentiation. The Israelite thinkers did not indeed differentiate the idea of history to the point of developing a theoretical vocabulary. Nevertheless, with due precautions, the modern vocabulary may be used without destroying the meaning of Israelite symbols, because the idea of history has its origin in the Covenant. The compact Mosaic symbolism of communal existence under the will of God as revealed through his instructions has in continuity, through the course of Israelite, Jewish, and Christian history, undergone a process of articulation from which resulted, among others, the idea of history. After three millenniums of defections and returns, of reforms, renaissances, and revisions, of Christian gains and modern losses of substance, we are still living in the historical present of the Covenant. Moreover, the work of the Israelite historiographers is still going on, although, due to theoretical differentiation, the techniques have changed. For Israel has become mankind; and the accretion of the Instructions has become the revision of principles.

The use of such terms as "history," "historical present," and "historiography," however, is more than justified in an analysis of Israelite symbols—it is a matter of theoretical necessity. For if the differentiated vocabulary were rejected, there would be no instruments for critical analysis and interpretation. Confined to the use of the Hebrew symbols, our understanding would be locked up in the very compactness which, in Israelite history, has led into the disastrous impasses previously discussed. Nevertheless, while we cannot dispense with modern theoretical vocabulary, extreme caution is neces-

sary in its use, for the idea of history has absorbed experiences beyond
the Israelite range, and we run the risk of projecting later, e.g.
Christian, meanings into the earlier symbols. Hence, the interpretation must be kept as close as possible to the Biblical text. Moreover,
a brief reflection on the peculiar nature of Israelite compactness will
be in place . . .

> (Chapters 7 to 10, which comprise part three, introduce the reader
> to Voegelin's study of the period from Abraham to the Northern
> Kingdom's fall. In this part he takes his position "at the level of
> pragmatic events," following "the trail of their symbols." The
> reader should bear in mind that the pragmatic and the paradig-
> matic levels of history, in Voegelin's view, are able to be distin-
> guished, but they are not really separable. The study of Abraham's
> revelatory experience is one of Voegelin's most sustained treat
> ments of religious personalities and their experience. The Deborah
> Song study presents one of the most pristine views of Yahwist
> Israel. At the same time, it underscores the role of women in Israel's
> history.—Eds.)

## [185] PART THREE

### HISTORY AND THE TRAIL OF SYMBOLS

The historiographic work was originally dominated by the foundation of the monarchy. Under the impact of the Prophetic movement,
then, the focus of interest shifted from successful pragmatic existence
to the substantive order under the Covenant. The exilic and postexilic
historians, finally, weighted the Pentateuch heavily with additional
Codes, constructed the history of the Kingdom around the Temple of
Solomon and the purity of the cult of Yahweh, and superimposed the
speculation on periods of world-history.

The radical shift of interest, however, did not induce the historians
to abandon the work of earlier generations. The complete work, as a
consequence, assumed the symbolic form sui generis . . . On the one
hand, the form of the narrative absorbed into its medium the
variegated contents of myth and history and transformed it into the
paradigmatic world-history. On the other hand, the resulting
world-history was not the work of a single historian who digested
primary sources and imposed his personal literary style on them. The
late historians achieved the desired changes of meaning rather through
selection, repression, mutilation, interpolation, and the silent influence of context. In such fragmentized form, therefore, the narrative

contains a considerable amount of source materials which, isolated from their context, still reveal their original meaning.

The peculiarity of the literary form is intimately determined by the problems of an order that oscillated between the righteousness of a life in obedience to divine instructions and the organization of a people for existence in history. The compactness of the cosmological symbolism, to be sure, was broken by the Yahwist experience, but the elaboration of the experience through new symbols never completely penetrated the consequences of the leap in being for either the life of the spirit or the life in the world. Israelite symbols have, therefore, a baffling structure.

[186] And that is perhaps the reason why their nature rarely comes into clear view in the literature on the subject. The Yahwism of the Prophets still appears to be the best recognizable "contribution" of Israel to the civilization of mankind, whereas the symbols concerning organized existence seem so closely related to the cosmological myth of the time that the specific Israelite difference is difficult to determine.

That complexity of order must be faced just as the corresponding complexity of the historiographic work. There is neither a "religious" Israel of the Covenant and the Prophets, to which the love of theologians and Old Testament scholars reaches out, nor a "political" Israel which receives preferential treatment from pragmatic historians. There is only the one Israel, which tries to exist in the historical form centered in the Covenant, though at the same time the cosmological myth creeps back wherever the exigencies of pragmatic existence assert themselves. While the form elements can be well distinguished in the sources, one must resist the temptation to isolate them against each other and to speak, as is frequently done, of a genuine Israelite order under the Covenant and its vitiation through "oriental influences." For the people who had an incomplete understanding of their God, who deserted him for Canaanite, Assyrian, and Babylonian divinities, who even degraded him to a god of the same rank as the others, and perhaps not the most reliable one, were as much Israel as the Prophets and had as good reasons for their defection as the Prophets for their opposition. When reflecting on the tensions between the form elements, it will perhaps be better not to distinguish between the forms at all, but rather to descend to the level of experience and to speak of the two experiential forces which respectively pushed toward the full realization of a life in obedience to Yahweh, and pulled the people back toward existence in cosmological form. For if the tension is expressed in the language of experiential forces, it will become clearer that Israelite symbols, even when they approach closely to the cosmological symbolism of the neighboring civilizations, are still loaded with the opposition to, or regression from,Yahwism; while Prophetic symbols, even when they come closest to a universalist understanding of divine transcendence, are still loaded with the problems of Israel's pragmatic existence.

The two counteracting experiential forces met in the creation of the historiographic work. The fragments of traditions, oral and written, were incorporated in the great narrative because the history of Israel's [187] struggle for survival in pragmatic history was tinged, at every turn of events, by its relation to the order of the Covenant. The pragmatic events themselves had acquired symbolic meaning as fulfillments of, or defections from, the Covenant order, or as variegated compromises between the will of God and the conditions of worldly existence. And the events had left their trail of symbols in the traditions. The later historians could follow the trail and heighten the events paradigmatically in the light of the Covenant order, but they certainly did not want to destroy a history which itself had become a symbol of revelation.

The preceding reflections will guide the presentation of the Israelite symbols of order. In the present Part Three of the study we shall take our position at the level of the pragmatic events and follow the trail of their symbols from the Abraham traditions to the end of the Northern Kingdom. When the history of Israel had ended in worldly disaster, the weight of interest shifted, in the Judah of the eighth century, distinctly toward the clarification of the right order in the light of the Sinaitic revelation. The concluding Part Four of the study will, therefore, deal with the symbolism of Moses and the Prophets.

## [188] Chapter 7: From Clan Society to Kingship

### § 1. The Abram Story

The infiltration of Hebrew clans into Canaan, as it can be discerned in the stories of the Patriarchs, began in the first half of the second millennium B.C. For the Hebrew form of order in this early period no sources are extant that can be reliably dated as contemporary with the events. Nevertheless, an access to the political situation, as well as to the Hebrew ideas of the time, offers itself through the story of Abram as related in Genesis 14.

## 1. Yahweh's Berith with Abram

The Abram story opens with the brief information that a coalition of four Mesopotamian kings met in battle with a coalition of five Canaanite kings in the valley of the Dead Sea (Gen 14:1-3). For twelve years the group of Canaanite kings had paid tribute to Chedorlaomer of Elam; in the thirteenth year they rebelled; in the fourteenth year Chedorlaomer and his allies made war on the Canaanites (4-5). The war assumed the form of a raid on the southern tribes of Canaan, and the razzia approached the rebellious center (5-7). Battle was joined in the valley of Siddim. The Canaanite kings were defeated; Sodom and Gomorrah were plundered; and the victors departed, carrying with them Lot, Abram's nephew, who had dwelt in Sodom (8-12). The abduction of Lot caused Abram's intervention. A survivor of the battle reported the abduction, and Abram, with his confederates and retainers, went in pursuit of the Mesopotamian kings. He defeated them, recaptured the whole of the loot, including his nephew Lot, and returned (13-16). On his return he was met by the King of Sodom, as well as by Melchizedek, the king and priest of Jerusalem (17-18). To the blessing of Melchizedek Abram responded with the gift of a tithe (19-20). The King of Sodom requested return only of his people, saying that Abram could [189] keep the other loot (21). Abram, however, restored everything, with the exception of the sustenance for his own men and the portion of his confederates (22-24).

As a literary piece the story of Genesis 14 is an erratic block in so far as it cannot be assigned to any of the major sources of the Pentateuch. Up to Genesis 13 the narrative draws on the J and P sources; beginning with Genesis 15 the E source makes its first appearance. Genesis 14 is apparently an independent Jerusalemite tradition; and the assumption that it owes its present form to the recasting of an older Abram tradition for the purposes of Davidic propaganda is almost certainly the correct one. The role of the story in the context of Genesis envisages, through its present form, the original tradition of a patriarchal adventure. By that original content the story dates itself "in the days of Amraphel king of Shinar." The identification of Amraphel as Hammurabi is probable; and tentative identifications for the names of the other three Mesopotamian kings have been proposed. Nevertheless, from the side of the Babylonian sources, it is impossible to find a time when any four kings of these names were contemporaries and could have engaged in an expedition of this nature. Hence, the anti-Canaanite kings must not be considered historical personages but representatives of the four main peoples at the time of

Hammurabi—that is, of the Elamites, the Babylonians, the Mitanni, and the Hittites. One can retain of this part of the story no more than the intention to date the events before the Egyptian conquest of Palestine. The Melchizedek episode (14:18-20), furthermore, has long been suspected as a late interpolation, because the assumption of a high priest in Jerusalem in the first half of the second millennium was considered anachronistic. The suspicion can no longer be entertained, since we know now that Canaanite cities did have high priests. There is no reason why Jerusalem should not have had one, too, at the time. Hence, we shall assume that the story, however garbled with regard to [190] names and pragmatic details, contains a core of genuine tradition with regard to the typical features of the situation. And the meaning of the story, as conveyed by the context of patriarchal history in Genesis, must be accepted as authentic, since it contains nothing inherently improbable.

The story reveals a richly diversified political scene. There are, first, the kings of the Canaanite city-states of Sodom, Gomorrah, Admah, and Bela; and later enters a priest-king of Jerusalem. East of the Jordan and to the south live the aboriginal, primitive peoples who become the first victims of the Mesopotamian raid. They bear such names as Rephaim (giants), Emim (horrors), Horim (cave dwellers), and Zuzim (possibly the same as the Zamzummim of Deuteronomy 2:20, the howlers). The kings of the city-states must be considered originally independent rulers. But at the time of the story they have been collectively the "servants" of a foreign power for twelve years, and when they break their servitude they appear as allies, *chaberim*, on the field of battle. The reason for the raid against the aboriginal tribes to the east and south is not clear, unless the city-states exerted some kind of sovereignty over them, so that a plundering raid against the tribes would be an economic blow to the kings.

Besides the city-states there is presumed a countryside beyond their control. There the Amorites settle who appear as the confederates of Abram. And on the land leased or bought from the Amorites, finally, there lives a Hebrew chieftain like Abram who for a fight can muster more than three hundred trained retainers born in the household. The Amorites stand to Abram in the relation of berith-masters, that is, of lords of the land to their vassal. And, as the course of events reveals, the berith must have stipulated assistance in case of war; for, at the end of the story, the three Amorites appear as participants in Abram's expedition and as such entitled to a share of the loot. The berith relation between Abram and the Amorites, however, is not the only one possible for a Hebrew in Canaan. The nephew Lot is settled in the city of Sodom, though his status, probably that of a ger, a protected resident, is not [191] specified. The status of Lot in Sodom seems not to be connected with the status of Abram. Between Lot and Abram, however, there prevails the clan law which obliges Abram to come to the rescue of his abducted nephew; and as a consequence, the fighting force of the Amorite berith-masters, who otherwise would not seem to be concerned with the affairs of the Canaanite kings, comes into play. But such unconcern is not certain, for the raid of the Mesopotamians against the aboriginal tribes also extends to the Amorites of Hazazon-tamar. Hence, the berith-masters of Abram are perhaps after all involved in Abram's expedition through their Amorite connections.

The story thus partly indicates explicitly, partly implies, an intricate system of relations between the various political groups of Canaan which can hardly function properly without divine sanctions accepted in common by the groups of the region. The assumption of a common divinity as the guardian of political compacts, a *baal berith* in Hebrew, will perhaps explain the appearance of the priest-king of Jerusalem, after the battle. He is introduced as bringing forth bread and wine in his capacity as "priest of El Elyon." And he extends his blessing to Abram in the following verses:

> Blessed be Abram by El Elyon,
> The maker of the heavens and the earth!
> And blessed be El Elyon,
> Who delivered your enemies into your hands!

The god invoked by Melchizedek is distinguished by his name from the Israelite Yahweh or Elohim; but otherwise we receive no information about his nature. The English translations as "the highest God," while correct, are equally uninformative. But here again the Ugaritic discoveries come to our aid. The Canaanites had indeed a highest god, the storm-god Hadad, briefly referred to as the Baal, the king or lord of the gods; and one of the standard epithets of this Baal was Al'iyan, "the One who Prevails." The supremacy of the Baal as the highest divinity in the Canaanite pantheon was established very early, at the latest in the fifteenth century B.C. This Baal must be the El Elyon of the temple-state of Jerusalem who, through his priest-king Melchizedek, extends blessings [192] and, for his service of delivering enemies into the hands of the people who recognize him, receives tithes after a successful war.

Among those who recognize the Canaanite Baal is Abram. Nevertheless, while ready to let the Baal have his share of the war loot, Abram reserves his allegiance beyond this point. Subsequent to the Melchizedek episode (Gen 14:18-20) the King of Sodom offers to share the loot with Abram (21); but Abram rejects the offer, which must be supposed to have been generous, in violent, almost insulting language:

> I raise my hand to Yahweh, El Elyon,
> the maker of the heavens and the earth:
> If from a thread to a shoe-lace, if I take aught that is yours...!
> You shall not say: "I have made Abram rich."
> Not for me—
> Only what the young men have eaten,
> and the portion of the men who went with me, Aner, Eshcol,
>     and Mamre,—
> Let them take their portion.

It is a dramatic speech; an outburst, holding back on the verge of a betrayal, lapsing into silences to cover what already has been half said. It reveals more than the resentment of a proud nomad of being made rich by the generosity of a king—if this feeling plays an important role at all. For behind the overt rejection of the King's offer there lies the rejection of Melchizedek and his El Elyon. When Abram raises his hand to Yahweh, he pointedly arrogates the Baal's epithet for his own God. By Yahweh he swears his unfinished oath not to take anything of the King's possessions. His professed unwillingness to be made rich by the King, is in reality an indignant refusal to be made rich by the King's Baal. Yahweh is the god who delivers enemies into Abram's hands, not the god of Melchizedek; Yahweh blesses Abram, not the Baal of Jerusalem; and not to the El Elyon who watches over the relations between political allies in Canaan will Abram owe his prosperity, but to Yahweh alone. Hence, Abram reduces the King's offer to the payment of an ascetic expense account.

Any doubt about the intention of the story will be dispelled by a glance at its context. When Abram indignantly refuses to become rich with the blessing of the Baal, we may justly wonder how he ever will prosper in a political order under the protection of El Elyon. The concern will dissolve when we read the opening verse of Genesis 15:

> [193] After what just has been related, the word of Yahweh came
>         to Abram in a vision:
>     Fear not, Abram, I am your shield,
>     Your reward shall be rich.

In the further course of the chapter Yahweh makes a berith with Abram (15:18), promising the dominion of Canaan for his descendants (15:18-21) when the guilt of the Amorites is full (15:16). The meaning of Genesis 14 is clarified by this sequel beyond a doubt. Abram is in the difficult situation of the Exodus. Pragmatically he has left the former home in Chaldea, but in Canaan he has settled in an environment whose understanding of human and social order does not substantially differ from the Mesopotamian. He is still a foreigner, dependent for his status on his berith-masters, the Amorites, whose principal occupation in the spiritual order of things seems to be the accumulation of guilt, and he must accept the system of order under the Baal after a fashion. Spiritually he is profoundly disturbed. The Exodus from Chaldea shows that he no longer can live contentedly in the world of cosmological experiences and symbols but his movements in the new world that opened to him when his soul opened toward God lack yet in assurance. On the one hand, he makes concessions to the Baal—and he must, if he wants to survive; on the other hand, the new God has taken possession of him strongly enough to strain his soul and to cause, in a critical situation, the outburst of Genesis 14:22-24. The tension between god and God is severe indeed, especially since the nature of the new God and the strength of his assistance are not certain at all. The transfer of the El Elyon from the Baal of Jerusalem to Yahweh leaves in doubt whether Yahweh is God or only a highest god in rivalry with others. Moreover, while Abram rejects riches that come to him under the sanction of the Baal, he is not averse to prosperity; he does not want to be ruined for Yahweh. Hence, he must have gone home from the dramatic scene full of sorrows. He certainly has not made friends by his outburst. Will Yahweh now protect him against the possible consequences? And will he compensate him for the riches renounced? In this critical hour of his life the "word of Yahweh" comes to him with comfort for every disquieting aspect of the situation: (1) The generally assuaging "Fear not"; (2) the "I am your shield" in political difficulties; and (3) the promise "Your reward shall be rich" in compensation for the economic loss.

[194] The comforts and promises of Genesis 15 subtly dissolve the tenseness of Genesis 14. A masterpiece is the transformation of the berith symbol. In Genesis 14 Abram is in bondage through his involvement in the Canaanite system of political compacts. He lives under baals both human and divine: the Amorites are his berith masters (baal berith) in political relations, and the Baal of Jerusalem is the guardian of the political berith. In Genesis 15 the decisive step

of liberation occurs, when Yahweh makes his berith with Abram. The worldly situation, to be sure, remains what it is for the time being; but spiritually the bondage is broken with the change of berith-masters. The order in which Abram truly lives from now on has been transformed from the Canaan of the Baal to the domain of Yahweh. The symbol of bondage has become the symbol of freedom. On this occasion, furthermore, the peculiar nature of a berith with Yahweh reveals itself. In the mundane situation of Abram, as we said, nothing has changed. The new domain of Yahweh is not yet the political order of a people in Canaan; at the moment it does not extend beyond the soul of Abram. It is an order that originates in a man through the inrush of divine reality into his soul and from this point of origin expands into a social body in history. At the time of its inception it is no more than the life of a man who trusts in God; but this new existence, founded on the leap in being, is pregnant with future. In the case of Abram's experience this "future" is not yet understood as the eternity under whose judgement man exists in his present. To be sure, Yahweh's berith is already the flash of eternity into time; but the true nature of this "future" as transcendence is still veiled by the sensuous analogues of a glorious future in historical time. Abram receives the promises of numerous descendants and their political success in the dominion of Canaan. In this sense the experience of Abram is "futuristic." It is a component in the berith which lasts throughout Israelite into Judaic history and issues into the apocalypses. Nevertheless, [195] the lack of differentiation must not be seen as an imperfection only. For, as has been discussed previously, compact experiences contain the bond of compactness that holds the undifferentiated elements together—the bond that all too frequently is lost in the process of differentiation. While the promises of the berith still veil the meaning of transcendence, they at least preserve the awareness that eternity reaches indeed into the process of history, even though the operation of transcendent perfection through the mundane process is a paradox that cannot be solved through Canaans or Utopias of one kind or another.

Genesis 14 and 15 together are a precious document. They describe the situation in which the berith experience originates in opposition to the cosmological order of Canaanite civilization, as well as the content of the experience itself. The philological and archaeological questions of trustworthiness and date of the story will now appear in a different light. For clearly we are not interested in either the date of literary fixation or the reliability of the story, but in the authenticity of the experience that is communicated by means of the story, as well as in the probable date of the situation in which the experience originated. As far as the authenticity is concerned, the problem is not too difficult for nobody can describe an experience unless he has had it, either originally or through imaginative re-enactment. The writers to whom we owe the literary fixation certainly had the experience through re-enactment; and the masterly articulation of its meaning through the dramatic high points of the story proves that they were intimately familiar with it. The answer to the question of who had the experience originally will have to rely on the common-sense argument that religious personalities who have such experiences, and are able to submit to their authority, do not grow on trees. The spiritual sensitiveness of the man who opened his soul to the word of Yahweh, the trust and fortitude required to make this word the order of existence in opposition to the world, and the creative imagination used in transforming the symbol of civilizational bondage into the symbol of divine liberation—that combination is one of the great and rare events in the history of mankind. And this event bears the name of Abram. As far as the date of the event is concerned we have nothing to rely on but the Biblical tradition which places it in the pre-Egyptian period of Hebrew settlements in Canaan, that is, in the second millennium B.C. The date, therefore, must be accepted.

## [201] . . . 2. The Deborah Song

The earliest source for the ideas of order in the Israelite Confederacy is the Deborah Song, in Judges 5. It is contemporary with the events, *ca.* 1125, and probably was written by an eyewitness of the battle which it commemorates. It has considerable value as a source, as it has preserved not only the "facts" of the event but the drama of experience. Together with the prose account of the war in Judges 4 it furnishes, in spite of a corrupt text, a fairly clear picture of the early Yahwist order of Israel.

At the time of the Deborah Song the infiltration of Hebrew tribes into Canaan had resulted in the occupation of three distinct regions west of the Jordan. A northern settlement extended in an arc around the Sea of Galilee, touching on the Mediterranean coast; a central group had penetrated across the Jordan into Samaria; and a penetration from the south had led to the settlement of Judah. The three Hebrew areas were separated by the territories of the Canaanite towns. Between the northern and central settlements a broad Canaanite strip wedged in from the coast, through the plain of Esdraelon, to the Jordan, while Judah in the [202] south was separated from the

Ephraimite region in the center by a belt of towns that included the mountain-fortress Jerusalem. The southern settlement was still weak and politically insignificant; Judah was not even mentioned in the Deborah Song and apparently did not yet belong to the Israelite Confederacy. The scene of important events was the north, where a coalition of Canaanite princes, under the leadership of Sisera of Harosheth-goiim, engaged in raids against Israelite villages in order to keep the northern and central tribes apart and, if possible, to restrict their territories. The tense situation exploded in a war between the Canaanite forces, equipped with war chariots, and the primitive contingents of Israel. The main battle was fought near Megiddo, at the river Kishon. A violent thunderstorm made the ground sodden so that the war chariots could not operate; and the defeated Canaanites suffered heavy losses on their retreat across the Kishon that had changed from a dry bed to a torrent. The Canaanite leader Sisera was killed on his flight by a Kenite woman in whose tent he had sought refuge.

The song describes the suffering of the Israelite countryside under the Canaanite raids:

> In the days of Shamgar, the son of Anath,
> Traffic on the highways had ceased,
> Travellers went by the by-ways;
> The work of the peasants had ceased in Israel, had ceased,
> Until you arose, O Deborah, arose as a mother in Israel.

Deborah was a prophetess who by her songs (probably appeals for action and curses against the enemy) aroused the people to resistance. Since the Confederacy had no permanent organization for either peace or war, the lyrical activity of the prophetess had to incite a leader and to move the people to follow him:

> Awake, awake, Deborah!
> Awake, awake, utter a song!

The leader was found in Barak, who had been the captive of Sisera for a while and now had an opportunity to settle some personal accounts. But the tribes did not all participate in the common enterprise. The song accordingly distributes praises and blames:

> Ephraim surged into the valley . . .
> The chieftains of Issachar were with Deborah and Barak . . .

Zebulum were a people who exposed themselves to death . . .

[203] But others held back:

> In the clans of Reuben great were the debates . . .
> Gilead remained beyond the Jordan . . .
> Asher stayed by the sea-coast . . .

Still, it was a great uprising. The clans descended from the hills, the warriors' hair let down, according to the war ritual:

> When they let stream their hair in Israel,
> when the men volunteered, bless Yahweh,
> hear, O kings, give ear, O princes,
> I—unto Yahweh—will I sing,
> I will sing to Yahweh, the God of Israel.

And from his seat far in the south, Yahweh came to the aid of his people, driving the war chariot of his storm:

> Yahweh—when you came forth from Seir,
> when you advanced from the fields of Edom;
> The earth trembled, the heavens poured,
> the clouds poured down their waters;
> The mountains streamed down before Yahweh,
> before Yahweh, the God of Israel.

On the Canaanite side he was met by the celestial rulers, the Meleks, of the country:
[For the following verses 5:19-20 I am using the translation suggested by Nyberg 1935:6, 47: "The war between Sisera and the Israelites is depicted as a battle between the city-gods of Canaan and Yahweh."]

> The Meleks came and they fought,
> then fought the Meleks of Canaan,
> at Taanach, at the waters of Megiddo.
>  They won no booty of silver.
> From the heavens down they fought,
> the stars down from their courses,
> they fought on the side of Sisera.

But their help was of no avail to Sisera and his allies, for the storm and flood of Yahweh had done its work:

> The torrent Kishon swept them away,
> The ancient torrent, the torrent Kishon.

The defeat of the Canaanites was crushing. Sisera, on his flight, took refuge with Jael, a Kenite woman. She offered him hospitality, and when he felt safe, she drove a tentpin through his head:

> [204] Blessed be among women, Jael, the woman of Heber, the Kenite,
> Among the women who live in a tent, blessed she be!

From the end of Sisera in the bedouin tent, the scene shifts to his palace, where his mother waited for him and wondered about the delay. The song dwells with gusto on the expectations of the women, soon to be shattered by the terrible news:

> Are they not finding,
> Are they not dividing the spoil,
> A girl, two girls, for each man?
> A spoil of dyed stuffs for Sisera,
> A spoil of dyed stuffs embroidered,
> Dyed and embroidered, from the necks of the spoiled?

The song ends with the lines, perhaps added later:

> Thus perish all your enemies, Yahweh!
> But your friends be like the sun when he rises in his might!

The Deborah Song is unencumbered by interpretations and redactions of the later historical schools; and it is so early that it has not yet suffered from Israelite-Canaanite syncretism. It is the only document extant which conveys a coherent picture of Yahwist Israel in its pristine form. Hence, in its every detail it is of immeasurable value for the historian who wants to distinguish between early Israelite ideas and later developments, between original Israelite ideas and Canaanite accretions. The main characteristics of this early order as they become visible in the song are the following:

An Israelite Confederacy existed, indeed, but without political organization. This fact alone sheds a flood of light over the genesis of the people and its order. For if there was no permanent organization, and if the improvisation in case of an emergency functioned as haphazardly as the Deborah Song reveals, "Israel" never can have "conquered" Canaan; the component tribes can only have slowly infiltrated, in a process made possible by the disintegration of Egyptian power in the area. While the infiltration was not entirely peaceable, it can have involved only minor clashes of clans and tribes with local enemies, not any major conflict with the Canaanites that could have been met only by the organized forces of the whole Confederacy. There was no political organization because no military effort on a national scale had been [205] necessary. As a consequence, the Yahweh of the Confederacy can hardly have been a war god. And one can, indeed, find in the narrative traces of pleased surprise when, in a critical situation, the "God of the fathers" revealed himself unexpectedly as a mighty war lord, as in Miriam's outcry in Exodus 15:

> Yahweh is a man of war,
> Yahweh is his name . . .
> Sing to Yahweh,
> For he has triumphed gloriously;
> The horse and his rider
> He has hurled into the sea.

The same experience of surprise pervades the Deborah Song with its repeated accents on the voluntary participation of the tribes in a general war of Israel and on Yahweh's aid. It would be rash to conclude from this note of surprise that Israel as a whole had never fought a common war before the Sisera battle (and thus, in a strict sense, had never existed politically), but certainly such previous events were not impressive enough to leave their trace in the memory of the people. The Deborah Song can hardly be considered an accidental piece of poetry accidentally preserved. It must be understood as celebrating the great event in which Israel for the first time experienced itself as a people united in political action under Yahweh. [The suggestions in the text follow the study by von Rad 1951].

If the interpretation is correct, if the war with Sisera was indeed the occasion for a decisive advance in the constitution of Israel under Yahweh, the details of the song gain added importance as a source of information on the genesis of a people. To be sure, the information is spotty, for the song is a poem, not a treatise. Still, a few things become clear.

The warriors assembled in camp for battle were called *am Yahweh*, the people of Yahweh (Judges 5:11,13). The god himself was not present with his people in Canaan, but came to their aid from his seat far in the south (5:4). The ark as the seat of Yahweh is not mentioned in the song; but since the ark in general was a questionable piece of war equipment, it is difficult to draw any conclusions from its omission. In the later Philistine wars it had an important function, but it proved so ineffective that the enemy captured it. Once it had been captured, it became quite [206] active in spreading pestilences wherever it was placed; and the Philistines were glad to return it. When it then continued to make a nuisance of itself among its own people, it was deposited in a barn and abandoned; and Israel concluded the Philistine wars quite well without the dangerous object. And, finally, after the conquest of Jerusalem, it was remembered by David and put in a tent in the city. Its strange absence from Deborah's war is perhaps a further indication that Yahweh had not previously been a war god and that his usefulness in this capacity was discovered on the occasion.

Yahweh himself was experienced as a god who manifested himself in natural forces. His appearance brought an upheaval of nature: the clouds poured down, the earth trembled, the mountains released floods, and even the stars joined in the fight. Yet, the presence of Yahweh in his storm differed from the storm which Enlil spread like a shroud over Ur. In the "Lamentations over the Destruction of Ur" the attack of Elam was experienced as the cosmic storm of Enlil; in the Deborah Song the real storm was experienced as the presence of Yahweh. And what revealed itself as Yahweh in the real storm was not a cosmic storm but the *zidekoth Yahweh* (Judges 5:11), literally: the righteousnesses of Yahweh. The meaning of the term can only be conjectured as the righteous acts of the god by which he established just order among men. Yahweh was a god who revealed himself in historical action as the creator of true order. This conception, now, seems to be not too far from the Egyptian *maat* of both the god and the mediating Pharaoh. But again, the righteousness of Yahweh had a different complexion because there was no human mediator who would transform the cosmic into social order. One of the oddities not only of the Deborah Song but of the Book of Judges in general is the absence of a term for the human functionaries of political order in time of crisis. The designation of Deborah as a *shophet*, a judge, is probably anachronistic, for the term *shophet* belongs to the Deuteronomist redactions. But Deborah at least owes her public influence to her recognizable spiritual authority as a prophetess, a *nebijah* (4:4). For Barak, however, the war leader, there is no term at all to designate his function. The charismatic leadership, on which the actlon of the Confederacy in war depended, obviously was not conceived as an analogue of cosmic order in society that would require appropriate [207] expression through symbols. Hence, in spite of its brevity, the Deborah Song unmistakably reveals Israel's break with the cosmological civilizations.

The song celebrates a victory in a war. The ideas concerning warfare under the leadership of Yahweh are presupposed in the song, but their full understanding requires the use of additional sources. Military actions were numerous, but not all of them were *milhamoth Yahweh* (1 Sam 18:17; 25:28), wars of Yahweh, even though the Book of Judges sometimes gives this impression; with a rare exception, it tells only the story of the holy wars. The wars of Yahweh were engagements of the whole people, if not in fact, at least in their intention. And they were conducted according to a certain ritual. The component parts of the ritual are nowhere enumerated in their entirety but must be gathered from their fragmentary appearance on the various occasions of military action. Still, the general structure of the ritual can be discerned in the abbreviated account preserved in Judges 4:14-16:

> And Deborah said to Barak:
> "Up! For this is the day,
> on which Yahweh has given Sisera into your hand.
> Has Yahweh not gone forth before you?"
> So Barak went down from Mount Tabor, and ten thousand
>     men after him.
> And Yahweh brought confusion [or panic] to Sisera, and all his
>     chariots, and all his host; and Sisera alighted from his
>     chariot,  and fled on foot.
> But Barak pursued, after the chariots, after the host, unto
>     Harosheth-goiim;
> and the whole host of Sisera fell by the edge of the sword;
> there was not a man left.

The beginning of the ritual is missing in the account; and some features that are known from other contexts are omitted. At the opening of the account the army stands ready to go into battle. But the moment when the *am Yahweh* stood ready for battle had to be preceded by a number of preparatory steps. There had to be a declaration, not of war against the enemy but of a state of emergency to the people, through prophetic authorities who issued a call for war. Then a charismatic leader had to be incited to action, as was Barak by Deborah; and the leader had to have sufficient authority to summon the people to action through messengers, as for instance in Judges 3:27 or 6:34. The tribes and clans deliberated and acted on the summons, with varying results, as the [208] Deborah song indicates. The warrior community in camp had to be ritually pure, in particular submitting to sexual abstinence, for Yahweh was present with his people. Sacrifices were offered and oracles were obtained. Only then, when everything seemed favorable, would a leader (in the present case, Deborah to Barak) issue the verdict: "Yahweh has given the enemy in your hand"; and the army could proceed to the execution of the verdict with complete certainty of victory. For Yahweh was "going forth before them," he was conducting the war, and the army was no more than the instrument of execution. The character of the warriors as the instruments of Yahweh required their spiritual qualification. They had to have confidence in Yahweh; and they had to be conscious that not they themselves but their god was fighting and winning the war. Hence, in the war against the Midianites (Judges 7), Yahweh informed the war leader that his army was too large to give the enemy into his hand. Israel might vaunt itself to have won the war by its own human strength. The vast bulk of the army had to be dismissed, in particular those who were afraid and did not trust Yahweh sufficiently; and the victory had to be won by a few companies of hardened warriors with complete faith in their God. When the ritual and spiritual preconditions were fulfilled, the battle could begin. In the various holy wars, the external circumstances of the battles differed widely, but uniformly Yahweh came to the aid of his people by throwing a panic into the ranks of the enemy (Judges 4:15 or 7:22), a "confusion," a "terror," a bewilderment in which the enemies sometimes started fighting against one another. A numinous horror gripped the enemy, so that he was unable to offer resistance— perhaps not too surprising when a horde of seminude, fanatical dervishes came bearing down, screaming and screeching, with their hair flowing in the wind. After the defeat of the enemy in battle, the holy war came to a conclusion through the ritual of the *cherem*, the ban. Since Yahweh had won the war, the loot was his; all gold and silver went into the treasury of the god; all living beings, human and animal, were slaughtered in his honor . . .

[210] . . . The experience of Yahweh's help could blend with the spirit of a warrior community without inducing reflections on the consistency of the conception. But obviously, there was a crack in the symbolism. The war spirit of the tribes and the experience of a god who comes to the aid of an essentially passive community could part company. The development need not go in the direction of an

effectively organized people, conducting its political affairs with success under the guidance of its god. It also could go in the direction of a pacifist community that would sit back and expect the discomfiture of its enemies from divine interventions without military actions of its own.

In fact the history of Israel has followed both of these courses. And we venture to say that the recognition of this double course is the key to the understanding of Israelite history. The improvised organization of defensive wars under charismatic leaders proved inadequate against the rising pressure of foreign powers after the Philistine invasion. The improvisations had to be replaced by the permanent kingship. But as soon as the monarchy was organized, the potential tensions that could be discerned in the Deborah Song became actual. In the situation described by the song, the prophetess and the war leader co-operated in the organization of the war. The prophetess mobilized and crystallized the sentiments of the people (today we should say, the public opinion) by her songs; and the war leader let himself be induced to assume his function. The prophetess rendered the verdict that Yahweh had given the enemy into the hand of the leader; and the leader was ready to execute the verdict. But the mere articulation of these steps in the procedure makes it obvious that an organized government with a king, his policy-making officials, and his military staff could not, in making its decision, politely request the opinion of some prophet whether a war should be undertaken or not, and whether, according to the prophet's information about the intentions of Yahweh, the time was propitious for engaging in battle or not. Serious conflicts were bound to break out when prophetic and governmental opinions about the right order and policy should differ . . .

> (This important selection, on the occasion of Voegelin's interpretation of the place of the witch of Endor story [1 Sam 28:3-25] in Saul's kingship, provides us with a sustained study of the development of the soul or "human self" in Israel's thought. The fact that Saul has recourse to this witch, who is a ghost-master, even though one of his ordinances had banished ghost-masters from his territory [1 Sam 28:3,9], perplexes Voegelin. Did Saul consider ghosts to be minor gods [elohim], and so a threat to true Yahwism? But then, why does he have recourse to the witch? Perhaps, suggests Voegelin, his "was not a well-organized soul living in the faith in a transcendent God." This suggestion leads Voegelin to a study of the steps in the differentiation of the soul in Israel.—Eds.)

[CHAPTER 8: THE STRUGGLE FOR EMPIRE]

[§ 2. The Kingship of Saul] [2. Spiritual Order of the Soul]

[234] . . . The ghost-elohim must have played an important role in the spiritual life of the Israelites, or it would not have been necessary to sanction their consultation so severely, and the ordinance of Saul must have been a correspondingly grave disturbance of spiritual life. Such interventions in the economy of the psyche have consequences. What we know about the experiences and actions of Saul is sufficient proof that his was not a well-organized soul living in the faith in a transcendent God, but that his psyche was a field of diversifed sensitiveness for orgiastic contagion, priestly oracles, and [235] advice from seers, for divine dreams and voices, and messages from ghost-elohim. He was a man but also "another man" when in trance, and above all he was a part of the nonpersonal, diffuse humanity that went by the name of Israel and had to atone collectively for royal misconduct. In Saul's difficulties with a Yahwist order it is clear that the problems of a personal soul were involved—the same problems which, contemporaneously with Saul, became acute in the troubles of the Mycenaean civilization, in the epics of Homer. In Israelite history, however, these problems were bent in a direction widely divergent from the Greek, and in determining this bent the ordinance of Saul apparently was a causative factor of the first order. The issue, as well as the different forms which it assumed in Israel and Hellas, must be briefly characterized.

The leap in being, the experience of divine being as world-transcendent, is inseparable from the understanding of man as human. The personal soul as the sensorium of transcendence must develop parallel with the understanding of a transcendent God. Now, wherever the leap in being occurs experientially, the articulation of the experience has to grapple with the mystery of death and immortality. Men are mortal; and what is immortal is divine. This holds true for both Greeks and Israelites. Into this clean ontological division, however, does never quite fit the postexistence of man. In the Homeric epic, afterlife is the existence of the psyche, of the life-force, as an eidolon, a shadow in Hades; and in the same manner, Israelite afterlife is a shadowy, ghostlike existence in Sheol. In neither case is it an existence that would bring ultimate perfection to the order of the human personality. From this initial situation was developed, in Hellas, the understanding of the psyche as an immortal substance, capable of achieving increasingly perfect order, if necessary through repeated embodiments, until it reached permanent transmundane status. This development was due to the philosophers from Pythagoras and Heraclitus onward and achieved its climax in the dialogues of Plato. Without a doubt, the polytheistic culture of Hellas facilitated the speculative construction of the problem, since there was no deeprooted resistance to conceiving the immortal soul as a daimon, that is, as a divine being of lower rank. In Israel a parallel development was barred by the early, even if imperfect, understanding of the true nature of a universal, transcendent God. The dead were *elohim*, and no man was supposed to be an *elohim*. Genesis 3:22-24 was uncompromising on the point: "Then Yahweh-Elohim said: 'See, the man has become like one [236] of us, in knowing good from evil; and now suppose he were to reach out his hand and take the fruit of the tree of life also and, eating it, live forever!' So Yahweh-Elohim expelled him from the garden of Eden."

This incompatibility of human and divine status seems to have been realized fully for the first time by Saul. Since the dead were *elohim*, and since the belief that they were continued unshaken, these gods had to be relegated by means of a royal ordinance to a kind of public subconscious. Ancestor worship, the myth of a *heros eponymos*, and above all the evocation of such gods as rival authorities to Yahweh had to be suppressed. As a consequence the understanding of a personal soul, of its internal order through divine guidance, and of its perfection through grace in death that will heal the imperfection of mundane existence, could not develop. The relation to Yahweh, precarious in this life, was completely broken by death; what was not achieved in life was never achieved. A pathetic expression of this plight was the psalm of Hezekiah (late eighth century) by which the King thanked Yahweh for recovery from a sickness (Isa 39:18-19):

> For Sheol cannot praise thee,
>  Death cannot celebrate thee:
> They that go down to the Pit
>  Can not hope for thy truth.
> The living, the living, he shall praise thee,
>  As I do this day.
> The father to the children
>  Shall make known thy truth.

Throughout the history of the Kingdom the question of the soul remained in this submersion of a "public subconscious," and even the prophets were unable to deal with it. Only in the time of Ezekiel (late sixth century), the first step toward a solution became noticeable, from the side of ethics, in the hesitant admission of personal responsibility and retribution according to a man's merit (Ezek 14, 18, and 33). But even the break with the principle of collective responsibility did not break the impasse of experience with regard to the order of the soul and its salvation. Only under Persian influence, in the third century, did the rigid position weaken and could the idea of immortality enter the Jewish orbit.

The state of suspension in which the issue of the soul remained in Israelite history had curious consequences in the realm of symbols. On [237] the one hand, it favored the advance of historical realism. On the other hand, it prevented the development of philosophy.

With regard to historical realism, the suppression of the ghost-elohim eliminated the ancestor myth as a constitutive form from the public sphere. This, to be sure, does not mean that ancestor-worship or even hero-worship were unknown to the Hebrew tribes. A sufficient number of traces of such cults have survived in the Bible (and been confirmed by archaeological discoveries) to prove that the Hebrew clans, before they came within the range of Yahwist religiousness, were constituted by their ancestor cults just as any Hellenic genos. In the Yahwist period we find such sanctuaries of ancestors as the Cave of Machpelah, where Sarah and Abraham were buried (Gen 23 and 25:9); the Pillar of Rachel's Grave (Gen 35:20); and the burial place of Joseph at Shechem (Josh 24:32). And we find, furthermore, sanctuaries of heroes, such as the sanctuary of Deborah, Rebekah's nurse (Gen 35:8); the grave of Miriam at Kadesh, the "holy place" (Num 20:1); and the burial place of Samuel at Ramah (1 Sam 28:3). Nevertheless, while the ancestors and heroes were elohim on the popular level of Israelite religion, they never became mythological figures on the Yahwist level on which the narrative moves. On the contrary, those who had already disappeared behind the veil of the myth in pre-Mosaic times, such as the Jacob-el, or Joseph-el, of the Egyptian lists of Canaanite place names, were recovered as historical figures. Certainly Jacob, perhaps Joseph, and probably others of whom no records are preserved were transfigured from historical chieftains into mythical ancestors and then restored to their former status much in the manner in which a modern, critical historian recaptures pragmatic events from the myth. As a result, the Israelites developed a symbolic form without parallel in other civilizations, that is, the History of the Patriarchs.

The extraordinary character of the phenomenon must be realized in order to understand its extraordinary sequel. On the "public" level, the *elohim* had become the historical Patriarchs who now were definitely dead and no longer could influence mundane events. On this level the belief in an afterlife was blotted out so drastically that the late Kohelet could say: "A living dog is better than a dead lion. For the living know that they will die; but the dead know nothing at all, nor have they anything for their labor, for their memory is forgotten. Their love has vanished with their hate and jealousy, and they have no share in anything [238] that goes on under the sun" (Eccles 9:4-6). The radical historization of the elohim thus ran, by the logic of experience, into the impasse of nihilism and hedonistic existentialism that we can observe in the Kohelet.

On the lower, popular level, however, the community of the living with the dead, that is, the substance of continuous social order among men, was maintained through the cults of clan ancestors and national heroes, as well as by the faith in their help as advisers and avengers. Though the historians did their best to erase all traditions of this faith, numerous passages have escaped which manifest the belief in the "fathers" or the "people" to whom in death a man is gathered. [For instance Gen 25:8, 17; 35:29; 47:30; 49:29.] From this popular, living experience a prophetic spirit could break through to the insight that the community of the *elohim* to whom man was assembled in death was the community with the divine father himself. While dodging the issue of the ancestral *elohim* and their status, a prayer of Trito-Isaiah transferred their function in the human community to God in person (Isa 63:16):

> You are our father,
> though Abraham knows us not,
> and Israel is not mindful of us.
> You, Yahweh, are our father,
> Our Redeemer is, from the beginning, your name.

Yahweh in this prayer takes the place of the redeemer—that is, of the *goel*, the close relative and avenger under clan law—since the function no longer is fulfilled by the *elohim* of Abraham and Jacob. And Yahweh can help, as he did in the days of Moses, through the presence of his *ruach*, his spirit, with the shepherds of his people. Searchingly the prophet asks (Isa 63:11 ff.):

> Where is he who brought them up from the sea,
> with the shepherds of his flock?
> Where is he who put his holy spirit
> in the midst of them;

> Who caused his glorious arm to go
>    at the right hand of Moses;
> Who divided the waters before them,
>    to make himself an everlasting name;
> Who led them through the deep, without stumbling?
>    As a horse through the wilderness,
>    as cattle going down to the valley,
> [239]  the spirit of Yahweh guided them safe.
> So was it you guided your people,
>    to make yourself a glorious name.

And as in the past, the prophet hopes, the spirit of Yahweh will guide his people in the future again, and he prays (Isa 63:17):

> Return for the sake of your servants,
> The tribes of your heritage!

One senses the animosity against the ancestral *elohim* of the preMosaic age. The author of the prayer struggled to escape from their atmosphere and to understand the presence of the one and only Elohim through his *ruach*, in history. And, partially at least, his endeavors were successful. To be sure, Yahweh was still the God of Israel, not of mankind; and the issue of the soul was not clarified at all; but at least the questions had been sharpened in such a manner that from an apparently desperate situation emerged the vision of a solution. Opinion is divided whether the prayer was written immediately after the return to Jerusalem in 538 or during the conflict with the Persians in the fourth century B.C. At any rate, Israel was in a politically difficult time. No help was to be expected from man, either from men in this world or from men gathered to their fathers. Moreover, the feeling still prevailed that divine help had to come to society in its worldly existence; only help to the people in its historical straits was of interest, not help to the individual soul. From such negations, shutting out the conceivable alternatives, arose the idea of the God who would return as our Redeemer into history in order to rectify a condition of man beyond hope.

With regard to the form a return of God into history would assume, the prayer is silent. And one should not read more into Trito-Isaiah than can actually be found there. Nevertheless, there is enough in the prayer to suggest the experiential mood in which men were receptive for the appearance of God on earth and to become the followers of the Christ. To be sure, there was a host of other symbols approximating the god-man which would make the appearance of Christ intelligible to the civilizationally mixed humanity of the Roman Empire: there were Egyptian Pharaohs, Hellenistic god-kings, and Jewish expectations of a Davidic Messiah. Still, none of them contained the specific ingredient that made Christianity a scandal, the ingredient to be found in Trito-Isaiah: the return of the world-transcendent God into a cosmos which had [240] become nondivine, and into a history which had become human. This gulf between God and the world, inherent in Yahwism from the Mosaic age, could be bridged through the Israelite centuries by the survivals of cosmological symbols, by the Canaanite agricultural gods, and by ancestor cults; but when the terrible implications of this separation of God from the world had been realized through the work of the prophets, and when the intramundane, political disasters had brought home the anguish of life in a god-forsaken world, the time was ripe for the return of God into a history from which the divine forces had been eliminated so drastically.

With regard to philosophy, one must say that its development in the Hellenic sense was prevented by the irresolution concerning the status of the soul. The *philia* reaching out toward the *sophon* presupposes a personalized soul: the soul must have disengaged itself sufficiently from the substance of particular human groups to experience its community with other men as established through the common participation in the divine Nous. As long as the spiritual life of the soul is so diffuse that its status under God can be experienced only compactly, through the mediation of clans and tribes, the personal love of God cannot become the ordering center of the soul. In Israel the spirit of God, the *ruach* of Yahweh, is present with the community and with individuals in their capacity as representatives of the community, but it is not present as the ordering force in the soul of every man, as the Nous of the mystic-philosophers or the Logos of Christ is present in every member of the Mystical Body, creating by its presence the *homonoia*, the likemindedness of the community. Only when man, living with his fellow men in the community of the spirit, has a personal destiny in relation to God can the spiritual eroticism of the soul achieve the self-interpretation which Plato called philosophy. In Israelite history a comparable development was impossible for the previously discussed reasons. When the soul has no destiny, when the relation of man with God is broken through death, even a revelation of the world-transcendent divinity as personal and intense as the Mosaic (more personal and intense than ever befell a Hellenic philosopher) will be blunted by the intramundane compactness of the tribe. The God of Israel revealed himself in his wrath and his grace; he caused the joy of loyal obedience as well as the anguish of disobedience, triumph of victory as well as despair of forsakenness; he manifested himself in natural phenomena as well as in his messengers in [241] human shape; he spoke audibly, distinctly, and at great length to the men of his choice; he was a will and he gave a law—but he was not the unseen Measure of the soul in the Platonic sense. A Prophet can hear and communicate the word of God, but he is neither a Philosopher nor a Saint.

No Platonic "practice of dying" developed in Israel. Still, the leap in being, when it created historical present as the existence of a people under the will of God, had also sharpened the sensitiveness for individual humanity. Perhaps because the soul had no destiny beyond death, triumph and defeat in life were experienced with a poignancy hitherto unknown to man. In the wake of Saul's kingship a new experiential mood made itself felt which, for lack of a better term, may be called the specifically Israelite humanism. The first great document of this mood was the grandiose *quinah*, the funeral elegy or dirge of David for Saul and Jonathan after the battle of Gilboa (2 Sam 1:19-27):

> Your beauty, O Israel, on your heights lies slain!
>  How have they fallen, the heroes!
> Tell it not in Gath,
>  Announce it not in the streets of Ashkelon,
> Lest rejoice the daughters of the Philistines,
>  Lest exult the daughters of the uncircumcised!
> Mountains of Gilboa,
>  Let there be upon you no dew nor rain,
>  Nor upsurging from the deep.
> For *there* was thrown aside the shield of the hero,
>  The shield of Saul, no longer salved with oil.
> From the blood of the slain,
>  From the fat of the heroes,
> The bow of Jonathan turned not back,
>  The sword of Saul returned not in vain!
> Saul and Jonathan, beloved and loved
>  In their lives, in their death they were not divided.
> They were swifter than eagles,
>  They were stronger than lions.
> Daughters of Israel, weep over Saul,
>  Who clothed you in scarlet, and other delights,
> Who put ornaments of gold upon your apparel!
> How have they fallen, the heroes,
>  In the midst of the battle!

[242] Jonathan lies slain upon your heights!
I am afflicted because of you,
  My brother Jonathan!
Very dear were you to me!
Your love was more precious to me
  Than the love of women!
How are they fallen, the heroes,
  How shattered the weapons of war!


There is no touch of spiritual drama in the *quinah*, no question of obedience or disobedience to Yahweh's will, no search for the grounds of divine action. God might as well not exist. The disaster of Gilboa is strictly an affair of man in his earthly habitat. A curse of sterility falls on the mountains of Gilboa because arms and the men of Israel have fallen on their heights. What has fallen with them is the beauty of Israel, the splendor of its manhood, the *gibborim*, in war as well as the enhancement of women when decked with plunder. Since it is a critical defeat in the struggle for empire, the joy of the enemy is as much cause for grief as the losses on the own side. And the defeat is a personal disaster, for the community of lovers, of father and son, of friend and friend is broken by death . . .


## [256] CHAPTER 9: THE MUNDANE CLIMAX

### §1. The Davidic Empire

From the position of the post-Solomonic historians the united kingdom was the climax toward which Israel had been moving ever since Exodus and Conquest. The actual course of events, however, as far as it can be discerned through the editorial manipulation of traditions, does not reveal such an entelechy at all. On the contrary, Israel's destiny was deflected toward a mundane adventure, with the character of an impasse if the struggle for empire be reduced to its pragmatic phases: In the first of these phases the Philistines expanded their dominion at the expense of Israel and provoked the Israelite war of liberation under Saul. The second phase, after the defeat of Gilboa, was the war between the "houses of Saul and David" for the prize of kingship over a united people. In the third phase, finally, the double victory of David over both Israel and the Philistines led to the conquest of Jerusalem and the united monarchy under a Judaite dynasty. If we survey the pragmatic course from the beginning to the end, the result seems to have been a disaster for Israel rather than a success. At the beginning, there existed an Israelite Confederacy, even though its Yahwism was in a state of decomposition and the ethnic amalgamation of the Hebrew clans with the Cannanite population had far advanced toward the making of a new nation. At the end of the struggle, the territory and population of the formerly independent Confederacy had been absorbed into a kingdom which included not only Judah but also further Canaanite areas and was ruled by a Judaite clan. Moreover, under the Solomonic administration the position of Israel degenerated even further through discrimination, in matters of taxation and services, in favor of Judah. To be sure, Israel regained its independence after the death of Solomon. But the very fact that it separated from the kingdom proved that the unification was not experienced as a climax of Israelite history proper. Nor could the restored independence be con- [257] sidered a solution of Israel's problems, since after a bloody internal history of little more than two centuries the independent kingdom fell under the Assyrian onslaught and, as a consequence, Israel ceased to exist as a distinguishable political and civilizational entity.

These are the stark facts of pragmatic history. But they have been so successfully overlaid by the pragmatic construction of the Biblical narrrative that even today the lack of critical concepts makes it difficult to treat adequately the problems of continuity and identity. On the one hand, the language of "Israelite history" must arouse misgivings in view of the fact that the most important event in its course was the disappearance of Israel. On the other hand, the language is justified because certainly something continued, even if the "something" defied identification by a name. The problems of this nature, however, will be treated in their proper place in the further course of this study. For the present, we need only draw attention to their existence, in order to conduct the analysis with awareness of the pragmatic context.

The pragmatic context for the period under discussion is furnished by the united monarchy of Israel and Judah which, for lack of a better name, we shall call the Davidic Empire. It does clearly not continue the monarchy which the Israelite Confederacy had developed as an emergency organization, but must be considered a new imperial foundation imposed by the conqueror, his army, and his clan, on the territories and peoples of Israel, Judah, and the Canaanite towns. The elements of conquest and force which entered into the making of the empire, however, were balanced, at least in the early years of David's reign, by a genuine popular support engendered by the relief from Philistine dominion as well as by the appeal of imperial power and courtly splendor. Nevertheless, the empire did not outlast the reigns of its founder (*ca.* 1004-966) and his son (*ca.* 966-926). And a careful observer of the eighty years might arrive at the conclusion that the empire in a stable form did not last for any time at all, for during David's reign the empire was still in the making, gradually expanding its dominion over Edom and Damascus through military governors, and over Moab and Ammon through tributary princes. But under Solomon, though the direct administration was extended over most of Ammon and Moab, the empire as a whole was crumbling, as Edom in the south and the Aramean Damascus in the north regained their independence. If the territories and peoples assembled by conquest at the time of David's death could have been held together [258] by his successors for a few generations, a stable Syriac Empire, comparable in type to the Egyptian and Mesopotamian empires, might have come into existence. But whether such an imperial organization of the Palestinian and Syrian territories and peoples, when stabilized, would have been an Empire of Israel, even if it should have adopted the style, may justly be doubted.

The rapid succession of rise and fall, without a breathing space for stable existence, left no time for problems of this kind to develop. The causes which determined the rapid decline and the division of the empire were rather variegated. Certainly David's weakness in dealing with his sons had something to do with it, as well as the personality of Solomon, which, through the rare openings in the veil of glorification thrown around it by the Biblical narrative, looks somewhat less than wise. But there is no profit in pursuing details difficult to ascertain at best. For even men of impeccable character and statesmanship might have floundered in the attempt to overcome the fundamental obstacle to the building of a durable empire, that is, the hopeless poverty of the Palestinian soil. Palestine was too poor to maintain a first-rate military power, not to mention a magnificent court, in the style of the rich river civilizations in Mesopotamia and Egypt. We have touched already on the financial aspects of Saul's warfare and David's conquest. Loot as a major source of revenue had to cease when the conquest had reached its limits and the dominion had to be administered rationally within its boundaries. Labor in the king's service, taxation, and income from the control of trade had to replace the unorthodox financial methods of the war period. And when that point had been reached, the scarcity of resources quickly proved to be the limiting factor.

The actual difficulties, as we have indicated, have disappeared behind the veil of glorification surrounding the reign of Solomon.

Nevertheless, certain incidents allow at least a glimpse of the true situation. We find in 1 Kings 9:15-22 that Solomon recruited his slave-labor force from the descendants of Amorites, Hittites, Perizzites, Hivites, and Jebusites, that is, of non-Israelitic peoples whom "the people of Israel were unable to destroy utterly." Neither the wholesale destruction of people who, when alive, could have produced revenue, nor the use of their survivors as slave laborers on royal building projects, can have improved the wealth of the country. Moreover, contrary to the suggestion of 1 Kings 9:22, Israel [259] was not a military aristocracy ruling over slave laborers, but the Chosen People itself was pressed into service by a "levy of forced labor out of all Israel" (1 Kings 5:13-18) for the unproductive purpose of building the Temple. And the twelve "officers over all Israel," at the head of twelve administrative districts, who each provided for the King's household for one month of the year (1 Kings 4:7-19) can hardly have levied the provisions from anybody but the Israelites themselves. The country suffered and the revenue for royal projects was running low. In the twentieth year of luxurious building, 1 Kings 9:10-14 reports, Solomon could obtain a sum of gold only by selling twenty cities in Galilee to Hiram of Tyre. But when Hiram inspected his new territory he found the cities in poor condition, and "so they are called Cabul [no good] to this day" (13). It is not surprising, therefore, that Israel broke away from the house of David when after Solomon's death the successor threatened to increase the burden, and that the superintendent of slave labor, Adoram, was stoned to death on the occasion (1 Kings 12:16-18) . . .

> (This selection will provide the reader with an example of how Voegelin maintains that the cosmological symbolism entered Israel under David.—Eds.)

## [§ 4. David and Jerusalem]

[279] . . . The Biblical narrative received its final form after the return from the Exile, when the high priests had usurped the former functions of the king. It is not surprising, therefore, that we learn little from the narrative about the king's position in general, and about his function as the high priest in particular, which David and his successors inherited from the Jebusite rulers of Jerusalem. Nevertheless, we have a fairly clear picture of the continuity, because a sufficient number of coronation oracles, liturgies, and hymns has survived. Psalm 110 is of special importance for [280] our present con-

text, as it establishes the continuity between Melchizedek and the Davidic institutions.

Psalm 110 is preceded by the rubric *ledawid* and thus is characterized as a piece to be used in a ceremony involving the King. The text itself consists of a series of oracles which, by their contents, reveal themselves as a coronation ritual, or at least as important parts of it:

(1) The Psalm opens with an oracle, ostensibly spoken by a temple prophet to the King on a ceremonial occasion which appears to be the first act of the coronation:

> The word of Yahweh to my lord
> "Sit at my right hand,
>     till I make your enemies your footstool."

Yahweh invites the King to sit at his right hand, and the throne to which the King must be imagined to ascend is understood as Yahweh's throne. Of this first act we can speak as the enthronement.

(2) When the King has followed the invitation and is presumed to be seated, the speaker continues with a description of effective rule under the power of the god, supported again by a direct word from Yahweh:

> The scepter of your strength will Yahweh stretch forth from
>     Zion:
> "Rule in the midst of your enemies!"

In this second act of the ceremony the King apparently is endowed with the scepter. It is stretched forth from Zion by Yahweh himself, and its principal effect is victory over enemies.

(3) The third oracle presents great difficulties of translation. It probably is to be rendered as:

> [281] Your people offer themselves freely on the day of your
>     strength.
>     In holy array go forth!
>         "From the womb of the Dawn, as Dew have I brought
>         you forth!"

In the third act the King is endowed with the robe of the cosmocrator, after the usurpation described as the robe of the high priest, the "holy array," in which he is now to go forth to show himself to the people. The "day of your strength" is probably the coronation day, on which the people offer themselves freely to the King's rule, but possibly a day of war on which the people volunteer in the militia. In either case, the third act makes effective the King's domestic rule, as the second act makes him victorious over enemies. Again the picture of effective rule is supported by the oracle from its source in Yahweh who certifies the King as the newborn son, fathered by the god with his divine consort.

(4) The ritual reaches its climax with the declaration of the King as the priest of Yahweh:

> Yahweh has sworn and will not repent it:
> "You shall be a priest forever, after the manner of Melchizedek!"

Geo Widengren's translation follows the Septuagint (*kata ten taxin Melchizedek*), as most translations do, in speaking of a priesthood in the manner, or after the order, of Melchizedek. The Hebrew text, however, would render, instead, "You shall be a priest forever, because of me a Melchizedek." In that case the proper name Melchizedek would carry the overtones of "a King of Righteousness," deriving the righteousness (*zedek*) of the King from his priestly function and its source in Yahweh.

(5) Verses 5 and 6 resume the temple prophet's description of the King's dominion by the will of Yahweh:

> The lord at your right hand will shatter kings on the day of his wrath. He will execute judgment among the nations, filling with corpses, shattering heads, over the wide earth.

I assume "the lord at your right hand" to be the King, in accordance with the first oracle's request that the King take his seat at the right hand of Yahweh. Hence the prophet's words would be addressed to Yahweh, as a confirmation of the newly created King's proper functioning. The English translations (RSV, Jewish Publication Society, Chicago, Moffat) capitalize the "Lord," referring it, with several manuscripts, to Yahweh.

[282] (6) The concluding verse of the Psalm, "From the brook will he drink on his way; therefore will he lift up his head," seems to be a ritual direction for the king, who is supposed to drink from the brook Gihon the water of life.

Since an important phase in the creation of a king, the unction, is missing, Psalm 110 is perhaps a fragment. It will be good, however, to reserve judgment in such matters, because there are no independent sources for Israelite rituals; on the contrary the rituals must be reconstructed from sources like Psalm 110. The absence of the unction would be explained if the Psalm were a complete ritual for one day of a ceremony which extended over several days. It would also be explained if it were a ritual for the anointed David, who on this occasion entered into the cosmological symbolism of the Jerusalem priest-kings. Whatever the precise nature of the ritual in question may be, it shows conclusively how the imperial symbolism of the cosmological civilization entered Israel by way of the Jebusite succession ...

## [311] Chapter 10: The End of Israel's Worldly Existence

### § 1. The Divided Kingdoms

The revolt of Israel against Solomon's successor marked the end of the Davidic Empire. It was never to be restored. The northern part, comprising ten tribes, organized itself as the Kingdom of Israel. It lasted until 721 B.C., when it fell to the Assyrians. The southern part, comprising the tribe of Judah and the region of Jerusalem, continued as the Kingdom of Judah, under David's dynasty, to its final destruction by the Babylonians in 586 B.C.

Israel maintained its independent organization for more than two centuries. The newly won independence, however, did not bear fruit in a great political form. Even if allowance is made for a considerable amount of sources suppressed and destroyed by Judaite historians, it remains unlikely, in view of the known course of events, that a major symbolic literature has been lost. The Kingdom of Israel, to be sure, had its fleeting moments of glory, but the disorder of political existence was so profound that a stable form could hardly rise above the convulsions of war, murderous changes of dynasties, and social unrest. The worldly existence of Israel was drawing to its end. In the much smaller Southern Kingdom, where no allowance for the destruction of sources need be made, the symbolic landscape was equally arid during the two centuries. The symbolism of the Davidic kingship continued; but no noteworthy developments seem to have taken place.

Nevertheless, the period was not barren at all. It teemed with literary activity. This was the age in which Israelite intellectual and literary culture began to flourish. The David Memoirs received their final form and were given to the public. The songs and antiquities of Israel were col-[312] lected in the Book of Yashar and the Book of the Wars of Yahweh. The Royal Annals and Temple Records from the time of David and Solomon were continued; and they furnished the source materials for unofficial historical enterprises such as the Book of the Acts of Solomon. To a Book of the Acts of the Kings of Israel we owe the important sections in Kings on the fate of the Omride dynasty and on Jehu. The Yahwist and Elohist schools of historiography sprang into existence. The first law code, the Book of the Covenant, was collected and organized in written form. The prophetic revolt of the ninth century found its literary expression in the Elijah and Elisha stories. The first great "writing prophets," Amos (*ca.*750) and Hosea (*ca.*745-735), flourished toward the end of the period. And even the early years of Isaiah (from *ca.* 738 onward) still fell within its range.

As far as the distribution of the literary outburst over Israel and Judah is concerned, the Northern Kingdom seems to have had the greater share. That is hardly surprising. In spite of the passing ascendancy of Judah in the Empire, Israel was still the Chosen People of Yahweh. Israel was the ferment of history, not Judah; and the Northern Kingdom, furthermore, was much richer, more numerous in population, and more powerful than the southern late-comer to the expanding nation. That the capital of the Empire, with its court society and administrative personnel, remained with Judah did not seriously weight the balance against the spiritual and political preponderance of the North. For Jerusalem was at the time still the "city of David"; and Solomon's Temple was a royal chapel. Neither the city nor the sanctuary had yet the importance which it gained in the second half of the seventh century, through Josiah's reform and the monopoly of sacrifices. At any rate, the prophetic revolt of the ninth century occurred in the Northern Kingdom; the Book of the Covenant was a northern production; Hosea was an Israelite prophet; and even the Judaite Amos chose Beth-El in Israel as the place for his short public activity.

Behind the literary flowering there was a movement of experiences in search of expression; and the experiences pointed toward a communal order under Yahweh beyond the mundane existence of either Israel or Judah. The analysis of this class of experiences and their symbolic expression will occupy us in the present section. Before entering on it, however, we must consider certain formal aspects of the process in which Israel, while losing its existence as a power in pragmatic history, became a greater power in [313] the order of mankind. The problem of Israel's continuity and identity that had intruded itself in the preceding section must now receive some further clarification.

The first formal aspect to be considered is the combination, in Israelite history, of intensive with lateral growth. On the scale of civilizational intensity Israel grew from a clan society on the nomad level to an imperial nation with a rational administrative and military organization, as well as a differentiated intellectual and literary culture. At the same time it expanded laterally from a nucleus of Hebrew clans to an empire people with a fairly homogeneous civilization, through absorption of both the Canaanites and Judah. This process, moving in two directions at once, endangered the proportionate growth of Israelite society. The infiltration of the Hebrew clans west of the Jordan had, through amalgamation with the Canaanites, led to the formation of a new society with enough national coherence, by the eleventh century, to conduct common wars against Midianites and Philistines, to organize itself under a king, and to develop even such expressions of national consciousness as the bands of ecstatic prophets. Whereas this phase of growth, to be sure, had seriously impaired the pristine purity of the Yahwist order, the various manifestations of syncretism had not endangered the mundane existence of Israel. The Canaanites apparently were well digested, and they even added to the strength of Israel in pragmatic politics. In the second phase the dangers of rapid growth became unmistakable. By ways no longer traceable in detail Judah had been drawn into the national orbit of Israel during the reign of Saul. And this second increase of pragmatic power could no longer be digested organizationally—Israel, as part of the united kingdom, had to submit to a foreign dynasty. In the third phase, organizational freedom of a sort had been regained at the price of withdrawal from the Empire. But on the cultural level the growth of Israel continued with unbroken vitality, in both the Northern and Southern kingdoms. The impulses imparted by the luxurious and humanistic rule of Solomon, by the administrative and temple scribes of an imperial civilization, by the increased literacy of a well-to-do upper class, by the consequent literary activity of private persons who wrote court memoirs and survey histories of the reign, did not lose their effectiveness with the end of the Empire. On the contrary, they set moving the massive literary production that we have briefly sketched. While in the realm of organization for action the growth of the people had suffered a severe setback, a literary [314] dimension had been acquired in which Israelites and Judaites could move in common in spite of their political separation. And in that dimension the expansion and unification of the people, including the southerners, advanced. The cultural absorption of Judah was so successful, indeed, that in the literary construction of Israel's preDavidic history the Yahwist school of the south preceded the northern Elohists.

By means of a common literature historians and prophets created an Israel that could survive in Judah even after the ethnic Israel had disappeared from history. This ultimate transformation brings to our attention the second formal aspect of Israel's growth. There is a pattern of death and survival running through Israelite history. That is not surprising in itself, for every growth, to be sure, is the death of the phases outgrown. The growth of the Chosen People, however, left a peculiar paradigmatic trail in history. The forms of existence superseded by further growth did not sink back into a dead past, but survived as symbolic forms. From the original Yahwist Confederacy that had occupied Canaan emerged the charismatic kingship of Saul. The old theopolity had to be replaced by a more effective organization of the people. But its symbolism, the Kingdom of God, remained a living force so forcefully living indeed that the symbol of God's *mamlakah* motivated the further symbolism of a theocracy, that is, of a political organization adjusted to the exigencies of the original theopolitical idea. From the charismatic kingship, then, emerged under the pressure of the Philistine wars the Davidic Empire. Again the older forms of existence had been organizationally outgrown, but again the symbolisms of theopolity and theocracy survived with such strength that a further symbol, through the extension of the berith idea, had to be created so as to include the house of David in the system. And with the breakdown of David's organization that new component of the symbolism did not disappear either, but became the starting point for the Messianic idea with its long chain of metamorphoses ending in Christ the Messiah. From the Davidic Empire, finally, emerged the Kingdoms of Israel and Judah. And during the period of this further organizational adjustment, the surviving older symbols proved, in the revolt of the ninth century, strong enough to check the politics of the Omride dynasty and to prepare the growth of an Israel beyond the troubles of political organization. The sequence of symbols on occasion of organizational changes certainly falls into a pattern. It looks as if it had been the destiny of Israel, during the short five [315] centuries of its pragmatic existence, to create an offspring of living symbols and then to die.

The word "destiny" as just used signifies the meaning which the order of an existent has in relation to its own lasting and passing, as well as in relation to the order of mankind in historical existence. No romantic connotations should be evoked by the term. Such mysteries as there really attach to the destiny of Israel are profound beyond penetration and at the same time flat on the surface of facts.

The first of the mysteries is the conspiracy of historical contingencies with the survival of meaningful order. In that respect the destiny of Israel is indeed peculiar in so far as it found in Judah, with its meteoric rise from nonexistence to political rivalry and cultural equality, the partner that could develop the inheritance with brilliance and authority after the demise of the older people. Even so the success of survival was achieved by a hair's breath. If Jerusalem had fallen to the Assyrian power in 721 together with the Northern Kingdom, the upper class of the one southern tribe would have disappeared in the Asiatic hinterland as deeply as that of the ten northern tribes, leaving no more memory than they. The contingency of Jerusalem's escape in 721 granted the breathing space, until 586, in which the national substance of Judah grew firm enough to survive the Exile.

Even historical contingencies, however, could not have secured the survival of Israel in its symbols unless there had been something worth transmitting. That is the second of the mysteries attaching to the destiny of Israel: Here was a people that began its existence in history with a radical leap in being; and only after the people had been constituted by that initial experience did it acquire, in the course of centuries, a mundane body of organization to sustain itself in existence. This sequence, reversing the ordinary course of social evolution, is unique in history. It is so unbelievable that positivist historians, as for instance Eduard Meyer, do not believe it at all; while even more sensitive historians, as sensitive for instance as Adolphe Lods, have difficulties in adhering to their own belief when it comes to such a crucial test as admitting the possibility that the Decalogue of Exodus 20 is really Mosaic in content (though not in form), and not a late Deuteronomist creation. A society is supposed to start from primitive rites and myths, and thence to advance gradually, if at all, to the spirituality of a transcendent religion; it is not supposed to [316] start where a respectable society has difficulties even ending. Nevertheless, the mystery of Israel's start at the wrong end of evolution must be accepted, the progressivist thesis that first things come always first notwithstanding. In this one case the sequence actually was reversed; and the reversal was the cause of Israel's extraordinary creativity in the realm of symbols. For the disorderly beginning of existence with a leap in being provided the experiential motivations for the people to respond to its gradual descent into Sheol with the creation of symbols that would preserve its attunement with transcendent being on each new level of mundane involvement. Each step of further adjustment to the pragmatic conditions of existence had to be measured by the standards of the initial existence as the Chosen People under God. The result was something in the nature of a model experiment in the creation of symbols of mundane existence under the conditions of an already enacted leap in being.

In the ninth century, the exigencies of the power game brought the experiment to an end. The diplomacy of the Omrides had to compromise with the cosmological order of the surrounding powers to such a degree that a solution to the problem could no longer be found within the range of Yahwist symbols. At the risk of destroying the conditions of Israel's mundane existence, the response had to be a revolutionary return to the origins. The archaic Israel reasserted itself in the political revolt of Elijah, Elisha, and the Rechabites. On the level of pragmatic history the movement was a ruinous reaction that broke all hopes for a recovery of Israelite power; on the spiritual level, however, it preserved Israel from sinking insignificantly into a morass of ephemeral success.

On the following pages we shall first sketch the pragmatic situation that faced Israel with the dilemma of spiritual or worldly suicide. We shall then deal with the Book of the Covenant as our principal source for the general mood of discontent with the internal development of Israelite society, and finally with the revolt against the Omride dynasty.

## § 2. The Pragmatic Situation

When Israel withdrew from the Empire, Judah was left in possession of the capital, its administration, and the Davidic dynasty, and continued to exist with a minimum of internal difficulties. The Israelites themselves, however, were faced with the task of organizing themselves as a state. It was a throwback to pre-imperial times; and the social forces that could [317] be observed at work in the rise of David to kingship were released to find a new balance. Jeroboam, the first king, belonged to the tribe of Ephraim. The struggle of the clans for control of the kingship was renewed. Jeroboam's son, Nadab, lasted only two years. He was assassinated by Baasha, from Issachar, the founder of the next dynasty, whose son Elah was also assassinated after a reign of only two years. With the end of the Baashide dynasty the role of the army became more marked. Elah was murdered by an ambitious officer, Zimri, one of the two generals of the war chariots. But the new king had apparently acted without securing the consent of his superior officers. The commander in chief, Omri, marched on the capital; and Zimri died in the flames of the palace after a reign of only seven days. Omri, who because of his position must be assumed to have been a member of the murdered king's clan, became the founder of the next dynasty, but had to fight for four years against Tibni, another pretender who had wide support. The domestic and foreign policy of the Omride dynasty (886-841), finally, brought into play the forces of the archaic Israel that had caused the difficulties and the undoing of David's Empire. The movement found its royal executor in one of the generals, Jehu, who exterminated the Omrides and founded his own dynasty (841-747). The following years of brief regimes and civil wars ended with the Assyrian Conquest in 721 . . .

> (These selections from chapters 11 to 13, which make up part four and conclude *IR*, position themselves at the level of paradigmatic history. With the fall of the Northern Kingdom, Voegelin holds that the "weight of interest shifted, in the Judah of the eighth century, distinctly toward the clarification of right order in the light of the Sinaitic revelation." Voegelin explores the emergence of the Deuteronomic Torah, of Moses, and of the prophets, respectively, in and through the "paradigmatic heightening" of events as they are available to us through the texts.—Eds. )

## [PART IV: MOSES AND THE PROPHETS]

### [355] CHAPTER 2: THE DEUTERONOMIC TORAH

### 1. The Prophets and the Order of Israel

History as the present under God was the inner form of Israel's existence. As it had been gained through Moses and the Berith it also could be lost through defection of the people from Yahweh and his instructions. Whenever such a crisis of defection occurred, it would be the function of the "*malakh* of the *berith*" to recall the people to its obligations, to restore its inner form. While the phenomenon of prophetism is far from exhausted by this characterization, the *malakh* function must be the guide for its interpretation in a study of Israelite order.

When the function of the prophet is defined in such terms, the precariousness of Israelite order, as well as the difficulties of the prophet's task, become clear. Above all, the prophet to whom Yahweh spoke his word might arrive at the conclusion that the situation was hopeless and return his mandate to his God. That was the conclusion at which Elijah arrived; and on the level of pragmatic history, it was a possibility that the potential prophets renounced their mission in face of its futility. Israel might, indeed, have relapsed into a nation among others, and Yahweh might have ended as one of the many Near Eastern divinities. The spirit of Yahweh, however, proved a power of its own in the person of Elijah. The prophet could not despair of his people without despairing of the spirit; he could not go into the desert in order to die in God. The spirit, while not of this world, was nevertheless experienced as the source of its order; and the solitude from which it suffered in historical existence could not be relieved by the solitude of escape. The flight to Mount Horeb was halted by the question "What are you doing here?"

The experience of Elijah precluded the reversal of the leap in being. The place of the *malakh* was with his people. Still, when the prophet, in obedience to the injunction of the divine question, retraced his steps, he met on his return with the other question, what he and his successors [356] should do in the world. The situation in which the prophets found themselves was indeed desperate because it was fraught with the complications of Israel's pragmatic existence. For on the one hand, when the prophets were successful to a certain degree, as they were in the revolt of Jehu, they endangered the diplomatic relations on which the survival of the country depended; and when on the other hand, the existence of the people as an organized community was threatened with annihilation, the value of a covenant with Yahweh, which included the promise of a glorious future in Canaan, became doubtful.

Hence, under the impact of the prophetic movement, there developed the vacillations in the adherence to Yahwist order which accompanied the history of the people from the ninth century into the Hellenistic and Roman periods. Under the pressure of the Empires, Israel would assimilate itself to the culture of the more powerful neighbors, and then suffer a revival of Yahwist nationalism which precipitated a political disaster. The diplomatic loosening of the Yahwist order under the Omride dynasty, in the ninth century, provoked the prophetic revolt which made a policy of alliances impossible. Two centuries later the assimilation to the Assyrian pantheon, under the reign of Manasseh in Judah, provoked the Deuteronomist reform which stiffened disastrously the resistance to Babylon. And the same tension was still present, in the Maccabaean period, in the struggles between Hellenizers and nationalist zealots. The prophets themselves were more or less helplessly caught between the forces of the age. A Jeremiah, for instance, was first a propagandist for the Deuteronomist reform because it enacted prophetic demands for the purification of Yahwism; he then was its opponent, when he recognized the Deuteronomic Torah as an ossification of the prophetic spirit; and the tradition, finally, is believable that he was killed in Egypt by Jews who attributed the fall of Jerusalem to the wrath of the foreign divinities that had been insulted by the prophetic reforms. The present under God had become a suicidal impasse when it was conceived as the institution of a small people in opposition to empires.

The scriptures of Israel have become the Old Testament of Christianity, and the prophetic *dabar* of Yahweh to his people has become the word of God to mankind. It requires today an effort of imagination to realize that the prophets were concerned with the spiritual order of a concrete people, of the people with whom Yahweh had entered into the [357] Berith. Under the conditions of Israel's history, the concreteness of their task faced them with problems that were never quite resolved. On the one hand, the prophetic experience moved toward the clarity of understanding that Yahweh was not only the one God beside whom Israel must have no other gods, but the one God for all men beside whom no other gods existed. On the other hand, the concrete Israel was changing its identity from the Hebrew clans of the conquest and the amalgamation with Canaanites, to the people of the Davidic Empire that included Judah, further to the divided Kingdoms and then to Judah alone, and finally to the organization of the postexilic community around the restored Temple. Yahweh tended to become a universal God of mankind, while the protean Israel became smaller and smaller. Hence the prophets were torn by the conflict between spiritual universalism and patriotic parochialism that had been inherent from the beginning in the conception of a Chosen People.

The tension was to reach tragic proportions when it became fully conscious, in the exilic Deutero-Isaiah's symbol of the Suffering Servant for mankind, before it dissolved anticlimactically in the restrictive reforms of Nehemiah and Ezra. Nevertheless, even when the remnant had thus withdrawn into its shell, the consciousness of the dilemma remained alive, as in the unknown author of the Book of Jonah. At this late date, however, in the story of a prophet who received Yahweh's order to save Nineveh through his preaching but tried to evade the divine command by fleeing in the opposite direction, the consciousness had become ironic:

> The word of Yahweh came to Jonah . . . Arise, go to Nineveh,
> that great city, and preach against it . . . Then Jonah arose and
> fled to Tarshish, from the presence of Yahweh . . .

One need not agree with enlightened critics who consider Jonah the profoundest book of the Old Testament, but neither should one forget that by the fourth century, within the orbit of the canonized literature, the tragic dilemma of Israel had acquired a comic touch.

While in the pre-exilic literature of Judah the dilemma certainly had nothing comic, one sometimes wonders to what degree the tragic implications became ever fully conscious. To be sure, the problems were clearly articulated, but the articulation provoked no reflection; the conflicts were submerged, as it were, by a fanatical will of collective existence. The catastrophe of the Northern Kingdom had the serious repercussions in the Judaite experience of order that expressed themselves in [358] the creation of the Deuteronomic Torah, and one should suppose that such a radical reorganization of symbols would have aroused some critical observation, expression of grief, or reflective apology. Israel, after all, had perished; and Judah was the surviving heir to its traditions. The transfer, though, caused nothing more than the slight ripple of terminology that can be observed in Isaiah and Micah. In a phrase like "The Holy One of Israel," for instance, the term "Israel" still meant for Isaiah the community that had been constituted by Yahweh through the Berith. But it also could absorb the political contingencies and mean the people as organized in the two Kingdoms, as in the verse 5:7:

> For the vineyard of Yahweh of the hosts is the house of Israel,
> And the men of Judah are his cherished plantation.

And once the Yahweh of Israel had become the Yahweh of the Kingdoms, the politically separate Judah could slip into the symbolism of Israel, as in 8:14:

> For to both the houses of Israel shall he prove a holy place,
> A stone to strike against, and a rock to stumble upon.

From the Judah that had become one of the houses of Israel, then, it was only a small step further to the Judah which in political fact had become the only house of Israel after the disasters of 734 and 722, as in Micah 3: 1:

> Hear now, you heads of Jacob,
> And rulers of the house of Israel.

The ease of the transition, the sleight of hand by which the Israel that had lost its political existence was thrown out of its symbolic existence and replaced by Judah, recalls the charismatic brutality of David in his acceptance of success and survival.

With a similar brutality the splendid rhetoric of Deuteronomy rolls over the tension between the one God of mankind and the Yahweh who is Israel's (now, Judah's) personal possession. Deuteronomy 4:35 admonishes the people: "You were made to see, that you know that Yahweh is God, none beside him"; and 4:39 continues: "Know it this day, and lay it to your heart, that Yahweh is God, in the heavens above and on earth below, none else." Since the language is unrestrained by qualifications, the verses can be understood (as by some historians indeed they are) as the first formulation of theoretical monotheism. And yet, doubts [359] with regard to their precise meaning will arise when we read in 6:4-5 the famous invocation:

> Hear, O Israel: Yahweh—Our God, Yahweh—One!
> And you shall love Yahweh your God with all your heart, and
> all your soul, and all your might!

For the oneness of Yahweh, as the context shows, is compatible with the existence of the gods of other peoples whom Israel is warned [not] to follow (6: 13-15). And the oneness and universality of a God of all mankind is, furthermore, difficult to reconcile with the surrender of other peoples' cities, houses, and property to Israel (6:10-12), or with the injunction to exterminate the conquered peoples in order not to be contaminated by their gods (7:1-5; 7:16-26). But then again it seems to be the universal God who, through a free act of love, has singled out Israel for the covenant (5:2) and consecrated it as his people in preference to other peoples whom he might have chosen as well (7:6-8). And Israel is assured that "Yahweh, your God, he is God; the trustworthy God, who keeps covenant and faith with those who love him and keep his commandments, to a thousand generations" (7:9). From the conflict of formulations one can only conclude that the level of doctrinal articulation, of a "theology," was reached by Deuteronomy no more than by the earlier documents we have studied. To be sure, the tendency toward a differentiated understanding of the one, universal God is marked, but still it is so deeply embedded in the compact experience of the people and its destiny, that the context deprives the monotheistic passages of the meaning they would have in isolation. The fierceness of collective existence will not yet admit dissolution into the freedom of individual souls, whether Israelite or not, under God . . .

## [CHAPTER 12: MOSES]

### [388] . . . § 2. The Son of God

Through the analysis of forms, both of the Torah and of prophetic legends, we have penetrated to the common historical substance. It proves to be the clash between the Yahwist experience of Moses and the cosmological order of the Egyptian empire. From the result falls a new light on the difficulties which beset a critical understanding of Moses. Since the clash between the two orders, as well as its issue into the actual constitution of a people under the order that had its origin in the soul of Moses, was a unique event in history, general categories do not apply to Moses, on principle, but can be used only as approximations with careful qualifications. There was something of the *nabi* in the man in whose soul occurred the leap in being when he heard the word of Yahweh; but the man who concluded the Berith with Yahweh for his people was not one of the indefinite number of "messengers of the Berith" who came after him. There was something of the legislator in the man who on innumerable occasions rendered judgment in the spirit of the *debharim*, which he perhaps had formulated himself, on cases submitted to him; but he was not himself a codemaker, though many of his decisions may have become precedents for later codifiers. There was something of the historian in the man who [389] made history and, in the course of a long life, must have had frequent occasion to correct the stories that were forming around the memorable events in which he had been an actor; but he certainly was not the historian as which he appears in Deuteronomy. There was something of the liberator in the man who led his people from servitude to political independence; but he was not an Israelite Garibaldi, for the people, in order to be freed by him from the bondage of Pharaoh, had to enter the service of Yahweh. And finally, while he was a spiritual founder he did not found "a religion," but a people in the present under God. Hence, in order to characterize adequately the essence of the Mosaic person and work, we are forced back from the type concepts to the symbols by which the unknown authors of the respective sections of the Biblical narrative tried to express the unique essence of the issue in continuity with their traditions. That essence is contained in the formula: Yahweh brought Israel, through Moses, up from Egypt. And we must look for the symbols in which the meaning of the terse formula is made explicit.

Fortunately such symbols can be found embedded in the narrative. The decisive passage is Exodus 4:21-23:

> (21) Yahweh said to Moses:
> As you go to turn toward Egypt, see:
> All the portents, which I lay in your hand, you will do before Pharaoh,
> but I shall strengthen his heart, that he will not let the people go.
> (22) Then you will say to Pharaoh:
> Thus Yahweh has said:
> My son, my first-born, is Israel;
> (23 ) I said to you: "Let my son go, that he may serve me";
> and you refused to let him go;
> So now I shall slay your son, your first-born . . .

[398] . . . The unique position of Moses has resisted classification by type concepts, as well as articulation through the symbols of the Biblical tradition. He moves in a peculiar empty space between the old Pharaonic and the new collective sons of God, between the Egyptian empire and the Israelite theopolity. On the obscurities surrounding the position of Moses now falls a flood rather than a ray of light, if we recognize in him the man who, in the order of revelation, prefigured, but did not figurate himself, the Son of God. It is the compactness of this intermediate position which resists articulation and makes it impossible, even in symbols of his own time, to answer the question: Who was Moses?

Once we have become aware of the problem, however, we can search the Biblical text for attempts to overcome the difficulty and to break through, however imperfectly, to a symbolization of the man who stands between the compactness of the Egyptian and the lucidity of the Christian order . . .

## [§ 3. The God]

[405] . . . The second source, the thornbush episode of Exodus 3:1-4:17, does not at first sight show the clarity of construction which distinguishes the prologue [Exodus 2, the first source]. The text as it stands today is linked through the previously discussed summary of leitmotifs with the episode of the plagues, and is intended to balance the story of the encounter between Moses and Pharaoh in the larger

unit of the exodus narrative. With that layer of meaning we shall deal in the subsequent analysis of the Berith. The purpose, now, of balancing the encounters of Moses with God and with Pharaoh has been achieved through the expansion of an original account of the revelation by additions which point toward the later events. Fortunately, however, the interpolations are clearly recognizable by contents and style, and we shall follow Martin Buber [1948] in eliminating the following passages as additions: (a) 3:15-22, as it is partly repetitious, partly anticipates details of the conflict with Pharaoh; (b) 4:1-9, as it anticipates the *portenta* of Moses which have no inner connection with the divine revelation; and (c) 4:13-17, as it prepares the participation of Aaron in the conflict with Pharaoh. What remains, that is, the body of text comprising 3:1-14 and 4:10-12, is again a spiritual drama of the first rank, though we do not know whether it was written by the same hand as Exodus 2. It is this remaining text that we now shall analyze. As in the case of the prologue, it should be mentioned, the attribution of component parts to the J and E sources is of no assistance for the understanding of the composition.

The drama of the revelation is organized as a sequence of clearly distinguishable scenes:

(1) Exodus 3:1-3: Moses, while tending the flocks of his father-in-law, comes to the Horeb, the Mountain of God:

> [406] And the messenger of Yahweh let himself be seen by
>     him, in a flame of fire from the midst of a bush [*seneh*].
> And he looked: Behold, the bush [*seneh*] burned with fire,
>     and the bush [*seneh*] was not consumed.
> And Moses said: I will turn aside and see this great sight,
>     why the bush [*seneh*] is not burned up.

The repetitious insistence on the *seneh*, with its allusion to *Sinai*, draws attention to the two stages of the revelation. God reveals himself first to Moses from the *seneh*, then to the people from the *Sinai*. *Seneh* (Exod 3) and *Sinai* (Exod 19) are linked as the two acts in which the constitution of Israel is completed.

(2) Exodus 3:4: The divine presence has brought itself to the attention of Moses by arousing in general the awareness of his senses. It now makes itself a presence meant for him personally:

> When Yahweh saw that he turned aside to look,
> God called to him from the bush [*seneh*],

> and said: Moses! Moses!
> And he said: Here I am!

Through the plain answer Moses puts himself in the presence of the voice, whoever the speaker may be, and is ready to hear.

(3) Exodus 3:5-6: The voice reveals itself as divine and thereby introduces the proper distance into the mutual presence. Moses is on holy ground and must not come nearer. When he has stopped accordingly and taken his sandals off, the voice then identifies itself as the god of his father, as the god of Abraham, Isaac, and Jacob. Whereupon Moses hid his face, for he was afraid to look at God.

(4) Exodus 3:7-10: To see God is to die. Moses has hidden his face from the terrifying sensual presence, and he listens, with his soul, to whatever the voice has to say. And the voice tells him of the divine knowledge that is action. The revelation opens: "Seen I have, seen the oppression of my people who are in Egypt"; and it closes: "Lead my people, the sons of Israel, out of Egypt!" Here, for the first time, appears the theme of "my people [*ammi*]," firmly framing the promise of freedom in 3:8. As the *seneh* points forward to *Sinai*, so the *ammi* points forward to the Berith through which the Hebrew clans, who as yet are ignorant of the fate in store for them, will be transformed into "my people." In the knowledge [407] of God the action distended in historical time is completed. Moreover, the historical action has subtly begun with the revelation, for the knowledge of God has now become the knowledge of the Moses who, in the course of his life, has grown to the point where he can hear the divine voice articulate its command. When Moses can hear the voice appoint him the servant of Yahweh, he has grown spiritually into the servant of Yahweh. The command could be rejected only by a man who could never hear it; the man who can hear cannot reject, because he has ontologically entered the will of God, as the will of God has entered him. When the consciousness of the divine will has reached clarity of revelation, the historical action has begun.

(5) Exodus 3:11-14 and 4:10-12: When the command strikes Moses it cannot be rejected, but it can be received with misgivings about his human ability to accomplish the apparently impossible. Who is he to persuade Pharaoh and bring Israel out of Egypt (3:11)? And how can he explain to the prospective people that the god of their fathers, who has taken his good time to hear their cries from bondage, is the God, who now will indeed help them (Exod 3:13)? Such misgivings are overcome when the god of the fathers reveals his true

nature through the self-interpretation of his name, "Yahweh." The interpretation is part of the action that has begun in Moses with the revelation, and it also determines the literary form of the scene. As in the preceding scene the promise of freedom was framed by the introductory and concluding references to "my people," so now the supreme revelation of God's nature is framed by the "I will be [*ehyeh*] with you" of Exodus 3:12 and 4:12. In the exegesis at the center, the meaning of God is then revealed as "I am who I am [*ehyeh asher ehyeh*]." To the skeptical sons of Israel Moses will have to say: "*Ehyeh* has sent me to you" (3:14). The people thus will break the bondage of Egypt and enter the present under God, once they have responded to the revelation of God's presence with them. The mutual presence of God and Moses in the thornbush dialogue will then have expanded into the mutual presence of God and his people, through the Berith, in history.

[408] The thornbush dialogue could be written only by a man who had an intimate knowledge of the spiritual events of divine revelation and human response. He was a prophetic mind of the first rank; and the fact that in the composition J and E sources were used allows us to place him at the earliest in the eighth century B.C. The question will have to be raised whether a work so distinctly prophetic in form contains a historical substance that can be assumed to go back in an unbroken tradition to the time of Moses. And in particular, we must ask whether the exegesis of the divine name as I AM WHO I AM can have had Moses as its author. Since these questions are today obscured by an immense controversy which, first, is not always too clear in the statement of the issues and, second, is all too frequently biased by progressive ideology, we must briefly clarify what in our opinion the nature of the problem is.

We must realize first of all that we are dealing with a revelation presumably received by Moses, and nothing but that revelation; and second, that with regard to the contents of the revelation we have no source but the episode just analyzed. Hence, the rich etymological debate concerning the name of Yahweh, with its variegated conjectures, some more plausible than others but none conclusive, must be excluded as irrelevant to our problem. The narrative itself does not refer to any meaning attached to the name of Yahweh that could have influenced the contents of the revelation. On the contrary, it presents the name as one whose meaning is unknown, so that an exegesis is necessary in order to endow it with spiritual vitality. The exegesis, furthermore, is not intended as an etymology. As far as we know, the *ehyeh* has etymologically no more to do with *yahweh*, than *mashah* with *mosheh*, that is, nothing at all. The exegesis plays with a phonetic allusion, but its meaning is autonomous.

As far as the autonomous meaning is concerned, a formidable issue is injected into the controversy through the fact that since the time of the Patres, the divine self-interpretation (*Ego sum, qui sum*) has been the [409] basis of Christian speculation on the nature of God. The primacy of the divine *esse*, in opposition to the Platonic primacy of the divine *bonum*, is so distinctively the great issue of Christian philosophy with regard to the essence of God that it has been justly called the philosophy of Exodus. The assumption now that the member of a nomad people in the thirteenth century B.C., or earlier, should have coined a formula which contains a metaphysics of being is preposterous to the enlightened, and too much even for more conservative historians. Oesterley and Robinson [1952, 153], for instance, say:

> We may be fairly sure that Israelite theology in Moses' day did not differ materially from that of other peoples at the same stage of development. The meaning of the name has evoked a good deal of discussion. The ancient Hebrew derivation suggested by Exod iii, 14—"I AM THAT I AM"—has been suspected, as implying too advanced a metaphysical conception of God for an early nomad people.

And even Lods [1948, 323], the most sensitive of the historians of Israel, says:

> The essential nature of the God of Israel is and must remain inscrutable. According to our account, the word Yahweh is merely a formal title which the God of Horeb revealed in answer to the practical needs of the cult, but it was intended to be a continual reminder of the phrase of which it was the epitome: "He is that he is," the Being whom none may know. While such an explanation is a lofty one, it seems too theological, too artificial to convey the original meaning of the name of the Midianite god.

The passages are illuminating for several reasons. In the first place, the authors take it for granted that nothing extraordinary can happen in history; no unique personality, even if God so wills it, can break the "stage of development." They can make their assumption, second, because they remain unaware that the revelation creates history as the inner form of human existence in the present under God and therefore inevitably must be a break with the "stage of development" at whatever time it occurs. The "development" would be no less broken if the break occurred a few centuries later. And third, since they are not aware of the nature of revelation as a "break," as the leap in being, they both confuse the exegesis of the name, which in fact is an explication, of the experience of divine presence, [410] with an etymology of the name "Yahweh." Obviously, the issue cannot be successfully treated on this rather low level of methodical precision.

And yet, while the arguments advanced in the two passages can hardly be called even debatable, they are motivated by a quite reasonable reluctance to read metaphysics into the thornbush revelation. Hence, we are faced with a dilemma. On the one hand, the authors just quoted (and many others) sense rightly that the exegesis of Exodus 3:14 cannot be a philosophical proposition concerning the nature of God—not because it presumably occurred in the thirteenth century B.C. among a nomad people, but because for reasons previously discussed no philosophical propositions occurred in the history of Israel at all. On the other hand, when we read in the Damascene [Damascenus 1864, 836]:

> The foremost of all names applied to God is "HE WHO IS." For, as it comprehends all in itself, it includes being itself as an infinite and indeterminate ocean of substance ;

we cannot deny that the Christian interpretation is well founded on the text. While we cannot escape the dilemma either by doubting the text or by moving it down a few centuries, a solution suggests itself if we consider a distinction made by Gilson [1948, 50 n. 1]:

> One can, of course, not maintain that the text of Exodus bestowed a metaphysical definition of God on mankind. Still, if there is no metaphysics in Exodus, there is a metaphysics of Exodus.

Gilson's distinction applies to a concrete case, in effect, our principle of evolution from compactness to differentiation. While the Exodus passage is not a metaphysical proposition, it contains in its compactness the meaning differentiated by the Christian philosophers.

Once we have recognized the exegesis of the thornbush episode as a compact symbolism in need of explication, not only will the philosophical interpretation appear well founded, but the labors of analysis bestowed by Christian thinkers on the episode in general can be accepted as an important aid for the understanding of the symbol. We shall use for this purpose the summary of the problem given by St. Thomas in the *Summa Theologiae* [I., q.13, 11]. Thomas considers the

HE WHO IS the most proper name [411] of God for three reasons: (a) because it signifies God according to his essence, that is, as being itself; (b) because it is universal and does not more closely determine the divine essence which is inaccessible to human intellect in this life; and (c) because it signifies being in the present which is appropriate to God, whose being has not past or future. Thomas, however, goes beyond the implications which the *ehyeh* has for a philosophy of being and brings the other components of meaning into play. While the name HE WHO IS is the most appropriate one with regard to the mode of signifying the divine essence, the name God is more appropriate with regard to the object intended to be signified by the name; and even more appropriate is the name *tetragrammaton* for the purpose of signifying the singular, incommunicable substance of God. The three names which occur in the last section of the thornbush episode—*ehyeh, elohim, YHWH*—are co-ordinated by St. Thomas with the structure of the divine being in depth, leading from the philosophically communicable essence, through the proper name of the object, into the depth of the incommunicable substance.

If now we place the issue of the "philosophical proposition" in the context of the Thomist analysis, the *ehyeh* will no longer appear as an incomprehensible philosophical outburst, but rather as an effort to articulate a compact experience of divine presence so as to express the essential omnipresence with man of a substantially hidden God. The "I will be with you," we may say, does not reveal the substance of God but the frontier of his presence with man; and precisely when the frontier of divine presence has become luminous through revelation, man will become sensitive to the abyss extending beyond into the incommunicable substance of the Tetragrammaton. As a matter of fact, the revelation of the thornbush episode, once the divine presence had become an historical experience of the people through the Berith, had no noteworthy sequel in the history of Israelite symbols and certainly no philosophical consequences. The unrevealed depth, however, that was implied in the revelation, has caused the name of God to become the unpronounceable Tetragrammaton YHWH. Philosophy can touch no more than the being of the substance whose order flows through the world.

The great issue of the "philosophical proposition" has given way to the insight that a metaphysics of being can be differentiated from Exodus 3:14, but is not the meaning of the compact symbol itself; and the sum- [412] mary of the problem by St. Thomas has led us back to the full meaning of the thornbush episode as the revelation to Moses of the divine presence with him and his people.

The revelation of the hidden God, through Moses, reveals his presence with his people; revelation and historical constitution of the people are inseparable. There is extant an interesting text, in the prophecies of Hosea, which proves beyond a doubt that this was indeed the sense in which the Israelites themselves understood the formulas of the thornbush episode. Hosea [ . . . ] diagnosed the "forgetfulness" of the people about their God and his instructions as the symptoms of impending disaster. The God and the people who had been brought historically into their mutual presence through the revelations from *seneh* and *sinai* could separate again. The God who had disclosed himself as present could also withdraw; and then he would be no longer the "I will be with you," and the people would be no longer "My people." The prophet knew that the separation was already in process and would be consummated by disaster in pragmatic history, unless the people returned and remembered their God. As in the revelation to Moses the divine knowledge had embraced the actual constitution of Israel in historical time, so the revelation to Hosea embraced the actual dissolution of the people, accompanied by the external destruction of the Northern Kingdom. In order now to bring the divine foreknowledge to the knowledge of the people, Hosea chose the method of giving his son a symbolic name (1:9):

> And he [Yahweh] said:
> Call his name Lo-ammi [not-my-people]:
> for you are not my people [*lo-ammi*];
> and I not I-am [*lo-ehyeh*] to you.

The text is important in that it proves not only the role of the symbolism in the constitution of the Israelite theopolity but also the existence of the formulas in the middle of the eighth century. Moreover, since the naming of the unfortunate child was meant to be generally understood as a revelatory action, the symbolism presumably was familiar to the people whom Hosea wanted to impress. Hence, it can hardly have been created by Hosea, but must belong to a tradition of considerable age.

The structure and date of the symbol have been clarified sufficiently to prepare the crucial question whether the *ehyeh asher ehyeh* can be at-[413] tributed to Moses himself. An affirmative answer can be based on the close relation between the thornbush symbol and the Amon Hymns of Dynasty XIX (*ca.* 1320-1205, B.C.). We shall briefly establish the parallel:

(1) In the framing passages of the thornbush episode, 3:12 and 4:12, the *ehyeh* has the meaning "I will be with you"; and the Chicago translation justly paraphrases the *ehyeh* in 4:12 as "I will help you"— though the paraphrase destroys the structure of the text. The meaning that God will be present as the helper, furthermore, is confirmed by the instruction to Moses to tell the people: "Ehyeh has sent me to you" (3:14). The passage would have to be paraphrased: "The one who is present as your helper has sent me to you." In the light of this meaning, supported by the prophecy of Hosea, must be understood the central *ehyeh asher ehyeh*, usually translated as I AM WHO I AM. Unless we introduce extraneous "philosophical" categories, the text can only mean that God reveals himself as the one who is present as the helper. While the God himself is hidden (the first *ehyeh*) and, therefore, must reveal himself, he will be manifest whenever, and in whatever form, he chooses (the second *ehyeh*).

(2) This conception of divinity as a being hidden in his depth and, at the same time, manifest in many forms of his choice, however, is precisely the conception of divine being that we have found in the Amon Hymns of Dynasty XIX. Let us recall some of the characteristic passages [Pritchard 1950, 368ff., 371]:

> The first to come into being in the earliest times,
> Amon, who came into being at the beginning,
> so that his mysterious nature is unknown . . .
> His image is not displayed in writing;
> no one bears witness to him . . .
> He is too mysterious that his majesty be disclosed,
> he is too great that men should ask about him,
> too powerful that he might be known.
> Mysterious of form, glistening of appearance,
> the marvelous god of many forms.
> "Hidden" [*amen*] is his name as Amon,
> he is Re in face,
> and his body is Ptah.

Moreover, even within the cosmological form there become apparent the motives which tend to transform the highest empire god into the God who is present to man in his needs:

> [414] Do not widows say: "Our husband art thou,"
> and little ones: "Our father and our mother"?
> The rich boast of thy beauty,
> and the poor worship thy face.

> He that is imprisoned turns about to thee,
> and he that has a sickness calls out to thee . . .
> Everybody is turned back to thy presence,
> so that they may make prayers to thee.

One must not forget, however, that approximations to an experience of divine presence of the type just quoted remain within the sphere of personal piety and prayer. They do not break with the cosmological myth of the Empire.

The parallel between the Yahwist and the Amon symbols is clear enough not to require elaboration. The tension between the hidden depth in God and his manifestations has been transposed, by the thornbush episode, from the form of cosmological myth to the form of revealed presence in history. Such a transposition could well have been the decisive work of Moses, if we consider the fundamental issue of his existence as it has emerged from the previous analysis, that is, the conflict between the orders of Yahweh and the Egyptian empire. It is highly probable that the revelation of the new order was couched in symbols which clearly abrogated the order of the Egyptian gods as it was understood at the time. It would be the same type of symbolic opposition that we could observe in the Abram episode of Genesis 14. The revelation could break with the cosmological experience, but it could not be communicable unless it continued the symbols while changing their meaning. The God of Moses had to make himself intelligible to his people, not only as the God of the fathers, but also as the God of the new historical dispensation in opposition to the Amon of the empire. Hence, we are inclined to attribute the symbolism of the thornbush episode to Moses; and since the Egyptian texts which supply the continuity are later than the Amarna period, a date for Moses will have to be assumed in the eighteenth century B.C.

## [§ 4. The New Dispensation]

[425] The meaning of the Decalogue [Exod 20] is determined by its own contents, as well as by the context of the drama which begins with the Message of Exodus 19:4-6. The Berith has been concluded, and Israel is accepted as the royal domain of Yahweh the King. Hence, the Decalogue is not a catechism of religious and moral precepts, but a proclamation of the God-King laying down the fundamental rules for the order of the new domain. It opens with a declaration of the authority from which the commands emanate:

I, Yahweh,
thy God who brought thee
out of the land of Egypt, out of the house of bondage.

Yahweh is the lord of history who has brought his people from the service of Egypt into his own service. In this capacity, as the new ruler, he issues a series of commands, organized by subject matter into three groups:

1. Thou shalt have no other gods before me (literally, to my face).
2. a. Thou shalt carve no image, or any likeness of what is in the heaven above, or on the earth beneath, or in the water under the earth.
   b. Thou shalt not bow down thyself to them.
   c. Thou shalt not serve them.
3. Thou shalt not invoke the name of Yahweh, thy God, to evil intent.
4. Remember the sabbath day, to keep it holy.
5. Honor thy father and thy mother.
[426] 6. Thou shalt not kill.
7. Thou shalt not commit adultery.
8. Thou shalt not steal.
9. Thou shalt not bear false witness against thy neighbor.
10. Thou shalt not covet thy neighbor's house.

The commands are addressed both to Israel collectively and to each member of the people individually. We have retained the form of the "Thou shalt," though recent translations have abandoned it, in order to stress the character of the word that is spoken personally to the individual man, in so far as he is a member of the divine domain. The commands are not general rules of conduct but the substance of divine order to be absorbed by the souls of those who listen to the call. Only to the degree to which the divine substance of the proclamation has entered the human substance will the people indeed have been transformed into the royal domain under God.

The first group of three or, with the subdivisions of the second one, of five commandments deals with the relation between God and man. The commandments contain no "monotheistic doctrine"; they rather prohibit fallacious conduct that would obscure the nature of the God who has revealed himself as the *ehyeh asher ehyeh*. Yahweh is the hidden God who manifests himself in the form, and at the times, of his choice. He must not be made manifest through images of human device, because his nature as the hidden God would be obscured—

and man cannot obscure the nature of God through symbolic action without affecting the order of his relation with God. Moreover, behind all attempts to image God in the likeness of anything within the visible cosmos, even though the attempts are apparently harmless, there lurks the desire to bring God within the reach of man. Man cannot bow to the image (2.b), or serve it (2.c), without substituting the imaged divine force for the divine reality that calls on men, at its own discretion, through the "word." And from such possessiveness, it is only a small step further to the magic misuse of a divine power that has been brought under the control of man (3). The author of the Decalogue has discerned the human desire to create a manageable God as the source of the attempts at representation, whatever form they may assume. In the first commandment he goes to the root of the issue, when he prohibits the "having of other gods," not because Yahweh is polytheistically jealous of rivals, or monotheistically denies their existence, but because man is in rebellion against God when he has other gods "in his face." The phrase "in the face," in the sense of rebellious or antagonistic [427] existence, occurs also in other contexts, as for instance in Genesis 16:12 and 25:18, where the outcast Ishmael lives and settles "in the face" of his brethren. The recognition of other gods is an act of rebellious self-assertion which disrupts the relation between God and man.

The third group of five commandments is self-explanatory. The commandments transfer the rules of internal clan solidarity to the new social body of the people of Israel. The injunctions protect the basic goods of life, marriage, property, and social honor. And the last commandment again penetrates to the source of disturbance when it prohibits the cherishing of covetous sentiments, of envy, which ultimately might break out in the specific disturbances.

The two groups of injunctions are skillfully linked by the positive commandments of the middle group. The order of a people lives not only in the here and now of man's right relations with God and fellow man but in the rhythms of the people's existence in time. The articulation of order in time, through both the divine rhythm of the holy day and the human rhythm of the generations, must be honored. The command to remember the divine rhythm (4) concludes the commandments concerning the relation with God; and the commandment to honor the human rhythm (5) opens the commandments concerning the relation with fellow man. [Voegelin follows Buber 1948, 93, 195ff., 194.]

Clearly, the Decalogue is not an accidental collection of "religious" and "moral" precepts, but a magnificent construction, with a firm grip on the essentials of human existence in society under God. While the compact symbol offers an explicit "philosophy of order" no more than the thornbush episode offered a "philosophy of being," it certainly is animated by the insight that right order will somehow grow in a community when the attunement to the hidden divine being is not disturbed by human self-assertion. Since it does not issue positive rules, either cultic or moral, the field remains wide open, in both respects, for civilizational growth. Nevertheless, the Decalogue restrains and directs the growth by its injunctions against rebellious existence. It is framed by the firm blocks of the first and tenth commandments with their injunctions against the antitheistic rebellion of pride and the antihuman rebellion of envy. Between the two protective dams, in the middle, can move the order of the people through the rhythm of time. Through the articulation of the divine will into the commandments of the Decalogue Moses, indeed, has given Israel its constitution as the people under God in historical existence.

## [428] Chapter 13: The Prophets

### § 1. The Prophetic Effort

Without the revelations from the Thornbush to Moses and from the Sinai to the people, there would have been no messengers of the Covenant; but without the messengers we would probably know little about Moses and the events of his time. The great question of the "historical Moses," which agitates the moderns, must be considered of secondary importance compared with the real issue, that is, the prophetic effort to regain, for the Chosen People, a presence under God that was on the point of being lost. It was in order to re-establish its meaning, as constituted by the Sinaitic events, that unknown authors elaborated such traditions as were preserved in cult legends, poems, and prose accounts into the paradigmatically heightened dramas that we have studied in the preceding Chapter. From those scenes of the "middle stratum" of the Biblical narrative emerges the Moses who lived, in historical continuity, in the medium of prophetic experience in Israel. The Moses of the prophets is not a figure of the past through whose mediation Israel was established once for all as the people under Yahweh the King, but the first of a line of prophets who in the present, under the revelatory word of Yahweh, continued to bring Israel up from Egypt into existence under God.

If we distinguish, thus, between the "historical" and the living Moses and, furthermore, define the prophetic experience as the medium of his life, the problems of the prophetic movement, from the crisis of the ninth to the exile of the sixth century, will come more clearly into focus:

(1) When prophetic authors recalled the work of Moses and heightened it paradigmatically in dramatic scenes, their work was not an end in itself. It serves the purpose of awakening the consciousness of the Chosen People for the mode of its existence in historical form. The people had to be reminded, first, of its origin in the response of the fathers to Yahweh's revelation through Moses and, second, of the fact that its [429] continued existence depended on its continued response to Yahweh's revelation through the prophets. The recall of the past blends, therefore, into the call in the present. They both belong to the same continuum of revelation which creates historical form when it meets with the continuum of the people's response. The historical form of the people unfolds in time; but it remains historical form only as long as the people, while lasting in time, lives in the tension of response to the timeless, eternal revelation of God.

(2) The prophetic blending of past and present in a continuum of living tension between time and eternity, however, has its dangers. For precisely when the defection of the people has reached such proportions that repeated, energetic reminders of the conditions of existence in historical form become necessary, the recall of the past may have effects as unexpected as they are undesired. We have studied such an unwanted effect in the chapter on the Deuteronomic Torah, when we traced the line that led from the recall of the origins to the Myth of Moses. Far from resulting in a new response of the people to the living word of Yahweh as pronounced by the messengers, the prophetic effort derailed into a constitution for the Kingdom of Judah which pretended to emanate from the "historical" Moses. The past that was meant to be revitalized in a continuous present now became really a dead past; and the living word to which the heart was supposed to respond became the body of the law to which the conduct could conform.

(3) This evolution toward the mythical Moses and the Torah, although caused by the persistent recall of Israel's theopolitical constitution and at times perhaps even favored by prophetic circles, was certainly not their ultimate intention. Hence, as the first symptoms of the derailment became noticeable, that is, as early as the eighth century, the recall of the origins was accompanied by warnings against the misapprehension that Yahweh would be satisfied with ritual

observances and a conformity which disregarded the spirit of the law. As a consequence, the struggle of the prophets for the historical form of Israel had to cope with two evils at the same time: On the one hand, the prophets had to bring Israel back from its defections to Canaanite and Mesopotamian gods, to the obedience of Yahweh; on the other hand, when in the first respect they were successful, they had to convert Israel from its chauvinism and reliance on external performance, to a communal life in the spirit of the Covenant.

[430] (4) The most serious problems of the prophets, however, arose from the very nature of their work, that is, from their effort to clarify the meaning of existence in historical form. When the revelations of the Mosaic period were studied and relived by men of such spiritual sensitivity as the authors of the thornbush episode and the Berith drama must have been, implications of the experience would unfold which required symbolizations of a new type. The universalist implications, for instance, which could be suppressed on the popular level by the fierceness of collective existence, had to loom large in the souls of solitary spiritualists tortured by the sorrow about the destiny of the Chosen People. When the syncretistic defections raised the question in what sense Israel could still be regarded by Yahweh as "My People," the possibility of God's choosing another people had to be considered. Moreover, when the rising danger from the neighboring empires had to be interpreted as divine castigations, the foreign peoples became instruments of Yahweh in the execution of a historical plan; and consequently the features of Yahweh as the universal God of mankind became increasingly marked. The appearance of prophetic personalities, succeeding one another through the generations in opposition to the people, furthermore, had to raise the problem of personal existence under Yahweh, in his spirit, independent of Israel's collective existence. If Israel as a people was doomed, could not a remnant, consisting perhaps of the followers of the prophets, escape and be saved for a better future? Could the people of God not contract into a group of spiritual personalities in free association under God? Should those who were willing to walk humbly with their God suffer the fate of the defectors? Was Israel really identical with the "historical" people? The implications, unfolding in such questions, would raise the ultimate issue: Had the Kingdom of God, of necessity, to assume the form of a political Israel; and if that question should be answered in the negative, had it, of necessity, to assume the form of a politically organized people at all? If Israel relegated Moses and the Covenant to a dead past by transforming them into a constitutional myth, the prophets were about to relegate Israel to a dead past by

transforming the Kingdom of God into something which, at the time, was no more than the shooting lights of a new dawn on the horizon.

In the present, concluding chapter we shall deal with the transformation of the theopolitical symbols of the Mosaic period through the [431] prophets. The first section will treat the unfolding of the problems, contained in a compact form in the older symbols, under the pressure of new experiences. For this section the prophecies of Jeremiah will be our guide. For at this late hour, in the last period of the Kingdom of Judah, the two and a half centuries of resistance to defection and chauvinism, as well as of continuous occupation with the meaning of the Sinaitic foundation, had differentiated the experiences to the point where new symbols for their adequate expression, though not always found, were clearly required. The second section will deal with the search for new means of expression. Beyond Jeremiah, with his clarity of issues and the veil yet drawn over the solutions, lead the prophecies of the unknown genius of the sixth century to whom philological convention refers as Deutero-Isaiah. His symbol of the Suffering Servant stands on the borderline between Prophetism and Christianity . . .

## [§ 2. The Unfolding of the Problem] [2. The Covenant]

[439] . . . The ambiguity of the prophetic appeal was inevitable in view of the compact form of the Decalogue, which did not allow for a distinction between existential and normative issues. While the construction as a whole made it clear that the concrete offenses were prohibited as manifestations of self-assertive existence in rebellion against God and man, the commandments which concentrated the existential issue were couched in the same normative form as the other ones. In particular, the positive relation between God and man, man and God, was expressed negatively in the injunction not to have other gods in the face of Yahweh. We have previously studied the meaning of this peculiarity when we reflected on the difference between Israelite Revelation and Hellenic Philosophy: A positive articulation of the existential issue would have required the experience of the soul and its right order through orientation toward the invisible God; and that experience never in Israelite history clearly is differentiated from the compact collectivism of the people's existence—not even in the prophetic age and certainly not in the age that formed the Decalogue. Hence, at a time when a theory of the psyche and a theology would have been required to unfold the meanings implied in the Sinaitic legislation, the prophets were badly handicapped by the want of a

positive vocabulary. They had at their disposition neither a theory of the *aretai* in the Platonic-Aristotelian sense so that they could have opposed character to conduct in human relations, nor a theory of faith, hope, and love in the Heraclitian sense so that they could have opposed the inversion of the soul toward God to ritual observance of his commandments. In particular, the lack of a differentiated theology must have been a tremendous obstacle to a proper articulation of the prophetic intentions: When reading the story of Jeremiah's squabbles with the Judaite refugees in Egypt (Jer 44), one wonders whether the Israelite common man, and even more so the common woman, had ever really understood why they should have no other gods besides Yahweh; and one begins to wonder whether the prophets had ever been able to make the reasons clear to them. The famous defections from Yahweh to Canaanite and Mesopotamian gods will appear in a new light if one considers that the people at large probably never had understood a Commandment whose spiritual meaning had remained inarticulate.

[440] The insight that existence under God means love, humility, and righteousness of action rather than legality of conduct was the great achievement of the prophets in the history of Israelite order. Even though their effort to disengage the existential issue from the decalogic form did not lead to expressions of ultimate, theoretical clarity, the symbols used in their pronouncements leave no doubt about the intended meaning: The normative component of the decalogic constitution was a source of evil in as much as it endowed the institutions and conduct of the people, which derived through interpretation from the Decalogue, with the authority of divinely willed order, however much the actual institutions perverted the will of God. Moreover, the prophets recognized that any letter, as it externalized the spirit, was in danger of becoming a dead letter, and that consequently the Covenant written on tablets had to give way to the Covenant written in the heart . . .

## [3. The Message]

[474] . . . Once the image of the ruler has become articulate, it can be converted into a standard by which the conduct of the concrete ruler is to be measured. This possibility, which also exists in cosmological civilizations, acquires a peculiar importance in Israel because the kingship was syncretistic in the sense that a rulership in cosmological form had to find its place in the theopolity created by the Sinaitic revelation. And the combination of the two forms was achieved, as we

have seen, through the prophetic institution of David and his house by a word of Yahweh which declared the king to be his son. Hence, while the monarchy developed its cosmological ritual, the restoration of order did not rely on the annual catharsis through the cult festivals alone, but was supplemented by prophetic criticisms and admonitions addressed to the King. The "Man who rules over man" had to conform to the model adumbrated in 2 Samuel 23:3-4 and further elaborated in Psalm 72; and the prophets, who had instituted him, could remind him of the model when his conduct fell short of it. Through the history of the monarchy runs, from its beginnings, the theocratic tension between prophet and king—from Samuel and Saul, through Nathan and David, to Elijah and Ahab, and to the revolt against the Omrides. And this theocratic tension in the royal institution forms the never-to-be-forgotten background for the concern of the great prophets, since the middle of the eighth century B.C., with the figure of the King.

In the prophetic occupation with the problem three phases can be distinguished: (1) an institutional phase, represented by Amos and Hosea; (2) a metastatic phase, represented by Isaiah; and (3) an existential phase, represented by Jeremiah.

[475] In the first phase, when the great prophets began to express the crisis of Israel in the alternatives of disaster and salvation, the criticism of the present order was no more than supplemented by the evocation of a future perfect order. The faith in a cultic restoration of the present order was broken, to be sure, when the restored order of the future was separated from the present state of things by an abyss of destruction. But the future was conceived as an institutional order, not so very different from the present one, minus its imperfections. When Israel had to be destroyed because of the misconduct of the people and the king, the end would be a restoration of the survivors under a king after the model held up by Yahweh in the oracle of David. With regard to the people, Amos 9:8 envisages the survival of a "remnant" as the ethnic nucleus for the future:

> Behold! the eyes of the Lord Yahweh are upon the sinful
>    kingdom—
> and I will destroy it from off the surface of the earth,
> save that I will not utterly destroy the house of Jacob.

With regard to institutions, the threats of destruction in Amos 9:9-10 are followed by the promise that "the fallen tabernacle of David" will be raised again from the ruins (9:11). With regard to the general state of things, the concluding oracles (9:13-15) envisage the fortunes of Israel restored, with the countryside flourishing and the cities rebuilt. And Hosea, finally, completes the picture with the oracle (Hos 3:4-5):

> Many days shall remain the children of Israel
>   with no king, and no prince,
>   no sacrifice, no pillar, no ephod, no teraphim.
> After that shall return the children of Israel,
>   and seek Yahweh their God, and David their King.

The last line confirms our previous reflections on the "Man who rules over man" as the paradigm, briefly called "David," that must be humanly realized through "seeking" as God must be realized existentially through faith.

In Amos and Hosea, the cosmological form still exerted a strong influence on their conception of the process of history. Although their alternatives of disaster and salvation went beyond the restoration of order through the cult, they substantially did no more than break the cosmic rhythm down to a sequence of disorder and order in historical [476] time. With Isaiah, the younger contemporary of Hosea, begins the insight that one cannot advance from the cycle, in which institutions are restored through the cult, to the irreversible emergence of ultimate order in history without radically recasting the symbols. When the ebb and flood of cosmic order becomes the darkness and light of successive periods in history, new expressions for the dynamics of order, not yet provided in the compactness of cosmological symbols, must be differentiated. With Isaiah the experience of metastasis, of the substantive transfiguration of order, that was inchoately present even in Amos and Hosea, enters the prophetic concern with Israel's rulership. The motivations of Israel's experience, as well as its evolution in the course of about four decades following the call of *ca.* 740/34, are still discernible in the sequence of prophecies which at present form the text of Isaiah 6-12. [The following interpretation of Isaiah relies strongly on Buber 1949.]

The first of the distinctive Isaianic symbols is the Lord, who sits on his throne "high and exalted," while the skirt of his robe fills the Temple. Yahweh is the thrice-holy King above the earth, while at the same time "the fullness of the whole earth is his *kabhod*," his glory or divine substance (6:1-5). The symbolism of the Trisagion passage is of cultic origin, but Isaiah employs it to express the presence of the divine *kabhod* over all the earth throughout the time of history. And from this ever-present *kabhod* derives the Isaianic dynamics of history. For the *kabhod* can become the substance of order in society and history only when men let themselves be penetrated by it through faith; order depends on the human response to the *kabhod*. The historical metastasis of the world, as distinguished from the cultic restoration, into the realm of God the King requires the responsive change of heart. Moreover, this knowledge of historical dynamics comes to Isaiah (and through him), because in the vision of the call he responds to the revelation of the *kabhod* by volunteering as the messenger of Yahweh to his people (6:8). The metastasis has actually begun in his person and is to expand through the prophecies that Isaiah will address to Israel, though the message will be effectively heard only after the terrible disasters caused by the stubbornness of the people (6:9-13)

How Isaiah's understanding of his call developed through the next five to ten years, we do not know. As the text stands, the account of the call is the preface to his great political intervention, to his appeal to King [477] Ahaz in the hour of danger to place his trust in Yahweh rather than in military preparations for the clash with the Northern Kingdom and Syria. The Davidic institution of the Anointed of Yahweh still has so much weight with Isaiah, at least at this time, that he re-enacts the encounter Prophet-King even now, when the King is to be drawn beyond the institution into transfiguration. The metastasis that has begun in the prophet can gain its social dimension of order in Israel only through co-operation of the "Man who rules over man," of the King of Judah. The trust of the King will transfigure the order of history, so that not only will the imminent disaster be averted, but the *kabhod* will actually fill the order of Israel forever (7:1-9). But the King responds to the appeal with eloquent silence, and the prophet is forced to offer him a "sign" of his choice to confirm the truth of the oracle (7:10-11). This time the King politely declines, for the acceptance of a "sign" would commit him and perhaps interfere with his more earthy plans for the defense of Jerusalem (7:12). With the King's refusal to have anything to do with Isaiah's appeal, the attempt to operate the metastasis through the present ruler has come to its end. At this juncture, Isaiah turns from the present to the future, without abandoning the conception of order through kingship. At the command of Yahweh he gives the King the "sign," though he does not want it, but it is a "sign" concerning Ahaz' successor in the kingship. "The young woman," says the oracle, presumably the queen, is about to bear a son. She will call him *immanu-el*, With-us-God—a symbolic name that spins out the theme of Isaiah's call, of the "Fullness of the whole earth—his *kabhod.*" This child, in whom the *kabhod* of God will be "with us," is the future King, who knows to refuse evil and to choose good. But by the time he will be able to make the choice, the country will have been devastated by wars so thoroughly that it has reverted from an agricultural to a pastoral economy, thanks to the present King, who refuses good and chooses evil (7:13-17). The scene between the Prophet and the King closes with this threat and this promise.

About the sequel to the encounter between Prophet and King again [478] we know nothing. Nevertheless, since the following text 7:18-8:10 brings a series of oracles which elaborate the Immanuel prophecy, we can surmise that Isaiah's situation must have become difficult: When a prophet, perhaps accompanied by a group of disciples, proclaims in public that he is waiting for an Immanuel to replace the reigning King, his activity can be construed as incitement to rebellion. Some friction of this kind must have developed indeed, for in 8:11 Yahweh has to grasp his prophet's hand strongly so that he will not give in to the ways of the people. He must not call a conspiracy what they call a conspiracy, nor fear what they fear (8:13). Difficulties of this kind must be assumed as the background for Isaiah's immediately following resolve to withhold his prophecies of a metastatic ruler from the public and to entrust them as a secret to his disciples (*limmudim*) (8:16). In the meanwhile, waiting for the coming of the *kabhod,* Isaiah and his children would "remain as signs and wonders in Israel from Yahweh of the hosts" (8:17-18). The remnant of Israel, as the bearer of the sealed message, thus has become historically present in Isaiah, his children, and his disciples.

The message itself, "the testimony bound up, and the instruction sealed," is contained in the prophecy of the Prince of Peace (9:1-6), beginning with the lines:

> The people that walk in darkness
> have seen a great light.

This light, shining brightly over those who dwell in the shadow of death, is the newborn child, the future ruler (9:5):

> For a child is born to us,
> a son is given to us.

On his shoulders will rest the *misrah*—a term which occurs in this context in the Old Testament and is perhaps best translated by the

Latin *principatus*; and his name will be—among others, which the difficult text does not permit us to separate with certainty—Prince of Peace (9:5). The zeal of Yahweh will bring this about (9:6)

> For the increase of lordship [*misrah*], and for peace without
>     end,
> upon the throne of David, and over his Kingdom,
> to establish it, and to uphold it,
> in justice, and in righteousness,
> henceforth, and forever.

This prophecy must be treated with caution, for its text is so terse that under pressure it will easily render any meaning desired. What can [479] be asserted safely is the continuity with the Immanuel oracle: The child is still a ruler on the throne of David and over his Kingdom, wielding his *misrah* over the remnant of Israel, though we must note that the descent from the royal house is no longer stressed and even the royal style is carefully avoided. Beyond this point the interpretation becomes hazardous, which is all the more regrettable since the injunction of secrecy indicates that a matter of some importance is involved. What is so dangerously new about the Prince of Peace, that the prophecy must not be communicated to the public which is already in possession of the Immanuel oracle? Or is really nothing back of that secrecy but a human fear of unpleasantness at the hands of an irate populace or the authorities? Following the suggestions of Martin Buber we suspect that the answer to such questions is to be found in the closing line (9:6) that "the zeal of Yahweh of the hosts will perform this." If this phrase is taken at its full weight, it means that the transfiguration of history will no longer remain in the suspense which characterizes the meeting with Ahaz. The time for appeals will come to an end; God will not wait forever for a response that is not forthcoming, but will himself provide the man who responds, so that his *kabhod* will fill the earth in its realized order. That would indeed be a fundamental change in the position of Isaiah, and it would also explain why this knowledge should be "bound up and sealed." For such knowledge would be of no use to the men who do not respond to the appeal, least of all to the recalcitrant Kings of Judah; it is of importance only for the remnant, that is, for Isaiah and his disciples, who will have to wait until the present crisis has run its course and Yahweh provides them with the child that will rule over them as the new Israel.

This interpretation is confirmed by the last of the great metastatic prophecies, in Isaiah 11:1-9. The text is neither related to a concrete situation nor is the continuity discernible that would link it with the Prince of Peace prophecy, as the latter one is linked with the Immanuel oracle. Its place as the last one in the series of great prophecies related by their contents indicates probably a late date; perhaps it is something like a "last word" of Isaiah on these questions. It opens with a passage that restores the connection with the Davidic dynasty (11:1):

> A shoot shall come forth from the stem of Jesse,
> and a sprout shall spring out of his roots.

A stem, or stump, of the dynasty, thus, will survive the disaster; and from this Davidic remnant, as from the people's remnant the new Israel, [480] its new ruler will spring forth. And he is the ruler not because he has refused evil and chosen good like Immanuel but because the spirit, the *ruach*, of God has descended upon him (11:2):

> There will come to rest upon him the *ruach* of Yahweh—
> The *ruach* of wisdom and understanding,
> The *ruach* of counsel and might,
> The *ruach* of knowledge [*da'ath*] and fear of Yahweh.

With this endowment he will be the King after the model of David, in fear of Yahweh and in righteousness, but yet something more than a David, for he will judge not by what he sees and hears, but by true justice and fairness (11:3-5). The *kabhod* has penetrated the structure of the world indeed, and the metastasis is complete:

> And the wolf shall dwell with the lamb,
> and the leopard shall lie down with the kid.

There will be no harm nor destruction on all the God's Holy Mountain, for the earth shall be full of the *da'ath* of Yahweh, as the waters cover the sea (11:9).

The symbols of Isaiah 11:1-9, finally, are resumed in Isaiah 2:2-4 in order to enlarge the vision of the transfigured Israel into a vision of metastatic world peace. For in "the end of days" it shall come to pass that the nations will stream to it, saying (2:3):

> Come! let us go up to the mountain of Yahweh,
> to the house of the God of Jacob;
> and he will teach of his ways,
> that we may walk in his paths;
> for from Zion goes forth Instruction [*torah*],
> Word-of-Yahweh from Jerusalem.

Yahweh himself will be the judge between the nations; "they will beat their swords into plowshares" and learn no more the art of war (2:4). Governmental institutions and their human incumbents are no longer mentioned.

The prophecies of Isaiah thus move from the appeal to the historically real King Ahaz to the "sign" of a more responsive, future Immanuel; from Immanuel to the Prince of Peace who will rule on the throne of David, not over the contemporary, empirical Israel, but over the remnant that is gaining historical concreteness in Isaiah and his disciples; [481] from the Prince of Peace to a "remnant" of the Davidic dynasty on whom the *ruach* has descended; and, finally to a vision of world peace in which the institutions have lost their distinctness. With the articulation of the metastatic experience, with the unfolding of its consequences, the institutional problems arising from human recalcitrance to the realization of the *kabhod* must indeed become irrelevant. For the *ruach* of Yahweh has transfigured human nature, so that the order of society and history has become substantively the order of the *kabhod*.

When the metastatic experience had been explored to its limits by Isaiah, prophetism had arrived at an existential impasse. While Amos and Hosea could still envisage a restoration of the Kingdom after the Davidic model, Isaiah had thoroughly eliminated the cultic tension of institutional order from the sequence of darkness and light; within two generations, the pressure of historical form had driven the cultic symbolism against the blank wall of the metastatic vision. The prophet's situation was no longer that of an Egyptian sage in the breakdown of empire between the Old and Middle Kingdoms. Since in the Egyptian crisis the cosmological form was not broken, the expectation of a Savior-Pharaoh— "Ameni, the triumphant, his name," "the son of a woman from the land of Nubia"—could be fulfilled through the re-establishment of imperial order. The metastatic faith of the prophet, on the contrary, precluded fulfillment through any pragmatic establishment. Once the faith in the metastasis of social and cosmic order through an act of God had achieved the rigidity of full articulation, there was nothing one could do but sit down and wait for the miracle to happen. If it did not happen—and it has not happened to this day—the prophet would die while waiting; and if he had formed a group of disciples, who would transmit his faith to future disciples, generations might pass before the experience of their passing would become a motive of sufficient strength to reexamine the validity of what had become an article of faith. Hence, [482] it was perhaps not merely a question of suppression by the new regime under Menasseh that no prophets appeared in the generation following Isaiah and Micah. Moreover, an abeyance of prophetism as a consequence of the metastatic impasse is suggested by the peculiar structure of the Book of Isaiah. In the collection that goes in the Bible under the name of "Isaiah" one can distinguish between the Isaianic prophecies proper (Isa 1-35) with its appendixes (Isa 36-39); the prophecies of the anonymous Deutero-Isaiah (Isa 40-55), to be dated in the middle of the sixth century B.C.; and a collection of later oracles, of various unknown authorship, usually called the Trito-Isaiah (Isa 56-66). If it is assumed that the three parts of the collection were not assembled by accident but that they represent the body of traditions preserved by a prophetic circle which in continuity derived from Isaiah and his disciples, there would be a gap of about a century and a half in the tradition between Isaiah himself and the Anonymous of the sixth century. If it be further assumed that the gap is not due to the accidental loss of the sayings of one or more great prophets but that indeed no prophet of sayings of note arose within the Isaianic circle during this time, the long silence would indicate the sterility of waiting for the metastasis. And finally, it is even doubtful whether the mere waiting and the lapse of time would have furnished a sufficient motive for the re-examination of symbols. For when prophecy is at last resumed in Deutero-Isaiah, the symbols of the anonymous prophet bear the imprint not only of the Isaianic tradition but distinctly of the work of Jeremiah.

In Jeremiah we have to look for the experiences which advanced the understanding of order beyond the metastatic visions of Isaiah. As the first motive must be noted the lapse of time, though its effect is difficult to gauge. Between the calls of Isaiah and Jeremiah more than a hundred years had passed. That was time enough for a prophetic personality which did not belong to the inner circle of Isaiah's disciples, but rather formed itself through the study of Hosea, to relax the tension of gazing into a future which never became present. For the order of being is the order in which man participates through his existence while it lasts; and the consciousness of passing, the presence of death in life, is the great cor- [483] rective for futuristic dreams—

though it may require a strong personality to break such dreams, once they have become a social power in the form of accepted creeds. The fundamental concern of man is with the attunement of his existence, in the present tense, to the order of being. And Jeremiah indeed returned from the metastatic vision of the future to the experience of the untransfigured present. In this return, however, he did not have to break altogether with Isaiah. For his great predecessor, in spite of the extreme articulation of his experience in the symbols of the metastatic ruler, had achieved a solid advance, never to be abandoned, in the understanding of order: that the order of society in history is reconstituted in fact through the men who challenge the disorder of the surrounding society with the order they experience as living in themselves. The word of the prophet is not spoken to the wind, it is not futile or impotent, if it does not reform the society which he loves because it has given him birth. The Word that speaks through him is itself historical and forms the order of a new community wherever it is heard. In Isaiah, his sons and disciples, the "remnant" of Israel, which had been the contents of prophecies of salvation, had become the reality of salvation. The prophetic word about the future became historical present in the men who spoke and preserved it in community. And while the Israel that was pragmatically organized as the Kingdom of Judah went the way of all organizations, their governments, and kings in history, the Word spoken by the prophets and preserved by the communities which heard it, still forms the "remnant" of Israel in the present. This insight into the meaning of prophetic existence as the continuation of order in history, when its realization in the pragmatic order of a people is in crisis, was the heritage from Isaiah to be increased by Jeremiah.

Isaiah had received the "Messianic problem" from Amos and Hosea in its institutional form of an Israel under a king after the model of David. In his own experience of order the institutional form was preserved, even though it was now burdened with the metastatic act of trust he demanded of King Ahaz. When the King had the good sense not to make experiments in transfiguration, Isaiah neither abandoned the institutional form nor the metastatic will, but the metastasis had to be drawn out into the formation of a remnant by the prophet himself and its completion through the future appearance of a ruler. Moreover, in so far as being the carrier of the secret concerning the future ruler was the essence of the remnant, its formation had the characteristics of a first [484] step toward the complete metastasis— in this respect the procedure of Isaiah foreshadows the later types of metastasis by "installment." If the problem of order was to be restored to its concreteness, Jeremiah had to reverse the futuristic projection of Isaiah and to bring the King back into the present. This he did, as we have seen, when in the oracles of his call he transferred the royal symbolism to himself. The order of Israel was complete in the present again, though contracted into the existence of the Jeremiah who enacted the fate of the people while carrying the burden of the Anointed. This is the third, the existential, phase in the prophetic occupation with the "Messianic problem."

The effort that went into this achievement must have been enormous. In order to see it in its true proportions, it should be recalled that this *tour de force* of recapturing the present was conducted within the limits which the compactness of the prophetic experience set to Jeremiah as much as to Amos, Hosea, or Isaiah. The prophetic symbolism, we remember, derived from the rites of defeat and victory in the New Year's festivals; under the pressure of the historical form, the cultic tension of order had dissolved into the successive periods of disaster and salvation. The prophetic experience, thus, was essentially metastatic. And we have traced the expression of this character in the prophets' criticism of conduct under decalogic categories, in their struggle for the existential order of man through virtues, and in their creation of the symbol of a new Covenant that will transfigure world and society. In all of these respects the prophecies of Jeremiah not only conformed to the type but even brought it to perfection. And no more than in the general structure of his prophecy did Jeremiah deviate from the type in his articulation of the "Messianic problem," especially in Jeremiah 23:1-8. That the problem had undergone a change of complexion for him became noticeable only in the fact that his prophecies did not continue or elaborate the Isaianic symbols but reverted to the prediction of a remnant under a Davidic model-king, as we found them in Amos and Hosea. This firmness of the prophetic form was the burden that had to be carried by Jeremiah; it must be taken into account if one wants to estimate the strength that was necessary, not to break it—even a Jeremiah could not [485] do that—but to become aware that the problems of order did not revolve around the empirical Israel and its institutions but around the man who suffered concretely under the disorder. Hence the greatness of Jeremiah's achievement does not become manifest in the general body of his oracles which run true to a standardized form, but in the oracles of his call, in the enactment of Israel's fate, in the Temple Address and the trial. Above all, however, it must be sought in his creation of a new form of prophetic expression: What is new in his extant work are the pieces of spiritual biography in which the problems of prophetic existence, the concentration of order in the man who speaks the word of God, become articulate. The great motive that had animated the prophetic criticism of conduct and commendation of the virtues had at last been traced to its source in the concern with the order of personal existence under God. In Jeremiah the human personality had broken the compactness of collective existence and recognized itself as the authoritative source of order in society.

The type of experiences which forced Jeremiah back on himself and into the recognition of his personality as the battlefield of order and disorder in history, can be gathered from the notice about a conspiracy against his life (18:18):

Then they said:

> Come, and let us devise devices against Jeremiah.
> For the law shall not pass from the priest,
> nor counsel from the wise, nor the word from the prophet.
> Come, and let us smite him with the tongue,
> and let us not listen to any of his words.

The motive of the plot was Jeremiah's assumption of personal authority under God, which invalidated the people's traditional sources of authority in the priests, the wise, and the prophets (the "false prophets" of Jeremiah); and its purpose was to silence the word emanating from the new authority. In this danger Jeremiah turned to Yahweh with the question: "Shall evil be repaid for good, that they have dug a pit for my life?" (18:20). And assuming that this could not be God's intention he implored him to visit the conspirators, their wives, and their children with famine, pestilence, and violent death (18:21-23). In another notice of a plot to murder him, Jeremiah formulated the motive in the demand of his enemies: "You shall not prophesy in the name of Yahweh, lest you die by our hands" (11:21); and the notice is accompanied by the same [486] heartfelt plea to see his enemies come to grief (11:20, 22-23). This vengefulness of Jeremiah must not be covered with charitable silence, or treated with genteel discreteness, as if it were a weakness unbecoming a distinguished public figure. For it is precious evidence of the spiritual passion that burned in him. The man who predicted the destruction of Israel, Jerusalem, and the Temple; who wished on the King of Judah (22:19):

> With the burial of an ass shall he be buried,
> dragged about and flung out beyond the gates of Jerusalem;

was not the man to make exceptions for personal enemies. On the contrary, since he was the representative of divine order, forgiveness for an attack on his life would have been a presumptuous attribution of importance to his private sentiments and a betrayal of his status. The prophet of Israel could not condone an attack on the life that served Yahweh.

Moreover, the justice of God was at stake. In the vengeful wishes of Jeremiah was involved, as the text has shown, the torturing question of repayment for good and evil. To be sure, Israel deserved punishment for its sins, but how should order ever be restored if the punishment of the wicked was visited on Israel collectively and engulfed the good? Josiah, the Reformer-King, had fallen in the battle of Megiddo against Egypt; and Jeremiah was the target of plots against his life. There always would be some wicked around, and if the divine punishment did not become more discriminate, there would be no end of suffering. Jeremiah put his questions before God in the complaints of 15:10, 15:

> Woe is me, my mother, that you bore me,
> a man of strife and a man of contention to the whole earth!
> I have not lent, nor have men lent to me,
> yet all of them curse me.
> You well know of it,
> Yahweh, think of me, remember me,
> and avenge me of my persecutors.

God knows that the prophet suffers for his sake: Jeremiah cannot join the company of the sportive and make merry with them, because the hand of God is on him and forces him to sit alone (15:16-17). Why then is his pain unceasing, and his wound incurable? Will God be to him like a treacherous brook, like waters that are not sure? (15:18). To such questioning Yahweh answers (15:19):

> [487] If you turn back, I shall take you back,
> and before my face shall you stand;
> and if you bring forth the precious from the vile,
> as my mouth shall you be.

There is no answer to the questions: The questioning itself is the defection, from which Jeremiah must return to the presence of God; only when, through the return from questioning, he has brought forth the precious from the vile will he be the speaker of God's word.

The prophet has to live with the mystery of iniquity. But that is not easy: "My grief is incurable, my heart is sick within me" (8:18).

Jeremiah found no peace from these questions. He elaborated them most profoundly in the great dialogue of Jeremiah 12, where he presented them as a legal case for judgment to the God with whom he had the quarrel (12:1):

> In the right you are, Yahweh,
> if I contend with you—
> and yet of this case I must speak with you:
> Why is the way of the wicked happy?
> Why do those prosper who deal most treacherously?

Why does God not punish them individually but inflict misery collectively on the faithful together with the wicked? (12:4):

> How long shall the land mourn,
> and the herb of the whole field wither?
> Because of the wickedness of those who dwell in it,
> the beasts are consumed, and the birds.
> For they said: "He will not see our way."

To the question again comes no answer that would solve the mystery of iniquity, but the counterquestion (12:5):

> If you have run with the footmen,
> and they have wearied you,
> how then will you compete with horses?
> And if in the land of peace you fall down,
> how will you do in the jungle of Jordan?

Much more terrible things will happen than Jeremiah has experienced as yet—and he will have to live through them, the questions unanswered. But then the tension is relieved by the words of God, which must be understood as a soliloquy to which Jeremiah is permitted to listen (12:7 ff.):

> [488] I have forsaken my house,
>       have abandoned my heritage;
> I have given the beloved of my soul
>       into the hands of her enemies . . .
> My heritage has become to me
>       as a lion in the forest . . .

> Many shepherds have destroyed my vineyard,
>      they have trodden my portion under foot . . .
> The whole land is desolate,
>      yet no man lays it to heart.

What is the suffering of Jeremiah, compared with the suffering of God?

Prophetic existence is participation in the suffering of God. Beyond this insight gained by Jeremiah for his own person lies its application to everyman's existence. The prophet's secretary Baruch apparently was inclined sympathetically to experience the same sorrows as his master. When he had finished writing the words of Jeremiah, at his dictation, in a book, he must have complained often enough (45:3):

> Woe is me now!
> For Yahweh has added sorrow to my pain;
> I am weary with my groaning,
> and I find no rest.

For Jeremiah was authorized to transmit to him the succinct information, coming from Yahweh himself (45:4-5):

> Behold! What I have built, I will pull down;
> and what I have planted, I will tear up—
> and you seek great things for yourself?
> Seek them not!
> For behold! I will bring evil upon all flesh—
> says Yahweh—
> But your life will I give you, as a prize of war,
> in every place where you go . . .

## [§ 3. The Suffering Servant]

[491] . . . The metastatic experience of Isaiah, which hitherto has been considered under the aspect of a sterile withdrawal from the realities of Israel's order, will appear in a new light if it is considered as an experience of the gulf between true order and the order realized concretely by any society, even Israel. And Jeremiah's experience of the tension between the two orders, his suffering participation in the divine suffering, is even articulate enough to make it certain that the prophet had at least a glimpse of the terrible truth: that the existence of a concrete society in a definite form will not resolve the problem of order in history, that no Chosen People in any form will be the

ultimate omphalos of the true order of mankind. When Abram emigrated from Ur of the Chaldaeans, the Exodus from imperial civilization had begun. When Israel was brought forth from Egypt, by Yahweh and Moses his servant, and constituted as the people under God, the Exodus had reached the form of a people's theopolitical existence in rivalry with the cosmological form. With Isaiah's and Jeremiah's movement away from the concrete Israel begins the anguish of the third procreative act of divine order in history: The Exodus of Israel from itself. The anguish of this last Exodus was lived through by the unknown prophet who by a modern convention is designated as Deutero-Isaiah, because he is the author of Isaiah 40-55 . . .

[494] The text of Isaiah 40-55 is an accomplished literary composition *sui generis* which expresses certain experiences by means of the symbolic language developed in classical prophetism from Amos to Jeremiah. In the experiences expressed, clusters of motives can be distinguished. A first one is furnished by the historical events: the exile, the liberation through Cyrus, the fall of Babylon, and the vicissitudes of empire in general. A second cluster stems from the heritage of the great predecessors: the contraction of Israel into the solitary suffering of the prophet, the message to mankind that embraces both Israel and the nations, and above all the Isaianic secret of the *kabhod* that will fill the earth. A third cluster, finally, is formed by the motives to which the author himself refers as the "new things": the message of salvation; the self-revelation of God in three stages as the Creator of the world, as the Lord and Judge of history, and as the Redeemer (*goel*); the consciousness that the present is the epoch between the second and third stages; the suffering of the second stage as the way to redemption; redemption as the existential response to the third revelation of God as the Savior and Redeemer; the role of Israel as the representative sufferer for mankind on the way to the response; and the climax in Isaiah 52:13-53:12, in recognition of the Servant as the representative sufferer. While the distinction and classification of the motivating experiences is so amply supported by pieces of a meditative nature that the results are reasonably certain, the book as a whole is not a treatise in *oratio directa* on definite "doctrines." It is a symbolic drama which does not permit the separation of a contents from the manner of its presentation. Moreover, while the single motives can be distinguished, they have merged in the comprehensive experience of the movement that we have briefly characterized as the Exodus of Israel from itself. The text does not consist of a series of symbols expressing successive states of experience, so that it would be

left to the reader to reconstruct from them a spiritual biography of the author. The construction is done by the author himself, to whom the movement is given as completed in the retrospect of his work. Beyond the component symbols, the drama as a whole is a unit of meaning. The [495] Exodus has happened in the soul of the author, and his work is the symbol of a historical event.

If this is the nature of the work, the methods most frequently used in its interpretation must be considered inadequate:

(1) The drama, to be sure, is autobiographical in substance, but the evolution of experience is mediated by the author's interpretation in retrospect. Hence, we know nothing about that experience except what the author chooses to reveal. It is reasonable to assume that the experience of the exile and the victories of Cyrus sparked the movement that reached its climax in the Fourth Song, and also that the beginning and the end were not joined in a flash of insight but were separated by a considerable number of years—but it is reasonable only because the text itself suggests this evolution over the years. Any attempt to go beyond the drama and to reconstruct the author as a "historical" person is therefore not only hazardous but contributes nothing to the understanding of the work.

(2) The meaning of the drama cannot be found by tearing an important symbol out of its context and treating it as if it were a piece of somewhat enigmatic information. There exists a library of studies on the question "Who is the Suffering Servant?" Is he the author himself, or some other suffering personage, or does the symbol prophetically envisage Christ—or is he no individual at all but Israel, and if that should be the case is he the empirical or the ideal Israel, and is he the whole of Israel or a remnant? Such attempts to understand the Deutero-Isaianic work through solving the puzzle of the Servant is, on principle, not different from an attempt to understand an Aeschylean tragedy by means of a study on the question "Who is Prometheus" or "Who is Zeus?" And even when Glaucon in the *Republic* (361e) draws the figure of the just man "who will have to endure the lash, the rack, chains, the branding iron in his eyes, and at last, after suffering every kind of torture, will be impaled," nobody will search for the historical model of the sufferer, though the allusion to the suffering of the "historical" Socrates is considerably more probable than any lines that can be drawn from the Suffering Servant to a historical figure. If such studies can be undertaken in the case of Deutero-Isaiah nevertheless with at least a measure of sense, the reason must be sought in the difference between the Israelite historical and the Hellenic mythical form of order. The Aeschylean tragedy moves,

in search of order, from its compact expression in the [496] polytheistic myth toward the Logos of the psyche; the Deutero-Isaianic drama
moves from the compact revelation from Sinai toward the Logos of
God. From Aeschylus the movement goes toward the Platonic Vision
of the Agathon; from Deutero-Isaiah it goes toward the Incarnation
of the Logos. When man is in search of God, as in Hellas, the wisdom
gained remains generically human; when God is in search of man, as
in Israel, the responsive recipient of revelation becomes historically
unique. Since the human experience of revelation is an event in the
history constituted by revelation, historicity attaches to the recipient
of revelation, to the very historicity of Christ. As a consequence, the
question "Who is the Servant?" is not as outlandish in an Israelite
context as a comparable question with regard to an Hellenic literary
text would be. Nevertheless, while these reflections will cast some light
on the difference between the Logoi of philosophy and revelation, and
while they will make intelligible the tendency to search for the
historical figure behind the symbol of the Suffering Servant, they do
not justify the procedure. Isaiah 40-55 remains a literary composition;
and the symbols must be read as expressions of the author's evolving
experience, even though what he tries to communicate is an insight
concerning the revelation of God in history.

The various errors of interpretation, of which we have just adumbrated the two most important types, can be avoided only if one
penetrates to their root in the multiplicity of time levels running
through the work:

(1) The experience of the author evolves and matures over a period
of perhaps ten or more years. Hence, there runs through the work the
time of the experience from its inception to its completion. The
temptation is great, therefore, to isolate this level and to use the clues
of the text for a reconstruction of the "historical" course of the
experience. This attempt, however, is bound to fail, as we have
indicated, because the time of the experience has been absorbed into
the structure of the work. The author's own reconstruction bars this
possibility.

(2) The experience is inseparable from its expression in symbolic
form. In so far as the component oracles and songs originate at various
points of time in the course of the experience, the same argument
applies to them as to the time of the experience itself. The text as a
whole, however, is not a series of oracles in chronological order. It is
a composition in which the single pieces, regardless of the time of their
origin, are placed in such a manner that they express the meaning of
the experience [497] as it has accumulated during its course. The

compositorial work is itself part of the process in which the meaning of the experience is clarified; the revelation is received by the author completely only in the act of composition. Hence, the work is not the account of an experience that lies in the past, but the revelation itself at the moment of its supreme aliveness. From the human side, the time of the composition is the time which accumulates, the time in which one grows old and matures, the *durée* in the Bergsonian sense; from the divine side, it is the present under God in eternity. This is the time level to which in the literature on the subject practically no attention is given.

(3) The human response is an event in the history constituted by revelation. With the response begins the divine work of salvation, spreading through communication in space and time from the responsive human center. Since the symbols of the work picture the process of salvation, there is running through the work the time of salvation. And this time of salvation is not the inner time of a work of fiction, but the real time of the order of revelation in history. Hence, the symbols of the work, first, touch on the past history of revelation; they furthermore are concerned with the present revelation as received by the author, with the "new things" in the light of which the "former things" become a past of revelation; and they finally envisage the process of salvation as completed in the future through earthwide acceptance of the message that is received by the author, and communicated by his work, in the present. The time of salvation thus absorbs both the time of the experience and the time of the composition in so far as the historical process of the "new things" has its beginning in the experience of the author and continues in the composition of the work which communicates the revelation. This nature of the work as an event in the history of salvation, as the beginning of a process which in its symbols is imaged as extending into the future, is the inexhaustible source of difficulties for the interpreter. For there can hardly be a doubt that the Servant who dies in the Fourth Song is the same man who speaks of his call and his fate, in the first person, as the prophet in the Second and Third Songs. And is it not against common sense that a man gives an account of his death, as well as of its effects in the process of salvation? Such common-sense arguments have indeed become the basis for the assumption that the Fourth Song was written by a member of the circle after the death of the prophet who wrote the other three songs, and *a fortiori* that the work [498] as a whole (if it is a literary unit at all) could not have been written by the prophet to whom certain parts of it may be conceded.

The structure of the work is so intricate that only an extended commentary could do justice to it. For the purpose of this study it is sufficient to indicate the main parts of the organization and then to analyze the substantive problem which determines the detail of the composition.

The main organization of the work is easily to be discerned, because the incisions are marked by the position of the Servant Songs. The major subdivisions are: (1) A Prologue (Isa 40-41); (2) a First Part (Isa 42-48, barring the dubious Isa 47); (3) a Second Part (Isa 49-53); and (4) an Epilogue (Isa 44-55). The Prologue sets forth the message of salvation and its implications. The First Part, beginning with the First Song, deals with the salvation of Israel. It culminates in the exhortation to the exiles to leave Babylon and to let the news of the redemption spread to the ends of the earth (Isa 48:20-22). The spreading of the news of Israel's redemption forms the transition to the Second Part, beginning with the Second Song. The process of salvation now expands to the nations and culminates, in the Fourth Song, in the recognition of the Servant as the representative Sufferer by the kings of the gentiles. The hymns of the Epilogue, finally, envisage the process of salvation as completed for Israel (Isa 54) and the nations (Isa 55). A redeemed mankind will surround Jerusalem, in response to the Holy One of Israel.

The composition itself emerges from the substance of the revelation; and this substance is to be found in the opening oracle of the book (Isa 40:1-2):

> Comfort, O comfort my people—
>    says your God—
> Speak to the heart of Jerusalem,
>    and call to her:
> That her time of service is ended,
>    that her guilt is paid in full,
> That she has received from Yahweh,
>    double for all her sins.

The oracle marks an epoch in the history of prophetism inasmuch as it breaks with the classic form of the great prophets from Amos to Jeremiah and creates a new symbolic form. In the first place, it is not a "word [499] of Yahweh" spoken to the prophet, and through him, but a divine command of which the recipient is informed by heavenly voices. And to the mediation of the command in heaven there corresponds, second, a new mediating function of the prophet. For the hearer of the heavenly voices is no longer the mouth through which Yahweh warns his people to return to order, but the mediator of a message which supersedes the alternatives of punishment and salvation hinging on the existential appeal.

The meaning of this new type of prophecy will best be clarified through the elimination of suggestive misunderstandings:

(1) Since the guilt of Israel is atoned and the prophet has to bring the news of salvation without regard to the people's conduct, it is tempting to understand the message of the oracle as a prophecy of salvation of the older type. The new form would then not be so very "new," but a plain promise of salvation, unconditioned by reform of conduct; and it would become difficult to distinguish between Deutero-Isaiah and the "false prophets" of the eighth and seventh centuries. The new form, however, is not a mere matter of dropping one of the alternatives from the dual symbolism. For the suffering of Israel, far from having disappeared from the new prophecy, is one of its two major problems, balancing the concern with salvation. Hence, suffering and salvation are both present, but they have changed their complexion, as we may say provisionally, in as much as they are no longer "alternatives" linked by the appeal.

(2) Is the new complexion of suffering and salvation, then, due to the disappearance of the appeal? This assumption would be the second misunderstanding. For the salvation announced by Deutero-Isaiah is not a divine act that transfigures the order of Israel and mankind, but a revelation of God as the Redeemer. And since the revelation requires human response, the prophet has to appeal very energetically to the people not to reject the message of salvation (Isa 44:22):

> I have blotted out, as a vapor, your transgressions,
>     and, as a cloud, your sins;
> Return to me, for I have redeemed you.

And the appeal is resumed in the Epilogue (Isa 55:6):

> Seek Yahweh while he may be found,
> call upon him while he is near!

[500] Hence, the appeal has disappeared no more than the alternative, though it also has changed its complexion. For the whole question of the people's conduct lies now in the past: Israel *has* suffered for its defection, and it *has* been forgiven. The appeal is therefore no

longer concerned with conduct measured by the Sinaitic legislation, but with the acceptance of God the Redeemer.

(3) The form elements of the classic prophetic symbolism thus are all present, though in a different mode. Moreover, through the elimination of the misunderstandings, the cause of the change has been traced to the shift of the prophet's interest from the order of the Chosen People under the Sinaitic *berith* to an order under the Redeemer God. The character of this new order is flashlike illuminated by the prophet's use of the *berith* symbol. In Isa 42:6 the Servant is appointed as "a *berith* to the people, as a light to the nations." And more elaborately, in Isaiah 55:3-5, the prophet lets God say:

> Incline your ear, and come to me;
> hear, and your soul shall live!
> For I shall make you a berith forever,
> the mercies of David [*dwd*] which are sure.
> Behold, I have given him as a witness to the peoples,
> a prince and commander to the peoples.
> Behold, a nation you know not shall you call,
> and a nation that knows you not shall run to you,
> for the sake of Yahweh, your God
> and the Holy One of Israel, for he has glorified you.

If the two texts be conjoined, the "*berith* forever" of 55:3 is the Servant who was appointed, in 42:6, as the "light to the nations" and is now given as the "witness, prince, and commander" to the peoples. This princely Servant, who is glorified by Yahweh, will call to the nations, and his call will be heard for the sake of the Holy One of Israel. In this manner there will be established the order of mankind envisaged at the beginning of the work (Isa 40:5):

> Then shall be revealed the *kabhod* of Yahweh,
> and all flesh shall see it together,
> for the mouth of Yahweh has spoken it.

[501] The type of the new prophecy has now been sufficiently clarified to be placed in the history of Israelite order. From the imperial order in cosmological form emerged, through the Mosaic leap in being, the Chosen People in historical form. The meaning of existence in the present under God was differentiated from the rhythmic attunement to divine-cosmic order through the cult of the empire. The theopolity, supplemented by kingship for survival in

pragmatic history, however, still suffered under the compactness of its order. The order of the spirit had not yet differentiated from the order of the people's institutions and mores. First, in his attempt to clarify the mystery of the tension, Isaiah split the time of history into the compactly unregenerate present, and a quite as compactly transfigured future, of the concrete society. Through Jeremiah this unregenerate present then gained its existential meaning, in as much as the prophet's participation in divine suffering became the omphalos of Israelite order beyond the concrete society. And through Deutero-Isaiah, finally, there emerged from existential suffering the experience of redemption in the present, right here and now. The movement that we called the Exodus of Israel from itself, the movement from the order of the concrete society toward the order of redemption was thus completed. The term "completion" must be properly understood. It means that the order of being has revealed its mystery of redemption as the flower of suffering. It does not mean, however, that the vision of the mystery is the reality of redemption in history: the participation of man in divine suffering has yet to encounter the participation of God in human suffering . . .

[512] . . . The Servant's situation in the Third Song is transferred to the people at large. They are now those "in whose hearts is my instruction [*toroth*]" (51:7) and who, therefore, need not fear the reproaches of mortal men; and even the satisfaction of seeing their enemies consumed by the moth like a woolen garment is now granted to everybody (51:8). Finally, even the heralds with the good news of salvation reappear, announcing to Zion: "Your God has become King" (52:7). The section concludes with the exhortation to go out from the midst of the redeemed Jerusalem, from the omphalos of mankind, to bring the news of salvation to the nations and to spread it to the ends of the earth (52:8-12):

> Depart you! depart you! go out from thence!
>    Touch nothing unclean!
> Go out of the midst of her; keep yourselves pure,
>    you who bear the vessels of Yahweh!
> For you shall not go out in haste,
>    nor depart in flight,
> for Yahweh will go before you,
>    and the God of Israel will be your rearguard.

With the imagery of the Exodus from Egypt Israel is urged on to its Exodus from itself.

[513] In the Second and Third Songs the prophet is the speaker; in the First and Fourth Songs it is God. The Exodus that is now to be undertaken leads into the future, beyond the time of the prophet and his work. The time of salvation which entered the time of the prophet runs beyond it toward fulfillment. In the First Song, God presented the Servant to the heavenly audience and revealed his intention of salvation; in the Fourth Song, God presents the Servant as their representative sufferer to the kings and the nations, so that all can accept him and be saved. The God who is first and last has the first and last words in the drama of salvation that reaches from heaven to earth.

In the first part of the Song, God presents the Servant as the exalted ruler over mankind (Isa 52:13-15; the second and third lines of 52:14 are placed after 53:2):

> Behold! My servant shall prosper,
> he shall be exalted and lifted up, and be very high,
> As many were appalled at him
>
> . . . . . . . . . . . . . . . . .
> So shall he startle many nations,
> because of him kings shall shut their mouth,
> for what has not been told them shall they see,
> and what they have not heard shall they understand.

The presentation is answered by a chorus which consists of the kings and the nations, and perhaps also of the prophet's own people. We can speak of it as a chorus of mankind. They at last believe what they have been told about the Servant and his representative suffering (53:1-9):

> Who could have believed what we were told?
> And the arm of Yahweh—to whom was it revealed?
> For he grew up as a small shoot before us,
> and as a root out of dry land.
> No form had he nor comeliness, that we should look at him,
> no appearance that we should delight in him,
> so disfigured his appearance, unlike that of men,
> and his form unlike that of the sons of man.
> Despised and forsaken of men,
> a man afflicted by pains, and marked by sickness,
> and as one from whom men avert their faces,
> he was despised and we regarded him not.
> [514] Yet ours were the sicknesses he carried,
> and ours the pains he bore,

> while we regarded him stricken,
> smitten of God, and afflicted.
> He was wounded for our transgressions,
> he was bruised for our iniquities,
> the chastisement for our weal was upon him,
> and through his stripes we were healed.
> All we like sheep went astray,
> everyone his own way we turned,
> and Yahweh made fall on him
> the iniquity of us all.
> He was oppressed—and he humbled himself
>     and opened not his mouth—
> as a sheep that is led to the slaughter,
> and as a ewe before her shearers,
>     he was dumb,
>     and opened not his mouth.
> Through violence in judgment he was taken off,
> and to his fate who gave thought?
> He was cut off from the land of the living,
> for our transgressions the stroke fell on him.
> And they made his grave with the wicked,
> and with the rich in his deaths,
> although he had done no violence
> and there was no deceit in his mouth.

The unbelievable tale that now is believed, the mystery of representative suffering, is handed over from marveling mankind to heavenly voices which reflect (53:10):

> Yet Yahweh was pleased to crush him with sickness,
> truly he gave himself as a guilt-offering.
> He shall see seed that prolongs days,
> and the purpose of Yahweh shall prosper in his hand.

And from the heavenly voices the theme is finally taken over by God himself (53:11-12):

> Out of the travail of his soul he shall see light,
> he shall be satisfied with his knowledge:
> My Servant shall bring deliverance to many,
> and their iniquities he shall bear.
> [515] Therefore will I assign as his portion the many,
> and numberless shall be his spoil:
> Because he bared his soul unto death,

and with the transgressors he was numbered,
while he bore the sin of the many
and for the transgressors he interposed.

The Exodus from the cosmic-divine order of empire is completed. The Servant who suffers many a death to live, who is humili-
ated to be exalted, who bears the guile of the many to see them saved
as his offspring, is the King above the kings, the representative of
divine above imperial order. And the history of Israel as the people
under God is consummated in the vision of the unknown genius, for
as the representative sufferer Israel has gone beyond itself and become
the light of salvation to mankind.

About the effectiveness of the prophet's vision in the history of
Judaism almost nothing is known for the next five centuries. A trace
here and there in the apocalyptic literature reveals that there are "wise
among the people who bring understanding to the many" (Dan
11:33) in the tradition of Deutero-Isaiah. And such discoveries as the
Zadokite fragment and the Dead Sea scrolls prove that movements
related to this tradition must have been much stronger than the
canonical and rabbinical literature would let us suspect. These movements break to the historical surface again in Christianity. A prayer of
such intenseness as the Nunc dimittis of Luke 2:29-34 cannot be
explained as a literary reminiscence; it belongs to a living tradition of
Deutero-Isaiah. And the preoccupation with the problem of the
Suffering Servant is attested by the story of Acts 8: The Ethiopian
eunuch of the queen, sitting on his cart and reading Isaiah, ponders
on the passage: "Like a sheep he was led away to the slaughter." He
inquires of Philip: "Tell me, of whom is the prophet speaking? of
himself, or of someone else?" Then Philip began, reports the historian
of the Apostles, and starting from this passage he told him the good
news about Jesus.

# REFERENCES
## WRITINGS OF ERIC VOEGELIN

*A Anamnesis: Zur Theorie der Geschichte und Politik.* Munich: Piper, 1966.

*AE Anamnesis.* Trans. and ed. Gerhart Niemeyer. Notre Dame: University of Notre Dame Press, 1978. Reprint, Columbia: University of Missouri Press, 1990.

*AR Autobiographical Reflections.* Ed. Ellis Sandoz. Baton Rouge: Louisiana State University Press, 1989. Reprint with index, 1996.

BB The beginning and the beyond: A meditation on truth. In *CW*, vol. 28, *What Is History? and Other Late Published Writings*, ed. Thomas A. Hollweck and Paul Caringella, 1990.

*CEV Conversations with Eric Voegelin.* Thomas More Institute Papers, 1976. Ed. R. Eric O'Connor. Montreal: Thomas More Institute, 1980.

*CW The Collected Works of Eric Voegelin.* 34 vols. planned. Series ed. Paul Caringella et al. Vols. 1-3, 12, 27-28, Baton Rouge: Louisiana State University Press, 1990-98; remaining vols., Columbia: University of Missouri Press, 1997-.

EESH Equivalences of experience and symbolization in history. In *CW*, vol. 12, *Published Essays 1966-1985*, ed. Ellis Sandoz, 1990.

ER The eclipse of reality. In *CW*, vol. 28.

GC The gospel and culture. In *CW*, vol. 12.

GUOGS The German university and the order of German society: A reconsideration of the Nazi Era. In *CW*, vol. 12.

HG History and gnosis. In *The Old Testament and Christian Faith: A Theological Discussion*, ed. Bernhard W. Anderson. New York: Herder and Herder, 1969.

*HGe* Hitler and the Germans. Trans. and ed. Detlev Clemens and Brendan Purcell. In *CW*, vol. 31, 1999.

*HPI History of Political Ideas.* 8 vols. Series ed. Ellis Sandoz. Columbia: University of Missouri Press, 1997-99. In *The Collected Works of Eric Voegelin*, vols. 19-26, ed. Paul Caringella et al. Vol. 1, *Hellenism, Rome, and Early Christianity* (1997), ed. Athanasios Moulakis.

IES Immortality: Experience and symbol. In *CW*, vol. 12.

*IR Israel and Revelation.* See *OH* I.

MOPKO The meditative origin of the philosophical knowledge of order. In *The Beginning and the Beyond: Papers from the Gadamer and Voegelin Conferences.* Supplementary Issue of *Lonergan Workshop*, vol. 4. Trans. and ed. Frederick Lawrence. Chico: Scholars Press, 1984.

*NSP The New Science of Politics: An Introduction.* Charles R. Walgreen Foundation Lectures. Chicago: University of Chicago Press. 1952. Reprint with a foreword by Dante Germino, 1987.

*OBG Ordnung, Bewußtsein, Geschichte: Späte Schriften—Eine Auswahl.* Ed. Peter J. Opitz. Stuttgart: Klett-Cotta, 1988.

*OH I-V Order and History.* 5 vols. Baton Rouge: Louisiana State University Press, Vol. 1, *Israel and Revelation* (1956); vol. 2, *The World of the Polis* (1957); vol. 3, *Plato and Aristotle* (1957); vol. 4, *The Ecumenic Age* (1974); vol. 5, *In Search of Order* (1987).

OPP The Oxford political philosophers. *Philosophical Quarterly* 3 (1953): 97-114.

QDD Quod Deus dicitur. In *CW*, vol. 12.
RANH Response to Professor Altizer's "A new history and a new but ancient God?"
    In *CW*, vol. 12.
RCE Reason: The classic experience. In *CW*, vol. 12.
*RS Race and State*. *CW*, vol. 2. Trans. Ruth Hein. Ed. Klaus Vondung. 1997.
*SPG Science, Politics and Gnosticism: Two Essays*. First essay trans. William J.
    Fitzpatrick. Chicago: Henry Regnery, A Gateway Edition, 1968.
THST Toynbee's history as a search for truth. In *The Intent of Toynbee's History*, ed.
    Edward T. Gargan. Chicago: LoyolaUniversity Press, 1961.
WME Wisdom and the magic of the extreme: A meditation. In *CW*, vol. 12.
*WPG Wissenschaft, Politik und Gnosis*. Munich: Kösel-Verlag, 1959.
ZLS Zur Lehre von der Staatsform. *Zeitschrift für öffentliches Recht* 6 (1927):
    572-608.

## OTHER REFERENCES

Aaron, Raymond. 1961. *L'Histoire et ses interpretations: Entretiens autour de Arnold
    Toynbee sous la direction de Raymond Aaron*. Paris: Mouton et Cie.
Albrektson, Bertil. 1967. *History and the Gods: An Essay on the Idea of Historical
    Events as Divine Manifestations in the Ancient Near East and in Israel*. Lund: C.
    W. K. Gleerup.
Altizer, Thomas J. J. 1975. A new history and a new but ancient God? A review essay.
    *Journal of the American Academy of Religion* 43:757-72.
Anderson, Bernhard W. 1967. *Creation versus Chaos*. New York: Association Press.
———. 1971. Introduction to *A History of Pentateuchal Traditions*, by Martin
    Noth, trans. Bernhard W. Anderson. Englewood Cliffs: Prentice-Hall.
———. 1972. Review of *Genesis 1-11*, by Claus Westermann. *Journal of Biblical
    Literature* 91:243-45.
———. 1975. Myth and the biblical tradition. *Theology Today* 27:44-62.
———. 1976a. Biblical faith and political responsibility. *Theological Bulletin*
    [McMaster Divinity College] 4:5-11.
———. 1976b. Exodus and covenant in Second Isaiah and prophetic tradition. In
    *Magnalia Dei: The Mighty Acts of God: Essays on the Bible and Archaeology in
    Memory of G. Ernest Wright*, ed. Frank M. Cross, Werner E. Lemke, and Patrick
    D. Miller, Jr. Garden City, New York: Doubleday.
———. 1976c. Human dominion over nature. In *Biblical Studies in Contemporary
    Thought*, ed. Miriam Ward. Boston: Greeno, Hadden and Co.
———. 1985. Biblical theology and sociological interpretation. *Theology Today*
    42:292-306.
———. 1994. Human dominion over nature. In *From Creation to New Creation*.
    Philadelphia: Fortress.
———. 1995. Standing of God's promises: covenant and continuity in biblical
    theology. In *Biblical Theology: Problems and Perspectives*, ed. Steven J. Kraftchick
    et. al. Philadelphia: Fortress.
———. 1997. *Understanding the Old Testament*. 4th ed. Englewood Cliffs:
    Prentice-Hall.
———. 1999. *The Contours of Old Testament Theology*. Minneapolis: Augsburg/
    Fortress.
Augustine. 1972. *City of God*. Pelican Classics. Trans. Henry Bettenson. Ed. David
    Knowles. Baltimore: Penguin.

Baek, Seung-Hyun. 1989. Reality and knowledge in Voegelin's political philosophy. Ph.D. diss., Louisiana State University.

Baltzar, Klaus. 1960. *Das Bundesformular*. Neukirchen-Vluyn: Neukirchener Verlag.

Bandstra, Barry L. 1995. *Reading the Old Testament: An Introduction to the Hebrew
Bible*. Belmont: Wadsworth.

Barr, James. 1963. Revelation through history in the old testament and modern
theology. *Interpretation* 17:193-205.

———. 1966. *Old and New in Interpretation*. New York: Harper and Row.

———. 1968. Le Judaisme postbiblique et la théologie de la Ancien Testament.
*Revue de théologie et de philosophie* 18:209-17.

———. 1976. Story and history in biblical theology. *Journal of Religion* 56:1-17.

Barth, Christoph. 1947. *Die Errettung vom Tode in den Individuellen Klage- und
Dankliedern des Alten Testaments*. Zollikon: Evangelischer Verlag.

Bentzen, Aage. 1948. *Messias, Moses redivivus, Menschensohn: Skizzen zum Thema
Weissagung und Erf llung*. Zurich: Zwingli Verlag.

Berger, Peter L. 1969. *A Rumor of Angels: Modern Society and the Rediscovery of the
Supernatural*. Expanded ed., 1990. Garden City, New York: Doubleday.

Bergson, Henri. 1932. *Les deux sources de la morale et de la religion*. Paris: Librairie
Felix Alcan. Eng.: *The Two Sources of Morality and Religion*, trans. R. Ashley
Audra and Cloudesley Brereton with W. Horsfall Carter (Notre Dame: Univer-
sity of Notre Dame Press, 1963).

Blenkinsopp, Joseph. 1977. *Prophecy and Canon: A Contribution to the Study of
Jewish Origins*. Notre Dame: University of Notre Dame Press.

———. 1980. Tanakh and the New Testament: A Christian perspective. In *Biblical
Studies: Meeting Ground of Jews and Christians*, ed. Lawrence A. Boadt, Helga
Croner, and Leon Klenicki. New York: Paulist.

Bright, John. 1984. *Jeremiah*. Anchor Bible. 2d ed. Garden City, New York:
Doubleday.

Brooks, Roger, and John J. Collins, eds. 1990. *Hebrew Bible or Old Testament?:
Studying the Bible in Judaism and Christianity*. Notre Dame: University of Notre
Dame Press.

Brown, Peter. 1969. *Augustine of Hippo: A Biography*. Berkeley: University of
California Press.

Brueggemann, Walter. 1977. *Theology of the Old Testament: Testimony, Dispute,
Advocacy*. Minneapolis: Augsburg/Fortress.

———. 1978. *The Prophetic Imagination*. Minneapolis: Fortress.

Buber, Martin. 1948. *Moses*. Zurich: G. Muller.

———. 1949. *The Prophetic Faith*. Trans. Carlyle Witton-Davies. New York:
Macmillan.

———. 1963. *Israel and the World*. 2d ed. New York: Schocken.

Bultmann, Rudolf. 1962. Das Verständnis der Geschichte im Griechentum und im
Christentum. In *Politische Ordnung und menschliche Existenz: Festgabe für Eric
Voegelin zum 60. Geburtstag*, ed. Alois Dempf, Hannah Arendt, and Friedrich
Engel-Janosi. Munich: C. H. Beck.

———. 1963. Prophecy and fulfillment. In *Essays on Old Testament Hermeneutics*,
by Claus Westermann, ed. J. L. Mays. Richmond: John Knox Press.

Burchfield, Charles Warren. 1989. Eric Voegelin's mystical epistemology and its
influence on his theories of ethics and politics. Ph.D. diss., Louisiana State
University.

Burke, Edmund. 1993. *Reflections on the Revolution in France*. The World's Classics. Ed. L. G. Mitchell. New York: Oxford University Press.

Cahill, Michael. 1996. Reader-Response criticism and the allegorizing reader. *Theological Studies* 57:89-96.

Caputo, John D. 1993. *Demythologizing Heidegger*. Indianapolis: Indiana University Press.

Caringella, Paul. 1991. Voegelin: philosopher of divine presence. In *Eric Voegelin's Significance for the Modern Mind*, ed. Ellis Sandoz. Baton Rouge: Louisiana State University Press.

Chignola, Sandro. 1993. Fetischismus der Normen: Tra normativismo e sociologia; Eric Voegelin e la dottrina dello stato (1924-1938). *Rivista internazionale di filosofia del dritto*, 4th series, 70: 515-65.

Childs, Brevard. 1992. *Biblical Theology of the Old and New Testaments: Theological Reflection on the Christian Bible*. Minneapolis: Fortress.

Clements, R. E. 1965. *God and Temple*. Philadelphia: Fortress Press.

Cohn, Norman. 1981. *The Pursuit of the Millennium: Revolutionary Millenarians and Mystical Anarchists of the Middle Ages*. Rev. and expanded ed. New York: Oxford University Press, 1957, 1971. Reprint.

Cooper, Barry. 1986. *The Political Theory of Eric Voegelin*. Lewiston: Edwin Mellen.

———. 1989. *The Restoration of Political Science and the Crisis of Modernity*. Toronto: Edwin Mellen.

———. 1999. Eric Voegelin and the foundations of modern political science.

Corrington, John W. 1987. Order and consciousness/consciousness and history: The new program of Voegelin. In *Eric Voegelin's Search for Order in History*, expanded ed., ed. Stephen A. McKnight. Lanham, Md.: University Press of America.

Cross, Frank M. 1966. The divine warrior in Israel's early cult. In *Biblical Motifs*, ed. Alexander Altmann. Cambridge: Harvard University Press.

Damascenus, Johannes. *De fide orthodoxa*. Patrologia Graeca 94, 836. Paris: Migne, 1864.

Dempf, Alois, Hannah Arendt, and Friedrich Engel-Janosi, eds. 1962. *Politische Ordnung und Menschliche Existenz: Festgabe für Eric Voegelin zum 60. Geburtstag*. Munich: C. H. Beck.

Doran, Robert M. 1990. Theology and the Dialectics of History. Toronto: University of Toronto Press.

Douglass, Bruce. 1976. The gospel and political order: Eric Voegelin on the political role of Christianity. *Journal of Politics* 38:25-45.

———. 1977. The break in Voegelin's program. *Political Science Reviewer* 7:1-21.

———. 1987. A diminished gospel: A critique of Voegelin's interpretation of Christianity. In *Eric Voegelin's Search for Order in History*, expanded ed., ed. Stephen A. McKnight. Lanham, Md.: University Press of America.

Dworkin, Ronald. 1986. *Laws Empire*. Cambridge: Harvard University Press.

Eichrodt, Walther. 1955. Les Rapports du Nouveau et de l'Ancien Testament. In *Le problème biblique dans le protestantisme*, ed. Jean Boisset. Les Problèmes de la pensée chrétienne, vol. 7. Paris: Presses universitaires de France.

———. 1961. *Theology of the Old Testament*. Trans. J. A. Baker. Philadelphia: Westminster.

Emberley, Peter, and Barry Cooper, trans. and ed. 1993. *Faith and Political Philosophy: The Correspondence between Leo Strauss and Eric Voegelin, 1934-1964*. University Park: Pennsylvania State University Press.

Engnell, Ivan. 1969. *A Rigid Scrutiny: Critical Essays on the Old Testament*. Trans. and ed. John T. Willis. Nashville: Vanderbilt University Press.

Fackenheim, Emil L. 1972. *God's Presence in History: Jewish Affirmations and Philosophical Reflections*. New York: Harper and Row.

Fohrer, Georg. 1957. *Messiasfrage und Bibelverständnis*. Tübingen: J. C. B. Mohr.

Forster, Karl, ed. 1960. *Christentum und Liberalismus: Eric Voegelin, Erich Mende, Paul Mikat, Gustav Gundlach, Alexander Rhstow, Paul Luchtenberg, Wilhelm Geiger*. Munich: Karl Zink Verlag.

Frankfort, H., et al. 1946. *The Intellectual Adventure of Ancient Man*. Chicago:University of Chicago Press.

Franz, Michael. 1992. *Eric Voegelin and the Politics of Spiritual Revolt: The Roots of Modern Ideology*. Baton Rouge: Louisiana State University Press.

Gabler, Johann P. 1992. On the proper distinction between biblical and dogmatic Theology and the specific objectives of each. In *The Flowering of Old Testament Theology: A Reader in Twentieth-Century Old Testament Theology, 1930-1990*, ed. Ben C. Ollenburger, Elmer A. Martens, and Gerhard F. Hasel. Winona Lake, Ind.: Eisenbrauns.

Gadamer, Hans-Georg. 1989. *Truth and Method*. 2d rev. ed. Trans. Joel Weinsheimer and Donald G. Marshall. New York: Crossroad.

Germino, Dante. 1972. *Beyond Ideology: The Revival of Political Theory*. Chicago: University of Chicago Press, 1967. Reprint.

———. 1982. *Political Philosophy and the Open Society*. Baton Rouge: Louisiana State University Press.

———. 1995. Leo Strauss *versus* Eric Voegelin on faith and political philosophy. *Rivista internazionale di filosofia del dritto*, 4th series, 72:527-48.

Gillman, Neil. 1990. *Sacred Fragments: Recovering Theology for the Modern Jew*. Philadelphia: Jewish Publication Society.

Gilson, Étienne. 1948. *L'Esprit de la philosophie médiévale*. Gifford Lectures. 2d ed. rev. Paris: Vrin.

Gowan, Donald E. 1975. *When Man Becomes God: Humanism and Hubris in the Old Testament*. Pittsburgh: Pickwick Press.

Greenstein, Edward L. 1984. Biblical law. In *Back to the Sources*, ed. Barry W. Holtz. New York: Simon and Schuster, Summit Books.

Hanson, Paul D. 1971. Old Testament apocalyptic reexamined. *Interpretation* 25:454-79.

———. 1975. *The Dawn of Apocalyptic: The Historical and Sociological Roots of Jewish Apocalyptic Eschatology*. Philadelphia: Fortress.

———. 1986. *The People Called: The Growth of Community in the Bible*. San Francisco: Harper and Row.

Havard, William C. 1962. The disenchantment of the intellectuals. In *Politische Ordnung und menschliche Existenz: Festgabe für Eric Voegelin*, ed. Alois Dempf, Hannah Arendt, and Frederich Engel-Janosi. Munich: C. H. Beck, 1962.

———. 1984. *The Recovery of Political Theory: Limits and Possibilities*. Baton Rouge: Louisiana State University Press.

Hayes, John H., and Frederick Prussner. 1985. *Old Testament Theology: Its History and Development*. Atlanta: John Knox Press.

Heilke, Thomas W. 1990. *Voegelin on the Idea of Race: An Analysis of Modern European Racism*. Baton Rouge: Louisiana State University Press.

Henriques, Mendo Castro. 1992. Filosofia civil de Eric Voegelin. Ph.D. diss., Catholic University of Portugal (Lisbon).

Herberg, Will. 1976a. The Christian mythology of socialism. In *Faith Enacted as History: Essays in Biblical Theology*, ed. Bernhard W. Anderson. Philadelphia: Westminster.

———. 1976b. Society, democracy, and the state: A biblical-realist view. In *Faith Enacted as History*.

Heschel, Abraham Joshua. 1951. *Man Is Not Alone: A Philosophy of Judaism*. New York: Farrar, Straus and Young.

———. 1955. *God in Search of Man: A Philosophy of Judaism*. New York: Farrar, Straus and Cudahy.

———. 1962. *The Prophets: An Introduction*. Vol. 1. New York: Harper and Row.

———. 1996. *Moral Grandeur and Spiritual Audacity*. Ed. Susannah Heschel. New York: Farrar, Straus, Giroux.

Heschel, Susannah. 1994. The image of Judaism in nineteenth-century Christian New Testament scholarship in Germany. In *Jewish-Christian Encounters over the Centuries: Symbiosis, Prejudice, Holocaust, and Dialogue*, ed. Marvin Perry and Frederick M. Schweitzer. New York: Peter Lang.

Hillers, Delbert. 1969. *Covenant: The History of a Biblical Idea*. Baltimore: Johns Hopkins University Press.

Hollweck, Thomas A., and Ellis Sandoz, eds. 1997. A general introduction to the series. In *History of Political Ideas*, vol. 1, by Eric Voegelin. Vol. 19 of *The Collected Works of Eric Voegelin*, ed. Athanasios Moulakis. Columbia: University of Missouri Press.

Hughes, Glenn. 1993. *Mystery and Myth in the Philosophy of Eric Voegelin*. Columbia: University of Missouri Press.

Johnson, Aubrey. 1949. *The Vitality of the Individual in the Thought of Ancient Israel*. Cardiff: University of Wales Press.

Johnson, Elizabeth A. 1994. *She Who Is: The Mystery of God in Feminist Theological Discourse*. New York: Crossroad.

Kessler, Udo. 1995. *Die Wiederentdeckung der Transzendenz: Ordnung von Mensch und Gesellschaft im Denken Eric Voegelins*. Würzburg: Könighausen und Neumann Verlag.

Keulman, Kenneth. 1990. *The Balance of Consciousness: Eric Voegelin's Political Theory*. University Park: Pennsylvania State University Press.

King, Martin Luther, Jr. 1986. Letter from Birmingham City Jail. In *A Testament of Hope: The Essential Writings and Speeches of Martin Luther King, Jr.*, ed. James Melvin Washington. New York: HarperCollins.

Kirby, John, and William M. Thompson. 1983. *Voegelin and the Theologian: Ten Studies in Interpretation*. Toronto Studies in Theology, vol. 10. New York: Edwin Mellen.

Klein, Charlotte. 1978. *Anti-Judaism in Christian Theology*. Trans. Edward Quinn. Philadelphia: Fortress.

Kroeker, P. Travis. 1993. The theological politics of Plato and Isaiah: A debate rejoined. *Journal of Religion* 73:16-30.

Lacocque, André. 1957. The Old Testament in the Protestant tradition. In *Biblical Studies: Meeting Ground of Jews and Christians*, ed. Lawrence Boadt, Helga Croner, and Leon Klenicki. New York: Paulist.

Langan, Thomas. 1996. *Being and Truth*. Columbia: University of Missouri Press.

Lemke, Werner E. 1992. Theology (Old Testament). In *The Anchor Bible Dictionary*, vol. 6, ed. David Noel Freedman. New York: Doubleday.

Levenson, Jon. 1993. *The Hebrew Bible, the Old Testament, and Historical Criticism: Jews and Christians in Biblical Studies.* Louisville: Westminster/John Knox.

Levinas, Emmanuel. 1969. *Totality and Infinity: An Essay on Exteriority.* Trans. Alphonso Lingis. Pittsburgh: Duquesne University Press.

———. 1985. *Ethics and Infinity: Conversations with Philippe Nemo.* Trans. Richard A. Cohen. Pittsburgh: Duquesne University Press.

———. 1987. *Time and the Other.* Trans. Richard A. Cohen. Pittsburgh: Duquesne University Press.

———. 1989. *The Levinas Reader.* Ed. Sean Hand. Oxford: Blackwell.

Levy, David J. 1981. *Realism: An Essay in Interpretation and Social Reality.* Manchester: Carcanet New Press.

———. 1987. *Political Order: Philosophical Anthropology, Modernity, and the Challenge of Ideology.* Baton Rouge: Louisiana State University Press.

———. 1993. *The Measure of Man: Incursions in Philosophical and Political Anthropology.* Columbia: University of Missouri Press.

Lods, Adolphe. 1948. *Israel from Its Beginnings to the Middle of the Eighth Century.* Trans. S. H. Hooke. New York: Knopf, 1932. Reprint.

Mackler, Aaron. 1980. Bridge or barrier? Martin Buber on halakhah, man and God. *Conservative Judaism* 33:38-43.

———. 1991. Symbols, reality, and God: Heschel's rejection of a Tillichian understanding of religious symbols. *Judaism* 40:290-300.

Macquarrie, John. 1994. *Heidegger and Christianity.* New York: Continuum.

Maimonides, Moses. 1963. *The Guide of the Perplexed.* Trans. Shlomo Pines. Chicago: University of Chicago Press.

Mann, Thomas. 1963. *Joseph and His Brothers.* Trans. H. T. Lowe-Porter. New York: Alfred A. Knopf.

McAllister, Ted V. 1996. *Revolt against Modernity: Leo Strauss, Eric Voegelin and the Search for a Postliberal Order.* Lawrence: University of Kansas Press.

McGinn, Bernard. 1991. *The Presence of God: A History of Western Christian Mysticism.* Vol. 1, *The Foundations of Mysticism: Origins to the Fifth Century.* New York: Crossroad.

McGregor, Bede, and Thomas Norris, eds. 1994. *The Beauty of Christ: An Introduction to the Theology of Hans Urs von Balthasar.* Edinburgh: T and T Clark.

McKnight, Stephen A. 1975. Recent developments in Voegelin's philosophy of history. *Sociological Analysis* 36:36.

———. 1987. *Eric Voegelin's Search for Order in History.* Baton Rouge: Louisiana State University Press, 1978. Expanded ed., Lanham, Md.: University Press of America.

———. 1991. *The Modern Age and the Recovery of Ancient Wisdom: A Reconsideration of Historical Consciousness, 1450-1650.* Columbia: University of Missouri Press.

———. ed. 1992. *Science, Pseudo-Science, and Utopianism in Early Modern Thought.* Columbia: University of Missouri Press.

McKnight, Stephen A., and Geoffrey L. Price, eds. 1997. *International and Interdisciplinary Perspectives on Eric Voegelin.* Columbia: University of Missouri Press.

Mendenhall, George E. 1954. Law and covenant in Israel and the Ancient Near East. *Biblical Archaeologist* 12:nos. 2 and 3.

Miller, Patrick. 1977. Editorial. *Theology Today* 29 (March).

Miskotte, Kornelis H. 1967. *When the Gods Are Silent*. New York: Harper and Row.

Morrissey, Michael P. 1994. *Consciousness and Transcendence: The Theology of Eric Voegelin*. Notre Dame: University of Notre Dame Press.

Myers, Todd Eric. 1997. Nature and the divine: Classical Greek philosophy and the political in the thought of Leo Strauss and Eric Voegelin. Ph.D. diss., Louisiana State University.

Nazianzus, Gregory. 1989. *A Select Library of the Nicene and Post-Nicene Fathers of The Christian Church*. Second Series. Vol. 7. Ed. Philip Schaff and Henry Wace. New York: Christian Literature Publishing Co., 1890. Reprint, Grand Rapids: Wm. B. Eerdmans.

Niebuhr, H. Richard. 1941. *The Meaning of Revelation*. New York: Macmillan.

Niemeyer, Gerhart. 1976. Eric Voegelin's philosophy and the drama of mankind. *Modern Age* 20: 28-39.

Noth, Martin. 1960. *The History of Israel*. Trans. Stanley Godman and rev. P. R. Ackroyd. New York: Harper and Row.

Nyberg, H. S. 1935. *Studien zum Hoseabuche, Zugleich ein Beitrag zur Klärung des Problems der Alttestamentlichen Textkritik*. Uppsala: A. B. Lundequistska.

Ochs, Peter. 1997. Judaism and Christian theology. In *The Modern Theologians: An Introduction to Christian Theology in the Twentieth Century*. 2d ed. Ed. David F. Ford. Cambridge: Blackwell.

Oesterley, W. O. E., and Theodore H. Robinson. 1952. *Hebrew Religion: Its Origins and Development*. 2d ed. rev. and enlarged. New York: Macmillan, 1937. Reprint.

Opitz, Peter J., ed. 1993. *Eric Voegelin, Alfred Schütz, Leo Strauss, Aaron Gurwitsch: Briefwechsel über* Die Neue Wissenschaft der Politik. Freiburg: Karl Alber Verlag.

Opitz, Peter J., and Gregor Sebba, eds. 1981. *The Philosophy of Order: Essays on History, Consciousness and Politics*. Eightieth birthday Festschrift. Stuttgart: Klett-Cotta.

Pannenberg, Wolfhart. 1977. *Human Nature, Election, and History*. Philadelphia: Westminster.

Perdue, Leo G. 1994. *The Collapse of History: Reconstructing Old Testament Theology*. Overtures to Biblical Theology. Philadelphia: Fortress.

Petropoulos, William. 1993. The person as *imago Dei*: Augustine and Max Scheler in Eric Voegelin's *Herrschaftslehre* and *The Political Religions*. Unpublished conference paper.

Polybius. 1979. *The Rise of the Roman Empire*. Penguin Classics. Trans. Ian Scott-Kilvert. Ed. F. W. Walbank. London: Penguin.

Poulssen, Niek. 1967. *König und Tempel im Glaubenszeugnis des Alten Testaments*. Stuttgarter Biblische Monographien, vol. 3. Stuttgart: Katholisches Bibelwerk.

Price, Geoffrey L., ed. 1994. Eric Voegelin: A classified bibliography. In *Bulletin of The John Rylands University Library of Manchester* 76: no. 2.

Pritchard, J. B. 1969. *Ancient Near Eastern Texts Relating to the Old Testament*. Princeton: Princeton University Press, 1950. 3d ed. with supplements.

Rad, Gerhard von. 1951. *Der Heilige Krieg im Alten Israel*. Zurich: Zwingli-Verlag.

———. 1962. *Old Testament Theology*. Vol. 1, *The Theology of Israel's Historical Traditions*. Trans. D. M. G. Stalker. New York: Harper and Row.

———. 1963. Typological interpretation of the Old Testament. In *Essays on Old Testament Hermeneutics*, trans. John Bright, ed. Claus Westermann. Richmond: John Knox Press.

———. 1965. *Old Testament Theology.* Vol. 2, *The Theology of Israel's Prophetic Traditions.* Trans. D. M. G. Stalker. New York: Harper and Row.

———. 1970. *Weisheit in Israel.* Neukirchen-Vluyn: Neukirchener Verlag. Eng.: *Wisdom in Israel,* trans. James D. Martin (New York: Abingdon, 1973).

Ranieri, John J. 1995. *Eric Voegelin and the Good Society.* Columbia: University of Missouri Press.

Rendtorff, Rolf. 1992. The image of postexilic Israel in German Bible scholarship from Wellhausen to von Rad. In *Sha'arei Talmon: Studies in the Bible, Qumran, and the Ancient Near East Presented to Shemaryahu Talmon,* ed. Michael Fishbane and Emanuel Tov. Winona Lake, Ind.: Eisenbrauns.

Reventlow, Henning Graf. 1992. Theology (Biblical), history of. In *The Anchor Bible Dictionary,* vol. 6, ed. David Noel Freedman, trans. Frederick H. Cryer.

Rosenzweig, Franz. 1955. *On Jewish Learning.* Ed. Nahum N. Glazer. New York: Schocken.

Rothschild, Fritz A. 1975, ed. *Between God and Man: An Interpretation of Judaism from the Writings of Abraham Joshua Heschel.* New York: Macmillan, The Free Press.

———. 1990. *Jewish Perspectives on Christianity.* New York: Crossroad.

Ruler, Arnold van. 1971. *The Christian Church and the Old Testament.* Trans. Geoffrey W. Bromiley. Grand Rapids: Wm. B. Eerdmans.

Rylaarsdam, J. C. 1972. Jewish-Christian relationships: The two covenants and the Dilemmas of christology. *Ecumenical Studies* 9:249-79.

Sandoz, Ellis. 1971a. The philosophical science of politics beyond behavioralism. In *The Post-Behavioral Era: Perspectives on Political Science,* ed. George J. Graham and George W. Carey. New York: David McKay.

———. 1971b. *Political Apocalypse: A Study of Dostoyevsky's Grand Inquisitor.* Baton Rouge: Louisiana State University Press.

———. 1981. *The Voegelinian Revolution: A Biographical Introduction.* Baton Rouge: Louisiana State University Press.

———. ed. 1982. *Eric Voegelin's Thought: A Critical Appraisal.* Durham: Duke University Press.

———. 1990. *A Government of Laws: Political Theory, Religion, and the American Founding.* Baton Rouge: Louisiana State University Press.

———. 1993. Medieval rationalism or mystic philosophy? Reflections on the Strauss-Voegelin Correspondence. In *Faith and Political Philosophy: The Correspondence Between Leo Strauss and Eric Voegelin, 1934-1964.* Trans. and ed. Peter Emberley and Barry Cooper. University Park: Pennsylvania State University Press.

———. 1996. The crisis of civic consciousness: Nihilism and political science as resistance. *Political Science Reviewer* 25:22-42.

Schall, James V. 1987. *Reason, Revelation, and the Foundations of Political Philosophy.* Baton Rouge: Louisiana State University Press.

Scheler, Max. 1913-16. *Der Formalismus in der Ethik und die Materiale Wertethik.* In *Gesammelte Werke.* 9 vols. Zurich: Francke Verlag, 1954-76.

———. 1915. *Vom Umsturz der Werte.* In *Gesammelte Werke.*

———. 1921. *Vom Ewigen im Menschen.* In *Gesammelte Werke.*

———. 1923. *Vom Wesen der Sympathie.* 2d ed. In *Gesammelte Werke.*

———. 1928. *Die Stellung des Menschen im Kosmos.* In *Gesammelte Werke.*

Schleiermacher, Friedrich. 1996. *On Religion: Speeches to Its Cultured Despisers.* Trans. and ed. Richard Croutier. Cambridge: Cambridge University Press.

Schmidt, W. L. 1964. *Die Schöpfungsgeschichte der Priesterschrift.* Neukirchen-Vluyn: Neukirchener Verlag.

Schultz, Hermann. 1892. *Old Testament Theology.* Edinburgh: T. and T. Clark.

Sebba, Gregor. 1968. The present state of political theory. *Polity* 1:259-70.

———. 1991. *The Collected Essays of Gregor Sebba: Truth, History and the Imagination.* Ed. Helen Sebba, Anibal A. Bueno, and Hendrikus Boers. Baton Rouge: Louisiana State University Press.

Spann, Othmar. 1923. *Gesellschaftslehre.* Leipzig: Quelle und Meyer.

Speiser, E. A. People and nation of Israel. *Journal of Biblical Literature* 79:157-63.

Syse, Henrik. 1996. Natural law, religion, and rights: An exploration of the relationship between natural law and natural rights, with special emphasis on the teachings of Thomas Hobbes and John Locke. Doctor Artium diss., University of Oslo.

Tanakh. 1985. Philadelphia: Jewish Publication Society.

Thompson, William M. 1991. *Christology and Spirituality.* New York: Crossroad.

———. 1996. *The Struggle for Theology's Soul: Contesting Scripture in Christology.* New York: Crossroad, A Crossroad Herder Book.

*Time Magazine.* 1953. 61 (March 9): 57-60.

Tocqueville, Alexis de. 1969. *Democracy in America.* Trans. George Lawrence. Ed. J. P. Mayer. New York: HarperCollins.

Toynbee, Arnold J. 1935. *A Study of History.* Vol. 1. 2d ed. London: Oxford University Press.

Vondung, Klaus. 1988. *Die Apokalypse in Deutschland.* Munich: Deutscher Taschenbuch Verlag.

Walsh, David. 1983. *The Mysticism of Inner-Wordly Fulfillment: A Study of Jacob Boehme.* Gainesville: University Press of Florida.

———. 1995. *After Ideology: Recovering the Spiritual Foundations of Freedom.* San Francisco: Harper and Row, 1990. Reprint, Washington, D.C.: Catholic University of America Press.

———. 1997. *The Growth of the Liberal Soul.* Columbia: University of Missouri Press.

Webb, Eugene. 1981. *Eric Voegelin: Philosopher of History.* Seattle: University of Washington Press.

———. 1988. *Philosophers of Consciousness: Polanyi, Lonergan, Voegelin, Ricoeur, Girard, Kierkegaard.* Seattle: University of Washington Press.

Wellhausen, Julius. 1957. *Prolegomena to the History of Ancient Israel.* Trans. A. Menzies and J. S. Black. Cleveland: World Publishing, Meridien.

West, Charles. 1970. Theological guidelines for the future. *Theology Today* 27: 277-91.

Westermann, Claus. 1975. *Genesis 1-11.* Neukirchen-Vluyn: Neukirchener Verlag.

Wilhelmsen, Frederick D. 1975. The new Voegelin. *Triumph* 10:32-35.

———. 1978. Professor Voegelin and the Christian tradition. In *Christianity and Political Philosophy.* Athens: University of Georgia Press.

Wildberger, H. 1965. Das Abbild Gottes. *Theologische Zeitschrift* 21:245-59, 481-501.

Winkler, Nils. 1997. Philosophische Aspekte der Rassismus-Kritik Voegelins von 1933. Magister Artium thesis, University of Hamburg.

Wright, G. Ernest. 1952. *God Who Acts: Biblical Theology as Recital.* London: SCM Press.

Zanetti, Gianfrancesco. 1989. *La Trascendenza e L'Ordine Saggio su Eric Voegelin.* Bologna: Cooperative Libraria Universitaria.

# INDEX

**Marquette Studies in Philosophy**
Andrew Tallon, Editor
Standing orders accepted
* *denotes available as eBook*

Harry Klocker, S.J. *William of Ockham and the Divine Freedom.* ISBN 0-87462-001-5. 141 pages, pp., index. $15. Second edition, reviewed, corrected and with a new Introduction.*

Margaret Monahan Hogan. *Finality and Marriage.* ISBN 0-87462-600-5. 122 pp. Paper. $15.*

Gerald A. McCool, S.J. *The Neo-Thomists.* ISBN 0-87462-601-1. 175 pp. Paper. $20.*

Max Scheler. *Ressentiment.* ISBN 0-87462-602-1. 172 pp. Paper. $20. New Introduction by Manfred S. Frings.*

Knud Løgstrup. *Metaphysics.* Translated by Dr. Russell Dees ISBN 0-87462-603-X. Volume I, 342 pp. Paper. $35.* ISBN 0-67462-607-2. Volume II, 402 pp. Paper. $40. Two volume set priced at $70.*

Howard P. Kainz. *Democracy and the "Kingdom of God".* ISBN 0-87462-610-2. 250 pp. Paper. $25.

Manfred Frings. *Max Scheler. A Concise Introduction into the World of a Great Thinker* ISBN 0-87462-605-6. 200 pp. Paper. $20. Second ed., rev. New Foreword by the author.*

G. Heath King. *Existence Thought Style: Perspectives of a Primary Relation, portrayed through the work of Søren Kierkegaard.* English edition by Timothy Kircher. ISBN 0-87462-606-4. 187 pp., index. Paper. $20.*

Augustine Shutte. *Philosophy for Africa.* ISBN 0-87462-608-0. 184 pp. Paper. $20.

Paul Ricoeur. *Key to Husserl's Ideas I.* Translated by Bond Harris and Jacqueline Bouchard Spurlock. With a Foreword by Pol Vandevelde. ISBN 0-87462-609-9. 176 pp., index. Paper. $20.*

Karl Jaspers. *Reason and Existenz.* Afterword by Pol Vandevelde. ISBN 0-87462-611-0. 180 pp. Paper. $20.

Gregory R. Beabout. *Freedom and Its Misuses: Kierkegaard on Anxiety and Despair* ISBN 0-87462-612-9. 192 pp., index. Paper. $20.*

Manfred S. Frings. *The Mind of Max Scheler. The First Comprehensive Guide Based on the Complete Works* ISBN 0-87462-613-7. 328 pp. Paper. $35.*

Claude Pavur. *Nietzsche Humanist.* ISBN 0-87462-614-5. 214 pp., index. Paper. $25.*

Pierre Rousselot. *Intelligence: Sense of Being, Faculty of God.* Translation of *L'Intellectualisme de saint Thomas* with a Foreword and Notes by Andrew Tallon. ISBN 0-87462-615-3. 236 pp., index. Paper. $25.*

Immanuel Kant. *Critique of Practical Reason.* Translation by H.W. Cassirer. Edited by G. Heath King and Ronald Weitzman and with an Introduction by D.M. MacKinnon. ISBN 0-87462-616-1. Paper. 218 pp. $20.*

*Gabriel Marcel's Perspectives on The Broken World.* Translated by Katharine Rose Hanley. *The Broken World,* A Four-Act Play followed by "Concrete Approaches to Investigating the Ontological Mystery." Six orignal illustrations by Stephen Healy. Commentaries by Henri Gouhier and Marcel Belay. Eight Appendices. Introduction by Ralph McInerny. Bibliographies. ISBN 0-87462-617-X. paperbound. 242 pp. $25.*

Karl-Otto Apel. *Towards a Transformation of Philosophy.* New Foreword by Pol Vandevelde. ISBN 0-87462-619-6. Paper. 308 pp. $35.

Gene Fendt. *Is Hamlet a Religious Drama? As Essay on a Question in Kierkegaard.* ISBN 0-87462-620-X. Paper. 264 pp. $30.*

## Marquette Studies in Theology
Andrew Tallon, Editor
Standing orders accepted
* denotes available as eBook

Frederick M. Bliss. *Understanding Reception.* ISBN 0-87462-625-0. 180 pp., index, bibliography. Paper. $20.*

Martin Albl, Paul Eddy, Renée Mirkes, OSF, editors. *Directions in New Testament Methods* ISBN 0-87462-626-9. 129 pp. Annotated bibliography. Paper. $15. Foreword by William S. Kurz.*

Robert M. Doran. *Subject and Psyche.* ISBN 0-87462-627-7. 285 pp. Paper. $25. Second ed., rev. With a new Foreword by the author.*

Kenneth Hagen, editor. *The Bible in the Churches. How Various Christians Interpret the Scriptures* ISBN 0-87462-628-5. 218 pp. Paper. $25. Third, revised editon. New chapter on Reformed tradition. Index.*

Jamie T. Phelps, O.P., editor. *Black and Catholic: The Challenge and Gift of Black Folk. Contributions of African American Experience and Thought to Catholic Theology.* ISBN 0-87462-629-3. 182 pp. Index. Paper. $20. Foreword by Patrick Carey.*

Karl Rahner. *Spirit in the World.* New, Corrected Translation by William Dych. Foreword by Francis Fiorenza. ISBN 0-87462-630-7. COMPUTER DISK VERSION. $10. Available on 3.5 inch disk; specify Macintosh or Windows. By a special arrangement with Continuum Publishing Co.*

Karl Rahner. *Hearer of the Word.* New Translation of the First Edition by Joseph Donceel. Edited and with an Introduction by Andrew Tallon. COMPUTER DISK VERSION. Autumn, 1994. $10. Available on 3.5 inch disk; specify Macintosh or Windows. By a special arrangement with Continuum Publishing Co. ISBN 0-87462-631-5. *

Robert M. Doran. *Theological Foundations. Vol. 1 Intentionality and Psyche.* ISBN 0-87462-632-3. 484 pp. Paper. $50.*

Robert M. Doran. *Theological Foundations. Vol. 2 Theology and Culture.* ISBN 0-87462-633-1. 533 pp. Paper. $55.*

Patrick W. Carey. *Orestes A. Brownson: A Bibliography, 1826-1876.* ISBN 0-87462-634-X. 212 pp. Index. Paper. $25.*

John Martinetti, S.J. *Reason to Believe Today.* ISBN 0-87462-635-8. 216 pp. Paper. $25.*

George H. Tavard. *Trina Deitas: The Controversy between Hincmar and Gottschalk* ISBN 0-87462-636-6. 160 pp. Paper. $20.*

Jeanne Cover, IBVM. *Love–The Driving Force. Mary Ward's Spirituality. Its Significance for Moral Theology* ISBN 0-87462-637-4. 217 pp. Paper. $25.*

David A. Boileau, editor. *Principles of Catholic Social Teaching.* ISBN 0-87462-638-2. 204 pp. Paper. $25.*

Michael Purcell. *Mystery and Method: The Other in Rahner and Levinas.* With a Foreword by Andrew Tallon. ISBN 0-87462-639-0. Paper. 394 pp. $45.*

W.W. Meissner, S.J., M.D. *To the Greater Glory: A Psychological Study of Ignatian Spirituality.* ISBN 0-87462-640-4. Paper. 657 pp. $65.

Virginia M. Shaddy, editor. *Catholic Theology in the University: Source of Wholeness.* ISBN 0-87462-641-2. Paper. 120 pp. $15.*

**Subscibe to** *e-News from Marquette University Press*
Email universitypress@marquette.edu with the word "subscribe" as the subject.
*Visit Marquette University Press online:* **www.marquette.edu/mupress/**